The Great American Songbooks

Modernist Literature and Culture

Kevin J. H. Dettmar and Mark Wollaeger, Series Editors

The Great American Songbooks

*Musical Texts, Modernism,
and the Value of Popular Culture*

T. Austin Graham

OXFORD
UNIVERSITY PRESS

OXFORD
UNIVERSITY PRESS

Oxford University Press is a department of the University of Oxford.
It furthers the University's objective of excellence in research, scholarship,
and education by publishing worldwide.

Oxford New York
Auckland   Cape Town   Dar es Salaam   Hong Kong   Karachi
Kuala Lumpur   Madrid   Melbourne   Mexico City   Nairobi
New Delhi   Shanghai   Taipei   Toronto

With offices in
Argentina   Austria   Brazil   Chile Czech Republic   France   Greece
Guatemala   Hungary   Italy   Japan   Poland   Portugal   Singapore
South Korea   Switzerland   Thailand   Turkey   Ukraine   Vietnam

Oxford is a registered trademark of Oxford University Press in the UK and
certain other countries.

Published in the United States of America by
Oxford University Press
198 Madison Avenue, New York, NY 10016

© Oxford University Press 2013

Library of Congress Cataloging-in-Publication Data
Graham, T. Austin.
The great American songbooks : musical texts, modernism, and the value of popular
culture / T. Austin Graham.
p. cm.—(Modernist literature & culture)
Includes bibliographical references and index.
ISBN 978-0-19-986211-5—ISBN 978-0-19-996738-4—
ISBN 978-0-19-986212-2   1. American literature—20th century—History and
criticism.   2. Music in literature.   3. Songbooks, English—United States—History and
criticism.   4. Popular music—United States—History and criticism.   5. Music, Influence
of.   6. Sheet music—United States—History.   7. Modernism (Literature)—
United States.   I. Title.
PS228.M87G73 2013
810.9'3578—dc23
2012032582

ISBN 978-0-19-986211-5
ISBN 978-0-19-996738-4
ISBN 978-0-19-986212-2

9 8 7 6 5 4 3 2 1
Printed in the United States of America
on acid-free paper

For Peter, Kathryn, and James Graham

Contents

Series Editors' Foreword

Ever since modernist studies began its recent (re-)engagement with popular culture (David Chinitz's *T. S. Eliot and the Cultural Divide* [2005] might mark, if not the start, at least a signal moment in this resurgence), there's been music in the air—and that music has largely been jazz. "Jazz modernism," in fact—when not merely redundant—has been used to suggest both an aesthetic shift away from literature and the "high" arts, and a kind of synesthetic interdisciplinary approach to the field of modernist production. Alfred Appel Jr.'s *Jazz Modernism: From Ellington and Armstrong to Matisse and Joyce* (2004) is apposite here.

When Austin Graham reads modernism, he too hears things: but his approach, and his readings ("listenings"?), are far different from anything the scholarship had previously prepared us for. In *The Great American Songbooks*, Graham explores the suggestive idea that American literature in the decades pivoting around 1900 (from Whitman to the 1930s) made use of the widespread availability of mechanically reproduced popular music to engage in a musical/literary synesthesia that Graham calls the "literary soundtrack." Hence his title is not just a weird pluralizing of the Platonic notion of the Great American Songbook—a kind of Hit Parade in the Sky—but designates books whose very DNA is threaded through with the sounds and words and images of American popular song: Walt Whitman's poetry, and T. S. Eliot's poetry through *The Waste Land*; the first three of F. Scott Fitzgerald's novels, culminating in *The Great Gatsby*; the poetry of Jean Toomer and Langston Hughes; and the nearly forgotten popular genre of the chorus girl novel, especially in the hands of Theodore Dreiser and John Dos Passos. "When audiences can be depended on to know of and even 'play' a song in the mind upon receiving a written cue"—which, as Graham argues, readers can reliably be depended on to do beginning in this period—"a range of possibilities opens up for authors." As Graham points out, "the first major phase of [Eliot's] career . . . coincides almost exactly with the rise of the modern recording industry."

Part of the excitement of this study is Graham's narrative of how this new use of musical allusion develops across the writing of the authors he studies; we begin, chronologically, with Whitman's palpable operatic aspirations in a poem like "Proud Music of the Storm" (1869) and end with Dos Passos's rather bitter scrutiny of the musical theater: *Manhattan Transfer*, Graham writes, is "an exposé that asks its readers to scrutinize and then recoil from a rising chorus girl and the culture of entertainment she typifies."

Graham has worked to make this study itself a "songbook": when he refers to a popular tune that Fitzgerald expected his readers to hear in conjunction with a passage in *This Side of Paradise*, for instance, Graham has provided links on a website that allow the reader to play those tunes from various internet audio archives. It's a book that wouldn't have been possible just a decade or so ago: in the curatorial frenzy that the Internet has helped to fuel, much of the ephemeral popular music that sat as "unheard melodies" on wax cylinders in physical archives has been digitized and made easily available around the world. So that for the first time since the music's original demise, it's possible now, in the hands of a wise guide like Graham, to read, and hear, this literature in the way it might have been experienced at the moment of its publication.

Such a reading protocol—with Internet resources augmenting the potentially silent experience of reading *The Great American Songbooks*—requires an active and engaged reader, of course. And in this aspect, too, form mirrors content, for one of Graham's more important insights is that the "soundtracked" writing that is his subject "ask[ed] its readers to 'do' something beyond merely reading it." Writing of *This Side of Paradise*, for instance, Graham argues that "one of [Fitzgerald's] innovations in attempting this variety of musical-theatrical writing is the creation of an atmosphere in which readers may choose their level of emotional engagement rather than have it dictated to them, in which they can take it as seriously—or not—as they wish."

As American life has become ever more thoroughly mediated in the decades that follow those under scrutiny here, "soundtracked" writing has become even more prevalent; Graham closes with a briefly suggestive epilogue tracing the lineage forward to the present day, an introduction to the topic that cries out to be followed up on. The Great American Playlist, anyone?

We've sought out work for the Modernist Literature and Culture series that breaks down the disciplinary and generic boundaries that for too long kept modernist literary studies in sterile isolation; we're proud, with *The Great American Songbooks*, to bring to the scholarly community a book that illuminates the rich and mutually informing traffic between American letters and popular music during the heyday of modernism.

— Kevin J. H. Dettmar and Mark Wollaeger

Acknowledgments

To write this book, I spent years listening for harmonies between music and the written word, and I almost never did so alone. My greatest debt is to Eric Sundquist, who nurtured the project at every stage and has been a cherished mentor and friend. The manuscript was mostly written at the University of California-Los Angeles, where I received indispensable advice and direction from Michael North, Michael Colacurcio, and Robert Fink. I am also grateful to have had the chance to discuss these ideas at UCLA with Christopher Looby, Jennifer Fleissner, Mark McGurl, Sianne Ngai, Richard Yarborough, Mark Seltzer, Joseph Bristow, Frederick Burwick, Helen Deutsch, Jonathan Grossman, Felicity Nussbaum, Susan McClary, Mitchell Morris, Robert Walser, Joseph Dimuro, Christopher Mott, Adam Lowenstein, Michael Devine, Julian Knox, Adam Gordon, Matt Dubord, Jesse Johnson, Erin Templeton, Holly Moyer, Mac Harris, Dennis Tyler, Sam See, Jessica Pressman, Melanie Ho, Joyce Lee, J. D. Lopez, Sean Silver, Noah Comet, Kate Marshall, Beth Goodhue, the members of the Americanist Research Colloquium, and the late, much missed Barbara Packer. I also had helpful correspondence with Ryan Jerving, Erich Nunn, Cristina Ruotolo, and Angela J. Latham. I was kindly invited to present some of this material to the F. Scott Fitzgerald Society, the International Theodore Dreiser Society, the English departments at Case Western Reserve University and Virginia Polytechnic Institute and State University, and "The Past's Digital Presence" conference at Yale University. Finally, Gordon Hutner, Priscilla Wald, Kirk Curnutt, and Robert McParland were wise and insightful editors of my work in its early stages.

This project received generous funding and research support from the American Academy of Arts and Sciences and the American Council of Learned Societies

(ACLS). At the Academy, I had the distinct pleasure of working under the direction of Patricia Meyer Spacks, and alongside Thomas Crocker, Coleman Hutchison, Amy Lippert, Jason Sharples, Tracy Steffes, and Heather Tressler. ACLS funded a year of residency at the University of Virginia English Department, where I was supported by Cynthia Wall, mentored by Jahan Ramazani, and welcomed by Jerome McGann, Herbert Tucker, Eric Lott, Fred and Katharine Maus, Andrew Stauffer, Victoria Olwell, Jennifer Greeson, Anna Brickhouse, Sylvia Chong, Deborah McDowell, Jennifer Wicke, Caroline Rody, Stephen Arata, Lisa Goff, Lisa Russ Spaar, Susan Fraiman, Sandhya Shukla, Alison Booth, Mrinalini Chakravorty, Bruce Holsinger, Paul Cantor, Clare Kinney, David Gies, Laura Goldblatt, and Michael Pickard. Marc Campbell expertly prepared sound clips for the book's audio guide.

My thanks to the staffs at the following institutions, without whom books like this cannot be written: the Charles E. Young, Powell, and Music libraries at UCLA; Widener Library at Harvard University; the Rare Books and Special Collections Library at Princeton University; the Alderman and Clemons Libraries at the University of Virginia; and, within the New York Public Library system, the Stephen A. Schwartzman Library, the Library for the Performing Arts, and the Schomburg Center for Research in Black Culture.

At Oxford University Press, I have had the best support an author could ask for. Kevin Dettmar and Mark Wollaeger reviewed the manuscript, wrote the introduction, and did me a great honor in making *The Great American Songbooks* part of their Modernist Literature and Culture series. Brendan O'Neill patiently shepherded me through the publication process. Two anonymous readers gave me sage advice on the manuscript. Jashnie Jabson coordinated the production phase of the book, Patterson Lamb did copy editing, Stephen Bradley assisted with the cover art, and many others helped bring this project into being.

And most important of all: my thanks to my wife Susana, my parents, and my brother for a lifetime of love.

Some of this book was originally published elsewhere and can be found in the following volumes. My thanks to these journals and presses not only for their permission to reprint material, but also for supporting my work.

"O Cant: Singing the Race Music of Jean Toomer's *Cane*" in *American Literature*, vol. 82, issue 4, pp. 725–752. Copyright 2010. Reprinted by permission of the publisher, Duke University Press.

"The Literary Soundtrack; or, F. Scott Fitzgerald's Heard and Unheard Melodies" in *American Literary History*, vol. 21, issue 3, pp. 518–549. Copyright 2009. Reprinted by permission of the publisher, Oxford University Press.

"Fitzgerald's 'Riotous Mystery': *This Side of Paradise* as Musical Theater" in *The F. Scott Fitzgerald Review*, vol. 6, pp. 21–54. Copyright 2007–2008. Reprinted by permission of the F. Scott Fitzgerald Society.

"T. S. Eliot and Ubiquitous Music, 1909–1922," in *Music and Literary Modernism*, ed. Robert McParland, pp. 194–209. Copyright 2006. Reprinted by permission of the publisher, Cambridge Scholars Press.

A Note on Audio

WWW.OUP.COM/US/THEGREATAMERICANSONGBOOKS

This book discusses several sound recordings, and on occasion invites the reader to listen to them. An audio guide containing musical excerpts, marked in the text by a speaker icon ◉, can be found on the companion website. It can be accessed by using the username Music1 and password Book5983. Some of the recordings can be listened to free of charge in online archives, and so the audio guide directs readers to other music sites, as well.

The Great American Songbooks

1. Musical Literature, Its Theory and Practice

It is one of the most famous and influential ideas in the history of aesthetic theory: *"All art constantly aspires towards the condition of music."*[1] This pronouncement appears in "The School of Giorgione," an 1877 essay by the Oxford don Walter Pater that is nominally about painting, but is more broadly concerned with the interrelations and common aims of all the arts. Laying out the principles of true aesthetic appreciation, Pater begins by conceding that each art has "its own peculiar and untranslatable sensuous charm" (122). He also notes, however, that the arts "are able, not indeed to supply the place of each other, but reciprocally to lend each other new forces" (124). A sculpture can possess elements of tragic drama, a sonnet can call a picture to mind, and every artistic work that has ever been created attempts in some way to be like music, which Pater praises as "the typical, or ideally consummate art, the object . . . of all that is artistic, or partakes of artistic qualities." Music commands widespread emulation, Pater says, because of its abstract nature: it contains nothing in the way of worldly subject matter and therefore attains a purity that "all art constantly strives after, and achieves in different degrees" (125). Regardless of how devoted writers, painters, or actors might be to their particular crafts, then, Pater finds that they all are called to the same, fundamentally musical purpose, and that their works might contain something that can be heard as well as read, seen, or felt.

Pater's aphorism has inspired artists in every medium over the years, but for the American author of the late nineteenth and early twentieth century, his assertion of music's supremacy sometimes struck a discordant note. Ezra Pound gave it equal importance to his own theory of Imagism in the first issue of *Blast* (1914), but he did not think so well of it as to quote it correctly: "All arts approach the conditions of music," he wrote.[2] William Carlos Williams flatly declared in *Spring and All* (1923) that "I do not believe writing would gain in quality or force by seeking to attain to the conditions of music. I think the conditions of music are objects for the action of the writer's imagination."[3] T. S. Eliot mocked the works of Pater as "misch-masch potpourri" in an early version of *The Waste Land* (1922), and he later suggested that the true poet "aspires to the condition of the music-hall comedian" instead.[4] Even F. Scott Fitzgerald, whose undergraduate lyricism often showed the hallmarks of Pater's influence, seems to have regarded him as an out-of-date embarrassment, including his writings among the "misty side-streets of literature" wandered by Amory Blaine, the effete, dilettantish protagonist of his 1920 novel *This Side of Paradise*.[5]

There is something not a little odd about Pater's poor standing in the estimations of these and other American writers. In more friendly quarters, after all, his theory of aesthetic mutability is credited with having helped usher in the movement of cross-generic, interdisciplinary experimentation known as modernism, in which poems sometimes aspired to visuality, paintings to movement, and symphonies to color.[6] Moreover, a great many American writers during modernism's moment—including some of the ones just quoted—betrayed intensely musical aspirations in their works. Authors of the late nineteenth and early twentieth centuries sometimes took music up as subject matter, whether in discussing its effects on listeners, in using musicians as characters, or in demonstrating the social function of Pater's ultimate art in their own world and time. On other occasions they used music as a formal model for literature, attempting something like singing, record-playing, and soundtracking in their pages. And a considerable amount of American writing from this period reads as fundamentally hybrid in nature, bringing new, sounding dimensions to the silent act of reading and appealing to its audiences in distinctively non-textual ways. The anti-Paterians, it would seem, protested a bit too much. Indeed, if Pater's musical partisanship truly offended the turn-of-the-century American writer, it may well have been because it had come to seem overly abstract and insufficiently thought out, deaf to the many actual possibilities of musical literature that were then being realized.

The book that follows is the story of this musical literature, a study of the ways in which nineteenth- and twentieth-century American authors successfully achieved "the condition of music" in their writing. The idea of musical literature is an ancient one and has been part of the Western tradition since Homer, but this book will advance an argument that has seldom been made: namely, that certain works of American literary modernism are not merely about or influenced by music but can be considered works of music in and of themselves. The authors discussed here ask their readers to sing poems, to imagine fiction being accompanied by well-known melodies, to occupy unfamiliar roles and assume new perspectives through musical performance, and to inflect literary meaning with the techniques and associations of an admired sister art. In all cases, moreover, these authors write musically with the aim of making literature a more participatory, more audience-oriented, and therefore more authentically musical form. As the musicologist Christopher Small has put it, music is a distinctive art insofar as it emphasizes process over product, active involvement over passive reception: "The fundamental nature and meaning of music lie not in objects, not in musical works at all, but in action, in what people do," Small writes. "It is only by understanding what people do as they take part in a musical act that we can hope to understand its nature and the function it fulfills in human life."[7] Correspondingly, musical literature of the sort studied here asks its readers to "do" something beyond merely reading it, and in the process it challenges and transcends many of the Western world's most persistent cultural divisions, whether between author and audience, subject and object, material and ideal, black and white, or male and female.

In addition to asking why American modernist authors wrote musical literature, this book attends to the kind of music they invoked and emulated most frequently: that of the commercial, popular tradition. Most previous accounts of the relationship between music and literature have been highbrow and European in orientation, and they have tended to emphasize music's ineffability, its abstract autonomy, and the promise it offers of escaping the confines of language.[8] The authors studied in these pages, however, draw upon the popular arts for very different reasons, attracted by their immediacy, their familiarity, and the implicit welcome they extend to diverse audiences. In regard to musical accessibility we can turn again to Small, who notes that in popular idioms, "no-one is excluded through being unable to comprehend what the musicians are doing, and no-one seems to need formal instruction in order to do so. . . . As with speech, what the individual does in music is couched in a language that has to be learned, but that learning takes place not in a formal situation but in the encounters of everyday life."[9] Similarly, all of the authors discussed here depended on the music of "everyday life" in the hopes of reaching the greatest possible number of readers, and the coming chapters will therefore take up a popular culture that is usually considered too slight to be worthy of scholarly attention: sentimental Broadway numbers, forgotten novelty records, white travesties of African-American blues, overwrought opera highlights, and the like. Moreover, you, the reader of this book, will be asked at several points to listen to audio recordings, which will help you understand the musical effects that these authors are attempting in their works and will allow you to participate in the audience responses that such works demand. Much of this music will sound peculiar and even unappealing to the modern ear, but for these authors—many of whom had dreamed in their younger days of becoming song-writers and performers and Broadway stars—it was indispensible.

The book begins, in this chapter, with a critical overview of three broad questions, each of which pertains to American musical authors their boundary-crossing, multidisciplinary works. What did music represent to the American public and the literary establishment in the modernist period? What role does the sense of hearing play in the reading act? And what relative value does popular culture enjoy in comparison to the "high" arts? As regards the first question, this chapter will go on to discuss the many changes that writers heard occurring in music, its symbolic character, and its place in American culture between the nineteenth and twentieth centuries. Music had always been of interest to writers in previous eras, and in the nineteenth century it was admired as an almost cosmic art, one that offered a spiritual transport quite unavailable in the realms of everyday experience. But at the century's turn, Americans found themselves surrounded by music to an extent that earlier generations could scarcely have imagined, thanks to a spectacular expansion of commercial entertainment and various technological advances in producing and disseminating sound. The growing availability and new commodity status of music changed its perceived character and the uses to which it could be put in literature, with American writers attentive to and much affected by the change. Their musical fiction and poetry is therefore valuable in part because it registers a historical shift in American thinking about one of the most exalted of the arts.

The second question taken up in this chapter—on the audibility of the written word—can seem at first blush to be somewhat absurd. Excepting the case of a book being read aloud or the sound one makes when it is dropped on the floor, after all, few arts are more technically silent than literature. But in the late nineteenth and early twentieth centuries, artists across the international modernist movement made concerted efforts at interweaving modes of expression and at appropriating the varying demands that each makes on the human sensorium. Many works of American literature, meanwhile, were quite successful at triggering perceptible, aural stimulations in readers. As the reading public became increasingly acquainted with the same kinds of music (and even with the same versions of the same kinds of music), American writers found it easier to deploy musical sound effects and, in some cases, to construct entire soundtracks that their readers would mentally "fill in" upon receiving the necessary cues. The result was a literature that, depending on one's familiarity with the music it contained, could become remark-ably audible. And while the American works discussed in this book are exception-ally rich in their musicality, they suggest more generally how one might go about listening to other, less obviously musical novels and poems, as well.

Third and finally, this chapter will consider a sometimes bedeviling aesthetic problem, the place and relative value of the popular arts in literary culture. The very idea of a "popular culture" that was qualitatively different from both the high and folk arts was still fairly new in America at century's turn, and the attitudes of the literary establishment toward that culture were often ambivalent. In many American musical-literary works, however, one finds the stirrings of a broadmin-dedness that would eventually be a central part of the nation's collective thought: audible in them are the beginnings of a miscellaneous sensibility, a cultural per-spective that rejects rigid, categorical delineations of the "high" and the "low" and instead considers how "art" and "popular culture" can be appreciated and valued on their own, unique terms. This sensibility, moreover, is ultimately greater than the sum of its parts, concerned not just with evaluating music or literature but also with considering the problem of aesthetic apprehension in general. The writ-ers discussed in this book frequently use music as an occasion for pondering the larger, complex question of how one identifies the good and the bad in a crowded culture, and they suggest that to comment upon or engage effectively with such a culture is often to be contradictory and paradoxical. More often than not, these writers present themselves as modernist eclectics who are both guardians of an august literary tradition and connoisseurs of a popular one, and in many cases they are able to thrive in these dual roles precisely because they are aware how incongruous they might initially seem.

Subsequent chapters of this book focus more specifically on individual writers, and they will still be useful to readers who skip the historical, theoretical, and criti-cal material contained in the present one. The second chapter discusses the ways in which poetry, the most obviously musical of literary genres, was transformed between the middle of the nineteenth century and the beginning of the twentieth, with Walt Whitman's singing and T. S. Eliot's musical quotation serving as rep-resentative examples. Both men draw on popular music in their verse, and their bodies of work reflect their very different historical and cultural moments. When their writings are considered in tandem, several contrasts can be heard: opera and Tin Pan Alley, the expansive singing voice and the overwhelmed listening ear, and music's elusive ideality in live performance and its recorded materiality in the age of the phonograph. But there is common ground between Whitman and Eliot as well, a shared sense that poetry, when infused with the power of song, can become an inclusive, participatory process: both men use music to cross those boundaries usually thought to separate poets from their audiences, and both invite musical performances of their texts.

Turning to prose, the third chapter finds that novels of the early twentieth century frequently asked readers to bring their musical knowledge to bear upon fiction, thereby creating an inventive, multisensory experience. F. Scott Fitzgerald is the central figure here, as he was an early practitioner of what will be somewhat anachronistically referred to as "the literary soundtrack"—a series of identifiable, well-known pieces of music that punctuate plots and are intended to be listened to in conjunction with the reading act. Fitzgerald was fascinated by the ways that music could intrude upon or harmonize with narrative, and his novels often seem to emulate the method of the Broadway stage, the techniques of silent film, and the musically allusive, magpie-like aesthetic of James Joyce's novels. The resulting textual experience can be ecstatic, insidious, immediate, or ineffable in Fitzgerald's hands, but in all cases his fiction is strikingly audible, existing in states of cross-aesthetic tension that demand to be physically heard and responded to as well as read.

The fourth chapter explores the notion of sung poetry in relation to race, turning to Jean Toomer, Langston Hughes, and other poets of the Harlem Renaissance. Here, twentieth-century African American verse forms are studied alongside the slave spirituals, folk songs, and blues that they so frequently saluted and emulated. Toomer and Hughes, however, are shown to be using black music not just in the service of racial affirmation (as is commonly assumed) but also as a means of complicating the very idea of racial categorization. At the time of their publication, both men's works relied on musical forms—spirituals in the case of Toomer, blues in the case of Hughes—that could be recognized and sung by readers of various ethnic backgrounds. The musicality and performability of both men's texts, moreover, serve to promote interracial empathy and elide racial difference; for readers and writers of this literary tradition, to sing a race's music through the medium of poetry is to be made to identify with that race.

The fifth chapter is less about music per se than about musical theater, turning to a subgenre of fiction termed "the chorus girl novel." Such novels, among them Theodore Dreiser's *Sister Carrie* and John Dos Passos's *Manhattan Transfer*, depict lowly heroines who are in the process of becoming theater stars, and their plots are somewhat twisted adaptations of Broadway shows. While such novels are less literally audible than some of the other texts under review here, they are every bit as concerned with the ways in which popular music and the popular arts invite readerly participation. The "chorus girl novel," generally speaking, gives readers a backstage view of an archetypal variety of musical entertainment, and it inducts them into otherwise exclusive realms of artistic production. In the case of Dreiser, the view behind the curtain reveals a higher music than Broadway can itself provide, whereas in the case of Dos Passos, commercial entertainment is revealed to be bankrupt and deleterious to performers and consumers alike. For both novelists, however, the act of peeking into the backstages of musical theater presupposes readerly interest in popular culture, and it advances an argument that when all is said and done, the apprehension of such culture is of real and significant importance.

Taken together, these literary works will be referred to as the "Great American Songbooks," with the designation derived from the so-called Great American Songbook of the jazz era. For the uninitiated, the Great American Songbook was a collection of "standard" tunes that any musician worth his or her salt would have been expected to have mastered and been able to sing or play in the days before the rise of rock 'n' roll. Constituting something like a musical canon, the Great American Songbook depended above all else on audience familiarity, on listeners who were capable of recognizing and responding appreciatively to music that was performed for them. The literary Songbook, meanwhile, attempts to reach its readers in a similar way, relying on their common musical knowledge and asking them to bring that knowledge to bear on a poem, novel, or story. But the Great American Songbook was also a facilitator of cultural improvisation and change, as it invited vocalists, instrumentalists, and any number of other performers to make their own marks on the musical tradition, to tweak the established order, and to create something new and original out of something old and well known. And musical literature of the sort discussed in the pages that follow represents one of many possible responses to this invitation, with the Songbooks studied here often coming to sound as unique and distinctive as the great musicians of the twentieth century were. A fundamental tension between similitude and difference, accessibility and experimentation, and continuity and change was always at the heart of the Great American Songbook, and ultimately, it is the central motif of the Great American Songbooks taken up here, as well.

This story of modernism's moment should sound quite familiar to twenty-first-century audiences, for many of the techniques that these authors pioneered have become utterly commonplace in the years since. As long as the music in question is familiar to them, after all, most of today's readers understand instinctively what it means to inflect a novel or poem with popular song, and they have ample assistance in doing so from various quarters. When Thomas Pynchon's novel *Inherent Vice* was published in 2009, for example, his narrative of a stoned, 1960s-era California was so littered with references to specific musical pieces that the online merchant Amazon.com advertised a twenty-seven-song, downloadable playlist "designed exclusively" by the author, with Pynchon's selections promising an enriched reading experience when purchased and listened to in tandem with the text.[10] "Can't Buy Me Love" by the Beatles, "God Only Knows" by the Beach Boys, and "Interstellar Overdrive" by Pink Floyd were but a click away, and so too were several less famous songs by obscure bands that Pynchon's novel generously introduces to new audiences. Subsequent innovations in digitality have promised to streamline the practice of musical reading yet further: at the time of this writing, a start-up publisher called "Booktrack" is beginning to release e-books whose plots are synched to continuous musical accompaniments.[11]

But for all their cutting-edge intermediacy, Pynchon and Booktrack's experiments in merging literature with music have had a long foregrounding. At the end of his life more than a hundred years before, Whitman found a comparable but even larger dynamic of synthesis at work in every aesthetic mode that humanity had yet produced: "*Art is one*, is not partial, but includes all times and forms and sorts," he argued.[12] For Whitman, each individual artistic work, no matter how distinct it may seem, still has a place in a vast, all-containing aesthetic totality. And if he is correct, then the expansive, boundary-crossing Songbooks discussed in the pages that follow will not only have something to say to their present readers and listeners, but will also sing to any other kind of artist or audience, now or in the years to come.

Writing about Music

In surveying the last two hundred years of American literature, one notices a pronounced shift in the ways that writers think about music and the purposes to which they evoke it, with that shift coinciding with an extraordinary florescence of music at the century's turn. For much of the nineteenth century, music was considered to be the pinnacle of the arts, even a conduit to something beyond the realm of art entirely. In a journal entry from 1857, for instance, Henry David Thoreau describes the astonishing response that the strumming of a guitar had drawn from him one day:

> We hear the kindred vibrations, music! and we put out our dormant feelers unto the limits of the universe. We attain to a wisdom that passeth understanding. The stable continents undulate. The hard and fixed becomes fluid. . . . When I *hear* music I fear no danger, I am invulnerable, I see no foe. I am related to the earliest times and to the latest.[13]

Thoreau's description of an aesthetically inspired totality that transcends time, space, and consciousness has its oldest analogue in Pythagoras, whose theory of a universal music—also known as the music of the spheres—posited an all-encompassing harmonic perfection, an underlying, mathematical order of creation that the arts in turn gesture toward.[14] For Thoreau and others of the nineteenth century, music expressed a profound spirituality that, by definition, could not be accounted for by most worldly, material mediums. Indeed, authors were frequently willing to elevate the musical arts above their own literary productions, as in Ralph Waldo Emerson's skeptical evaluation of his life and career: "Underneath the inharmonious and trivial particulars, is a musical perfection, the Ideal journeying always with us, the heaven without rent or seam," he writes in his sober "Experience" of 1844.[15]

To this ideal, however, was a corollary, a literary conception of music that recognized its Pythagorean majesty but also had more sinister implications. Plato was its earliest exponent, warning in Book III of *The Republic* that music is so intoxicating and invasive that it is capable of dissolving the listener's self-possession entirely and dictating his or her moods and actions, to the point that in an ideal state it would be banned. (Where the Pythagorean theory has overtones of the universally sympathetic Orpheus, Plato's brings the seductive Pied Piper to mind.) Centuries later, Thoreau would express something similar in his journal, describing a musically inspired loss of internal coherence after having heard a simple birdsong: "No particulars survive this expansion; persons do not survive it. In the light of this strain there is no thou nor I. We are actually lifted above ourselves."[16] For the nineteenth-century sensibility, this experience of being "lifted above" oneself by music could be profoundly morbid, and music's intensity of effect often had connotations of insanity and oblivion in its literary invocations. Consider the battle scene of James Fenimore Cooper's *The Last of the Mohicans* (1826), in which a traveling minstrel's "death song" protects him during a massacre; or the tune whose "infinite significancies" coaxes the protagonist of Herman Melville's *Pierre* (1852) toward incest, madness, and suicide; or the parlor music that captivates Edna Pontillier in Kate Chopin's *The Awakening* (1899), penetrating "her whole being like an effulgence" and inducing a dreaminess that leads her to a fatal immersion in the sea.[17] In these cases the power of music is aligned with the infinitude of death, and it should therefore come as no surprise that one of the most formally, even entrancingly musical American poets of the period, Edgar Allan Poe, was also the most consumed with the occult and the limits of mortality.

It would be difficult indeed to overstate the extent to which nineteenth-century artists and thinkers across the Western world named music as a model for their works, aspiring toward the otherworldly abstraction that they considered unique to it. Whether evoked for its unitary Pythagorean properties, for its Platonic powers of direct emotional effect, or for both of these at once, an art that had once been regarded as a lower, less rational form than poetry came to achieve supremacy in philosophic circles and inspire interdisciplinary imitation well into the twentieth century. Music's ascendance was most pronounced in Germany: it was named the highest form of expression by Arthur Schopenhauer in *The World as Will and Idea* (1819), while Richard Wagner's mid-century conception of a totalizing aesthetic mode—or *Gesamtkunstwerk*—included other arts but was fundamentally musical. The Symbolist school in French poetics attempted to approximate the indefiniteness of music by emphasizing the sound-faculties of words rather than their referents, and Paul Verlaine's call in his "Art Poétique" for "music above all else" has proven an enduring statement of the movement.[18] In the visual arts, James Whistler painted a series of "Nocturnes" and "Symphonies," Henri Matisse emphasized direct primary colors that were meant to affect viewers as musical tones do, and Vassily Kandinsky attempted to capture musical abstraction itself. Even modernist musical experiments with atonal, grating compositional techniques—such as Arnold Schoenberg's twelve-tone method or the Futurist "Art of Noises"—betrayed a similar sense that music could go beyond traditional boundaries and become a much more expansive, "pantonal" art than had hitherto been realized. From there, it was but a few steps forward to John Cage's *4'33"* (1952), a "silent" American piece whose musicality lies not in the creation of tones but in the ambient sound of its performance space. In his implication that any sound can be music to a listener's ears if perceived with sufficient attention, Cage reaches the theoretical end of composition but also goes back to the very beginning, suggesting a Pythagorean, universal music even more profound than "music" as it is commonly understood.[19]

It is this sense of music's ineffability, otherworldliness, and resistance to aesthetic limitations that tends to occupy scholars who study musical-literary correspondences in the late nineteenth and early twentieth centuries. Daniel Albright, for example, has noted that much of music's allure for modernism lay in the fact that it formally contains a tension between fixity and flux: it can be apprehended in both a frozen, "vertical" sense and a fluid, "horizontal" one, either as a construction of stacked, perfected chords or as an unfolding, temporal process.[20] Similarly, Brad Bucknell has argued that music's unique stability-in-instability made it a useful model for modernist authors with a taste for the wavering and the paradoxical: music's synthesis of oppositional qualities would give rise to such slippery literary paradigms as Pater's "hard gem-like flame" of aesthetic experience or Pound's definition of a poetic Image as "an intellectual and emotional complex in an instant of time."[21] Add to this Eric Prieto's argument that modernist authors harnessed music in an attempt at transcending the mere "denotata of words" in their works, and one finds a healthy scholarly narrative of one art consistently urging another toward greater abstraction.[22]

This sense that music is capable of expressing emotions or states of being that words cannot is yet more evident in the field of African American letters. In the decades since Amiri Baraka—then writing under the name LeRoi Jones—memorably classified black Americans as a "blues people" whose songs reveal "something about the essential nature of the Negro's existence in this country," scholars have shown just how indebted African American writing of the nineteenth and twentieth century was to the musical legacy that grew out of the field hollers, spirituals, and folk songs of the antebellum South.[23] As is the case with criticism that takes up musical-literary correspondences in modernism, this line of study emphasizes music and musical literature's ability to say the unsayable. Here, however, music is usually represented as a means not of aesthetic escape but rather of cultural recovery, of articulating or tapping into those racial feelings, remembrances, and spiritual urges that cannot be meaningfully translated into a Western literary idiom. Paul Gilroy has influentially argued that the "power and significance" of modern black musical practice grew "in inverse proportion to the limited expressive power of language," but African American writers since emancipation have still frequently sought to merge words with music. From the spirituals that W. E. B. Du Bois sounds throughout *The Souls of Black Folk* (1903) to the many acts of musical communion in the works of Toni Morrison, African American literature registers a powerful conviction that music can move literature beyond its generic limitations and help writers express what Gilroy calls "the phatic and the ineffable."[24]

On a related but less frequently studied note, music's abstract qualities also offered literary artists an opportunity to transcend their sexes and overcome traditional strictures of gender during modernism's moment. Readers of this book have no doubt already ascertained that it focuses rather narrowly on male authors. But while women do not provide many of the literary voices under review here, they provide virtually all of the musical ones. Whitman claimed that his poetry was awakened by the operatic career of Marietta Alboni; Eliot's verse was significantly indebted to the music-hall performances of Marie Lloyd; Hughes's favorite blues singer was Bessie Smith; Dreiser and Dos Passos were far more interested in chorus girls than in male actors; and Fitzgerald's commitment to the Broadway musical was such that he had himself photographed in drag during his theater days at Princeton. In all of these cases, male writers were not only reaching beyond literary boundaries by invoking music but were also tapping into wellsprings of

female creativity and talent, perhaps even attempting to occupy differently gen-
dered subject positions entirely. Consequently, even an all-male study of musical
writers can still illustrate what Rita Felski has called the "hybrid and often contradictory identities" of gender so fundamental to modernist art, with the writing male's channeling of singing female voices demonstrating the degree to which
the movement was what Virginia Woolf famously termed "woman-manly" and
"man-womanly."[25]

The associations of universality, spirituality, abstraction, and transcendence
that turn-of-the-century authors admired and envied in music have been of interest to scholars for quite some time, and there is no reason that critics ought not
continue investigating them. But when music is studied as an ecstatic art capable
of taking listeners and readers out of the world, the very terms and assumptions
of the conversation obscure one of the most dramatic musical developments of
modern times: the emergence of a society in which music was so palpably present
that the experience of it came to be unmistakably worldly, even quotidian. The
late nineteenth and early twentieth centuries witnessed the expansion of music
publishing, recording, and production in the United States; the rapid exportation
of music into the global economy; and the increased availability of music of all
kinds in any number of media, developments that profoundly changed the ways in
which music could be invoked in literature. The nineteenth-century belief in music's lofty character did not disappear in this new musical environment, as authors
could be as captivated by their Victrolas as Thoreau was by his birdsong. But the
experience of music was changed considerably by the everyday musicality that had
come to characterize American life: music had become so audible, so available,
and so familiar that the sonic environment—or "soundscape," to use R. Murray
Schafer's neologism—had realized Emerson's theory of musical omnipresence to
an almost unsettlingly literal extent.[26] The literature of late nineteenth- and early
twentieth-century America was correspondingly shaped by this newly musical
world, but a full accounting of musical writing under these changed conditions
has not until now been attempted.

These were the years in which music, especially that of the popular variety,
began to achieve the saturation of American life that characterizes its place in
culture today.[27] Indeed, it is often called the "golden age" of popular music, not
because it saw its invention but rather because music achieved a new ubiquity
during the period. The 1890s marked the emergence of what would be the first
group of publishers devoted entirely to popular music (New York City's famed
"Tin Pan Alley," so nicknamed in 1903) as well as the concurrent realization that
music could be an immensely profitable commodity, with both developments

dramatically raising the profile of music in public, private, and literary life. In contrast to the ephemerality praised by Thoreau, music came increasingly to be thought of as something that could be owned by individual consumers, in large part because the possibilities for its material dissemination had never been greater: it was available in sheet music or in its newest incarnation, the phonograph record. (Coming decades would see radio added to the mix of musical media.) By the 1920s—also known as "The Jazz Age" and "The Roaring Twenties"—the American condition was inseparable from its musical character and volume, and its songs, having already conquered America, seemed to be nearly as prevalent the world over. In 1922, for example, the journalist Burnet Hershey declared that a "jazz latitude" had come to encircle not just America, but the globe itself.[28] Indeed, he argued, the best way for a disoriented American traveler to fix his or her location was not to consult a map but rather to ascertain how up-to-date the local imports from Tin Pan Alley were and then calculate the distance from New York accordingly.

Music was therefore integral to a pressing problem of the era and its literature: the character of the nation's soundscape and its effect on Americans. The turn of the century heard the first large-scale debates over noise in American life and the methods for managing it, with the underlying assumption being that changes in what Emily Thompson has dubbed the "culture of listening" would in turn change listeners themselves.[29] This concern for the American psyche in an increasingly loud culture can be traced back to George M. Beard's *American Nervousness* of 1881, which found that the increasingly frenetic pace of American life had left the population jittery and distracted; Beard singled out Thomas Edison—who had completed his first model of the phonograph three years earlier—for "making constant and exhausting draughts on the nervous forces of America and Europe."[30] Of particular concern to turn-of-the-century observers of American culture was the sheer presence of music, in large part because of the Platonic, mood-altering effect that it had always been believed to have on audiences. Some feared that too much musical exposure would result in a dull, passive, and standardized American mind highly susceptible to outside influence, with the esteemed art increasingly thought to inspire states of spiritual torpor rather than of ecstasy.

One of the most famous of these pessimists was the "March King" John Philip Sousa, who claimed that recording technology—and its products, "canned music"— would transform Americans into machine-dependent automatons and rob them of their capacity for profound aesthetic experience, thereby weakening the "national throat" and "national chest."[31] The novelist Willa Cather sounded a similar note in worrying that "We have music by machines, we travel by machines—soon we will be having machines to do our thinking."[32] In the realm of popular music, meanwhile, descriptions of Tin Pan Alley as mechanistic, avaricious, and highly invasive were at the time practically a matter of course. The *New York Times* in 1910 described for its readers "How Popular Song Factories Manufacture a Hit," and it was no great secret that music advertising was most effective when it was aggressively and repetitively imposed upon listeners.[33] In a 1926 memoir, for example, the tunesmith Charles K. Harris—the man responsible for "After the Ball" (1891), one of the most popular songs of the nineteenth century—observed without any apparent sense of discomfort that a melody "must be sung, played, hummed, and drummed into the ears of the public, not in one city alone, but in every city, town, and village, before it ever becomes popular."[34]

More and more, music was described as a pathological presence rather than as a portal to imaginative realms, with "catchiness" becoming the most commonly cited quality of successful popular songs. Indeed, it was not at all unusual for music to be thought of as something that was to be escaped from rather than into: there could be few things more unlike Thoreau's flights of musically inspired ecstasy, after all, than the productivity-enhancing, crowd-controlling background presence known as Muzak, which began to be conceptualized as a business venture in 1922. The state of American subjectivity under sometimes irritating, sometimes stupefying, and sometimes tyrannical musical stimulation therefore emerged as a favorite literary theme in this era. Some of its first memorable iterations arrived in the early novels of Frank Norris: the hulking protagonist of *McTeague* (1899), for example, habitually plays the same six "lugubrious airs" on his concertina over and over again as part of a highly scripted, never-changing, weirdly compulsive leisure routine, and his musically subjugated successors would come to populate later works by Eliot, Fitzgerald, Dos Passos, and many others.[35]

But while music's widespread presence and standardizing effects were objects of concern for literary artists and other listeners of the era, the new music also delivered what its sellers promised: a sense of vigor and variety that was then understood to be uniquely American. It was by no means clear that Sousa was correct in supposing that recorded song would stunt the nation's artistic growth, as the phonograph was often praised as a means of bringing musical culture to those Americans who, because of financial or geographic limitations, would otherwise have had little opportunity to hear it in any form. As Deems Taylor put it in the landmark 1922 essay collection *Civilization in the United States*, phonography was considered by many to be "a very real force in helping to civilize this country musically."[36] Nor was commercial music the exclusive domain of the upper and middle classes, for record companies offered the same pieces on discs of varying quality and price. And as to Sousa's supposition that passively listening to music was a lesser pursuit than actively playing it, Edward Bellamy's popular utopian novel *Looking Backward, 2000–1887* (1888) had posited a hopeful future in which professionally produced music is readily accessible over the telephone and the American public's taste is cultivated rather than narrowed. (Not for nothing would Bellamy's novel come to be cited in advertising copy for Muzak in 1937.)

But perhaps most important, the growing amount of music in American life often gave listeners a sense of exhilaration at the possibility of taking it all in, not in spite of but precisely because of the fact that its sheer variety, presence, and availability threatened the cultural divisions that had once separated the high from the low, the exceptional from the everyday, and the transcendent from the commercial. Dreiser, for example, would remember the jumbled musicality of the phonograph's early days with a certain fondness: "We sat in the 'front room,' or 'parlor,' and listened to the Victrola rendering pieces by Bert Williams and James Whitcomb Riley and Tchaikowsky and Weber and Fields and Beethoven—the usual medley of the sublime and the ridiculous found in so many musical collections," he recalls in one of his memoirs.[37] And just as in Dreiser's parlor, American literature of the late nineteenth and early twentieth centuries began to be punctured more and more by music of all kinds, with songs juxtaposed against one another in alternately intriguing, humorous, chaotic, and puzzling ways. The result was a jumpy and frequently exciting model of textuality that invoked various musical objects and styles in order to achieve a distinctively modern, multireferential, and audible effect.

Scholars often associate this musical-literary eclecticism with jazz, the famously inclusive, pieced-together American music of the era that delighted in drawing on and recontextualizing other musical traditions. Ronald Schleifer has argued that jazz musicians and songwriters can reveal as much about modernism as any writer, while Alfred Appel Jr. has theorized an entire school of "jazz modernism" whose rag-picking artists—musicians, writers, and painters alike—were "alchemists of the vernacular who have 'jazzed' the ordinary and given it new life."[38] To argue that a "jazz" sensibility existed in this period, however, is also to invite a certain degree of confusion, as the word was then defined much more broadly than it is today, used to describe everything from waltzes to *The Waste Land*. Fitzgerald, usually identified as the first to dub the 1920s a "Jazz Age," would note the word's slipperiness in 1931 when recalling that it "meant first sex, then dancing, then music" during his heyday,[39] and scholars generally agree that very little American literature before the century's midpoint could be described as meaningfully informed by what is now thought of as "true" jazz—a music that swings, that is characterized by an improvisational spirit, and that is associated with African American cultural practice.[40] At its best, however, musical literature of the period often shared an inclusive, freewheeling sense of cultural challenge and mastery with contemporary jazz, a sense that could only have come about in a busy, vibrantly musical culture. There may not have been many writers who were inspired directly by a Louis Armstrong or a Duke Ellington, but there were several who were of their party without knowing it.

By way of conclusion, consider the following range of responses to the musical din of early twentieth-century American life. In Dos Passos's 1925 novel *Manhattan Transfer*, the competing musical sounds in a New York apartment building are irritating and absurd: "Apartments round about emitted a querulous Sunday grinding of phonographs playing *It's a Bear*. The Sextette from *Lucia*, selections from *The Quaker Girl*."[41] Yet listen to the very different sense of play—inspired by one of the same songs—in the testimony of Jelly Roll Morton, the self-proclaimed "Inventor of Jazz":

> You have the finest ideas from the greatest operas, symphonies and overtures in jazz music. There is nothing finer than jazz music because it comes from everything of the finest class music. Take the *Sextet from Lucia* and the *Miserery from Ill Trovatore*, that they used to play in the French Opera House, tunes that have always lived in my mind as the greatest favorites of the opera singers; I transformed a lot of those numbers into jazz time, using different little variations and ideas to masquerade the tunes.[42]

Between Dos Passos and Morton is a sense that, in twentieth-century America, great things are possible for the cultural omnivore. The familiarity and immediacy of music reduced the celestial status it enjoyed in the hands of nineteenth-century authors, and sometimes bred wariness and contempt for it in those of the twentieth. But so too were there new possibilities of remaking and remodeling it into a textual art, one that would be as heterogeneous as the nation's soundscape had become. Music could suggest not only a world beyond, and not just a cheapening of the arts in the American market, but also a paradoxically transcendent aggregation of cultural objects, expressed in a patchwork literature whose unity would be all the more striking because its component nature would be so obvious. In these works one hears the emergence of distinctively modern sensibilities and types: the eclectic consumer of culture, the fan of aesthetic miscellany, the artist of multimedia pastiche. Ecstasy, annoyance, boredom, assurance, humor, irony, self-contradiction—these qualities, and all these qualities at once, characterized musically inflected American writing at the century's turn.

Listening to Books

In musical circles, few events have received as much scholarly attention as has the advent of Edison's sound-recording phonograph in the late nineteenth century. The possibility of capturing the most fleeting of the arts brought about any number of revolutionary developments: music became a commodity that could be "stock-piled" like any other, listeners came to live more musical lives than had hitherto been possible, and everything from performance techniques to methods of composition were altered in response to a new medium.[43] Less obvious but comparably significant were the opportunities that phonography afforded literature in the same period. Not long after they began purchasing the first records of their favorite songs and artists, Americans began encountering those same records and songs and artists on the page: fiction and poetry in the phonographic era had begun to develop a distinctive soundtrack, one that readers could reproduce and in a sense even "hear" with increasing fidelity. The new emphasis on music in American letters echoed the increasingly tuneful character of American life, but more important, it was also one of this generation's most successful methods of expanding the sensory possibilities of literature and of intensifying the embodied demands of the reading act. Writers had found a way to make literature audible.

The American modernists were of course not the first to attempt palpable and immediate sensory stimulation in their written works. When Irving Babbitt, the most prominent American literary critic of his day, surveyed the field in 1910, he found it to be wallowing in a confused and indulgent sensuality at least two centuries in the making. The problem for Babbitt was rooted in "an almost pathological keenness of sensation"—he dubbed it "hyperaesthesia"—that he argued had gestated in the eighteenth century, flourished in the Romantic years, and infected all of nineteenth-century literature.[44] In the French especially, Babbitt found a movement "toward a hypertrophy of sensation and an atrophy of ideas, toward a constantly expanding sensorium and a diminishing intellect," with those sensations tending not to remain distinct but rather to melt into a fantastical, all-feeling, even grotesque state of reverie in which sounds might be smelled, colors handled, and objectivity abandoned (145). In decrying this sloppiness in literature, Babbitt also noted that music had become particularly attractive to those writers whom he diagnosed with "eleutheromania," that is, an almost petulant refusal to respect boundaries or limitations of any kind (196). "Above all music has set itself to rendering the modern mood *par excellence*,—the mood of melting into outer nature. Music also reflects the suggestive interaction of all the sense-impressions upon one another," he wrote (162).

His contemptuous tone aside, Babbitt was a good reader of his moment. This was the era of international experiments in aesthetic fusion that were promising new varieties of bodily stimulation and that had only recently begun to be called "synaesthetic" art. Among them were Kandinsky's aforementioned attempts at painting visual music; Richard Strauss's confidence that he could tonally render colors; and Joseph Conrad's famous insistence that it is the function of literature "to make you hear, to make you feel . . . before all, to make you *see*," with direct sensory experience being of no less importance to American writers.[45] T. S. Eliot was certainly no Romantic, but Babbitt might have accused his former student of being one in 1921 when he lamented a modern "dissociation of sensibility" and praised the seventeenth-century "metaphysical" school for its resolutely embodied, even visceral poetics. "Those who object to the 'artificiality' of Milton or Dryden sometimes tell us to 'look into our hearts and write'. But that is not looking deep enough; Racine or Donne looked into a good deal more than the heart. One must look into the cerebral cortex, the nervous system, and the digestive tracts," Eliot asserted.[46] Five years later, Gertrude Stein defined the literary artwork—she called it a "composition"—as a fluctuating intersection of materiality, embodied subjectivity, and time, stating that a text is devoted to "what is seen" but also noting that "what is seen depends upon how everybody is doing everything."[47] The subject matter (the "thing seen") is for Stein contingent on the means by which it is seen ("how everybody is doing everything"), and Stein understood as well as anybody that the means by which something is seen has everything to do with the state of sensory experience in a particular culture, meaning that the writer must tailor her aesthetic accordingly. The question for Eliot, Stein, and other authors was therefore how one might go about evoking such experience on the page, and in the works of many American writers, music came to be an effective means of doing so.

The musical quality of American writing during this period leads to an array of larger questions that have only recently been explored by scholars. To what extent can literary synaesthesia be literally experiential, and to what extent is it metaphorical? What role does the aural sense play in the act of reading? How does a writer intent on evoking sound get it across, and what must a reader do to make it audible? At present, the answers are still preliminary. As Douglas Kahn has put it, the artistic output of the late nineteenth and early twentieth centuries "has been read and looked at in detail but rarely heard," and the difficulties that sound presents for critical inquiry are obvious: as Kahn notes, sound "inhabits its own time and dissipates quickly," excepting the fortuitous cases in which it has been recorded.[48] Nevertheless, the last fifteen years or so have seen a flowering of critical approaches devoted to audio culture and its relations to literature, history, and other disciplines.[49] It is still a young and, it must be said, a somewhat confrontational field. Audio culture manifestos are sometimes characterized by an aggrieved tone, arguing that scholarship on sensual aesthetics has lazily—perhaps even chauvinistically—tended to emphasize visuality above all else, placing it at the top of an ad hoc phenomenal hierarchy and relegating the study of sound to second-class status. But of late, the volume of literary study has been turned up.

Interest in the ways that one might go about listening to literature is sometimes traced back to modernism's historical moment, specifically Milman Parry's 1928 argument that the most distinctive formal features of Homer's epics were derived from the rhythms, musicality, and mnemonic devices often found in oral cultures. From there, interest in the fundamental ways that orality (in which hearing is the dominant sense) differs from literacy (in which vision reigns) grew until reaching a breakthrough in the 1960s work of Eric A. Havelock, Walter J. Ong, and Marshall McLuhan.[50] All three argued to various effects that the mediation of language has crucial implications for its meaning, and that even in a print-dominated age— McLuhan's "Gutenberg Galaxy"—the oral and aural qualities of language remain crucial if not always acknowledged influences on the reading act. "Written texts all have to be related somehow, directly or indirectly, to the world of sound, the natural habitat of language, to yield their meanings," Ong concluded a few years later. "'Reading' a text means converting it to sound, aloud or in the imagination, syllable-by-syllable in slow reading or sketchily in the rapid reading common to high-technology cultures. Writing can never dispense with orality."[51] In noting this dimension of written language, of course, these theorists were in some ways simply catching up to the field of African American letters, as such writers as Paul Laurence Dunbar, James Weldon Johnson, Zora Neale Hurston, and Richard Wright had been debating the vernacular character of black authorship since at least the late nineteenth century.[52]

This insistence on the multisensual character of written language in the 1960s came hand in hand with an increased understanding of textual meaning as less a fixed object than an ongoing, participatory, and interpretive process, one that is shaped by the reader's imagination as well as by authors. The seminal theory in this regard was Roland Barthes's formulation of the "writerly text," an ever-evolving collaborative progression—he called it a "production without product"—that is in large part constructed by, rather than simply communicated to, the reading individual.[53] Sound, moreover, is a crucial part of the participatory, writerly text: Garrett Stewart has extended Barthes's theory by arguing that the act of reading takes place in a kind of middle area between text and subjectivity—he calls it "the zone of evocalization"—in which readers construct a hybrid "phonotext" by combining written cues from an author with the "sounded," inner voicings of those cues that they produce themselves. According to Stewart's formulation, readers add sound to texts in a publicly silent but privately audible manner, much as a singer might scan a piece of sheet music in preparation for a performance. "When we read to ourselves, our ears hear nothing. Where we read, however, we listen," he asserts.[54]

Stewart's model of phonotextuality is as literal a claim as has yet been made for the sound-producing capacity of the written word, and it represents something of an end point for this particular line of criticism. More recently, studies of sound and its relation to literature have tended in more figurative directions, often concerned with what William R. Paulson has termed informational "noise," or in his words, "not loud or obnoxious sounds but anything that gets mixed up with messages as they are sent."[55] "Noise," according to Paulson, is that which introduces disturbance, perturbation, or chaos into a system of communication, something like the "white noise" that degrades clarity in an electronic transmission. A literary work is therefore to be considered "noisy" if—as tends to be the case—its meaning is ambiguous or veiled or unclear, and in recent years scholars have rather ingeniously applied this definition of "noise" to those American texts that are explicitly concerned with representing actual noises and actual sounds. Juan A. Suárez, for example, has argued that the din of everyday life in the early twentieth century became a favorite subject for the American modernists because it represented cultural, Paulsonain "noise" as well; these writers were fascinated, Suárez argues, by that which "simply refused to yield sense," and they therefore sought to create a literature that would be "at once knowable and enigmatic, predictable and contingent."[56] Philipp Schweighauser, on the other hand, finds an ideological quality to the sound-oriented works of American modernism, arguing that their attention to grating frequencies and the accents of racial and ethnic "others"—literally noisy sounds to some ears—allowed them to take "noisy," unruly positions within their political moment. Such literature, Schweighauser notes, is "strictly speaking, silent," but in a metaphorical sense it "negotiates, affirms, critiques, *and* becomes an integral part of the acoustics of modernity."[57]

American literature at the century's turn, according to these and other such accounts, is often about sound, and it can function as a kind of disruptive, symbolic "noise" within its broader cultural context, but it cannot be said to be truly audible. As it stands, then, the idea of a sounding text remains fanciful and perhaps even comical, rather like René Magritte's painting *The Subjugated Reader* (1928), whose horrified female subject, her mouth agape in mid-shriek and her eyes bulging with terror, fixes her gaze on the open pages of a slim and very innocuous-looking book. At the risk of treating Schweighauser's claims more literally than he intends them, however, one might ask whether the advent of recording technology did not in fact allow literature to become "an integral part of the acoustics of modernity" in a very real, physical sense. In some critical circles, after all, it has become all but obvious that the new possibilities afforded by inscriptive technologies of the period led to significant changes in the ways that listeners heard, responded to, and thought about aural stimuli. McLuhan's argument that information technologies create "extensions" of the human senses and Susan Gitelman's declaration that new media allow for the development of "new subjectivities" have become such common underpinnings of scholarship on late nineteenth- and early twentieth-century literature that, as Michael North has noted, "supposed changes in the human sensorium have come to represent modernity itself" in the present critical paradigm.[58] Leaving aside the question of whether the collective American sense of hearing was in fact altered in any measurable, quantifiably physical manner in this period, those who lived during modernism's moment were undeniably listening to new sounds in new ways, and these changes in listening behavior correspondingly created new, audible possibilities in turn-of-the-century literature.

Certainly no one has done more to consider the impact of phonography on embodied experience and literary practice than Friedrich A. Kittler, who has in many ways established the terms for discussing these intertwined issues. For Kittler, the gramophone and its production of precise, faithfully recorded sounds led to a desiccation of those "voiced," participatory reading practices so central to the 1960s debates on orality and the written word. Before the advent of phonography, Kittler argues, an idea had to pass through the "bottleneck" of written language in order to reach an audience, with a writer's meaning being transformed into letters and words that would in turn be re-formed into sensation within the reader's imagination.[59] As Kittler puts it, "words quivered with sensuality and memory. It was the passion of all reading to hallucinate meaning between lines and letters."[60] But once sound could be captured by the phonograph, the evocative quality of the written word ceased to be important or even viable: "readers and writers no longer need the powers of hallucination" in such an environment because the sounds represented by letters can all be reproduced faithfully in a new medium. As a consequence of this epochal shift, Kittler finds writers faced with two options, only one of which would go on to be associated with serious literary practice. The unambitious would write in such a way as to anticipate their works being translated into other media forms (a poem to be read aloud on record, for instance), while other, more adventurous authors would reject mimesis and referentiality altogether, often in order to reflect upon the arbitrary nature of language (the nonsense verse of the Dadaists, for example).[61]

One might question, however, whether the crisis of language that Kittler describes was really so pressing for the American writer and whether recording technology might not have had quite the opposite effect, enriching the sensory possibilities of language instead. Could not the phonograph also be utilized by writers within their literary works? In his history of sound recording technology in the nineteenth and twentieth centuries, for example, Jonathan Sterne emphasizes not how revolutionary but rather how banal and expected this technological step forward turned out to be for many Americans of the period. Arguing that the allegedly baffling consequences of recording had for years been anticipated by an American public that wanted more and more control over its sonic environment, Sterne posits that "[i]f modernity, in part, names the experience of rapid social and cultural change, then its 'shocking emblems' may very well have been taken in stride by some of its people."[62]

Similarly, critics have shown that writers frequently attempted to yoke and deploy information technologies at the century's turn, usually in order to have uniquely direct sensory impacts upon their readers. At least as far back as McLuhan, scholars have pointed to electronic media as being directly responsible for a certain richness in modernist writing: "The printed book had encouraged artists to reduce all forms of expression as much as possible to the single descriptive and narrative plane of the printed word. The advent of electric media released art from this straitjacket at once, creating the world of Paul Klee, Picasso, Braque, Eisenstein, the Marx Brothers, and James Joyce," he argues.[63] More recently, Sara Danius has discussed the ways in which the gramophone, telephone, and cinema led to a strain of modernism dedicated to "the inherent value of perception exercised for perception's sake,"[64] while others have shown how the so-called sensation fiction of the nineteenth century delivered sensation to a quite literal extent, stimulating quickened pulses, shortness of breath, and heightened adrenaline in readers. And while there was no precise American equivalent of the Italian Futurist movement—which celebrated "the complete renewal of human sensibility that has occurred as an effect of science's major discoveries"[65]—the modernist era saw more than a few artists who believed it their duty to take on the latest scientific advances in the United States. As Hart Crane put it, poets began to account not just for new technologies but also for new, technologically assisted methods of thinking in their verse: "to fool one's self that definitions are being reached by merely referring frequently to skyscrapers, radio antennae, steam whistles, or other surface phenomena of our time is merely to paint a photograph," he argued, suggesting instead that writers concern themselves with "the organic effects on us of these and other fundamental factors of our experience."[66]

If one bears in mind that Edison's aim in creating the phonograph was to fuse writing and sound in a form that could be "read" by a needle (as is implied by the very word "phonography"), one ought not be surprised that American writers of this period attempted a similar synthesis in their works. There was, of course, a palpable excitement at the time over the possibility of authors recording their words in their own voices, as well as a sense that a new, technological orality could enhance literature. Ford Madox Ford, for example, went so far as to suggest that the difficult, multiclausal late works of Henry James would become positively accessible—"limpid" was his word—if listened to on record in "the indefinitely distant future," a future, it must be said, that in James's case still seems as distant as ever.[67] But it was recorded music that offered authors the simplest and most direct means of delivering audible sensations to their readers on the printed page. There are, after all, few things that can invade and possess the imagination so completely as a well-known, catchy song, and this was a historical moment at which literary references to such songs, especially to ones that existed in standardized formats on records, could practically demand musical responses in the readerly mind, sounding with an almost occult degree of exactness and force.

A case in point from the period: when the acoustician Dayton Clarence Miller—known in his day as "The Wizard of Visible Sound"—was preparing to publish his first-of-its-kind collection of sound wave drawings for a general audience, his most effective means of appealing to readers was to depict the vibrations produced by an instantly recognizable piece of music. The first thing a reader of Miller's *The Science of Musical Sound* (1916) would therefore have found upon opening the book was a fold-out frontispiece emblazoned with the wave produced by a single note from that aforementioned popular favorite, the Sextette from *Lucia di Lammermoor* (see Image 1). What is more, readers may well have been familiar with the individual voice being depicted, as Miller went out of his way to mention that he had used a recording by Enrico Caruso, one of the most famous opera singers of his or any other day. Indeed, depending on the degree of their familiarity with Caruso's record, some readers might even have been able to listen mentally to the isolated syllable being graphically rendered, "chi." And when audiences can be depended on to know of and even "play" a song in the mind upon receiving a written cue, a range of possibilities opens up for authors: in this case, Miller is able to make his readers imagine not just a hypothetical voice but rather a particular, famous one, and he can presume that they will have more or less the same idea of what that voice sounds like.

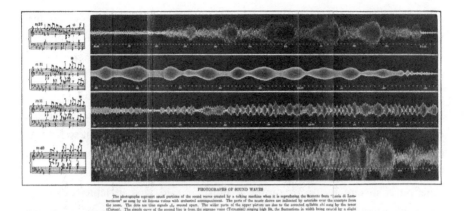

PHOTOGRAPHS OF SOUND WAVES

The photographs represent small portions of the sound waves created by a talking machine when it is reproducing the Sextette from "Lucia di Lammermoor" as sung by six famous voices with orchestral accompaniment. The parts of the music shown are indicated by asterisks over the excerpts from the score. The dots are time signals ⅟₁₀₀ second apart. The wider parts of the upper picture are due to the accented syllable *ché* sung by the tenor (Caruso). The simple curve of the second line is from the soprano voice (Tetrazzini) singing high B♭, the fluctuations in width being caused by a slight *tremolo*. The whole sound for this one note is nearly four times as long as the part here shown. The third line is produced by the soprano and baritone (Amato) voices singing softly. The fourth line shows the complex wave due to the six solo voices singing loudly. See pages 311 and 312.

A graphical rendering of a single note sung by Enrico Caruso, one of many early twentieth-century attempts at representing audio-visual experience on the printed page. From Dayton Clarence Miller's *The Science of Musical Sounds* (New York: Macmillan, 1916).

As is hopefully being made clear by the sheer regularity with which *Lucia* was taken up in the period, a well-known song's referentiality had considerable value for artists at the century's turn, able as it was to establish a powerful and precise aural intimacy with audiences. Writers were and remain able to use music in the service of such effects because it has always had a pronounced capacity for being internalized by listeners. It has become something of a critical commonplace, moreover, that this process of internalization was intensified by the invention of phonographic recording. Walter Benjamin's landmark essay "The Work of Art in the Age of Its Mechanical Reproducibility" (1935) notes the "shattering of tradition" represented by the listener's ability to play whatever music he or she likes at any time, and his influential formulation of "distracted" consumers of art depends on their absorbing mass-produced works into themselves rather than being absorbed by one-of-a-kind performances.[68] More recently, Kittler has argued in his inimitable style that the mind of the record listener becomes "stamped" with sound in the same way that a vinyl disc is: "Records turn and turn until phonographic inscriptions inscribe themselves into brain physiology. We all know hits and rock songs by heart precisely because there is no reason to memorize them anymore."[69] And if one of the distinctive qualities of popular music at the century's turn was that it had insinuated itself into the American public's collective consciousness, then writers of the period had a unique opportunity to "play" their audiences by referring to and activating those remembered songs and voices, almost as though readers had become jukeboxes that could be manipulated at will.

By way of conclusion, consider Fitzgerald's *This Side of Paradise*, one of many texts of the period that models how the process of musical-literary audience stimulation works. Here Fitzgerald's protagonist, Amory Blaine, writes a love letter from his dorm room at Princeton, taking care to specify what is to be heard during the act of reading his words:

> Oh Isabelle, dear—it's a wonderful night. Somebody is playing "Love Moon" on a mandolin far across the campus, and the music seems to bring you into the window. Now he's playing "Good-bye Boys, I'm Through," and how well it suits me. For I *am* through with everything.[70]

Of course, readers cannot know precisely what these songs sound like, as they are performed by a remote, live musician. But Isabelle is every bit as removed from the scene, and Amory's expectations for her are the very same ones that Fitzgerald has for his audience: in both cases, a reader is asked to "fill in" music from memory and match it with a text, to bring familiar songs into a productive relationship with narrative so as to create a multilayered aesthetic complex. The power of this moment in the novel has been lessened over the years, as few twenty-first-century readers are likely to have a working knowledge of the song Fitzgerald mentions. Yet the effects that Fitzgerald produced in his time were surely no different from those achieved by Salman Rushdie in his contemporary rock 'n' roll novel *The Ground Beneath Her Feet* (1999), as when his Indian rock star protagonist Ormus Cama gains telepathic access to "Like a Rolling Stone" and scoops Bob Dylan by performing his own version of it years before its real-world composition in 1965. There is no doubt that many readers, when encountering Rushdie's fanciful scene, still hear the original version's opening snare drum shot, its organ wail, and Dylan's distinctively American tone of accusation, even as they attempt to imagine what Cama's different take on it might be like. And in these and other such moments, the possibility of a sound-producing literary text comes to seem very real indeed.

Valuing Popular Culture

To talk about "popular culture" in regard to literature or music is also to talk about value judgments. The term came into existence so as to differentiate an artistic category from a worthier "high" culture and a more esteemed "folk" one, and the musical literature taken up in this book appeared at a time when the question of how Americans ought to balance their tastes and predilections was being debated widely.[71] Musically inclined writers tended to be idiosyncratic and contradictory on the subject of cultural value, with the same author who admired his era's popular arts at one moment being quite likely to deride them the next. The tastes and sensibilities of these and other American modernists were ongoing, never-ceasing balancing acts, and they can be difficult to understand and appreciate as a result. But while musical literature from this period is seldom consistent in its critiques of popular culture, this is precisely why it offers so much insight into the ways that turn-of-the-century Americans regarded entertainment and made sense—or nonsense, as the case may be—of their crowded, demanding era.

Before we can hear this, however, there is a "Great Divide" to cross. There was once a point in the scholarly discussion of modernism when that resonant phrase was used primarily to denote a nineteenth-century historical transition, a point at which a Victorian cultural sensibility gave way to a variously defined "modern" one.[72] But later it began to carry connotations of value and taste, increasingly being used to refer to the distance that literary artists were alleged to have created between their works and those of the market at century's turn. Now critics spoke of a "Great Divide" between art and popular culture, arguing that modernist artists were almost fanatically concerned with dissociating themselves from the masses and retreating into a zone of superiority and privilege. Today, few scholars believe this diagnosis was correct or that the modernists ever perceived such a yawning chasm between the high and low arts, but the "Great Divide" theorists are nevertheless worth revisiting here because they had such a profound impact on subsequent discussions of American literature and popular culture.

In essence, these thinkers found that the modernist movement had caught itself in a double bind, dismissing the popular, "low" arts but failing to realize that in pursuing "high" cultural autonomy, it had aligned itself with and helped shore up the very social order that it sought to transcend. Truly revolutionary art, the "Great Divide" critics asserted, confronts capitalist systems, mass taste, and popular culture directly rather than fleeing them, and it attempts to integrate art into what Peter Bürger—a key thinker in advancing this thesis—called the "praxis of life" in 1974.[73] The American modernists, however, were argued to have been notable failures in this regard. Particularly vehement was Andreas Huyssen, whose influential *After the Great Divide* (1986) charged American authors of the early twentieth century with refusing to acknowledge "jazz, sports, cars, technology, movies, and photography," and by extension the people to whom such things mattered.[74] It was only the advent of mid-century postmodernism and Pop Art, according to Huyssen, that returned high cultural expression to social relevance in America, and when that occurred the modernists were said to have been victims of their own snobbery. The irony of modernism's arc, concluded Terry Eagleton, is that it "escapes from one form of commodification only to fall prey to another. If it avoids the humiliation of becoming an abstract, serialized, instantly exchangeable thing, it does so only by virtue of reproducing that other side of the commodity which is fetishism."[75]

To a degree, the "Great Divide" thinkers were simply extending a line of thought that had enjoyed considerable currency in the decades leading up to the advent of American modernism. As Lawrence Levine has shown in his classic study *Highbrow/Lowbrow*, the late nineteenth century saw cultural reformers distancing themselves from the masses by elevating and sanctifying several forms and genres that had once been enjoyed by a broad cross-section of Americans—Italian opera and the plays of Shakespeare, for example. Writing in 1915, the critic Van Wyck Brooks theorized that a "highbrow" sensibility had separated itself from a "lowbrow" one even further back in the nation's history, and he argued that the United States had always been characterized by "two main currents in the American mind running side by side but rarely mingling."[76] Brooks used the terms "highbrow" and "lowbrow" somewhat generally and was not only referring to conceptions of cultural or aesthetic value when he did so, but his concern over what he called "a glassy inflexible priggishness on the upper levels" and his admonishment that "the lower levels have a certain humanity, flexibility, tangibility" to them would eventually become staples of "Great Divide" criticism (29). Looking back on the late nineteenth and early twentieth centuries, a great many scholars have, like Brooks, seen America's artists facing polarized cultural camps, "the one so fantastically above, the other so fantastically below the level of right reason" (35), and the modernists have frequently been accused of being too much inclined toward the former group.

In today's critical conversation, however, the notion of a "Great Divide" in modernism is discussed mainly as a straw man argument to be knocked down, especially in relation to American literature. Critics of the last two decades or so have tended to collapse its binary logic in two ways. First has been the identification of American writers of the period whose works were both aesthetically daring and socially engaged, many of them dedicated to proletarian and race advancement: the authors associated with the Washington Square circle of the 1910s, for example, or the Harlem Renaissance artists of the 1920s.[77] Second has been the demonstration of just how frequently modernist writers engaged popular culture, in both formal and thematic ways. Lawrence Rainey has shown how bound up even the most notoriously difficult modernist texts were with mass publishing, periodical culture, and advertising; Michael North has chronicled the wide-ranging, "ironic interdependence" of experimental literary works and popular phenomena;

and Juan Suárez has delineated a canon of "pop modernism" whose task was to "reinvent the practice of everyday life" in America, to name but a few examples.[78] While opinions vary as to what extent American modernist literature embraced popular culture at the century's turn, it is now very difficult to argue that the relationship can be ignored or dismissed as one of pat condescension.[79]

A key insight of recent scholarship has been modernism's formal debt to popular culture, with the experimental techniques of this "high" literary movement frequently resembling or aspiring to those of the "low." It has been noted, for example, that such popular venues as the music hall, the revue, and the nickelodeon depended on the same bricolage and pastiche effects as any number of quick-cutting modernist works. So too has it been pointed out that American entertainment was then characterized by a certain jumpy over-stuffedness that was different in intention from but not entirely unlike Eliot's mania of cultural juxtaposition in *The Waste Land*. Contemporary accounts of popular music, for example, often characterized it as an Eliotic vortex of cultural quotation: the famed dance band leader and self-proclaimed "King of Jazz" Paul Whiteman emphasized its alignment of the very high with the very low, noting that "everybody knows now that Handel's Messiah furnished the main theme of the well-known 'Yes, We Have No Bananas.'"[80] Similarly, Burnet Hershey, theorizer of the aforementioned global "jazz latitude," understood American music to be a racial and national magpie's nest: "Natives of far-off tropical lands eagerly nod their approval of Tinpan Alley's latest masterpieces. They prick up their ears in recognition of something strangely familiar to the plaintive melodies of their homelands."[81] If the goal of forward-looking literature in this period was, as Harold Stearns put it in *America and the Young Intellectual* (1921), to resist an essentially conservative American "institutional life" bent on "blackjacking our youth into the acceptance of the *status quo*," then popular music's veneration of brashness, cheek, and incongruity—so irritating to many of the day's cultural guardians—offered one means of rebellion.[82]

Simply pointing out the formal correspondences between the popular arts and American writing ought not be enough for the contemporary critic, however, for stopping there means overlooking issues that are frequently avoided in accounts of literary modernism: the ways these writers went about evaluating popular culture, their deeply personal relationships with entertainment, and their insights into the nature of fandom. These issues, so central to the field of musicology, are underemphasized in literary scholarship, which tends to concentrate so much on the formal or thematic uses to which the popular arts are put in texts that writers can come to seem not a little calculating in their invocations of them. Popular culture emerges in many critical accounts as a stalking horse for the serious author, a shadow presence whose dynamism was imitated by writers as a clever means of differentiating themselves from it (as Thomas Strychacz has asserted), or whose emphasis on marketability and product differentiation was manipulated in such a way as to increase the aesthetic and intellectual value of literary labor (as Mark McGurl has shown).

Such scholarly work is of course productive and insightful, but in regard to the musical-literary writing of this period, it is important also to take up the question of what it means for an author to like or dislike popular culture, to value or devalue it. As the musicologist Simon Frith has argued, the act of listening to or thinking about popular music is in many ways nothing more or less than an exercise in personal reaction, judgment, and taste, a never-ceasing reevaluation of the "good" and the "bad" that is as complex and unique to the individual listener as it is ongoing. The American writers under review here, moreover, understood this dimension of popular music and listening especially well. The music suffusing their works not only provides sonic ambiance and a model for experimental form, but it also questions what it means to have meaningful relationships with a mode of popular expression—a mode no less powerful or significant to audiences for its being marketable, widespread, and frequently unrepentant in its aesthetic "lowness."

It is easy to shy away from these matters in relation to the American modernists because their attitudes often seem so mixed, in states of such contradictory and even incoherent tension. There is no denying the fact, after all, that the popular arts are often depicted as dreary affairs in modernist novels and poetry. The records that punctuate *The Waste Land* can seem cheap and aligned with sordid circumstances; the lovelorn ballads floating through Fitzgerald's novels can seem to offer only unreal and unattainable fantasies to their frequently disappointed listeners; the songs of Langston Hughes can seem violent and misogynistic; and the chorus girls who populate the novels of Theodore Dreiser and John Dos Passos can seem materialistic and shallow. Is it not therefore the case, one might reasonably ask, that these unflattering musical portrayals reveal the haughtiness so often attributed to this generation? Yet even the briefest search through these authors' biographies reveals that all of them spent a significant amount of time with and in some cases cared passionately about popular music: Dreiser's brother was one of Tin Pan Alley's most famous songwriters, Fitzgerald harbored dreams of producing musicals for most of his early career, and Hughes traded his New York cosmopolitanism to experience the itinerant life of the bluesman. A disconnection appears to exist between the attitudes that these authors communicated in their works and those that they held in life, and this can make the question of taste difficult to take up.

Yet disconnection is in many ways the point of musical literature, not the problem. When exploring cultural value in the early twentieth century, the American
modernists often concluded that it is not strange or inappropriate for people's tastes
to be paradoxical, but rather that tastes in fact tend toward inconsistency. James
Weldon Johnson, in his novel *The Autobiography of an Ex-Colored Man* (1912),
revealed a seemingly peculiar but in some ways representative attitude by writing
in the voice of a classically trained musician who excels at ragtime and, crucially,
perceives little contradiction in his mixed talents. Early in the novel, the narrator
condemns snobbery thus:

> American musicians, instead of investigating ragtime, attempt to ignore it or
> dismiss it with a contemptuous word. But that has always been the course of
> scholasticism in every branch of art. Whatever new thing the *people* like is
> pooh-poohed; whatever is *popular* is spoken of as not worth the while. The
> fact is, nothing great or enduring, especially in music, has ever sprung full-
> fledged and unprecedented from the brain of any master; the best that he gives
> to the world he gathers from the hearts of the people, and runs it through the
> alembic of his genius. In spite of the bans which musicians and music teachers
> have placed upon it, the people still demand and enjoy ragtime.[83]

Johnson's protagonist, moreover, is precisely the kind of "master" he describes,
able to mix Tin Pan Alley and the classics with ease: at his club gig, he recalls,
"I used to play Mendelssohn's 'Wedding March' in a manner that never failed to
arouse enthusiasm," and he eventually concludes that he has been accorded greater
musical opportunities by ragtime than by Beethoven or Chopin.[84] It is his omnivorous cultural appetite and his ability to navigate high and low culture alike that
makes him a distinctively modern figure, and in combining idioms he undertakes
what Richard Middleton has identified as the fundamental task of popular music,
"to put a finger on that space, that terrain, of contradiction—between 'imposed'
and 'authentic,' 'elite' and 'common,' predominant and subordinate, then and now,
theirs and ours, and so on—and to organize it in particular ways."[85]
    Many other American modernists demonstrate a similar cultural flexibil-
ity in their works, and if critics have sometimes been reluctant to think in kind,
part of the reason lies in the discourses of commercialism, standardization, and
social control that so often surrounded popular music and culture at the century's turn. This was, after all, the period that saw the advent of a new, pejorative
cultural classification—"mass culture"—that referred to works that were alleged
to create passive, "receptive" audiences rather than active, participatory ones.[86]
It also witnessed the first works of music criticism by Theodor W. Adorno, the

Frankfurt School theorist who pioneered the notion that popular music is a shoddy, fraudulent product manufactured by a monolithic "Culture Industry" and forced upon a powerless, deluded population of listeners. "In our present society the masses themselves are kneaded by the same mode of production as the articraft material foisted upon them. The customers of musical entertainment are themselves objects or, indeed, products of the same mechanisms which determine the production of popular music," he wrote some years later in his landmark essay, "On Popular Music."[87] Adorno's was a powerful, influential, and in many ways convincing polemic, and in the years since there has been no shortage of those who associate—or imagine that others associate—such music with aesthetic and intellectual bankruptcy.

It is often tempting to presume that modernist authors shared Adorno's outlook on commercial music, particularly given the gloomy tone of so much of their writing. But the story of high literature, popular culture, and the relationships of authors to both at century's turn was far more complex than this. As Barry J. Faulk has argued, such institutions as the music hall not only offered vivacious, compelling models of artistry for writers, but also taught cultural observers how to appreciate and analyze the "low" on its own terms, as opposed to simply dismissing it outright.[88] Popular entertainments were increasingly understood to be distinct forms of cultural practice and even "art," with a new breed of thinker appreciating them for their own sakes and feeling free to engage with them without becoming compromised in other aesthetic arenas. For a representative figure in criticism one might point to Edmund Wilson, who penned crucial early reviews of such modernist giants as Eliot and Joyce even as he was writing articles on the Ziegfeld Follies and other ostensible fluff. For Wilson, appreciating both the high and the low could lead to a greater understanding of American culture as a whole, as theorized in his 1926 article "The All-Star Literary Vaudeville":

> When time shall have weeded out our less important writers, it is probable that those who remain will give the impression of a literary vaudeville: H. L. Mencken hoarse with preaching in his act making fun of preachers; Edna St. Vincent Millay, the soloist, a contralto with deep notes of pathos; Sherwood Anderson holding his audience with naïve but disquieting bedtime stories; Theodore Dreiser with his newspaper narrative of commonplace scandals and crimes and obituaries of millionaires, in which the reporter astonishes the readers by being rash enough to try to tell the truth; T. S. Eliot patching from many cultures a dazzling and variegated disguise for the shrinking and scrupulous soul of a hero out of Henry James.[89]

The writers mentioned by Wilson, moreover, sometimes saw themselves in similar terms, as when Eliot claimed to seek "the satisfaction of having a part to play
in society as worthy as that of the music-hall comedian" and hoped for a broad
popularity:

> I believe that the poet naturally prefers to write for as large and miscel-
> laneous an audience as possible, and that it is the half-educated and
> ill-educated, rather than the uneducated, who stand in his way: I myself
> should like an audience which could neither read nor write. The most use-
> ful poetry, socially, would be one which could cut across all the present
> stratifications of public taste—stratifications which are perhaps a sign of
> social disintegration.[90]

Eliot often enacted meetings of the high and the low during his career, as when he
wrote both *The Waste Land* and an appreciation of the music-hall star Marie Lloyd
in the same year. And in resisting "stratifications of public taste," he and other
authors of the American modernist movement can sometimes seem to be theorizing what has recently been termed a "nobrow" aesthetic, defined by Peter Swirski
as "an intentional stance whereby authors simultaneously target both extremes of
the literary spectrum."[91]

Apparent paradoxes in taste or concurrent inclinations toward the high and
low arts are often explained away, and a frequent method of doing so is to argue
that "low" arts are, in fact, something else entirely. Certain popular musics—
African American jazz and blues at the beginning of the twentieth century, punk
and indie rock toward the end—are sometimes said to have been valuable to listeners because they offered resistance to the hegemonic mainstream that Adorno
despised.[92] Other artists are critically praised insofar as they have "transcended"
the dubious category of pop: Duke Ellington is argued to have been a composer
in addition to a dance band leader, Bob Dylan a poet as well as a rock star, and in
such cases a popular performer is understood to have become more than "just"
that.[93] But as the best works of musicology in recent years have tended to claim, a
listener's relationship to popular music is often interesting not in spite of the fact
that such music has commercial origins and entertains rather than edifies, but
precisely because of this. The Adorno thesis of manipulated, brainwashed listeners has by and large been superseded by a belief that audiences are sophisticated
enough to make their own, independent judgments about the range of cultural
forms they are faced with. And assessing turn-of-the-century musical authors
requires a willingness to accept their consciously, even proudly messy states of
mind and emotion for what they are.

This chapter ends where it began, with Walter Pater's paean to music's preeminence. Here we find him invoked in *The Seven Lively Arts*, a 1924 volume of criticism by Gilbert Seldes that has been identified as the first serious study of American popular culture. Seldes alludes to Pater's famous definition of the aesthetic life ("to burn always with this hard gem-like flame, to maintain this ecstasy"), but he provocatively argues that it is the light, popular arts, and not the sublime, elevated ones, that best light the fire. There is a crucial difference, Seldes writes, "between burning and burning up—of which Pater was aware."[94] Whereas we feel we must "defend ourselves from the impact of great beauty, of nobility, of high tragedy, because we feel ourselves incompetent to master them," the lighter arts satisfy us because they are ephemeral, dependent on the tides of fashion, and so profuse that they are never especially difficult to encounter:

> Our experience of perfection is so limited that even when it occurs in a secondary field we hail its coming. Yet the minor arts are all transient, and these moments have no lasting record, and their creators are unrewarded even by the tribute of a word. A moment comes when everything is exactly right, and you have an occurrence—it may be something exquisite or something unnamably gross; there is in it an ecstasy which sets it apart from everything else. . . . All of those I am writing about here have given me that thrill at least once—and my memory goes back to these occasions, trying to catch the incredible moment again.[95]

What is the nature of this ecstasy that popular culture creates? What difference does it make for it to be inspired by the "exquisite" or the "unnamably gross"? And can the transient experience of standing outside of oneself, the "incredible moment" that Seldes describes, ever be felt again? It was the aim of American modernist writers to ponder these questions in their musical literary works, and it is the aim of the following book to listen.

2. Songs Not in Thy Songs
Musical Forms and American Free Verse

Of all the arts, poetry and music may have the longest-standing and most intimate association with one another. That association, however, has frequently gone unheard over the centuries. The problem dates back to the time of the Renaissance, when the works of Western poets and composers began to diverge and the differences between the two forms started to become more apparent than their commonality. As James William Johnson has shown in an authoritative essay, the spread of literacy some five hundred years ago tended to detach poetry from its roots in oral practice and to confine it to the silent page. At the same time, the rise of "such primarily melodic forms as the madrigal, glee, catch, and round" shored up a separate class of sung language, in which words were of secondary importance to musical sound and performance.[1] From this came our modern, generally distinct categories of poetry and song, and with them the pervasive sense that the influence of music on poetry is at best a "largely vestigial" one.[2]

Yet there have always been those who attend to the harmonies between the arts. As Marjorie Perloff has recently noted, the very terminology we use to discuss poetic verse suggests its ancient aurality: the word "*poetry* . . . comes from the Greek *poiesis*, a making or creation; in Medieval Latin, *poetria*, the art of verbal creation."[3] So too does "lyric" poetry intimate the accompaniment of a lyre, just as the concept of a metrical "foot" does a danceable tune. It should therefore not be too surprising that in the nineteenth and twentieth centuries, versifiers as far apart in history, geography, and sensibility as Homer and Baudelaire were sometimes discussed as similarly musical writers. Indeed, the nineteenth-century American poet Sidney Lanier went so far as to declare in 1880 "that the sound-relations which constitute music are the same with those which constitute verse, and that the main distinction between music and verse is, when stated with scientific precision, the difference between the scale of tones used in music and the scale of tones used by the human speaking-voice."[4] Closer to our own time, the composer and conductor Leonard Bernstein has provocatively argued that poetry constitutes a "true parallel" to music, and he has drawn extensively on the syntax of the former, linguistic art in attempting to explain how the latter, nonlinguistic one communicates to its listeners.[5]

For some of the most prominent American poets before and during modernism's moment, achieving musicality was of nothing less than central importance. The question was how to compose musical verse without going too far and crossing the line into songwriting, as had the many earlier writers who worked in the context of New England hymnody or whose works were sung to the tunes of popular "airs." Would-be musical poets frequently arrived at counterintuitive or difficult-to-explain prosodic theories when attempting this synthesis, most especially in regard to rhythm. Consider the case of Edgar Allan Poe: his famously regular meter earned him the pejorative nickname of "jingle man" from Ralph Waldo Emerson, yet he nonetheless believed that his poetry's music arose not from its steady beat but rather from its elusive abstraction.[6] "Music is the perfection of the soul, or idea, of Poetry," he wrote to James Russell Lowell in 1844. "The *vagueness* of exaltation aroused by a sweet air (which should be strictly indefinite and never too strongly suggestive) is precisely what we should aim at in poetry."[7] Ezra Pound attempted a similarly difficult balance some seventy years later, modeling his verse on the songs of the Provençal troubadours but also arguing that truly musical writing avoids singsong rhythms. As he famously put it in his rules of Imagism in 1912, a poet ought to "compose in the sequence of the musical phrase, not in the sequence of a metronome."[8] In both cases one hears something of a paradox: according to Poe and Pound, a "musical" poem would not be easily identifiable as such, at least not by the most obvious formal markers of musical composition.

The following chapter will address two bodies of work that demonstrate the challenges and possibilities of musical poetry, Walt Whitman's *Leaves of Grass* (written and revised over his lifetime) and T. S. Eliot's early verse (up to and including *The Waste Land*). These poets are seldom studied alongside one another for a variety of reasons,[9] but both illustrate the often-surprising uses to which musical forms, particularly popular ones, can be put in poetic contexts. Crucially, their works do not seem to be especially musical upon first listen. Both men are famous for avoiding traditionally songlike meters and verse forms, in spite of the fact that Whitman's words have been adapted for vocal performance many times and Eliot's were the basis for the Broadway extravaganza *Cats*. So too did both warn explicitly against poetry's falling too much under the influence of certain musics. Whitman complained in 1876 that "the prevailing flow of poetry for the last fifty or eighty years, and now at its height, has been and is (like the music) an expression of mere surface melody, within narrow limits," which he considered at odds with "the sturdy, the universal, and the democratic" character of his own work.[10] For his part, Eliot conceded in 1942 that purely instrumental compositions could model important structural techniques for poets, but he found that songs and other texted forms of music were not especially helpful. A poem, he writes, "may tend to realize itself first as a particular rhythm before it reaches expression in words," and as a result it is "in the concert room, rather than in the opera house, that the germ of a poem may be quickened."[11]

Both poets followed their own advice, and their compositions are seldom constructed according to preexisting musical models. Instead, Whitman and Eliot achieve musicality by situating specific, named pieces of music within the larger free verse frameworks of their poems, usually by quotation or allusion: Whitman's verse contains arias from his favorite Italian operas, while Eliot's incorporates Tin Pan Alley hits, passages of Wagner, and a great many other sounds. Thus are poetic forms brought into direct contact with musical ones on the printed page, with the two authors arranging these meetings of the arts for several shared reasons. Each draws on the uniquely suggestive power of a sister art to inflect and enliven his verse; each deploys recognizable, widely known music so as to appeal to a broad swath of readers and to elicit musical responses or performances from them; and each makes an implicit argument about the relative value of popular culture. Their differences are equally striking. For the nineteenth-century Whitman, opera is a portal to realms of spiritual experience beyond the reach of virtually any other art, a musical form that allows the poet to escape "form" altogether. For the twentieth-century Eliot, however, the dynamic is almost entirely reversed, with his verse demonstrating how popular song can colonize the mind and leave its subjects subdued, even imprisoned, by music. But for all this, Whitman and Eliot are united by a remarkable shared achievement: both men break from what is usually thought of as musical poetry, and in so doing they write some of the most musical poems in the language.

Songs Awaked: *Leaves of Grass*

Few American authors have so enthusiastically declared their writings to be "musical" as Walt Whitman. Styling himself as more bard than poet throughout his career, he included some two dozen titled "songs" or acts of "singing" in the final edition of his works, and according to him practically everything else in the collection was equally worthy of the designation. As reported by Horace Traubel in his epic seven-volume interview *With Walt Whitman in Camden*, the poet remembered his youth being "so saturated with the emotions, raptures, up-lifts" of musical inspiration that "it would be surprising indeed if all my future work had not been colored by them. A real musician running through Leaves of Grass— a philosopher musician—could put his finger on this and that anywhere in the text no doubt as indicating the activity of the influences I have spoken of."[12] Literary scholars have followed Whitman's lead in the intervening years and sought to identify musical structures in his writings, and some of his poems have been variously classified as symphonies, sonatas, and folk songs.[13] But Whitman might well have found such critical speculation to be idle, as his musical self-analysis tended to be bluntly (and somewhat unexpectedly) specific on the subject of form. In one of the anonymous "puffs" of his own work that he published in 1860, the patriotic, even chauvinistic American poet declared that his "method in the construction of his songs is strictly the method of the Italian Opera," and he continued to sound this note later in life, telling an acquaintance that "[b]ut for the opera . . . I could never have written Leaves of Grass."[14]

If Whitman is in fact the progenitor of modern American poetry that he is so frequently identified as being, then this self-styled literary opera singer must perforce be central to the nation's musical poetics, as well. His work and life, however, often suggest otherwise. At least since the days of F. O. Matthiessen's *American Renaissance* (1941), scholars have puzzled over this "musical" author's lack of interest in conventionally musical verse forms, his avoidance of even the most basic song rhythms, and his consistent use of unrhymed free verse. Indeed, he declared on more than one occasion that the bulk of American poetry during his time had, if anything, been excessively musical and overly reliant on "mere surface melody," and he dismissed Poe's works on precisely these grounds (*Poetry* 1021, 665). He was also known to criticize the very Italian opera that he claimed as an influence, at one point discouraging Americans from listening to its "stale, second-hand, foreign method, with its flourishes, its ridiculous sentimentality, its anti-republican spirit, and its sycophantic influence."[15] Finally and most problematically, he often signals in his poems that music is ultimately lacking as a form of artistic expression: he concludes "Eidólons," for example, by recalling the command of a mystic "seer" to chant "Thy very songs not in thy songs,/No special strains to sing, none for itself,/But from the whole resulting, rising at last and floating" (*Poetry* 168, 170). Whitman seems here to draw a distinction between music's familiar, formal structure and some better, more abstract variety of it, and he implies that the two need not be connected to one another. In this poem and elsewhere in Whitman's verse, "songs" as traditionally heard and understood are at best imperfect models for the true poet.

It is this simultaneous embrace of and distance from music that makes Whitman such an important and intriguing musical writer, giving rise to several productive contradictions in his work. The songs of *Leaves of Grass* are often studies in duality, whether in setting one art against another or in opposing American traditions with Italian ones. But as this chapter will go on to show, the central tension in Whitman's operatic poetry arises out of two, not easily reconciled notions of music's aesthetic value and function. On the one hand, Whitman is a consummately nineteenth-century romantic in his admiration for music, echoing his era's sense of it as a transcendent, even cosmic force capable of imparting meanings that exist on a higher plane than words can reach. On the other, he evinces a strikingly open-minded appreciation for worldly popular music, grounding his poetry in the sensational, internationally celebrated, and unabashedly commercial Italian opera of his day—a musical form that Lawrence Kramer has justifiably called "the nineteenth-century equivalent of music video."[16] Whitman contributes to musical poetics by denying the apparent incompatibility of these two attitudes, and he is original insofar as he finds that the worldly latter can in fact lead listeners and readers to the heavenly former. For Whitman, it is entirely possible for the popular arts to serve as conduits to the Absolute or the Ideal, and his poetry serves both to depict and enact this process.

Whitman's unique perspective is closely related to his larger sense that music and literature are not so much formal arts as they are invitations for audiences to behave and live artistically, and moreover that cultural distinctions of high and low ultimately cease to matter to people who have achieved such states. Just as the preface to the first edition of *Leaves of Grass* declares that they who are truly moved in the act of reading will find that their "very flesh shall be a great poem" (*Poetry* 11), so too does Whitman hold out the promise of a fundamentally musical existence for the initiated, an existence far more profound than actual, audible music could ever be. An early promulgator of the reader-response theory of art—"I seek less to state or display any theme or thought, and more to bring you, reader, into the atmosphere of the theme or thought—there to pursue your own flight," he writes (*Poetry* 667)—Whitman understands music to be both a creative stimulant and a force that can emanate from one's own being. Hence his eventual, crucial revision of "Song of Myself," which in its final form adds a second clause to its famous first line and reads, "I celebrate myself, and sing myself" (*Poetry* 188). Here Whitman understands himself not just as the subject of his song but as a song, full stop. And as we shall go on to see, Whitman embraces all types of music—whether popular, operatic, or otherwise—that can show audiences how to achieve this paramount, songlike condition.

Whitman's at once accessible and ineffable musicality is particularly well orchestrated in "Proud Music of the Storm" (1869), which first appeared in the *Atlantic Monthly* on Emerson's recommendation. An evocation of an alternately tuneful and cacophonous dream, the poem can in some of its most musical moments quite literally be heard and even sung by its readers. Whitman begins by introducing his governing conceit, which is that all of creation is patterned according to a higher, explicitly compositional plan:

> Proud music of the storm,
> Blast that careers so free, whistling across the prairies,
> Strong hum of forest tree-tops—wind of the mountains,
> Personified dim shapes—you hidden orchestras,
> You serenades of phantoms with instruments alert,
> Blending with Nature's rhythmus all the tongues of nations;
> You chords left as by vast composers—you choruses,
> You formless, free, religious dances—you from the Orient,
> You undertone of rivers, roar of pouring cataracts,
> You sounds from distant guns with galloping cavalry,
> Echoes of camps with all the different bugle-calls,
> Trooping tumultuous, filling the midnight late, bending me powerless,
> Entering my lonesome slumber-chamber, why have you seiz'd me?
>
> (*Poetry* 525)

What follows is an extraordinary array of sound and music, past and present alike, that washes over the poet. He might hear "airs antique and mediaeval" of "minstrels, gleemen, troubadours," or "the sound of the Hebrew lyre," or "the muezzin calling" from a mosque (*Poetry* 526-9), but he delights in everything the storm contains:

> Give me to hold all sounds, (I madly struggling cry,)
> Fill me with all the voices of the universe,
> Endow me with their throbbings, Nature's also,
> The tempests, waters, winds, operas and chants, marches and dances,
> Utter, pour in, for I would take them all!
>
> (*Poetry* 530)

The sublimity and multitudinous nature of this experience is of course meant to be overwhelming, communicated through sounds that, by Whitman's atemporal design, cannot all be familiar to or have been experienced by his audience. But snatches of the storm's music can still be heard and performed with relatively little difficulty, for sounding "o'er the rest" come some of Whitman's personal favorites, "Italia's peerless compositions."

> Across the stage with pallor on her face, yet lurid passion,
> Stalks Norma brandishing the dagger in her hand.
>
> I see poor crazed Lucia's eyes' unnatural gleam,
> Her hair down her back falls loose and dishevel'd.
>
> I see where Ernani walking the bridal garden,
> Amid the scene of night-roses, radiant, holding his bride by the hand,
> Hears the infernal call, the death-pledge of the horn.
>
> *(Poetry* 527)

Here Whitman alludes to the scenes from three of the most popular Italian operas of the nineteenth century, Vincenzo Bellini's *Norma* (1831), Gaetano Donizetti's *Lucia di Lammermoor* (1835), and Giuseppe Verdi's *Ernani* (1844). Each features frenzied emotions bordering on madness, shocking bloodshed (or the threat of it), and compelling music that, if familiar to the reader, adds to the poem's clamor in a variety of ways.

Perhaps most important here are the ways in which Whitman's opera highlights reinforce the intense, even violent emotional variability of "Proud Music of the Storm." Each oscillates between extreme and incongruous states of feeling: Norma is thinking of taking revenge on a lover by murdering the children they have had together, but she is restrained by her attachment to them; Lucia has just stabbed a man to whom she has been contracted against her will, and is escaping into a fantasy of marrying someone else; and Ernani is cavorting with his new wife on their wedding day, only to be confronted by a horn-blowing nemesis who drives him to suicide. The unsettled qualities of these scenes and plots are further amplified by their musical renderings, with their swerves of mood and action echoed in their compositions. Norma's aria alternates between sharp, angular outbursts when she is resolute to kill, and very high—and yet very quiet and controlled—melodiousness when she is less so, with the latter moments emerging as especially eerie. ◐ Lucia's singing grows ever more cheerful and ornamented as she drifts into her delusion, with her lighthearted trills, runs, and cadenzas made grotesque by the bloody context of the plot and Donizetti's brief shifts into minor. ◐ And while Ernani's part is less virtuosic than are the other two, its instability is just as striking, beginning as a passionate unison duet with his new wife in major but suddenly turning into an equally passionate outburst of anger upon hearing what would be, under different circumstances, the relatively benign tone of a horn. ◐

Each disorienting performance, then, reflects and contributes to the chaotic rush of Whitman's larger poem, both thematically and formally. And this moment in "Proud Music of the Storm" is rendered all the more audible—for its first readers, at least—by the historical popularity of the operas it refers to and the many different forms they had taken in Whitman's America.[17] His audiences might have seen them in any number of bowdlerized versions, as the promoters of his day, to put it mildly, seldom felt constrained to stay faithful to original scores and libretti. It was not at all unusual for one opera to be interpolated with songs or acts from another depending on the occasion, or for languages to shift without warning mid-performance. So too did Italian opera provide copious source material for American farce and burlesque: *Ernani* became *Herr Nanny*, *Norma* became *Mrs. Normer*, and *Lucia di Lammermoor* became *Lucy-did-Sham-Amour* and *Lucy did lam a Moor* (when performed as blackface minstrelsy) at points during the 1840s and 1850s. Moreover, the most admired melodies from these operas frequently took on lives of their own in new contexts, whether as band numbers, sheet music, or rolls for organ-grinders; indeed, Americans were often acquainted with Europe's most famous arias and choruses without ever having encountered the operas that contained them, as weddings, funerals, academic processions, and other public occasions "were inseparable from the music of Wagner or Handel or Verdi, even for people who had no idea what they were hearing."[18] As a consequence, the explicitly operatic moments in "Proud Music of the Storm" invite a broader range of readerly participation than one might initially assume, necessarily alluding to a profusion of related versions and allowing any number of audiences to share in the poem's musical experience.

Whitman makes a crucial shift, however, at the end of his work. The poet awakens from his dream "questioning all those reminiscences, the tempest in its fury,/And all the songs of sopranos and tenors" (*Poetry* 530), and he concludes that what was audible throughout the poem was not, in fact, what he ultimately comprehended.

> And I said, moreover,
> Haply what thou has heard O soul was not the sound of winds,
> Nor dream of raging storm, nor sea-hawk's flapping wings nor harsh
>   scream,
> Nor vocalism of sun-bright Italy,

> Nor German organ majestic, nor vast concourse of voices, nor layers of
>   harmonies,
> Nor strophes of husbands and wives, nor sound of marching soldiers,
> Nor flutes, nor harps, nor the bugle-calls of camps,
> But to a new rhythmus fitted for thee,
> Poems bridging the way from Life to Death, vaguely wafted in night air,
>   uncaught, unwritten,
> Which let us go forth in the bold day and write.

Behind all this music is another, more important art, a poetry set to a "new rhythmus" that is discernible in opera but is ultimately superior to it. "Proud Music of the Storm" is unclear on the question of how such poetry is to be brought into being—it may exist already and need only be caught, or it may be in a nebulous state and requires the guiding creativity of the poet—but the formal hierarchy is unmistakable. Readerly responses to the sounds of *Norma* or *Lucia* or *Ernani* turn out to be incomplete realizations of the poem's message, mere steps in the direction of a more significant aesthetic mode. Later in life Whitman would deemphasize the similarity of his artistry with Wagner's (*Poetry* 1288), but it is hard not to hear an echo of that composer's totalizing concept of *Gesamtkunstwerk* here, with Whitman imagining an art that is comprised of several others but is finally greater than each. As he would put it elsewhere in his unpublished notes, "Proud Music of the Storm" seems to conclude that "To sing well your part of opera is well; but it is not enough. You should be master of the composers of all operas—and of all tenors—and of all violins and first violins."[19]

This is the intriguing paradox of opera in Whitman's works: it is a palpable, audible presence that contributes to a grand design, yet it is also something of a disappointment, perhaps even an aesthetic failure. His ambivalence becomes easier to understand, however, when considered in light of the nineteenth-century discourses that shaped his sense of music and the uses to which it could be put in poetry. The fleeting nexus of musical sound and universal revelation in "Proud Music of the Storm" has its closest analogue in the Germanic intellectual movement that William Weber has termed "musical idealism," a school of thought that, in Whitman's lifetime, was becoming more and more central to theories of "classical" music.[20] In what are still some of the most extravagant claims that have ever been made for any art in any historical period, idealists throughout the Western world argued from the late eighteenth century onward that music, in its perfected form, was capable of nothing less than spanning "the gulf between subject and object, the particular and the universal, the phenomenal and the noumenal."[21] As the philosopher Arthur Schopenhauer famously put it in his 1818 theorization of an all-encompassing metaphysical "will,"

> music is by no means like the other arts, namely a copy of the Ideas, but a *copy of the will itself,* the objectivity of which are the Ideas. For this reason the effect of music is so very much more powerful and penetrating than is that of the other arts, for these others speak only of the shadow, but music of the essence.[22]

According to an idealist, listeners of music hear not representations of higher forces, but higher forces directly. And for all his insistence on poetry's supremacy in "Proud Music of the Storm," Whitman often invokes music or deploys musical symbolism with a similar amazement at its vast power. In verse he might ponder "the clef of the universes and of the future" (*Poetry* 400), while in journalism he might confess an

> overwhelming desire for measureless sound—a sublime orchestra of a myr-iad orchestras—a colossal volume of harmony, in which the thunder might roll in its proper place; and above it, the vast, pure Tenor,—identity of the Creative Power itself—rising through the universe, until the boundless and unspeakable capacities of that mystery, the human soul, should be filled to the uttermost, and the problem of human cravingness be satisfied and destroyed.[23]

Nor was Whitman any kind of American standout in describing music with such heady language, as similar hyperbole could be found throughout the Transcen-dentalist publishing circuit. One of the most prominent idealists of the era was John Sullivan Dwight, an erstwhile Brook Farm participant and eventual founder of *Dwight's Journal of Music* who claimed music to be "the aspiration, the yearn-ings of the heart to the Infinite."[24] So too did Margaret Fuller sound distinctly Ger-manic notes in her series on great composers for the *The Dial,* and it was not unusual for Emerson to use Whitmanian musical metaphor in his works, many of them dedicated to considering "the choral harmony of the whole."[25]

Any reader of Whitman will immediately understand why the sheer aesthetic scale and stakes of musical idealism were attractive to this ambitious poet of "kos-mos" (*Poetry* 15). But there was an important corollary, one that problematized his aim of writing literary opera: vocal music was increasingly argued by idealists to be an essentially and unfortunately worldly art, incapable of reaching the heights that instrumental music could. As Carl Dahlhaus has put it, idealists tended to think of music in its purest form as a "language beyond language," one able to communicate "what words are not even capable of stammering."[26] Music might sometimes inspire composers, in Schopenhauer's phrase, "to clothe it with flesh and bone" in the "analogous example" of opera, but such translation was nonetheless regarded by him and others as a "great misconception" and "utter absurdity."[27] While Whitman was at work on his first poems, for example, the German theorist Eduard Hanslick was arguing in his influential study *The Beautiful in Music* (1854) that "while sound in speech is but a sign, that is, a means for the purpose of expressing something which is quite distinct from its medium, sound in music is the end, that is, the ultimate and absolute object," with this expressive difference making words and music logistically incapable of unification.[28] These and other celebrations of music's self-contained, untexted, "absolute" character had a decisive impact on American and European concert programming, which over the course of the century changed from what had once been presentations of musical variety into more homogenous, instrumental affairs, largely free of linguistic markings. Whereas concertgoing audiences of the eighteenth century had generally heard miscellanies of opera numbers, symphonic works, concerti, and songs, those of Whitman's nineteenth century heard vocal music waning in prominence and German composers elevated at the expense of Italian ones.

Given this bias toward abstraction and away from language in idealist musical circles, it is not surprising that Whitman would find the worth of opera somewhat diminished by the end of "Proud Music of the Storm" and elsewhere in his writing. Indeed, unease at opera's verbal explicitness and its tendency toward reification haunts even Whitman's most extravagant praise for the form, as in his otherwise enthusiastic 1851 review of Donizetti's *La Favorita* (1840) and his suggestion that Italian works are best understood when not understood at all:

> Listen. Pure and vast, that voice now rises, as on clouds, to the heaven where it claims audience. Now, firm and unbroken, it spreads like an ocean around us. Ah, welcome that I know not the mere language of the earthly words in which the melody is embodied; as all words are mean before the language of true music.[29]

The "language of true music" is all but wordless for Whitman here, and in spite of his occasional declarations of poetry's aesthetic superiority, an admiration for the musically abstract finds its way into many of his other works, including those on "earthly" prosody. In his preface to the 1876 *Leaves of Grass*, for example, Whitman argues that poets should avoid becoming overly concerned with clarity, and instead aspire to "leave dim escapes and outlets" and "possess a certain fluid, aerial character, akin to space itself" in their style; when properly addressed to the reader, a poem "is less definite form, outline, sculpture, and becomes vista, music, half-tints, and even less than half-tints" (*Poetry* 1013). Here Whitman seems closer to the elusive, connotative poetics of the Symbolists than anything else, and quite far from the method of the Italian opera.

Whitman's strain of musical idealism is especially pronounced in his untitled poems from the first, 1855 edition of *Leaves of Grass*, many of which posit an infinite harmony that transcends the "definite form" of the material world. The epic that would become "Song of Myself," for instance, theorizes a vast and ultimately musical order of existence, with Whitman's famous catalogs often containing correspondences between literal music and sounds that, while not obviously tonal, are nevertheless described in the same terms. In one, a "pure contralto sings in organloft" even as a "carpenter dresses his plank. . . . the tongue of his foreplane whistles its wild ascending lisp" (*Poetry* 39); similarly, a "bugle calls in the ballroom" at the same time that a "youth lies awake in the cedar-roofed garret and harks to the musical rain" (*Poetry* 40). The world's pervasive musical patterning, however, requires concentration and openness in those who would apprehend it. "I think I will do nothing for a long time but listen," Whitman resolves at one point, and "accrue what I hear into myself. . . . and let sounds contribute toward me" (*Poetry* 53). As if on cue, the attentive listener hears an extraordinary collection of "sounds as they are tuned to their uses," with birds singing "bravuras," merchants joining one another in a "recitative," and dockworkers singing a "refrain," seemingly to reward the poet for his belief a larger, harmonic whole (*Poetry* 53–54). So impressive is the world's vividness, sweep, and variety, Whitman concludes, that all this activity can be said to be nothing short of a "grand-opera . . . this indeed is music!"[30]

It is important to pause here and note that the music of this moment is not the same thing as the Italian arias and stage tableaux that Whitman would go on to invoke in "Proud Music of the Storm." "Song of Myself" instead imagines music on a dramatically expanded scale, a point that Whitman underscores by turning his attention from the universal "grand-opera" to an actual opera house. In the immediately following stanza, the metaphorical opera of existence is juxtaposed with the literal kind, but even in describing a vocal performance Whitman still takes an idealist's perspective on what he hears:

> A tenor large and fresh as the creation fills me,
> The orbic flex of his mouth is pouring and filling me full.

> I hear the trained soprano . . . she convulses me like the climax of my
>   love-grip;
> The orchestra whirls me wider than Uranus flies,
> It wrenches unnamable ardors from my breast,
> It throbs me to gulps of the farthest down horror,
> It sails me. . . . I dab with bare feet. . . . they are licked by the indolent
>   waves,
> I am exposed . . . cut by bitter and poisoned hail,
> Steeped amid honeyed morphine . . . my windpipe squeezed in the fakes
>   of death,
> Let up again to feel the puzzle of puzzles,
> And that we call Being.
>
> (Poetry 54–55)

It would be difficult to conceive of a musical experience more cosmic than this. Its performer is no less immense than all of "creation," the imaginative flight it inspires is quite literally universal, and its content is the puzzle of "Being" itself. Boundary after boundary dissolves as sound becomes palpable in a moment of synaesthesia; as limitations of time and space are defied; and as the soprano finds a method, as will the poet of "Proud Music of the Storm," of "bridging the way from Life to Death." But it is equally important to note what is rather conspicuously not included here, namely, lyrics, character names, plots, and even the barest hint of what this opera is or what the singers are singing about. Indeed, Whitman seems to have gone out of his way to scrub this scene of familiar operatic conventions, having removed a rather *Ernani*-esque line from an earlier draft that describes the music as "stabbing my heart with myriads of forked distractions."[31] Where "Proud Music of the Storm" is explicit in its references, "Song of Myself" is studiously vague, more concerned with the associations and emotional responses that opera inspires than with opera itself. Indeed, were the performers not explicitly identified as singers, there would be no particular reason to presume this overwhelming music to be opera at all.

In the end, the most important aspect of the opera in "Song of Myself"—and of music in the 1855 *Leaves of Grass* more generally—is its emphasis on the listener's response and capacity for subsequent aesthetic transformation. The singing, the performers, and the larger forces they evoke are one thing, but the poet's assumption of a new state of "Being" in his works is quite another. And Whitman's poems on the whole suggest that such states are themselves musical in some fundamental way, and that an artist's ultimate goal ought to be helping audiences achieve them.

As he puts it in the poem that would become "A Song for Occupations," there is a better music than the sounding, aural kind, and it lies within:

> All music is what awakens from you when you are reminded by the instruments,
> It is not the violins and the cornets. . . . it is not the oboe nor the beating drums—nor the notes of the baritone singer singing his sweet romanza. . . . nor those of the men's chorus, nor those of the women's chorus,
> It is nearer and farther than they.

> (*Poetry* 94)

"Music" is not an opera, nor an instrumental composition, nor a performance, for all these are external to the self; as with Whitman's famous description of death in "Song of Myself," a true, inward music is "different from what any one supposed" (*Poetry* 32). Moreover, if music is in fact a state of being rather than a collection of audible sounds and formal characteristics, then so too is musical poetry an art of readerly involvement rather than one of meter and rhyme. "You think it would be good to be the writer of melodious verses,/Well it would be good to be the writer of melodious verses;/But what are verses beyond the flowing character you could have?" Whitman asks (*Poetry* 132–133). In his schema, inspired readers and listeners can themselves achieve states of musical abstraction, "flowing" with a grace unlike anything to be found on the stage, in the air, or on the page.[32]

Insofar as there is an operatic method in the 1855 *Leaves of Grass*, then, it has been mostly shorn of its linguistic and narrative qualities, the better for Whitman to discuss it in the elevated terms that an idealist would "absolute" music. But Whitman's sleight of hand should not be allowed to disguise the strangeness of what he has done here, for not only has he used a texted art as a conduit to realms said to exist beyond textuality, but so too has he deployed a popular form in the service of a lofty aesthetic. Critics have in the past asserted that Whitman's embrace of Italian opera was a "conversion to classical music" that accompanied his construction of a "professionalist self-image," but such interpretations largely grow out of twentieth-century assumptions and overlook the degree to which opera was in fact part of a nineteenth-century "common culture."[33] Whitman lived, after all, in the age of P. T. Barnum and his sponsored tour of the celebrity soprano Jenny Lind, which sparked a national frenzy; of competing Manhattan opera houses that drove down prices for the cheap seats to twenty-five cents; and of New York audiences generally going "opera mad," leading modern music historians to describe Italian composition as nothing less than "the most potent force to hit the American musical world in the nineteenth century."³⁴ Of course, opera could also be associated with refinement and snobbery, and Whitman would on occasion link it with "the high life of New York—the aristocracy—the 'upper ten'" in his journalism.³⁵ But as Lawrence Levine has noted, the Italian opera of Whitman's day was "an art form that was *simultaneously* popular and elite," one that appealed to various audiences in a nation whose sense of cultural distinction was considerably less exacting than it would eventually become.³⁶ Opera could be regarded as a music of elevation, but so too was it an object of controversy because of its crowd-pleasing, violent spectacles, its salacious themes, and its foreign provenance.

Italian opera appealed to Whitman in large part because of this contradictory character, for he believed, in the words of Christopher Beach, that the best and most representatively American art was "distinct as a result, paradoxically, of its *lack* of (high) cultural distinction."³⁷ A poet determined to sing to Americans of all stations, he had heard a great many examples of what an egalitarian, broadly popular voice might sound like on the New York stage. The stars of European opera, who frequently toured the United States because of the hefty paychecks they could command there, often remarked upon the relative lack of audience stratification they encountered; as John Dizikes has put it, the "European opera house, clearly marked and ordered, was being replaced in America by a theater of social uncertainty."³⁸ Singers therefore made a habit of including American popular tunes in their performances, and Whitman was particularly inspired by the universal appeal of Marietta Alboni, an Italian contralto whom he claimed to have heard in all her New York City appearances and whom he would apostrophize by name in "Proud Music of the Storm" (see Image 2).

> All persons appreciated Alboni—the common crowd quite as well as the connoisseurs.—We used to go in the upper tiers of the theatre, (the Broadway,) on the nights of her performance, and remember seeing that part of the auditorium packed full of New York young men, mechanics, 'roughs,' &c., entirely oblivious of all except Alboni, from the time the great songstress came on the stage, till she left it again.³⁹

It is important to note, however, that Whitman was no through-and-through cultural relativist, as he ardently believed that audiences could be improved through exposure to superior music and literature. He might in the same breath extol the common culture of the opera and be condescending, even puritanical, about other popular forms, as when he praised *Ernani* at the expense of "the church choir, or the songs and playing on the piano, or the nigger songs" in 1855.

MARIETTA ALBONI, A QUARANTE ANS

The soprano Marietta Alboni, who inspired Whitman with her musical performances and her popular appeal. From Arthur Pougin's *Marietta Alboni, avec quatre gravures et une fac-similé* (Paris: Librairie Plon, 1912).

"A new world—a liquid world—rushes like a torrent through you," he writes of this ideal operatic experience. "If you have the true musical feeling in you, from this night you date a new era in your development, and, for the first time, receive your ideas of what the divine art of music really is."[40] Part of opera's allure for Whitman, then, lay in its unique ability to reveal the higher "divine" even as it appealed to the lower "roughs," a feat of synthesis that he envisioned for his poetry, as well.[41]

But no matter how freewheeling and omnivorous his culture may have been, Whitman was nevertheless aware of certain incongruities in his embrace of Italian opera and the central place he accorded it in his work. His brief, modestly dialectical poem "Italian Music in Dakota" makes this obvious, stumbling upon a performance of some favorite airs in the American territories and achieving its poetic effect by initially finding the music to be out of place.

Through the soft evening air enwinding all,
Rocks, woods, fort, cannon, pacing sentries, endless wilds,
In dulcet streams, in flutes' and cornets' notes,
Electric, pensive, turbulent, artificial,
(Yet strangely fitting even here, meanings unknown before,
Subtler than ever, more harmony, as if born here, related here,
Not to the city's fresco'd rooms, not to the audience of the opera house,
Sounds, echoes, wandering strains, as really here at home,
Sonnambula's innocent love, trios with *Norma's* anguish,
And thy ecstatic chorus *Poliuto;*)
Ray'd in the limpid yellow slanting sundown,
Music, Italian music in Dakota.

(*Poetry* 523)

Historically speaking, this scene is not so strange as Whitman wants it to sound, for Italian opera was in fact quite popular in mining towns, prairie villages, and West Coast settlements, in spite of the fact that there was little infrastructure to support it. Nevertheless, the problems the poem introduces are myriad, with Whitman asking his readers to note tensions between Italian culture and American wilderness, "artificial" forms and the natural world, and refinement and roughness. These gaps, however, are in fact crucial to the poem's larger aims, for out of these oppositions arise "meanings unknown before" and, ultimately, a sense of greater connection:

Nature, sovereign of this gnarl'd realm,
Lurking in hidden barbaric grim recesses,
Acknowledging rapport however far remov'd,
(As some old root or soil of earth its last-born flower or fruit,)
Listens well pleas'd.

In revealing the extent to which material forms are "remov'd" from one another, the contrast of Italian opera and the American landscape ultimately allows their fundamental "rapport" to emerge. This insistent locating of difference in sameness, so common in Whitman and termed "bipolar unity" by Howard J. Waskow,[42] helps explain why the poet was seldom entirely abstract in his musical writing: only through the juxtaposition of forms, foreign or low or reified though they may be, can a larger, pluralist harmony be shown to exist.

Whitman's demonstration of incompatibility and similitude in "Italian Music in Dakota" points to a final quality of opera that must be noted in his poetry: the challenge of comprehension it poses to American audiences. Nowhere is Whitman more explicit on this subject than in his essay "All about a Mocking-Bird," the aforementioned self-review in which he casts himself as the titular bird and declares his songs to obey "the method of the Italian Opera." In making this connection, Whitman emphasizes not the opera's tunefulness, universality, or popularity, but rather the difficulty it presents to the uninitiated. Such music is presumed to baffle the American ear; it "confounds the new person" and "impresses him as if all the sounds of earth and hell were tumbled promiscuously together."[43] The problem of opera, and by extension Whitman's poetry, resides primarily in its form, for it bears little resemblance to "previous-accustomed tunes." But it is precisely for this reason that audiences must redouble their efforts in listening to it:

> Then, in view of the latter words, bold American! in the ardor of youth, commit not yourself, too irretrievably, that there is nothing in the Italian composers, and nothing in the Mocking-Bird's chants. But pursue them awhile—listen—yield yourself—persevere. Strange as the shape of the suggestion may be, perhaps such free strains are to give to these United States, or commence giving them, the especial nourishments which, though all solid and mental and moral things are in boundless profusion provided, have hardly yet begun to be provided for them—hardly yet the idea of that kind of nourishment thought of, or the need of it suspected. Though it is the sweetest, strongest meat—pabulum of a race of giants—true pabulum of the children of the prairies.

Whitman's advice here is, of course, contradictory. On the one hand, audiences are asked to ignore their instincts and commit themselves to studying that which they do not immediately understand. (In this, Whitman resembles the musical idealists, who argued that listeners must ponder and attempt to ascertain the ultimate meaning of a composer's work rather than expect mere entertainment.) But so too does Whitman suggest that such music can be absorbed passively, if only audiences "yield" and allow this strange art to wash over them. Opera is to be admired because it both demands translation and allows for instant comprehension, with Whitman finding a balance of the elusive and the accessible in the form, just as he heard it fusing the ennobling with the popular and the universal with the material. To achieve this balance in verse and to compel readers to unify these oppositions in their own being were, therefore, crucial aims of his musical poetry.

Whitman's "Out of the Cradle Endlessly Rocking" is perhaps the best demonstration of the active aesthetic engagement he hoped to inspire in his readers, a poem that both shows the process by which one can become meaningfully musical and suggests the role opera can play in setting such a process in motion. The poetic consciousness of the work, a "chanter of pains and joys, uniter of here and hereafter," is remembering an artistic awakening he experienced as a child, with his description of it as a "scene" explicitly casting it as a moment of representational theater (*Poetry* 388). The memory involves two "feather'd guests from Alabama," a "he-bird" and "she-bird," whom the "curious boy" watches day after day as they attend to their nest (*Poetry* 389). The poem offers an account of their birdsong, but importantly, the music is rendered into italicized English by its "peering, absorbing, translating" listener:

> *Shine! shine! shine!*
> *Pour down your warmth, great sun!*
> *While we bask, we two together.*
>
> *Two together!*
> *Winds blow south, or winds blow north,*
> *Day come white, or night come black,*
> *Home, or rivers and mountains from home,*
> *Singing all time, minding no time,*
> *While we two keep together.*

These are emphatically not tweets and calls in and of themselves (as in the avian approximations of Gustav Mahler's *Third Symphony* or Oliver Messiaen's *Catalogue d'oiseaux*), but are instead something akin to the sounds of Wagner's *Siegfried*, in which the music of a woodbird is magically transmuted into German. The obvious discrepancy here between the natural, repetitive, unconscious tones of literal birdsong and the wordy apostrophe they become in the boy's mind is striking, even somewhat humorous; in one strange turn, the he-bird refers to his home region by its given human name, "Paumanok." A marked instability has therefore emerged in the mediating poem, which the poet freely acknowledges: "He pour'd forth the meanings which I of all men know./Yes my brother I know,/The rest might not, but I have treasur'd every note . . . Listen'd to keep, to sing, now translating the notes,/Following you my brother" (*Poetry* 389–390).

The poet then turns the "scene" into a kind of opera, beginning when the he-bird's mate flies away, never to return. Her departure inspires what

Whitman refers to as a grief-stricken "aria" from the bereft male, and it goes on for an astonishing fifteen stanzas, taking the "translating" listener through several explicitly described emotional states (*Poetry* 392, 390). Sometimes the bird calls to his absent partner:

> High and clear I shoot my voice over the waves,
> Surely you must know who is here, is here,
> You must know who I am, my love.

Sometimes he addresses the natural world:

> Land! land! O land!
> Whichever way I turn, O I think you could give me my mate back again if you
>   only would,
> For I am almost sure I see her dimly whichever way I look.

(Poetry 391)

Sometimes he exhorts himself to sing more effectively:

> O throat! O trembling throat!
> Sound clearer through the atmosphere!
> Pierce the woods, the earth,
> Somewhere listening to catch you must be the one I want.
>
> Shake out carols!
> Solitary here, the night's carols!
> Carols of lonesome love! death's carols!
> Carols under that lagging, yellow, waning moon!
> O under that moon where she droops almost down into the sea!
> O reckless despairing carols.

And sometimes he fears that his would-be listener will not hear the proper music:

> Do not be decoy'd elsewhere,
> That is the whistle of the wind, it is not my voice,
> That is the fluttering, the fluttering of the spray,
> Those are the shadows of leaves.

The sheer length and demonstrative quality of the bird's moment-by-moment, mood-by-mood vocalization may remind readers of one of the most frequently commented-upon peculiarities of opera: the spectacle of solitary characters breaking into song and declaiming impressions or passing sensations that would, under normal circumstances, remain internalized. Compare the bird's grief, for example, to the self-addressed exposition of *Norma*, as alluded to in "Proud Music of the Storm": "I cannot go nearer:/A chill seizes me, my hair/Stands with fright. To kill my children!/Tender babies, until now/The joy of my life?"[44] The bird's aria is eloquent, to be sure, but so too does it read as performative, artificial, and therefore all the more operatic.

Ultimately, however, this moment is less about the bird's perspective and more about that of the listening, anthropomorphizing boy, for whom the "aria" is in fact a mutual production. In "translating the notes" he hears into language, he shifts attention away from the performer and toward the meanings that reach the one-person audience.

> The boy ecstatic, with his bare feet the waves, with his hair the atmosphere dallying,
> The love in the heart long pent, now loose, now at last tumultuously bursting,
> The aria's meaning, the ears, the soul, swiftly depositing,
> The strange tears down the cheeks coursing,
> The colloquy there, the trio, each uttering,
> The undertone, the savage old mother incessantly crying,
> To the boy's soul's questions sullenly timing, some drown'd secret hissing,
> To the outsetting bard.
>
> (*Poetry* 392)

If the bird's song is in fact intended to communicate what it has been reported to, then the boy's "ecstatic" reaction would seem rather hardhearted. But such a response is entirely appropriate according to the standards of tragic opera, which promises staged suffering in the service of catharsis—with such catharsis arriving in the poem when the boy experiences an outburst of "love in the heart long pent" thanks to the revelatory "meaning," "undertone," and "secret" that he has taken from the scene. And Whitman emphasizes here that the boy has not apprehended these meanings intuitively and on his own, but has rather done so through the mediating, analogous structure of a musical art. As Whitman would later put it in his memoir *Specimen Days*, natural forces are capable of "striking emotional, impalpable depths, subtler than all the poems, paintings, music, I have ever read, seen, heard," but he also recognizes that his appreciation of such forces is possible in part "because I have read those poems and heard that music" (*Poetry* 796). Art, it would seem, offers a useful introductory model for how one goes about perceiving those meanings that exist beyond art. The natural world cannot be apprehended in exactly the same ways that *Lucia* and *Ernani* are, but there is a useful, salutary resemblance nonetheless.

Moreover, the boy of "Out of the Cradle Endlessly Rocking" has not simply perceived an important truth or experienced a significant emotion because of this "scene," but he has also achieved a state of "Being" like the one suggested by the operatic flight of "Song of Myself." The question of whether the bird's song has meaningful content or is instead a projection by the imaginative boy is never resolved, but in either case the result is the same: he who once only listened to singers has become a singer himself.

> Demon or bird! (said the boy's soul,)
> Is it indeed toward your mate you sing? or is it really to me?
> For I, that was a child, my tongue's use sleeping, now I have heard you,
> Now in a moment I know what I am for, I awake,
> And already a thousand singers, a thousand songs, clearer, louder and more
> sorrowful than yours,
> A thousand warbling echoes have started to life within me, never to
> die.

The boy has achieved the "fluid character" called for in the first *Leaves of Grass*, containing within himself a perpetually audible multitude of "singers" and "songs" alike. This is the ultimate purpose of opera and operatic poetry for Whitman: to reach an audience, to captivate it with song, and to lead it to a newly musical life. Once the bird's "aria" is concluded and the poem's retrospection is complete, the now-mature poet is able to testify that "My own songs awaked from that hour" (*Poetry* 393). And while the biographical sources of Whitman's inspiration were various and frequently mysterious, there is no question that his songs were similarly "awaked," at least in part, by the arias of the aforementioned Alboni. In a manuscript note he chose not to publish when writing *Specimen Days*, Whitman recalled the contralto thus: "I wonder if the lady will ever know that her singing, her method, gave the foundation, the start, thirty years ago to all my poetic literary effort since?"[45] The method of the opera, whether heard in the natural world or on the New York stage, is primarily one of transference, inspiration, and transformation, and for Whitman the process is endless.

Whitman never believed that the American public heeded his instructions in his "Mocking-Bird" essay, claiming to the end of his life that his verse had failed to attain anything like the popularity enjoyed by the Italian opera it was based on. And when his first great wave of posthumous recognition came in the early twentieth century, his operatic method generally went unheard. This is not to say that he was not perceived as being uniquely musical. Indeed, the editors of the journal *Musical America* declared him nothing less than a "musical prophet" in 1915, one who "clears the way for creations that are fresh, large and simple, and appropriate to our land and time."[46] For nationalist American writers and thinkers of the 1910s and 1920s, especially those associated with the *Seven Arts* journal, he was an almost messianic musical figure, a quasi-Beethoven whose inclusive spirit was capable of inspiring what Waldo Frank called a "symphonic nation in whom all selves and all visions adumbrate to Wholeness."[47] In a rather different vein, he was seized upon as a kind of proletarian folk singer by blues-influenced, African American artists of the Harlem Renaissance and, as Bryan K. Carman has argued, by a line of white working-class troubadours beginning with Woody Guthrie and extending to Bruce Springsteen. But while all these strains do in fact exist in Whitman's poetry, his verse's unique braiding of classical idealism and popular song had become largely unwound in the public's estimation.[48]

Ironically, the closest—and yet very off-base—realization of his musical achievement in the first half of the twentieth century came from the critic Esther Shephard, whose odd 1938 exposé *Walt Whitman's Pose* charged the poet with all but plagiarizing George Sand's *Consuelo* (1842–43) and its sequel, *La Comtesse de Rudolstadt* (1843). Whitman had named the complete, five-volume work as one of his favorite novels, the "noblest in many respects, on its own field, in all literature," and Shephard believed he had modeled his "poet-of-man" persona on an aesthetically minded carpenter who appears in Sand's pages.[49] Shephard might have noted instead, however, that Whitman would have been just as likely to have emulated the eponymous Consuelo, a modest Italian girl of the eighteenth century who distinguishes herself as a singer in the church choir, becomes an opera star, and roams the European countryside having chaste, picaresque adventures with a young Joseph Haydn. For Sand, her heroine is admirable precisely because she is able to move comfortably between radically different artistic spheres; Consuelo boasts at one point that her "whole education had been a mixture of sacred and profane studies, in both of which she took an equal interest, indifferent whether she ended in a nunnery or upon the stage."[50] No doubt the broad-minded American poet, to whom the "profane" opera had shown a way to a larger, "sacred" ideal, would have liked something similar said of him.

One Definite False Note: Eliot's Early Poetry and *The Waste Land*

If Whitman was the great symphonist of American poetry for Waldo Frank, then T. S. Eliot was its Tin Pan Alley songwriter. The critical difference lay in Eliot's aesthetic of allusion, juxtaposition, and recombination: just as the jazz of the 1920s was said by Frank to consist of "departures, angular, sporadic, in no way organic, from the old foundations," so too did Eliot's verse leave the Western tradition "disarrayed to bear the mood of a meagre modern soul." As a result, he concluded, "there is little to choose between the best of [Irving] Berlin and 'Mr. Prufrock' or 'The Waste Land.'"[51]

Frank's sense for Eliot's essential jazziness was, as it happens, somewhat common in the early twentieth century. Louis Untermeyer also found a musical "jumble" in Eliot's early work, describing it as a "mingling of willful obscurity and weak vaudeville" that contained "narratives, nursery-rhymes, criticism, jazz-rhythms . . . and a few lyrical moments."[52] So too did Clive Bell situate Eliot within "the Jazz movement," hearing the "ministrations of a black and grinning muse" in his verse.[53] Eliot would come to seem far more genteel than this in later critical accounts, often portrayed as an elite, stuffy classicist who recoiled at the popular arts and only "used vernacular lingo to connote vulgarity."[54] But contemporary scholars have been quite successful at rehabilitating the broad-minded Eliot of the 1920s and showing how significantly his poetry was indebted to vaudeville, the music hall, and African American verse forms.[55] Whether in noting how music helps amplify the urban noisiness, the nervy variety, or the sentimental belatedness of Eliot's works, today's interpreters are quite likely to agree with his argument that high modernist literature often represents "the *refinement*, not the antithesis, of popular art."[56]

As had Whitman, Eliot appreciated the uniquely powerful appeal of popular musical forms, and he incorporated those forms within his verse for many of the same reasons. Eliot's early poetry is punctuated with identifiable pop hits and many other sorts of music in a manner like that of "Proud Music of the Storm," aspiring to the Whitmanian condition of audibility. Eliot also follows Whitman by inviting (and sometimes taking a fiendish glee in compelling) musical responses and performances from his audiences. But if Eliot's musical poetry resembles Whitman's in its most basic elements, it also registers and is shaped by several historical changes that had occurred between the nineteenth and twentieth centuries and that had significantly altered the relationship between writers, readers, and musical-literary works. As we shall go on to hear, Eliot's use of popular song is frequently anxious and eerie, and it cannot be separated from his concerns over recording technology and mechanical methods of distributing music; from his understanding of music as an increasingly commodified product in a commercial culture; and from his sense that the human auditory process had been altered, perhaps irrevocably, by a new and ever more cluttered sonic environment. Yet for all of Eliot's uneasiness, and for all that his barrage of sound and text can overwhelm the listening reader, his musical poetry still searches for an aesthetic balance, ever seeking a means by which dissonant cultural forms can be brought into harmony.

For a sense of how starkly Eliot's musical poems can differ from Whitman's, consider the "First Debate between the Body and Soul" from his early, unpublished collection *Inventions of the March Hare* (1909–17). Once again the reader encounters a world in which music is as much a part of the environment as are buildings, nature, and people, but the overall effect is discomforting and explicitly anti-romantic. The poem begins with a metaphysically minded protagonist "yet devoted to the pure idea" who sits in a city square, "Forced to endure" the sound of "a street piano through the dusty trees/Insisting: 'Make the best of your position.'"[57] As is the case in many of Eliot's early poems, the sound of the piano is one in a series of sordid sensations intended to highlight the unpleasantness of an urban scene, equated with "leering" houses and a blind man who "coughs and spits sputters" in the alleyways. Here, however, Eliot has also gone to the trouble of including what is presumably a song lyric—"Make the best of your position"—to accompany the piano's tune, drawing a rather queasy contrast between the grimy milieu and the song's possibly sunny, possibly fatalistic platitudes. For reasons Eliot does not explain, the music is too much for the protagonist to bear, as his optimism "dies of inanition" immediately after it begins. He struggles for a moment to retain his faith in the "Absolute" and "pure idea," but the song blithely continues and, if anything, grows yet louder as the poem winds down: "Street pianos through the trees/Whine and wheeze" in response (*Inventions* 65). The idealist's final defeat comes not with a bang but a whimper, to the sound of a slight and yet unshakable song.

The exterior world as depicted in Eliot's early verse often features this variety of public (and usually annoying) music, and this is no doubt partially because the poet grew up experiencing a great deal of it in what was then one of America's most musical cities. His childhood home, as described in a biography, was "an unfashionable part of St. Louis, not far from the saloons and brothels of Chestnut and Market Streets, at a time when pianists in back rooms were joining 'rags' together as jolting tunes."[58] Jaunty, syncopated works by such local artists as Scott Joplin and Tom Turpin were all but unavoidable, with St. Louis caught up in a ragtime craze that would eventually serve as the foundation for virtually every subsequent form of American popular song. There was nothing unusual, of course, about a major urban area's being saturated with music in post–Civil War America; as early as the 1870s, *Dwight's Journal of Music* had irritably noted the omnipresence of bands "in the streets and gardens and on every steamboat" and found that "hand-organ grinders, whistlers of *Pinafore*, keep the air full of melodies that cross each other in all directions."[59] But most observers of the music scene agreed that there was something uniquely striking, almost insidious, about St. Louis ragtime, a music whose appeal was often described in compulsive or pathological terms. According to James Weldon Johnson—the poet, novelist, and song lyricist whose ditty "Under the Bamboo Tree" would later be quoted in Eliot's *Sweeney Agonistes* (1932)—ragtime was an "all-conquering" music, and its allure was in large part due to the fact that it "demanded physical response, patting of the feet, drumming of the fingers, or nodding of the head in time with the beat."[60] The environmental music of Eliot's youth, at least according to Johnson's description, was very easy to hear and very hard to ignore.

Just as ragtime suffused late nineteenth-century St. Louis, so too do snatches of song appear throughout Eliot's early poetry, creating the impression that they circulate freely in the culture at large. The *March Hare* poems contain a great many identifiable popular songs beyond those of the "street piano" variety: readers will find the title of "By the Light of the Silvery Moon" buried in "Suite Clownesque," a line from "You Found" quoted in the fragment "The smoke that gathers blue and sinks," and two musical theater productions (*The Chocolate Soldier* and *The Merry Widow*) referred to in "Goldfish (Essence of Summer Magazines)." To live in Eliot's world was to encounter popular music at frequent and sometimes random intervals, and his poetry dutifully reflects a culture in which song was quite literally in the air. Moreover, the music of the early poems also serves to delineate cultures within cultures, as Eliot often seems to use song references as a means of saluting other young, self-consciously modern readers. There is a cheeky, rebellious attitude in many of his musical settings, with the poet deploying popular culture in order to pit what he thinks of as "vulgar life against a romantic, genteel world of blue-delft china."[61] Indeed, when Eliot sets out to illustrate the superiority of his youthful perspective and to break with traditional literary convention in his poetry, music is one of his favorite means of doing so—few characters in the *March Hare* works come off as badly as their stuffy, pretentious opera fans.

Eliot's interest in the social presence and function of music continues in his published poetry, and is on particularly effective display in one of his first successful works, "Portrait of a Lady" (1915). The poem is an extended conflict of wills between a high society woman and a young, determinedly lowbrow male protagonist, with their relationship disintegrating to the sound of a somewhat motley musical accompaniment. Readers meet the ill-matched couple after they have taken a trip to hear "the latest Pole/Transmit the Preludes, through his hair and fingertips," with the lady going on for a few lines about the "intimate" quality of Chopin's piano works.[62] Her salon has a similarly delicate and classically oriented atmosphere, with the stiff conversation among her guests, their "velleities and carefully caught regrets," blending and rhyming with "attenuated tones of violins/Mingled with remote cornets." But as the lady's rhetorical meanderings become more irritating to the young protagonist, so too does the music. The violins grow aimless, with their melodies transformed into "windings," while the short "ariettes" now seem to come from unpleasant "cracked cornets" instead of pure-toned ones (*Poems* 9). And in what may be the cleverest musical turn of the entire poem, the lady's voice at one point becomes "the insistent out-of-tune/Of a broken violin on an August afternoon"—she and the classical tradition she enjoys have merged to become the entire category of tone-deafness itself.

Music is being invoked to reveal the lady's character here, and Eliot adds some variations to the theme by correspondingly associating the young man with sounds that are more public, less sophisticated, and heavy on percussion. In one of the poem's most famous lines, for example, he hears a "dull tom-tom" playing inside his head while the lady speaks, "Absurdly hammering a prelude of its own" in a "Capricious monotone/That is at least one definite 'false note'" (*Poems* 9). This semi-primitive, resolutely unsophisticated response to the lady's refined sensibility is but one moment of several in which he aligns himself with what he thinks of as low culture, with another occurring when he sits in a city park, listening to Eliot's ever-present street-piano:

> I keep my countenance,
> I remain self-possessed
> Except when a street piano, mechanical and tired
> Reiterates some worn-out common song
> With the smell of hyacinths across the garden
> Recalling things that other people have desired.
>
> (*Poems* 10)

The music is little better than generic here, and it is at least initially surprising that the young man could be moved—if that is what he means to indicate—by a "worn-out" song and its secondhand sentiments. It is music for "other people," not himself, but presumably anything is better than the lady and her Chopin.

The moment of the street-piano is additionally interesting because it points to a significant oddity in the poem: while the characters are associated with different kinds of music, and while those musics seem to oppose one another in much the same way that the lady and the young man do, the human subjects of "Portrait of a Lady" have very little in the way of aural agency. The youth does not seek out the street-piano, but rather it seizes him and robs him of his ability to "remain self-possessed." The tom-tom in his head, so often described by critics as an instrument of resistance to romantic culture, is even further from his control. There is no conscious decision on his part to enlist music in this conflict, no indication that he imagines or remembers the beat in order to drown out the lady's words. Instead, the "Capricious" drum simply "begins," as though it were in his mind already and needed no formal impetus to start its thumping (*Poems* 9). So too does the pianist who performs Chopin seem unable to manage the music: his fingers "Transmit the Preludes" passively like radio antennae, as opposed to summoning, interpreting, or simply playing them. Music may serve to reinforce identity and perspective in "Portrait of a Lady," but it nevertheless remains something of an independent force, one that appears whether Eliot's characters will it or not. They do not deploy musical forms so much as musical forms play upon them.

However, the unwieldiness of the musical ensemble aligned with the lady—a combination of horns and strings far too large for a tasteful parlor performance—points to one rather obvious instrument of musical control in the poem: she has presumably put on a record of her choosing to set the scene. Mechanical music would ultimately have a considerable impact upon Eliot's poetry, and so it is worth pausing here to note that the first major phase of his career (up to the publication of *The Waste Land* in 1922) coincided almost exactly with the rise of the modern recording industry and a corresponding increase in the kind of ambient music that "Portrait of a Lady" describes.[63] In 1889, when Eliot was one year old, the first coin-activated jukebox was patented and began appearing in public spaces all over America. In 1901, a so-called golden era of sound recording was under way, with record sales increasing steadily for two decades and radio broadcasting holding sway long after that.[64] By 1909, one year before Eliot began writing "Portrait of a Lady," more than 27 million records were being produced every year, even as sales of pianos and sheet music—Tin Pan Alley's most profitable product—continued apace. Consequently, the amount of recorded music in everyday life was increasing at a rapid rate, and it did not take long for the new, fuller sonic environment to register in literature.

American life was of course musical before recording technology existed—as in Whitman's New York City, for example—but several cultural observers have nonetheless argued that mechanized sound brought about a decisive cultural change during Eliot's early lifetime. A certain casualness seemed to be setting in among American listeners, a blasé, unappreciative attitude rooted in what the composer Constant Lambert would eventually term "The Appalling Popularity of Music" in 1934.[65] In the words of the musicologist Richard Middleton, "Until relatively recently, music punctuated life; often the performed time of the musical event stood in a dissociated, even liminal relationship to the experienced time of surrounding existence." But after the phonograph and its promise of constantly available song, no more: "the *specialness* of the musical event that we can recognize in many traditional contexts—its capacity to interrupt—has been attenuated by the vernacularization of musical experience in modern societies."[66] The problem, in other words, was that musical familiarity was breeding contempt in a century of previously unthinkable sonic abundance.

With the increasingly common presence of music in American cultural life came a presumption that the new environment was transforming the act of listening, and even listeners themselves. The most famous theorist of this change was Walter Benjamin, who understood the recording of music to be a process of artistic decontextualization, reification, and commodification: "the choral work performed in an auditorium or in the open air is enjoyed in a private room," he observed, resulting in a devaluation of "the here and now" in musical moments.[67] Benjamin therefore predicted the rise of "distracted" consumers who, because of the convenience offered by mechanical reproducibility, would tend to absorb music into themselves instead of the other way around, a reversal of the relationship that earlier generations had enjoyed.[68] And while it is somewhat difficult to know just how a "distracted," music-absorbing listener might actually behave or think in practice, Eliot provides some intriguing suggestions in "Portrait of a Lady," whose narrator is at once annoyed by recordings of classical music and overwhelmed by the "tom-tom" of his inward experience.

As one might expect, however, Eliot's most vivid depictions of music's presence and cultural significance at the beginning of the twentieth century are to be found *The Waste Land*, his famously fragmented, collage-like, multimedia long poem. Songs break out at several points to make it an unusually audible composition, with snatches of music frequently emerging from the poem's vocal clamor of prophets, barflies, and long-dead writers. So too is the influence of sound recording evident throughout, so much so that Juan A. Suárez has argued that the poem functions as a kind of phonograph in and of itself, capturing and playing back the noises, sensations, and ideas of contemporary and historical moments alike. And most important, the many varieties of music that Eliot deploys in the poem—from rags to operas to religious chants to bawdy drinking songs—serve both to intensify its sense of cultural welter and to suggest a means of weathering the storm. Music is part of modernity's din in *The Waste Land*, a powerful and often sinister force that overwhelms the listener from without and within. But it also represents an opportunity for readers to participate in the poem's ongoing, ever-unfolding process, and it provides a model for how they might make *The Waste Land* into something of their own.

In the poem's published version, popular music makes its first and most surprising appearance in the "Game of Chess" section. After a thirty-three-line, heavily allusive description of a gaudily decorated room, Eliot presents a squabbling couple. Theirs is a strange argument, at least insofar as it is staged, because only one side—consisting of a woman's rapid-fire admonitions—seems actually to be audible. "Speak to me. Why do you never speak. Speak./What are you thinking of? What thinking? What?" she demands of her silent partner (*Poems* 40). Only the reader is privy to the man's responses—they are presumably his internal thoughts—but they too have an off-kilter feel. On the question of what he thinks about, he is ominous and inscrutable: "I think we are in rats' alley/Where the dead men lost their bones." Asked whether he can remember anything, he quotes a line of Shakespeare: "I remember/Those are pearls that were his eyes" (*Poems* 41). But when asked, "Are you alive, or not? Is there nothing in your head?" his response is jarring:

> "Are you alive, or not? Is there nothing in your head?"
>
>   But
>
> O O O O that Shakespeherian Rag—
> It's so elegant
> So intelligent
>
>   (*Poems* 41)

The rag being referred to here is a decade-old novelty number from the *Ziegfeld Follies* of 1912, and in the judgment of David E. Chinitz it isn't a particularly good one, a "rather forced" collection of puns and rhymes about well-known characters from Shakespeare's plays.[69] But more important than the rag's quality are the inventive ways in which Eliot is using it to demonstrate a distinctively modern malady, one that James Joyce's *Ulysses* had also depicted some months before and that the physician Oliver Sacks has recently classified as a "brainworm"—the sensation of having a song stuck in one's head, one that has popped up unbidden and at the strangest of moments.[70]

Once readers get over the song's initial apparent randomness, they will likely notice the odd "O" sounds and fanciful spelling of "Shakespeherian," which are not to be found in the published sheet music. The devices are Eliot's inventions, and they serve both to locate the rag squarely within the man's mind and to create a uniquely musical effect. The repeated O's might be his mental rendition of an instrumental line, an attempt at something like scat singing, or the embarrassingly familiar practice of covering up forgotten words in mid-performance. The mis-spelling, in a similar vein, forces a vaguely British accent, a syncopated rhythm, and a satiric edge on the lyric, appropriate for a song impishly claiming, among other things, that Shakespeare's canonized works are an "old classical drag."[71] Unlike many of Eliot's other allusions to outside sources in *The Waste Land*, "That Shakespearian Rag" is not quoted faithfully. Rather, the man has improvised upon it as any singer might, reinterpreting the piece in the private space of his mind.

Further attention to this moment will show that, while the song's appearance is odd, it is anything but random—no more random, certainly, than the two pre-ceding mental digressions. The simplest explanation is that the man, having just quoted from *The Tempest* in one of his unspoken responses, now has Shakespeare on the brain and has made a mental association with one of the Bard's popular incarnations. (Indeed, the "pearls that were his eyes" line is itself taken from a song within the play, which makes it all the easier for the thinker to attempt some musical variations.) Alternately, this might be the man's way of adding onto or developing the woman's question: if punctuation and the long space separating the lines are ignored, the phrase reads as a complete sentence, thus becoming, "Is there nothing in your head but 'That Shakespearian Rag'?" (Read this way, the man would seem to be engaging in a kind of call-and-response, with Eliot rather wittily drawing attention to the fact that he does, in fact, seem to have little in his head besides the song.) But regardless of whether this bit of musicality is inspired by the woman's needling questions or represents a contin-uation of the man's private thoughts, it is a strangely equivocal presence in the scene, on the one hand inappropriately flip under the tense circumstances and yet on the other entirely unsung and, therefore, technically irrelevant to the action of the scene.

The sudden appearance of "That Shakespearian Rag" is similar to the tom-tom effect of "Portrait of a Lady," but it differs in one crucial respect: by using a real, identifiable piece of popular music, Eliot makes the man easier to empathize with and draws his audience more directly into the poem. It is difficult to say just how widely known "That Shakespearian Rag" was in 1922, among either the contempo-rary public or Eliot's cadre of readers. But for those who were already familiar with the song before encountering it in *The Waste Land*, the allusion would presum-ably have caused the rag to begin playing within their own minds as well, leaving them beset by the very same "brainworm" that has come upon Eliot's character.

Music creates an uncanny but powerful intimacy between the poem and its readers here, and the rag therefore emerges as a very successful example of what Eliot had earlier termed an "objective correlative" for emotion in literature: that is, "a situation . . . which shall be the formula of that *particular* emotion; such that when the external facts, which must terminate in sensory experience, are given, the emotion is immediately evoked."[72] Eliot would later complain that critics were exaggerating when they claimed that *The Waste Land* had captured the anxieties of an entire generation, but it is nevertheless the case that many of his first readers knew all too well what the "sensory experience" of having "That Shakespearian Rag" on the brain was like.[73]

The passage of time and shifts in musical taste have made "That Shakespearian Rag" largely inaudible to modern audiences—indeed, it would be scarcely remembered at all were it not for its place in *The Waste Land*—and the reactions it must have once inspired have therefore lessened over time. One need not be familiar with the rag, however, to note that there is something vaguely disturbing about this scene and its depiction of a crowded sensorium. In the world of *The Waste Land*, one does not need to be within range of a street-piano or in the presence of a phonograph to be sprung upon by a well-worn tune. Indeed, Eliot suggests here that the modern listener is already a walking collection of prefabricated popular music, something akin to a record player himself. It is unclear whether Eliot is going so far as to make the explicitly techno-deterministic argument, as has Friedrich Kittler, that records "turn and turn until phonographic inscriptions inscribe themselves into brain physiology."[74] But a similar uneasiness could be found in the works of other American authors of the period, many of whom heard a threat of standardization, endless repetition, and inauthentic experience in recorded music. Sinclair Lewis had already used the word "phonograph" to denote not just a musical device but also an unthinking, cliché-spouting conversationalist in his 1920 best seller *Main Street*, while the protagonist of John Dos Passos's *Three Soldiers* (1921) had experienced a very Eliotic stagnation one year before *The Waste Land*: "the same dull irritation of despair droned constantly in his head, grinding round and round like a broken phonograph record."[75] In these and other literary works, the human mind is at the mercy of mechanized music, in danger of being colonized by sounds and processes.[76]

Perhaps even more unnerving, however, is Eliot's suggestion in *The Waste Land* that music's ability to invade and subordinate the self does not tend to strike modern listeners as unnerving at all. In the poem's "Fire Sermon" section, for example, Eliot introduces a working woman (an anonymous typist) who provides an object lesson in how bleak, and yet how perversely attractive, the experience of distracted listening can be. Her self-absorbed lover, a "young man carbuncular," drops by her apartment for a visit, which culminates in an unpleasant but brief sex scene: "he assaults at once;/Exploring hands encounter no defence;/His vanity requires no response,/And makes a welcome of indifference" (*Poems* 44). He leaves after giving her "one final patronising kiss," and she reacts thus:

> Her brain allows one half-formed thought to pass:
> "Well now that's done: and I'm glad it's over."
> When lovely woman stoops to folly and
> Paces about her room again, alone,
> She smoothes her hair with automatic hand,
> And puts a record on the gramophone.

Readers cannot know what the typist's musical selection is, as the scene shifts focus immediately afterward. There are any number of possibilities: it might be a sad song that corresponds to the mood of lingering disappointment, or a peppy one that provides something of a corrective—"Make the best of your position"—to what has just transpired. It is crucial to notice, however, that in either case the typist is attempting to force a song into her head, hoping that music will enter into and overtake her consciousness as it has already done (unbidden) for another of Eliot's characters. In describing how her brain "allows one half-formed thought to pass," Eliot casts the typist as a policewoman of her own mind, creating a sense—if it were not clear already—that there are aspects of her life that she would prefer not to investigate too closely. And in these sorts of situations, canned music is her perception-altering drug of choice, a distraction as readily available as the "food in tins" she eats for dinner (*Poems* 44).

Indeed, Eliot depicts the typist as having all but merged with her music machine. In describing her "automatic hand" he simultaneously suggests her habitual behavior, her repetitive day job, and her gramophone's tone arm (which holds the needle that reads a record's groove). His uncharacteristically ordered prosody creates an atmosphere of both rigidity and authorial discomfort. And finally, he emphasizes the typist's almost robotic impassiveness, both in her deference to the man who has assaulted her and in her willingness to let a record emote in her stead. The obliqueness of the poem leaves it somewhat hard to say whether Eliot's attitude toward this empty woman is one of disapproval, or pity, or both. But in other contexts he spoke forthrightly about the toll he thought mechanical culture was taking on humanity, as in this essay for *The Dial*, published in the same year as *The Waste Land*:

> When every theatre has been replaced by 100 cinemas, when every musical instrument has been replaced by 100 gramaphones, when every horse has been replaced by 100 cheap motor cars, when electrical ingenuity has made it possible for every child to hear its bedtime stories through a wireless receiver attached to both ears, when applied science has done everything possible with the materials on this earth to make life as interesting as possible, it will not be surprising if the population of the entire civilized world rapidly follows the fate of the Melanesians.[77]

Which is to say, the entire civilized world will be "dying from pure boredom" ("Letter" 662). For Eliot, the price of mechanized cultural abundance is the decline of cultural pleasure, with his typist serving as the very model of the alienated, unsatisfied music listener. And if the record-playing woman who "stoops to folly" in his poem is anything like the one in the Oliver Goldsmith verse from which Eliot has borrowed this particular phrase, her fate will be quite grim: Goldsmith asks if any "art can wash her guilt away," and concludes that the only solution for her is "to die."[78]

To clarify this point, however, Eliot was suspicious not of popular culture per se but rather the variety of it that he believed encouraged passive consumption. In the same essay just quoted, after all, Eliot also mourns the celebrated British music-hall star Marie Lloyd, whose death he calls "the most important event which I have had to chronicle in these pages"—no small claim considering that he had also discussed the publication of Joyce's *Ulysses* and a performance of Igor Stravinsky's *Rite of Spring* in the same journal ("Letter" 659). Lloyd was a great popular artist, Eliot argues, because she was capable of connecting with crowds and inspiring them to sing along with her, which therefore meant that they were "performing part of the work of acting" and engaging "in that collaboration of the audience with the artist which is necessary in all art" ("Letter" 662) (see Image 3). Mechanical culture, on the other hand, requires no such collaboration, and Eliot worries over what will happen to the average Lloyd fan as a consequence of her passing:

> He will now go to the cinema, where his mind is lulled by continuous sense-less music and continuous action too rapid for the brain to act upon, and he will receive, without giving, in that same listless apathy with which the middle and upper classes regard any entertainment of the nature of art. He will also have lost some of his interest in life.

The music hall star Marie Lloyd, whose death in 1922 marked the end of an era of live, intimate theater for Eliot. Used by permission, The Billy Rose Theater Collection at the New York Public Library.

Bearing Eliot's distinction between active and passive entertainment in mind, one might return to the aforementioned musical moments in *The Waste Land* and hear them somewhat differently than before. In "That Shakespearian Rag" there is a possibility of recognition, improvisation, and open-ended participation on the reader's part, which lends the scene a certain Lloydian good cheer. But because Eliot offers no similarly explicit musical cue for his audience to follow and perform in the case of the typist and her gramophone, there are few ways of lightening the gloom.

There is a final observation about popular culture worth noting in Eliot's essay, one that has implications for how readers might go about approaching his poetic masterwork as a whole: the contrast he draws between the "continuous" music of the cinema and more jumbled variety he associates with Lloyd. Continuous music is condemned here because it is too easy to follow, with a fluid film accompaniment requiring little engagement from audiences and therefore rendering them dull. But the music hall was above all else a place of variety, with spectators exposed to multiple kinds of entertainment and not allowed to lapse into "listless apathy." Eliot's implication here is that a discontinuous aesthetic presents a productive challenge to audiences, who must expend some amount of effort to take it all in and therefore earn a corresponding sense of satisfaction. And Eliot, who on more than one occasion named the music hall as a worthy model for high art,[79] surely felt that *The Waste Land* was comparably valuable insofar as it invites readers to make what sense as they will of its discontinuous fragments, textual sources, and speakers. He would later claim that "what a poem means is as much what it means to others as what it means to the author," and if this is in fact the case, then locating a master plot, a consistent point of view, or any other organizing continuity in the multiply-voiced *Waste Land* serves to limit rather than intensify its poetic possibilities.[80] Far better to arrive at one's own, idiosyncratic interpretation of Eliot's miscellanies, responding in a more associative manner and using what he called one's "auditory imagination" to hear the ways in which the poem communicates "far below the conscious levels of thought and feeling."[81]

The poem becomes less a message to be understood than a network of loosely related ideas to be wandered through when read in such a way, and it is for this reason that early interpreters of *The Waste Land* sometimes reached for extra-literary musical analogies in trying to describe what Eliot had achieved. Here is how I. A. Richards put it in an influential study of the poem in 1934:

> The ideas are of all kinds, abstract and concrete, general and particular, and, like the musician's phrases, they are arranged, not that they may tell us something, but that their effects in us may combine into a coherent whole of feeling and attitude and produce a peculiar liberation of the will. They are to be responded to, not to be pondered or worked out.[82]

Music is invoked here as a kind of super-unifying force, a catchall category containing that which might initially seem discontinuous. Eliot's musical poem, moreover, is said to be uniquely freeing, allowing readers to concentrate not on what the poet says but on the associations he inspires in their minds.[83] And seldom has Eliot's ability to elicit such associations been more apparent than in the literally musical moments of *The Waste Land*, as when he includes lines from Wagner's *Tristan und Isolde* (1865) in the first section. Eliot provides just two snippets of this very long opera here, and yet the music has inspired critics to go to extraordinary lengths in showing just how many parts of *The Waste Land* can be plausibly connected to it. Wagner's leitmotifs are compared to Eliot's patterns of symbolism; the opera's relation to the Grail legend is said to reinforce Eliot's use of the same mythic narrative; the shepherd's description of the ocean ("*Oed' und leer das Meer*") is shown to echo the poem's pervasive water imagery (*Poems* 38); and the list goes on and on. Whether understood in these accounts as just one of many cultural presences within *The Waste Land* or as an overarching structure that governs the entire poem, music provides a means by which initial diffusion can be resolved into wholeness, anticipating the almost mystical harmony of Eliot's later *Four Quartets* (1936–42).[84]

Ultimately, Eliot's invocations of music in *The Waste Land* result in an unusually dynamic poem, both by adding to the accreted allusions on its pages and by spurring the imaginations of its readers. The poem is often a kind of freestyle improvisation in its musical moments, as when it jumps from a morbid scene to a garbled line from Andrew Marvell to a dirty street song about a notorious "Mrs. Porter" to the ecstatic sounds of a children's choir in the Grail Chapel, with the lines having little obvious connection to one other besides the rhymes or words they share:

> White bodies naked on the low damp ground
> And bones cast in a little low dry garret,
> Rattled by the rat's foot only, year to year.
> But at my back from time to time I hear
> The sound of horns and motors, which shall bring
> Sweeney to Mrs. Porter in the spring.
> O the moon shone bright on Mrs. Porter
> And on her daughter
> They wash their feet in soda water
> *Et O ces voix d'enfants, chantant dans la coupole!*
>
> (*Poetry* 43)

Whoever it is that speaks here, the poem reads as though a word ("Porter") or a sound ("eer") in one context reminds him of the same word or sound in a different one, and if the unfolding lines do not obey a narrative logic they still have a musical congruity. Even more significant is the way that this musical process of association sometimes provides a sense of liberation, perhaps even a cure for the enervation and hopelessness on display in so many other parts of *The Waste Land*. Just as compiling a series of linked references can transform a bone-filled garret into a jolly musical number and then into a profound hymn, so too can the mind create a musical pattern that escapes even the dreariness of modern mechanical culture. Here, for example, are the therapeutic sounds that follow the episode of the typist and her gramophone:

> She smoothes her hair with automatic hand,
> And puts a record on the gramophone.

"This music crept by me upon the waters"
And along the Strand, up Queen Victoria Street.
O City city, I can sometimes hear
Beside a public bar in Lower Thames Street,
The pleasant whining of a mandoline
And a clatter and a chatter from within
Where fishmen lounge at noon . . .

(Poems 44–45)

The typist's record player brings another, better music to mind, the kind said to be heard "upon the waters" of Prospero's Island in *The Tempest*. That musical setting evokes a memory of the riverside London streets that Eliot enjoyed walking during his workday lunch breaks, which in turn recalls the musical performances that could sometimes be found there. The sad episode of the typist has developed into a pleasant tune after just a few lines and mental digressions, with Eliot deploying three very different types of music and a larger musical pattern of association to bring about the transformation.

The listening reader of *The Waste Land* is therefore left with something of a conundrum by poem's end. Music is on the one hand a presence to be disliked and feared, an oppressive sonic force and an insinuating aesthetic form that seizes the mind and saps the will. It is on the other a means of transcendence and control, an art that demonstrates how one might reassemble the twentieth century's cultural noise in the service of something greater. But while this uneasy combination of antipathy and admiration for music's power has struck many readers as disorienting over the years, it seems to have taught a crucial lesson to the young Ralph Ellison, who as a college undergraduate found *The Waste Land* to be as catchy as the best music and instrumental in showing him what modern literature was capable of:

> *The Waste Land* seized my mind. I was intrigued by its power to move me while eluding my understanding. Somehow its rhythms were often closer to those of jazz than were those of the Negro poets, and even though I could not understand then, its range of allusion was as mixed and as varied as that of Louis Armstrong. Yet there were its discontinuities, its changes of pace and its hidden system of organization which escaped me.[85]

Like Waldo Frank before him, Ellison is attracted by a music of disconnection in Eliot, seduced by disarray. So too has he fallen under the poem's compulsive power, experiencing the ways in which a reader's mind can be played upon without his having a full awareness of what, precisely, has happened. And as any reader of his intensely musical novel *Invisible Man* (1952) knows, he has heard quite clearly the ways in which various arts can be brought together in the service of the new. The modern moment may require the artist to have a sense for discontinuity and fracture, but so too does its crowded culture offer him a chance at a greater, harmonizing mastery.

Beneath the Jazz: Linking Transcendentalism and Modernism

These two approaches to uniting poetry and music, the Whitmanian and the Eliotic, were at the most general level about the synecdotal relationship between parts and wholes. Each poet's body of work meditates upon the place of the individual artwork within the broader cultural tradition, of the present moment within the unfolding expanse of time, and of objective experience within a larger conception of ideality. And by aligning two media with one another, each poet asks whether distinct forms can work in concert and, in their being influenced by one another, achieve some larger, component aesthetic. There is little question that Whitman was affirmative on all these points: the contemporary sounds of Italian opera produced feelings in him that he was certain echoed those of civilization's earliest artists and presaged those of today's creative generation, with the boundary separating true music and true poetry being essentially nonexistent. Eliot, however, seems to have been considerably more ambivalent, suggesting at some points that the popular songs of the Jazz Age are but passing fancies and noise in a disorderly world.

This tension between a Transcendental sense of unity and a modernist sense of fragmentation could be heard in a great many other musical or musically inspired works of the early twentieth century, the moment that, among other things, saw Transcendentalism coming to attain its present reputation as a serious school of thought with which subsequent American artists must grapple. Consider the case of Ezra Pound, who in some moments was capable of a Whitmanian flexibility in regard to verse and meter: "I believe in an 'absolute rhythm,' a rhythm, that is, in poetry which corresponds exactly to the emotion or shade of emotion to be expressed," he wrote in an early, inclusive delineation of his poetic principles. "A man's rhythm must be interpretative, it will be, therefore, in the end, his own, uncounterfeiting, uncounterfeitable."[86] Yet in his first singing *Cantos,*

Pound goes out of his way to leave the impression that certain rhythms—and in particular certain musical rhythms—do not count. See, for example, this suggestion in Canto VII that contemporary sounds lack any vital relation to the art that came before:

> Another day, between walls of a sham Mycenian,
> "Toc" sphinxes, sham-Memphis columns,
> And beneath the jazz a cortex, a stiffness or stillness,
>   Shell of the older house.
> Brown-yellow wood, and the no colour plaster,
> Dry professorial talk . . .
>   now stilling the ill beat music,
> House expulsed by this house.[87]

Here the "ill beat music" and "jazz" of modernity are little more than sonic clutter within their poetic context, and at other moments Pound belittles contemporary rhythms by widening his scope, the better to show popular music's ultimate insignificance relative to historical and geologic time. Consider this verse from Canto XXIX:

> Past the house of the three retired clergymen
> Who were too cultured to keep their jobs.
> Languor has cried unto languor
>   about the marshmallow-roast
> (Let us speak of the osmosis of persons)
> The wail of the phonograph has penetrated their marrow
> (Let us . . .
> The wail of the pornograph . . .)
>   The cicadas continue uninterrupted.[88]

In contrasting the wail of the phono/pornograph with the sound of the cicadas, Pound is doubly dismissive. On the one hand, he draws on the insects' Provençal association with folklore and vernacular culture, thereby suggesting a tradition at odds with and unwilling to make way for cheap mechanical music. On the other, he evokes an organic, natural drone that remains essentially indifferent to human affairs, one that predated the popular hits of his moment and will continue long after today's artists are gone.

Hart Crane was not so technophobic as Pound could be, arguing that modern poetry needed to "absorb the machine" if it was to have any meaningful relationship to its era.[89] Yet in *The Bridge*—Crane's long poem of 1930 that synthe-sizes Whitman (who makes a cameo) and Eliot (whose *Waste Land* he was in part responding to)—he still seems to conclude that popular culture and much of the contemporary condition are rather meager in comparison with the most legiti-mately musical of the arts. The poem's first section begins by introducing the inan-ity and impersonality of a Manhattan business district, with office workers waiting for elevators to "drop us from our day," the "multitudes" entertaining themselves in front of the "panoramic sleights" of the cinema, and an insectoid "subway scuttle" conveying everyone from place to place (45). And how small this all appears in comparison with Crane's description of the "harp and altar" that is the Brooklyn Bridge, whose majesty is described in Pythagorean language:

> Again the traffic lights that skim thy swift
> Unfractioned idiom, immaculate sigh of stars,
> Beading thy path—condense eternity:
> And we have seen night lifted in thine arms.
>
> . . .
>
> O Sleepless as the river under thee,
> Vaulting the sea, the prairies' dreaming sod,
> Unto us lowliest sometime sweep, descend
> And of the curveship lend a myth to God.
>
> (46)

The bridge's suspension cables, suggested by Crane to resemble the strings of the Aeolian Harp, are tuned to an all-encompassing frequency: they span prairies in spite of the vast distance separating them, their "sigh of stars" produces a universal music, and they seem superior even to God in their ability to "condense eternity." Unlike the ephemera and urban monotony that came before, this is an "unfrac-tioned idiom," a unifying scheme that helps discrete objects and moments attain a greater harmony. And unlike his forefather Whitman, Crane seems to locate musical sublimity in exemplary, unusually accomplished cultural monuments, not in the arts of everyday life.

In these and other cases Eliot can seem to be the most influential, representative thinker, with the poet who seeks a musical totality in verse generally advised not to listen for it in the popular arts. Seldom in modernism do the songs of Tin Pan Alley inspire the ecstasy that the Italian opera did in Whitman, nor do they tend to speed verse of the early twentieth century to his heady heights. But poets were not the only artists of the era to juxtapose popular music with other forms in the hopes of creating a fused aesthetic, and in the realm of musical composition there was at least one extraordinarily successful example of the Whitmanian approach, leavened with an Eliotic modernism: Charles Ives and his short orchestral work *Central Park in the Dark* (1906). Whitman's "Italian Music in Dakota" had found opera to be initially incongruous but strangely in rapport with the wide-open spaces of rural America, and Ives's analogous piece aligns two distinct musics with one another to discordant and yet strikingly moving effect. *Central Park in the Dark* begins moodily, with a string section moving slowly from one drawn-out note to another, usually at eerie, unexpected intervals so as to evoke an otherworldly natural space in the middle of Manhattan. Their music is punctuated, however, by a series of wind instruments meant to represent a passing street band, some of them playing raucous, recognizable popular hits at an entirely different tempo from that of the strings. As "Hello! Ma Baby" and the "Washington Post March" ring out the listener suddenly feels grounded in a particular time and place, experiencing a sense of familiarity and recognition while at the same time left disoriented by the growing din. But then the clamor abruptly ends and the strings, which all the while had been wending their way onward at the same speed as before, continue unperturbedly until the piece's placid conclusion. 🎧

Central Park in the Dark implies that some deeper order exists beneath the flurry of everyday life, a greater unity that might not always be heard but cannot be drowned out. (Ives's personal interest in Transcendentalism—expressed most explicitly in his writings on Emerson, Henry David Thoreau, and Bronson Alcott in *Essays before a Sonata*—is particularly audible here.) One might interpret the piece as being about the irreconcilable differences between absolute and popular music or the incursions of urban space into the natural world, with the tones of the park having little meaningful relation to the strains of the band. But for all that the two, concurrent musics fail to correspond in the minutes that they overlap, they both resonate equally in the listener's mind after the piece has run its course, and they share one vital point in common—that is, an existence within the unifying space of Ives's composition. As did both Whitman and Eliot, Ives ingeniously demonstrates how new wholes can be created even with ill-fitting parts, how opposite sounds or media or cultural categories become all the more meaningful and strangely appropriate to one another when forced into proximity. Hearing the jazz, in other words, is sometimes the best way to appreciate what lies beneath the jazz, whether in verse or in music or in any other art.

3. The Literary Soundtrack
F. Scott Fitzgerald's Heard and Unheard Melodies

Anyone who writes about music is likely to have at some point been warned that words are limited instruments for describing the most evanescent and time-bound of the arts, that, as the old cliché of uncertain provenance would have it, "writing about music is like dancing about architecture."[1] A less discussed corollary to this problem is that reading about music makes for an odd experience as well. Consider the following excerpt from Richard Powers's *The Time of Our Singing* (2003), narrated by a mixed-race pianist whose artistic genealogy is at once classical and popular, traditional and modern, black and white:

> "Naw, naw. Play me that pretty one. The one with the string quartet." He hummed the first three notes of "Yesterday," with a schmaltz three years too late or thirty too soon. I'd heard the tune thousands of times. But I'd never played it. . . . The problem with pop tunes was that, in those rare moments when I did recreate them at the piano, as a break from more études, I tended to embellish the chord sequences. "Yesterday" came out half Baroque figured bass and half ballpark organ.[2]

It is hard to think of many better-known songs than "Yesterday," and upon encountering this scene readers are quite likely to hear, somewhere in the recesses of their minds, Paul McCartney singing its "first three notes" or the sound of his accompanying "string quartet." Yet the song has also been radically defamiliarized in Powers's treatment, still recognizable but rendered "half Baroque figured bass and half ballpark organ" by the improvising narrator. It is a counter-version of a popular song that, long before *The Time of Our Singing* took it up, was already among the most frequently covered in history, with Powers presenting a new "Yesterday" that his readers might be able to imagine but cannot actually hear. The result is a musical-textual moment that fluctuates between the known and the unknown, the familiar and the foreign, the literally audible and the suggestively abstract.

This peculiar combination of immediacy and ambiguity is typical of an authorial device that this chapter will refer to as the "literary soundtrack," defined as a series of written references to specific pieces of music that compel extra-literary responses in readers and thereby heighten, color, or otherwise comment upon the narrative that contains them. Over the course of the twentieth century more and more authors invoked music in their works to various literary effects, but precisely what are the stakes of a novel's reaching across aesthetic boundaries in this way? Most obviously, the literary soundtrack lends the resonance of a sister art to writers, allowing them to align two very different aesthetic forms with one another in ways more commonly associated with the stage or film. But it also cedes as much authorial control as it grants, dependent as it is on audiences to make the necessary connections between texts and a notoriously slippery mode of expression. Readers, after all, hear and remember songs in different ways, and in many cases they have utterly divergent reactions to the same pieces of music.[3] And if the contemporary public can even be said, as has recently been argued, to "think in soundtracks" because of its long exposure to popular song and musically accompanied narrative,[4] then this act of aesthetic doubling in relation to literature becomes all the more difficult to predict or classify because readers are as likely as not to engage in it intuitively. Just as the soundtracked novel puts two generically distinct arts into productive dialogue, so too does it represent a fluid complex of authorial intention and audience participation, a musicalized work of transmission or *poesis* that that depends to an unusual extent on reception or *esthesis*.

The literary soundtrack has afforded authors a great many opportunities over the years,[5] but it also poses a problem: what are readers to do when they encounter a literary soundtrack but are not able to hear it? Is not the novel that relies on musical recognition in any significant way also uniquely threatened by the possibility of unfamiliarity in audiences? These are especially pressing questions for those works that invoke popular music, as one of the defining characteristics of the popular tradition has been its dependence on tides of fashion, its unflagging emphasis on the new, and, all too often, its silencing of the old. To what extent, for example, are contemporary readers able to listen to E. L. Doctorow's historical novel *Ragtime*? It has a soundtrack, but while readers may have musical reactions when Doctorow mentions an enduring classic like Scott Joplin's "Maple Leaf Rag," his allusion to the all-but-forgotten "I Hear You Calling Me"—playing on a phonograph during a parlor scene—seems intended to signal just how far away the past has become.[6] This problem is still more pronounced in novels hailing from the early twentieth century, decades before the term "soundtrack" had even been coined. Authors then took it for granted that their audiences would be familiar with certain kinds of popular music, but they could not have foreseen the extent to which that music would eventually be supplanted. Very few of the songs mentioned in such texts ever became standards, and even those that did became much less known after the rise of rock 'n' roll some fifty years later. As a result, a great many literary soundtracks from otherwise familiar novels have become sequences of what would in internet parlance be called dead links, strangely inaudible musical moments that highlight the fact that entire cultural, aesthetic, and sensory dimensions of these texts have disappeared.

If a literary soundtrack depends on musical familiarity in readers and means little if it is not listened to, then it falls to scholars to do the necessary archival legwork and make audible those turn-of-the-century texts that have since been muted. And in the sphere of American letters, F. Scott Fitzgerald is one of the best authors with whom such musical archaeology and reengagement can begin. He was an exemplary practitioner of the literary soundtrack in the first half of the twentieth century, invoking the songs of his day not just for ambiance or as subject matter, but also as a means of creating a fresh, musical mode of reading and writing. A brief glance through the annotated Cambridge Edition of Fitzgerald's work reveals the sheer amount of music in his novels and stories, as well as the adroitness with which he uses it: the opening strains of *This Side of Paradise* (1920) faithfully reflect an idealized, prewar setting, while the most significant party song in *The Great Gatsby* (1925) very deliberately situates the plot in 1922, the *annus mirabilis* of literary modernism. Working in concert with his similarly song-mad contemporary James Joyce, Fitzgerald was instrumental in developing the musical dimension of twentieth-century fiction, and by extension the interdisciplinary character of the international modernist movement.[7]

The twenty-first-century reader's response to Fitzgerald's soundtracks, unfortunately, is not likely to go much beyond a kind of detached appreciation, as the feelings of musical recognition and immediacy that they were intended to inspire usually elude today's audiences. But Fitzgerald remains instructive even in his outmodedness. Tuneful though they may be, Fitzgerald's novels tend also to emphasize singular, time-bound, and ultimately unknowable qualities in music, thereby making his soundtracks play counterpoint to his central literary themes: the "sense of the passing present," the impossibility of preserving experience in a world of ceaseless change, and the value of impermanent states of being.[8] Fitzgerald seems to have deployed song not just to heighten the reading act for his contemporary audiences but also to veil his novels with a certain, mysterious liminality, at once inviting readers to hear something familiar in his scenes but also underscoring the difficulty of grasping their musical meaning. Consequently, he not only demonstrates the degree to which fiction can achieve musical effects, but he also anticipates the challenges his works now present nearly a century later.

In explaining why Fitzgerald was an innovator when it came to musical writing, one must first note that he was in many ways a product of his time, the beneficiary of various historical changes that made literary soundtracks considerably easier to construct than had been the case for most of the nineteenth century. His musical understanding was shaped by many of the same phenomena noted in relation to T. S. Eliot in the previous chapter, including the advent of sound recording technology, the widespread commercial availability of song, the preponderance of musical fads, and the increasing importance of music as a facet of personal identity, particularly among the young. Consider the following scene from *The Beautiful and Damned* (1922):

> In October Muriel came out for a two weeks' visit. Gloria had called her on long-distance, and Miss Kane ended the conversation characteristically by saying "All-ll-ll righty. I'll be there with bells!" She arrived with a dozen popular songs under her arm.
>
> "You ought to have a phonograph out here in the country," she said, "just a little Vic—they don't cost much. Then whenever you're lonesome you can have Caruso or Al Jolson right at your door."[9]

Muriel's casual, tossed-off tone only highlights the momentousness of the cultural shift she embodies. Her slangy comeback suggests that she will "be there with bells on," but so too does she allude to the old "Banbury Cross" nursery rhyme and its archaic notions of musical enticement ("With rings on her fingers and bells on her toes, she shall have music wherever she goes"). And how times have changed: music for Muriel is positively common, such that a song is not a sound or an event but a product that can be carried about by the armful. The jingling bells of old are being fast replaced by the bell horn of the phonograph, with Muriel pointing out—just as contemporary advertisers often did—that no one in twentieth-century America need wallow in silence or sing to oneself when the companionship of far greater and more famous musicians is both affordable and always at the ready. The unprecedented availability of music now offers Muriel the opportunity to be the architect of her aural surroundings, to harness the emotionally heightening powers of a famously transitory art, and to achieve what one scholar has called the "monumentalization" of everyday life through well-chosen, mood-matching songs.[10]

Fitzgerald's beloved New York City was the songwriting and performing capital of this increasingly musical America, and he threw himself into its cultural crescendo enthusiastically—Zelda Fitzgerald recalled that she and her husband visited Broadway so often that they reduced their income tax accordingly.[11] One might therefore say that he was simply in the right place at the right time, in a unique position to capture a turning point in the nation's aesthetic. No longer was a "musical" text bound to adhere to formal song structures (as in the long tradition of nineteenth-century poetry set to "airs"), nor need it aim at an abstract lyricism in emulation of music's much-vaunted, "absolute" beauty (as in the "decadent" verse that Fitzgerald admired as an undergraduate). Rather, Fitzgerald could presume his audiences to be as musically up-to-date as he was, their minds so suffused with the lyrics and voices and ditties of their age that the briefest of suggestions could set them playing in the imagination. The nation's culture of entertainment had expanded to the point that his novels could easily summon the unique feelings of ecstasy, humor, and pathos that he found in song, thereby yoking the associative powers of what so many nineteenth-century thinkers had argued was the highest of the arts.

Popular song, as was noted in the previous chapter, was certainly not what music's philosophical partisans had had in mind when they afforded it such a lofty position in its relation to literature, and Fitzgerald knew that many of his contemporaries found something insidious about America's hit tunes and their effects on the public consciousness. Zelda Fitzgerald's autobiographical novel *Save Me the Waltz* (1932) would look back upon a wife who cannot keep herself from irritating her artist husband with song: "She supposed it *was* annoying the way the music of the day kept running through her head. There was nothing else there."[12] So too had Fitzgerald heard the aforementioned "Shakespearean Rag" nattering away in *The Waste Land*, a poem that may have inspired his valley of ashes in *The Great Gatsby*. The problem of cultural value and judgment, of course, was implicit in these and other such apprehensive texts, and some of Fitzgerald's peers found him to be less than discerning on this subject: John Dos Passos, an inveterate soundtracker himself, would later describe him as having "no taste for food or wine or painting, little ear for music except for the most rudimentary popular songs."[13] But as will become apparent in this chapter, Fitzgerald's writing stakes out a middle position between fandom and concern in regard to entertainment, with his fiction's "rudimentary popular songs" allowing him to depict and engage with the complexities of his very busy cultural moment.

Dos Passos's verdict aside, literary scholars have been generous to Fitzgerald's supposedly tin ear over the years, with several noting an aural richness in his novels and discussing their music in compelling ways. But in all previous approaches to Fitzgerald and his soundtracks, critics have been hampered by an obvious methodological problem: they seldom give any indication that they have listened to the music he invokes, or that its actual, perceptible sound is especially important in relation to his work.[14] This oversight can be explained not only by the fall from grace that Fitzgerald's songs suffered as the decades wore on, but also by the significant media obstacles that have kept scholars from being able to hear them in their original incarnations. The days of the wax cylinder and phonograph record passed along with Tin Pan Alley's golden age, with both developments helping to wither the musical familiarity that any soundtracked novel of the 1920s depends on. But recent strides forward in digital music conversion and internet archiving have bestowed a significant gift to scholars, with most of Fitzgerald's selected songs widely available once more and free of charge. The permanent auditory record that Thomas Edison intended his technology to inaugurate has, after several decades of obsolescence, begun to be restored in a new form, and so too has the opportunity to hear Fitzgerald's texts (to say nothing of late nineteenth and early twentieth-century literature more broadly).

If the soundtracks of Fitzgerald and his literary contemporaries can be recovered today, what should readers now be listening for? Those who would hear such songs and retune such novels should first consider that music communicates in several ways, all of which would ideally be balanced in musical-textual analysis. Most obviously, a soundtrack can create meaning through words, and when song lyrics are quoted, implied, or otherwise used as accompaniment by authors they can be parsed in the same way that poems are. But words are only one aspect of musical performance and listening, with a song's lyrics additionally inflected by its melody, key, rhythm, timbre, and other structural features that must be heard or imagined aurally if they are to be grasped.[15] And finally, it does not do to think of a song merely as a self-contained aesthetic object, one whose meaning can be made entirely evident through formal explication. Over the last twenty years, musicologists have tended more and more to argue that music cannot be understood apart from its effects on and reception by audiences, even when it has been captured on a record: to borrow a distinction from Christopher Small, music is "not a thing at all but an activity, something that people do," an ongoing, reciprocal interaction between performers and listeners rather than a canon of autonomous works, "musicking" more than "music."[16] Accounting for musicking in a novel requires that readers think about songs not simply on their own terms but also in relation to literary context; that they ask what social role music plays in its fictional world; and that they engage in the musicking act themselves, listening and responding to songs in whatever way they are moved to. Taken together, these three methods of studying music—as language, as sound, and as action—can account for both its objective, semantic qualities and the subjective, variable associations it inspires. And all three should therefore be brought to bear on the literary soundtrack, which is in some ways a coded message and in others a process to be participated in.

The experiential quality of popular song makes it hard to say at the outset just what the "correct" way of listening to Fitzgerald's fiction might be, even with the help of previously unavailable cues. The following analysis will rely on records released during the first thirty years of his life and will draw conclusions accordingly, but there is no way of determining whether he was thinking of any of them while writing, to say nothing of what his early readers might have heard and reacted to. But while it is impossible, as Fitzgerald's best-known character might say, to "repeat the past" and listen to his works in the same ways that his first audiences did, there are still several conclusions that can be drawn from them.[17] Taken together, his first three novels offer a defense of the popular arts, demonstrating the value of what might initially seem to be a frivolous musical culture and the vital necessity of taking that culture seriously. In advancing this argument, his novels also model the different ways in which a literary soundtrack can be deployed: *This Side of Paradise* invokes musical selections that harmonize with its scenes (a method borrowed from the Broadway stage), *The Beautiful and Damned* contains ones that are jarring and inappropriate (in a manner analogous to the discontinuities of early film), and *The Great Gatsby* emphasizes the ultimate ineffability and mysteriousness of song (ever promising insights into characters even while making them more unknowable). Generally speaking, Fitzgerald's musical novels resist simple explanations and straightforward communication. And yet if the literary soundtrack's at once orchestrated and amorphous legacy in the twentieth century has been any indication, it is their invitation to musical interpretation and the act of carrying it out that ultimately matters most, and not their intended ends.

Riotous Mystery: *This Side of Paradise*

To begin, a confession that the forty-three-year-old Fitzgerald made in a letter to his daughter, Scottie, around the time she took up musical comedy writing for an undergraduate theater company at Vassar: "Again let me repeat that if you start any kind of a career following the footsteps of Cole Porter and Rodgers and Hart, it might be an excellent try. Sometimes I wish I had gone along with that gang, but I guess I am too much a moralist at heart and really want to preach at people in some acceptable form rather than to entertain them."[18] This is an interesting statement for a variety of reasons, foremost among them the highly misleading distinction that Fitzgerald draws between literary edification on the one hand and musical-theatrical diversion on the other. Stark aesthetic oppositions of this sort are rarely very useful in the study of literature, but they are especially unhelpful in Fitzgerald's case, as there are few novelists with better claims to membership in the Broadway "gang" than he. And if ever there were a novel that could be profitably interpreted and listened to as a kind of musical theater, it would be *This Side of Paradise*, his first and most optimistic experiment in literary soundtracking.

This Side of Paradise, the story of Amory Blaine's aimless progress through a Princeton education, the first world war, and his growing feelings of malaise, is one of those novels whose plot seems in large part to be about the development of the novel's own aesthetic. Amory hopes above all else to make his life look, sound, and feel like the dreamlike world he has seen on the musical stage, and *This Side of Paradise* takes on a similarly theatrical atmosphere. Consider Amory's early visit to Broadway for a production of George M. Cohan's *The Little Millionaire* (1911), at which he is carried away by one seductive tune after another, imagines himself as a character in the play, and ultimately manages to become part of the act: "When the curtain fell for the last time he gave such a long sigh that the people in front of him twisted around and stared and said loud enough for him to hear: 'What a *remarkable*-looking boy!'"[19] Amory continues to behave in this showy fashion for most of the novel, ever attempting to recast his own experiences so that they seem more of a piece with the "sphere of epicurean delight" that he associates with the stage (*Paradise* 35), and one of the novel's most pressing questions comes to be whether life can in fact be lived at such an aesthetic pitch and, if so, how that pitch might be sustained.

There are many dimensions to Amory's ongoing, even perpetual performance in *This Side of Paradise*, but particularly important are his sensitivity to popular music and his desire for a life that has been set to or synchronized with it. During Amory's formative trip to the theater, musical accompaniment symbolizes the possibility of dramatic existence: "Oh, to fall in love like that, to the languorous magic melody of such a tune!" he privately effuses (*Paradise* 35). And at several other points Amory finds himself able to realize this fantasy with the help of his favorite songs, which allow him to achieve heightened states of being that approach (if only temporarily) the ecstatic and the sublime. Musical numbers therefore come to pervade the text and tend to have the effect of elevating its plot to unusually intense, frequently melodramatic levels of emotion, with Fitzgerald merging text and song in the service of a novel that reads like nothing so much as an adapted, highly self-conscious Broadway show.

A good demonstration of the novel's musical theatricality is its first moment of sustained romantic coupling, in which "Babes in the Wood"—a song first heard on Broadway during Fitzgerald's junior year at Princeton—serves as a prelude to a much-hoped for kiss and directs the almost ceremonial performance that the two listening characters stage in conjunction with it.[20] The first thing a reader is likely to notice about this scene is that Amory and his flame of the moment, Isabelle, are described in explicitly theatrical terms, their interaction suffused with posturing and other "little conventions" that they feel obliged to obey in this, "a very definite stage—nay, more, a very critical stage" in their affair (*Paradise* 68–69). Their conversation is exceedingly precious, and the question of whether their words are in any way sincere is largely beside the point. Eventually, however, the couple's silences grow "more frequent and more delicious," and at the point of highest tension the melody of "Babes in the Wood," sung by a "light tenor" in a nearby room, arrives as if on cue to bring the scene to what both Amory and Isabelle understand to be its dramatic climax (*Paradise* 70).◐

The song's lyrics are of the come-on variety, scored in the published sheet music for alternating male and female voices and modeled on the centuries-old "Babes in the Wood" children's tale (in which a boy and girl become lost in a forest, die in one another's arms, and are buried under leaves by a company of birds). Here are some representative lines:

> Little Lady don't be depressed and blue,
> After all, we're both in the same canoe.
> Have no fear, can't you see I'm here?
> And till our journey is through
> Little Lady I will take care of you.
> Give me your hand, here where we stand
> We're off to Slumberland,
> Come, dry your eyes, I'll sympathize
> Like a father, mother, brother,
> Moonlight is bright, kiss me goodnight,
> Just like a sister should,
> Then put on your little hood,
> And we'll both be, Oh, so good!
> Like the babes in the wood.[21]

Fitzgerald quotes the song in the text and tends to emphasize its most imperative lyrics ("Give me your hand" and "Kiss me good-night"), but there is considerably more here that, if the reader is able to hear it, contributes to the scene's amorousness. Its merging of male and female voices has obvious implications for the listening lovers, and its chorus (beginning with "Give me your hand") tantalizingly delays its conclusion, with the pace of the lyrics slowing to half the speed of those in the expository verse. Small wonder, then, that Isabelle thrills at the "romantic scene," delighted by "their hands clinging and the inevitable looming charmingly close" and the manner in which Amory's whispered requests for a kiss become "blended in the music" (*Paradise* 71).

Yet there is a great deal about the song that seems strange, not least the fact that it is a remarkably chaste selection for a novel that was considered quite racy in its time. "Babes in the Wood" is strikingly anti-sexual, with the song's female addressee asked to kiss her companion "just like a sister should" and the supposed paramour announcing himself as a familial comforter "like a father, mother, brother." "Babes in the Wood" is innocent enough when heard on its own, but when the fraternal affection of the music is juxtaposed with the fictional scene's pervasive sense of titillation, one wonders whether any seduction perpetrated to this tune might not be taboo, even whether Amory and Isabelle are considering something akin to incest as they draw ever closer to one another. And if the reader is inclined to react to the song in this way, it comes as a relief to find out that Fitzgerald's tableau ends, as so many Broadway numbers of this period did, in a comic interruption and reversal: a company of Amory's friends bursts into the darkened room, the lights go on, and the possibility of coupling ends abruptly.

When listened to less literally, however, "Babes in the Wood" seems ultimately to be about the suspension of passion at its highest point rather than the consummation of it, a celebration of anticipatory emotion. The song's singers find themselves at a threshold, afforded a final opportunity to express themselves before an impending sleep. The desires of Amory and Isabelle, meanwhile, are to be similarly put to rest by the physical satisfaction that they both know is coming, and while the two could hardly be said to be children there is nevertheless a death of innocence implicit in their much-awaited fall into experience. But in the minutes that the song plays, the affection of these "Babes" is of a Platonic variety that allows for chemistry but not reaction, with the surging melody and the singers' intimate harmony indicating that such feelings are no less powerful for their not being acted upon.[22] Indeed, it is an open question as to whether Amory even wants to kiss at all: it is Isabelle, not Amory, who is most petulant after the song is interrupted. Many readers of this novel have noticed that Amory seldom becomes physically involved with sexually forward or available women, with Pearl James suggesting that he is stymied by a "labile, feminine nervousness," and possibly a latent attachment to his own sex.[23] But the "Babes in the Wood" interlude ultimately suggests that Amory's conception of desire is a radically idealized one and that he is more concerned with achieving an abstract aesthetic condition, one in which sexuality might exist as a stimulus but must not be an end in and of itself. Amory's life philosophy, after all, is that "It was always the becoming he dreamed of, never the being" (*Paradise* 24), and so it seems reasonable to conclude that his duet with Isabelle has in fact reached the best of all possible conclusions, allowing him to revel in feelings of potentiality without ever having to enter the realm of the actual and the defined. Music, moreover, assists in heightening the moment and transcending physical expressions of sexuality: Fitzgerald knew and admired Keats's "Ode on a Grecian Urn" as an undergraduate, and his treatment of romance seems to be echoing that poem's suggestion that "Heard melodies are sweet, but those unheard/Are sweeter."[24]

The emotional tenor of this scene may well strike the present-day listener as silly and out of proportion to a song like "Babes in the Wood," and it is therefore useful to pause for a moment and consider why Fitzgerald was so enamored of what he called the "facile froth-like comedy" of the Broadway stage and its associated music (*Paradise* 35). Generally speaking, he seems to have been attracted to a pronounced artificiality in the musical and theatrical entertainments of his day, an aesthetic of flagrant unreality that he attempted to capture as well as critique in his own novel-writing. The value of high art over the other kind is largely predicated on the assumption that the former is concerned with and produces "real" feeling while the latter is but an exercise in cheap and cynical fakery, and yet one of the central questions of *This Side of Paradise* is whether such a thing as "real" feeling actually exists and, if it does, whether art ought to concern itself with something so quotidian when it could instead attempt to achieve fantastic, impossible, and out-of-the-world heights.[25] Fitzgerald's protagonist chooses and embraces performativity; declines to separate what he calls "The fundamental Amory" from the personae he takes up (*Paradise* 97); regards himself as less a stable, fixed personality than a magpie-like "personage" who collects "glittering" exterior identities (*Paradise* 101); and agrees with Oscar Wilde that a young man's ultimate ambition ought not to be producing art but rather becoming a work of art himself. *This Side of Paradise* ponders what it means to view the world as theater and life as an act, and popular entertainment—and the genre of the musical in particular—helps Fitzgerald explore these questions in several ways.

To begin, Fitzgerald regarded drama as a particularly effective portal for the imagination in the early years of his career. He had begun writing plays at the age of fourteen and continued into the 1920s, recalling some years later that even lowbrow works struck him as being "enormously suggestive, opening out into a world much larger and more brilliant than themselves that existed outside their windows and beyond their doors."[26] Through their very design, high and low theater alike promised flight from the everyday. But the musical theater, imbued with the "power of music" that Fitzgerald had begun to realize as a teenager,[27] went a step further, elevating a fundamentally imaginative experience to almost utopian heights where speech blended into song, sound into harmony, and movement into dance. Nor did such an experience, once enjoyed, have to be confined to the physical boundaries of the stage, as Amory makes plain after he takes in *The Little Millionaire* and, in a moment of flâneurie, comes to understand all of New York City as an extension of the show: "They wandered on, mixing in the Broadway crowd, dreaming on the music that eddied out of the cafés. New faces flashed on and off like myriad lights; pale or rouged faces, tired, yet sustained by a weary excitement. Amory watched them in fascination. He was planning his life" (*Paradise* 36).

Equally enticing to Fitzgerald was the hodgepodge format of so much early twentieth-century musical drama, which was generally characterized by what Rick Altman has called an "aesthetic of discontinuity" in the years before the 1927 production of *Show Boat*.[28] One old hand observed in 1915 that stage productions of the period tended to be "not so much written as put together,"[29] and Broadway's relative lack of concern with causality, psychological motivation, plot structure, and dramatic unity all find analogues in the abstract associativeness of *This Side of Paradise*. In composing the somewhat slapdash manuscript, Fitzgerald took the opportunity to recycle much of his undergraduate scribbling—"poetry, prose, vers libre and every mood of a tempermental temperature [*sic*]"[30]—such that the novel quite literally became a kind of variety show. Even those readers who find the finished product to be little more than a glorified grab-bag of incidents and scenes would seem to be on more or less the same page as Fitzgerald was: he tended to refer to *This Side of Paradise* in somewhat vaudevillian terms as he wrote and revised it, alternately classifying it (with characteristically bad spelling) as "pot-pouri," "a prose, modernistic Childe Harolde," a "tedius, disconnected casserole," and "crowded (in the best sense)."[31]

Fitzgerald raises the specter of modernism in explaining the heterogeneity of *This Side of Paradise*, but a more immediate source of inspiration lay in the three comparably crowded musical comedies—*Fie! Fie! Fi-Fi!* (1914), *The Evil Eye* (1915), and *Safety First* (1916)—whose song lyrics he had penned some years earlier for Princeton's Triangle Club. (Two moments of literally dramatic writing in *This Side of Paradise*, complete with scripted dialogue and interspersed stage directions, make the connection between his collegiate theatrical work and the novel's structure all the more obvious.) The strain of musical comedy that Fitzgerald was familiar with in this period was freewheeling and even ramshackle in its organization, with the shows he contributed to at Princeton tending to bounce from song to song with very little in the way of narrative coherence. Yet the allure of such shows for audiences and performers alike lay in precisely this unsettledness, with Fitzgerald's description of a Triangle Club rehearsal in the novel emphasizing the "riotous mystery" that theater represented to him: "a big, barn-like auditorium, dotted with boys as girls, boys as pirates, boys as babies; the scenery in course of being violently set up; the spotlight man rehearsing by throwing weird shafts into angry eyes; over all the constant tuning of the orchestra or the cheerful tumpty-tump of a Triangle tune" (*Paradise* 59). *This Side of Paradise*, of course, makes for something of a "riotous mystery" itself, and while some scholars have found the novel "anything but dramatic" because of his its lack of verisimilitude, organization, and economy, Fitzgerald was more interested in emulating the musical theater's excessiveness and impossibility, its strange amalgamation of the antic and the transcendent (see Image 4).[32]

SCOTT FITZGERALD,
Considered the Most Beautiful "Show Girl" in the Princeton Triangle Club's New Musical Play, "The Evil Eye," Coming to the Waldorf on Next Tuesday. He Is Also the Author of the Lyrics of the Play.   (Photo by W.)

An undergraduate Fitzgerald in costume, promoting a musical comedy production by the Princeton Triangle Club. Used by permission, Rare Books and Special Collections, Princeton University.

Perhaps most evocative of all to Fitzgerald, however, was the doubled, frequently ironic perspective that the musical theater of his day demanded from its audiences, a combination of sophistication and credulity that today tends to be associated with such aesthetic categories as camp or kitsch. On the one hand, the musical theater surrenders all claims to realism through its very design, and spectators are seldom likely to mistake narratives in which characters frequently break into song for anything other than unalloyed fantasy. Yet on the other, its extreme and readily apparent artifice does not preclude emotional responses, even profound ones. As Raymond Knapp has theorized, musicals offer audiences a choice: they may accept them as spectacles and appreciate them on those terms, or they may acknowledge their unreality and then, armed with the assurance that comes of awareness, give themselves leave to be swept up in them and respond to what they hear with a particularly intense degree of feeling. Watching a musical can lead, depending on the viewer, to a kind of self-conscious ecstasy: as Knapp puts it, audiences have "access to a heightened emotionality and permission either to feel the moment more deeply or to laugh at it—or, somehow, to do both at once, in which case we are also laughing at and with ourselves and, perhaps, more fully embracing our humanity."[33]

The peculiar duality of such an experience was especially pronounced in the musicals of Fitzgerald's youth, which routinely trumpeted their own fakery. At *The Little Millionaire*, for example, Amory would have seen a number titled "We Do All the Dirty Work," in which Cohan's villains boast that "all of the trouble in the play we cause" and that "we create the hero by the dirty work we do."[34] Viewers of Cohan's musical—which at points becomes a play-within-a-play not unlike the meta-fictional *This Side of Paradise*—were reminded again and again by the performers themselves that the stage is a zone of artifice and that it demands the conscious suspension of disbelief. Yet for Amory, the play is nevertheless one of the defining experiences of his life, a work of art that achieves profundity in spite of the fact that it is deliberately and explicitly inauthentic. In this and other musical-theatrical works, perspective and decision making on the part of the audience play vital roles in constructing meanings, whether those meanings be frivolous or profound. And this aspect of musical theater matters in relation to *This Side of Paradise* because Fitzgerald's own attempts at it—particularly in his musical interludes—render great swaths of the novel nearly impossible to read "straight," forcing the question of whether audiences are meant to take Amory's emotional predicaments seriously or be amused by them.[35]

This Side of Paradise is unquestionably excessive and profoundly artificial, but its deliberate emulation of Broadway also suggests that these qualities are not limitations, that Fitzgerald was attempting to commingle dramatic impossibility and emotional sincerity in his text. Moreover, he seems to have known that he was playing with fire and that musical-theatrical artistry—whether on the stage or page—is as likely to strike audiences as being supremely hokey as it is to move them in unaccountable ways. Almost as though in anticipation of the jibes and bad reviews that *This Side of Paradise* would receive, Fitzgerald punctuates the novel with numerous aesthetic judgments and divergences of opinion, repeatedly asking why a song, play, or story might mean the world to one person and almost nothing to another. He implies throughout that the way one reacts to aesthetic stimulation constitutes a category of aesthetics in and of itself, and *This Side of Paradise* thus comes to theorize what might be called an art of openness or of receptivity. What is more, this marked interest in the nature of interpretation—particularly insofar as it relates to popular song and the musical stage—not only comes to bear on Amory's theatrical life but also has larger implications for how Fitzgerald's theatrical novel ought to be read.

This question of how best to interpret entertainment—and its corollary, whether audiences should take it seriously—is particularly evident in "The Débutante," a chapter in which Fitzgerald shifts from fiction to stage writing and uses a song called "Kiss Me Again" to illustrate, among other things, how variously listeners sometimes react to the same musical stimuli. Here Amory meets Rosalind Connage, a girl whose talent for dramatic posing is suggested by both the Shakespearian overtones of her first name and the first syllable of her last. Amory begins another scene of stagy, performative seduction very much like the "Babes in the Wood" duet, and then, after a few lines of banter, "*Very deliberately they kiss*" (*Paradise* 173). As was the case earlier in the novel, music arrives just when it is needed and makes the moment seem yet more over-the-top, with the strains of "Kiss Me Again" audible in another room and pushing the drama to a yet-higher intensity. The lyrical content of this particular song is more straightforward than that of "Babes in the Wood," and it initially seems to be a better fit for this interaction: its singer recalls a lost love, describes a romantic setting, and concludes by asking the addressee to do what the song's title suggests. The key to understanding this particular musical moment, however, lies in noticing its instability rather than its appropriateness, as Amory and Rosalind seem to have rather different ideas of what the song is saying and, by extension, what sort of play it is that they have cast themselves in.◑

Amory is the more obviously changed of the two when the song begins, suddenly becoming much less verbose and witty. His quips fall away, and he is able to say little more than "I love you. . . . I don't know why or how, but I love you—from the moment I saw you" (*Paradise* 173). Moreover, it seems as though the song compels him to speak as he does. Certainly "Kiss Me Again" is, depending on one's perspective, an affecting piece of music, largely because so much of its emotion is conveyed in simple, matter-of-fact lyrics that lend it an air of sincerity and distinguish it from other, more conspicuously poetic hits of this frequently mawkish musical era. Its singer is addressing a former lover whose tenderness has waned, but her wistfulness is sympathetic because she does not exaggerate it, indulging only occasionally in fanciful language: she describes actions—thinking, dreaming, and of course kissing—more than she does feelings, she acknowledges the foolishness of her dwelling on something that was "too wondrous to last," and she avoids weighty, more obvious minor keys so as to create an atmosphere of mature melancholy.[36] The song's narration, meanwhile, engages in a temporal sleight of hand by blurring the boundaries of past and present, making it unclear whether the singer is remembering the "sweet summer breeze, whispering trees" of an old romance or is perceiving these things in the moment of performance.[37] Indeterminacy is a large part of the song's allure, and this vagueness appears to have conjured a dreamlike scene into which Amory can easily project himself.

The problem, however, is that Amory appears to be the only one in this scene with an un-ironic attachment to the song. Rosalind's lines are still freighted with dramatic signification after she hears it, suggesting that she appreciates "Kiss Me Again" as little more than an accompaniment to her own performance. "I love you—now," she ominously declares before delivering what Fitzgerald's stage directions identify as "*an odd burst of prophesy*" in histrionic fashion: "Oh—I am very youthful, thank God—and rather beautiful, thank God—and happy, thank God, thank God—Poor Amory!" (*Paradise* 173–174) Rosalind, it would seem, is still in character, less inclined than Amory to take the song to heart and more aware than he that the moment's seductive atmosphere and musically inspired charge will be fleeting. And listening to "Kiss Me Again" for a second time with Rosalind's more theatrical reaction to it in mind makes its many high-wire aspects considerably more evident, raising the question of whether the sincerity announced by its lyrics is not in conflict with its considerable formal sophistication. Most striking of all is the song's virtuosic melody, which requires two vocal leaps of an octave or more (not to mention several smaller but still-challenging ones) and a range of two. Marie Tiffany's 1919 recording of the song amplifies the difficulty even more by adding swooping portamentos and fluttering grace notes, with "Kiss Me Again" coming to sound less like an honest revelation of emotion than a showstopper, one that requires talent, training, and poise to deliver artfully.

Based on Amory and Rosalind's responses to the music, then, "Kiss Me Again" can be heard as a from-the-heart profession, a piece of showmanship, or some combination of the two, with Fitzgerald demonstrating that musical meaning is in large part constructed by the listeners who hear it.[38] Fitzgerald's point in this scene is to some extent an argument about American youth and its savvy relationship to consumer culture: as Kirk Curnutt has noted, *This Side of Paradise* presumes that to be young in the twentieth century is to be adept at manipulating commercial entertainment and using it to construct a working identity for oneself. But Fitzgerald is also hinting here that popular song is able to satisfy emotional needs in listeners not in spite of the fact that it can seem extravagant and overwrought in character, but precisely because of this. A song can be an expression of true feeling for one and an instrument of fantasy for another, but both reactions are "legitimate" according to the conventions of musical theater, a genre whose stories are only as affecting and "true" as listeners allow them to be.

Make-believe of the sort that "Kiss Me Again" inspires is very serious business in *This Side of Paradise*, a practice that Fitzgerald's characters engage in repeatedly, consciously, and sometimes desperately. Indeed, the idealized existence that Amory desires for himself is shown to be so demonstrably, even painfully out of reach throughout *This Side of Paradise* that fantasy can at points come to seem positively healthy, nothing so much as a vital act of self-preservation. The twentieth century as experienced by Amory and his peers is an era in which a scenic nighttime car ride might veer off into a fatal crash; in which expressions of sexual desire can be prosecuted under the Mann Act; and in which the first world war consumes its share of Princeton undergraduates. That Amory, upon experiencing these and other intrusions of real-world tragedy, attempts to bury them so quickly and unproblematically under a veneer of theatricality only makes the fear that they have presumably inflicted upon him seem all the more conspicuous. Unreality in *This Side of Paradise* can therefore be understood as productive and illusion as palliative, with popular song and the musical stage having value because they are uniquely able to divert a damaged generation of American youth. They offer a variety of psychic glue, a cultural pressure valve, a means of temporary but nevertheless therapeutic escape.

That Fitzgerald would champion popular culture for the very fakery and affectedness that usually constitute the grounds for its dismissal might at first seem odd, but as the novel draws to a close it becomes increasingly evident that vacuity is more useful for his characters than most of what passes for "serious" art. All references to popular song disappear about two thirds of the way through *This Side of Paradise*, and when Amory no longer has access to the fantasy that such music offers, he loses control over his life and is left to make one of his greatest mistakes.

It arrives, significantly enough, after he becomes entranced by a new kind of "music," not the commercial sort that he has thrilled to in the past but something considerably more sinister, emanating from an "evil" presence hidden "under the mask of beauty" (*Paradise* 206). Its agent is a Lamia-like girl named Eleanor who is distinctive primarily for sharing Amory's taste in Romantic and Symbolist verse: in a chapter that is by turns grotesque and utterly absurd, the two meet, wander the forests of Maryland, succumb wholeheartedly to the lyricism of Poe and Verlaine, and eventually come to believe that they have become attuned to an infinite, Emersonian musicality underlying all of creation. Amory begins to wonder whether he has found a new and deeper state of being, and is for once in danger of lending excessive credence to something. "He didn't at all feel like a character in a play, the appropriate feeling in an unconventional situation—instead, he had a sense of coming home," Fitzgerald writes (*Paradise* 211). And that "home," at least according to Eleanor, is a state of perception in which the natural world, the senses, and emotion all "harmonize" into perfect musical suspension (*Paradise* 216).

This feels to Amory like a much longed-for experience of musical universality, real transcendence as compared to the mere artifice that the theater and popular song represent. His dalliance with Eleanor, however, is in fact a decisive cultural retreat, a desperate attempt at experiencing the grand, all-encompassing unity more commonly associated with nineteenth-century thought than that of the twentieth. And no amount of declaiming "Ulalume" and boasting of one's own unconventionality can change the fact that, in Fitzgerald's reckoning, these two alleged aesthetes have become so excessively sincere that they have committed the worst offense of all: unconscious and un-ironic self-delusion. The breaking point comes when Eleanor, on horseback and determined to prove the strength of her principles through ecstatic self-obliteration, shrieks, "*I'm going over the cliff!*" and rides toward a precipice (*Paradise* 221, emphasis original). At the last moment, she realizes that her convictions are not quite so firm as she had thought and throws herself from the saddle, leaving only the horse to plunge off the mountain to its spectacular death. This, it seems, is the price of pretending to seriousness rather than simply pretending, and the scene concludes with Eleanor's fraudulence revealed, the music of the spheres turning dissonant, and the couple's once-convincing "poses" left shattered, "strewn about the pale dawn like broken glass" (*Paradise* 222).

Thus does the flexible, self-aware, and ultimately harmless popular song of the novel's first half come to sound far better than the allegedly profound, more abstract "music" of the second, with Fitzgerald offering an implicit defense of frivolity and superficiality. And if Fitzgerald's argument is taken one step further, his admiration for the consciously artificial amusements of popular culture is in many ways analogous to the question of how *This Side of Paradise* is to be read more broadly, as he was very much aware that his delirious novel would appear "a tremendously conceited affair" to many readers and yet also hoped it would stir them in some unique, extra-literary way.[39] There has been no end of commentators who have found Fitzgerald's characters impossible, their dialogue pretentious, and the general atmosphere of this novel exasperating, but one of his innovations in attempting this variety of musical-theatrical writing is the creation of an atmosphere in which readers may choose their level of emotional engagement rather than have it dictated to them, in which they can take it as seriously—or not—as they wish. Certainly this was clear to Edmund Wilson, who seems to have understood better than most that the excessiveness of *This Side of Paradise* is in many ways its greatest strength and that its effectiveness depends in large part on how exacting readers decide to be. It should be obvious, Wilson observed in 1922, that Amory is a "wavering quantity in a phantasmagoria of incident," that Fitzgerald's plot "is always just verging on the ludicrous," and that the novel is on the whole "one of the most illiterate books of any merit ever published." Yet for all its faults, the novel "does not fail to live. The whole preposterous farrago is animated with life."[40] *This Side of Paradise*, for Wilson, does not hold up under traditional literary scrutiny, but it does when a different standard is applied, one that does not condemn artificiality but rather takes the same, indulgent satisfaction that Fitzgerald does in Amory's musical fantasies.

Amory's extravagant visions have dimmed by novel's end, and as he gropes toward a more humble philosophy, music once again emerges as a possible model. The key, Amory concludes, is to avoid extremity: "in this new loneness of his that had been selected for what greatness he might achieve, beauty must be relative or, itself a harmony, it would make only a discord" (*Paradise* 258-9). Whether Amory can return to it or not at novel's end, the happy, self-aware, and safe unreality of popular song and the musical stage would seem to be well suited to the more balanced, "relative" life that he has in mind. And as Fitzgerald later came to believe, much the same might be said for the frequently overwrought musical theater that *This Side of Paradise* represents more broadly. Returning to the novel in 1925, the year in which he would publish his most famous and enduring work, Fitzgerald inscribed the following observation in the margins of one of his copies: "I like this book for the enormous emotion, mostly immature and bogus, that gives every incident a sort of silly 'life.'"[41] "Silly" life, and life in quotation marks—this is what *This Side of Paradise* celebrates and offers at its musical-theatrical best, and if it is "bogus," so much the better.

What You'd Call Cheapness: *The Beautiful and Damned*

The Beautiful and Damned, published two years after *This Side of Paradise*, represented a step forward not just for Fitzgerald but for musical literature more broadly, one of the first and most sustained examples in fiction of an aesthetic phenomenon that should be familiar to any film or television viewer today: a musically accompanied narrative whose songs and plots seem frequently to be at cross-purposes. Far from inspiring ecstasy or perfected emotional states, music in this novel tends to create irony and puzzlement, with Fitzgerald recontextualizing the hits of his cultural moment and juxtaposing them with his characters and scenes to seemingly inappropriate, odd, or uneasy effects. His realization that songs have lives of their own that may or may not harmonize with those of their listeners was not entirely original, of course. Pablo Picasso's use of "Ma Jolie" sheet music in collage and Erik Satie's inclusion of popular snippets in his larger compositions come to mind as avant-garde analogues, and the "Shakespearean Rag" of *The Waste Land*, as has already been discussed, sounded a similarly out-of-tune note in the year that *The Beautiful and Damned* was published. Nor was Fitzgerald's experiment in disjointed musicality the final word on the subject, as musical incongruence could in later years be found in all categories of American storytelling, ranging from the Tin Pan Alley–inflected "Newsreel" sections of John Dos Passos's *U.S.A.* trilogy (1930–36) to the combinations of peppy music and disturbing, violent imagery in the films of Martin Scorsese, David Lynch, and Quentin Tarantino.

But for all this, there is no other American writer of the early twentieth century who used music as wryly as Fitzgerald did, nor a novel that makes musical departure as central to its subject matter as *The Beautiful and Damned* does. The plot is somewhat similar to that of *This Side of Paradise* in its general contours: it follows the decline and fall of a privileged young New Yorker of the 1910s named Anthony Patch, whose life is marked by hedonism and frustrated artistic ambitions. A rich dilettante with no immediate need to earn a living, Anthony fancies himself to have the makings of a great writer, but the novel is mainly a record of his multiplying failures. Over the course of the decade he loses his inheritance, enlists in the army, worries that his wife is unfaithful to him, finds himself incapable of holding down a job, and never manages to produce his long-promised literary work. As the plot meanders from one disappointment to another, Anthony constantly evaluates his cultural surroundings, ever passing judgment upon the novel's cast of writers, movie producers, and commercial artists—all of whom, irritatingly, turn out to be far more successful than he. Fitzgerald's overall achievement in *The Beautiful and Damned* is to bring a culture of abundance and excess to life, demonstrating just how crowded and even overwhelming the early twentieth century could be for the young. And in its many, frequently perverse musical scenes, the novel suggests that only the most flexible thinkers will be able to make sense of their times.

To understand just how much Fitzgerald's use of the literary soundtrack did and did not change between his first and second novels, the reader should listen to the opening song of *The Beautiful and Damned*, a 1911 composition titled "My Beautiful Lady."◐ It is on the whole a pleasant piece, with its singer imagining what it might be like to entrance "the prettiest girls in France" with violin playing and much of its compositional structure contributing to an overall atmosphere of fantasy.[42] Most immediately striking is the song's variation in time signatures—4/4 in its verses, 3/4 in its chorus—which has the effect of reinforcing its lyrical description of musical experience: in Elizabeth Spencer's 1913 recording of the song, her precisely articulated, almost fussily ornamented verses take up the hypothetical possibilities of performance, while her vocal lines during the contrasting chorus are held for longer, more languid expanses, suggesting the heightened temporality of her "sweet, sweet waltz dream." So too does "My Beautiful Lady" as interpreted by Spencer emphasize the act of musically accompanied communication, with the pivotal lyric—"and while I'd play, my yearning eyes would say"—turned into a vocal cadenza and the word "say" drawn out at the song's highest pitch. Ultimately, this commingling of form, content, and delivery has a self-referential quality to it, as if to suggest that the musical flights of fancy described by "My Beautiful Lady" would wind up sounding a great deal like "My Beautiful Lady" itself. Such a song would therefore not be at all out of place in the earlier, effusive pages of *This Side of Paradise*.

The social context in which a song is "musicked" to, however, is as important to musical meaning as the song itself, and in *The Beautiful and Damned* the reader encounters "My Beautiful Lady" in an unexpected one. Here it is sung by Anthony as he luxuriates in his bathroom, admires the portraits of various Broadway actresses that he has hung on the wall, and draws some water:

> "To . . . you . . . beaut-if-ul la-a-dy
> My . . . heart . . . cries—"

He raised his voice to compete with the flood of water pouring into the tub, and as he looked at the picture of Hazel Dawn upon the wall he put an imaginary violin to his shoulder and softly caressed it with a phantom bow. Through his closed lips he made a humming noise, which he vaguely imagined resembled the sound of a violin. After a moment his hands ceased their gyrations and wandered to his shirt, which he began to unfasten. Stripped, and adopting an athletic posture like the tiger-skin man in the advertisement, he regarded himself with some satisfaction in the mirror, breaking off to dabble a tentative foot in the tub. Readjusting a faucet and indulging in a few preliminary grunts, he slid in.

(*Damned* 22)

The striptease, the vaguely primitivist posturing, the grunting—very little of this is likely to have been what the songwriting team of Ivan Caryll and C. M. S. McLellan had in mind as they composed the "harmonies sweet and low" of "My Beautiful Lady," and the question of whether the song is a comfortable presence or an unsettling one in this scene therefore comes to the forefront.[43] Certainly there is nothing inherently wrong with Anthony's behavior here (let they who have never acted thus in solitude cast the first stone), but Fitzgerald's decision to enter and linger in such an intimate setting is invasive, while his explicit reference to an identifiable song invites readers to judge its appropriateness in this supremely private moment.

If readers are inclined to take the bait, they might begin by observing—as a large contingent of Fitzgerald's 1920s audience would have done—that Anthony is engaged in an act of multilayered imitation here. Most obviously, he is imagining himself as the seductive violinist described in "My Beautiful Lady," but so too is he aping the photographed Hazel Dawn: it was she who first popularized the song in the musical *The Pink Lady* (1911) and who brought the house down night after night with her famous combination of singing, dancing, and feigned violin playing. (Indeed, if her publicity photos from the period are any indication, she may even be holding a violin in the portrait that Anthony is addressing himself to; see Image 5.) The listening reader might also note that Anthony seems to have cast himself as the song's audience as well as its performer. The subject of "My Beautiful Lady," after all, is aesthetically induced compulsion, with its lyrics concerned primarily with creating a quasi-hypnotic state in which "ladies would forget to eat, and Pommery cease to flow."[44] And in an obliging bit of mimicry, Anthony falls into a similar trance in this scene, gazing out his window after his song is through and fixing upon "a girl in a red negligée, silk surely" in a nearby apartment: "He watched her for several minutes. Something was stirred in him, something not accounted for by the warm smell of the afternoon or the triumphant vividness of red. . . . [F]or a not altogether explained second, posing perversely in time, his emotion had been nearer to adoration than in the deepest kiss he had ever known" (*Damned* 23). The musical entrancer, it would seem, has also become the musically entranced.

The actress Hazel Dawn, whose image and musical performances are vivid, unsettling presences in *The Beautiful and Damned*. Used by permission, The Billy Rose Theater Collection at the New York Public Library.

In many ways, then, "My Beautiful Lady" and Anthony's reaction to it can be easily explained: a young man is singing a song and experiencing the fantasy it describes. The fit between music and novel, however, is not so easy as that. To begin, the obvious disjunction between Anthony's exaggerated, masculine preening, Hazel Dawn's pinup femininity, and Elizabeth Spencer's soprano voice causes Fitzgerald's protagonist to seem positively unmoored from his gender. (The performance becomes yet more peculiar when one considers that the song, whose singer describes how she would go about seducing other women "if I were a man,"[45] also demanded a degree of gender impersonation from Dawn, making Anthony's bathroom act an imitation of an imitation.) Additionally significant is the fact that Anthony's desire to fall under the hypnotizing power of "My Beautiful Lady" is disappointed almost immediately, with the scene's supposed correspondences between music and action shown to be illusory: upon closer inspection, he ascertains that the object of his momentary fascination in the opposite window is, in fact, "fat, full thirty-five, utterly undistinguished" (*Damned* 23). Finally, there are the still-greater questions of why Fitzgerald has included this scene in his novel and whether he intends Anthony's performance to signify anything other than a passing caprice. "My Beautiful Lady" has captivated the young man, become a conduit for all manner of sexual fixation and cross-gendered fantasy, and clouded his perspective, but then the moment is over and Anthony is off to the Ritz-Carlton. The novel has presented a moment of musicalized text that, in its very strangeness, seems to demand interpretation, but it is difficult to say to what end.

As is the case with "My Beautiful Lady," the rest of the songs and musicking moments of *The Beautiful and Damned* tend to raise multiple interpretive possibilities without privileging any one of them. This open-endedness, moreover, frames a larger investigation on Fitzgerald's part into the relative value of popular culture and the vital—if unpredictable—role that audience reception plays in determining it. At points, the apparent randomness and incongruity of his soundtrack can seem a criticism of commercial entertainment's vacuity, with Fitzgerald arguing (as he would in an essay the following year) that popular culture is irrelevant at best and "the heroin of the soul" at worst.[46] He avoids the sorts of love songs that brightened his debut, turning instead to strange, sometimes threatening numbers: "Down in Jungle Town" and its tale of a parallel monkey universe, for example, or "The Yama-Yama Man" and its warnings of a nightmarish creature that hunts children. Equally striking is his tendency to align peppy songs with grim narrative, as when the jaunty "K-K-K-Katy" plays counterpoint to Anthony's growing suspicion that his wife, Gloria, has had an affair. Here and elsewhere, Fitzgerald's aim appears to be to question how well the profusion of music in American life ever "fits" its listeners' affairs, and in doing so he joins H. L. Mencken and other luminaries of the 1920s in finding the popular arts to be invasive and pathological.

But *The Beautiful and Damned* is not a purely didactic exercise, for Fitzgerald also has much in common with those writers of the 1920s who understood the popular arts to have what Gilbert Seldes called a "validity of their own," a value that resists facile oppositions of "high" and "low."[47] This distinctive "validity" was at the time being identified in the antics of Charlie Chaplin, the new rhythms of jazz, and even, as one character in *The Beautiful and Damned* suggests, the frothier writings of Fitzgerald himself; the key to evaluating such expression lay in recognizing that popular culture was at once simpler and more complex than it was usually given credit for, that it does not always have "pretensions to art," and that audiences judge it by alternative, often idiosyncratic standards.[48] Fitzgerald's novel, meanwhile, engages with the paradoxes, switchbacks, and flux of this cultural moment with unusual immediacy by deploying an unmistakably audible yet frequently inscrutable soundtrack, sounding the ambiguities of popular music and inviting its readers to explore the question of just how one is to "take" commercial entertainment. Unfortunately for Anthony, he often emerges in Fitzgerald's accounting as the most vivid example of what a young twentieth-century American ought not to do.

The Beautiful and Damned evinces an unmistakable distaste for popular song at several points, but so too does Fitzgerald indicate that many of his characters have been "damned" by it only insofar as they have chosen to be: they are self-conscious about themselves and their pastimes, amused by the alleged power of music to lead them astray, and singularly unconcerned that what they enjoy would by a great many people be considered cultural blight. Indeed, problems arise only when someone begins to take popular culture too seriously in the novel. In an early chapter, for example, Anthony and Gloria attend a third-rate cabaret, and the musical moment that occurs there provides an occasion for Fitzgerald to demonstrate the perversities and surprising divergences of taste that the popular arts often inspire. Surveying the scene, Anthony cultivates an ironic superiority, permitting himself to enjoy a dive and congratulating himself for having brought a woman with an "authentic distinction of face and form and manner that made her like a single flower amidst a collection of cheap bric-à-brac" (*Damned* 65). But when the band begins to play "Ring Ting-a-Ling," a novelty number of 1912 that praises the many conveniences made possible by the telephone, he is agog to hear the supposedly "authentic" Gloria enjoying the music. "I belong here. . . . I'm like these people," she murmurs, going so far as to identify herself not only with her fellow patrons but also with the show that Anthony is only deigning to attend: "I've got a streak of what you'd call cheapness. I don't know where I get it but it's—oh, things like this and bright colors and gaudy vulgarity" (*Damned* 66).

Hearing this admission is nothing short of a catastrophe for Anthony, and listening to Ada Jones's 1912 recording of "Ring Ting-a-Ling" helps explain why he reacts so strongly.◗ For Anthony, a trifle such as this can only be appreciated as a joke, as nearly everything in the orchestration and delivery of "Ring Ting-a-Ling" leaves an impression of sheer and unconstrained goofiness. Jones's backing band is almost cartoonish, replete with twittering flute lines and portentous brass. So too does Jones's tone of faux naughtiness, her knowing laughter, and her mock-confiding use of *sprechstimme* (or speech-song) transform every word into an unmistakable gag. And "Ring Ting-a-Ling" comes to sound all the more shallow in its literary context when Anthony reacts viscerally, even desperately to it. Gloria's attachment to the song leads him to shriek, "You're a young idiot!" (*Damned* 66), and his subsequent, pretentious attempt to explain away her taste is utterly out of proportion to the silly innocuousness of the music: "Out of the deep sophistication of Anthony an understanding formed, nothing atavistic or obscure, indeed scarcely physical at all. . . . The sheath that held her soul had assumed significance—that was all. She was a sun, radiant, growing, gathering light and storing it" (*Damned* 66–67). For Anthony, only someone capable of turning super-ficiality into an art form ought to be listening to such a fundamentally unserious song, and his wife's appreciation for it throws him into a panic.

Anthony hears something like kitsch in "Ring Ting-a-Ling" and attempts to rescue his "authentic" beloved by aestheticizing her identification with it, but according to Gloria he has missed the point. "These people," she says in reference to her fellow club-goers, "could appreciate me and take me for granted, and these men would fall in love with me and admire me, whereas the clever men I meet would just analyze me and tell me I'm this because of this or that because of that" (*Damned* 66). And if being taken for granted is what Gloria wants, then "Ring Ting-a-Ling" no doubt appeals to her because it is so happily and unapologetically vacant. Even the song's most inquisitive, searching lyrics—"I would give the world to know half the things you hear"[49]—ultimately circle back to nothing more than the telephone itself, with most of its verses centered around such banalities as get-ting numbers right, returning calls, describing where people are and what they are doing while they talk, and most important, hearing a "ring ting-a-ling" to respond to in the first place. Indeed, the song's fixation on the sound of the telephone causes it at times to veer toward utter nonsense, with Jones lapsing into a gabby but ulti-mately anti-expressive babble in promising that "If you don't ring-a-ling, ting-a-ling-a-ling-a-ling/Then I'll ring-a-ting-a-ling for you" at the end of each verse. The medium is the only message here: Gloria is attracted to empty signification in her music, in her fellow nightclubbers, and in herself, and nothing could be more beside the point than an intellectual search for content in the song or the woman.

Where Anthony listens for cultural significance, Gloria deliberately avoids it, and in doing so she profitably bypasses the familiar binaries of high and low cul-ture that her husband relies on. Fitzgerald is often credited with having revealed the hollowness of America's gaudy and hedonistic boom years, but here one of his own characters has beaten him to the punch and gone so far as to argue that such hollowness is in fact something to be enjoyed. Gloria's perspective on popular cul-ture would seem, moreover, to preempt any criticisms that the mocking Anthonys or highbrow Menckens of her era might make of popular culture and its consum-ers: there is little sense, after all, in exposing or attempting to correct someone's bad taste when she is aware of and happy to have it. As Gloria puts it, much of the fun of popular music lies in listening to the "wrong" songs rather than the "right" ones, in having proud, even defiantly shabby cultural predilections. "Ring Ting-a-Ling" is both a good song and a bad one by her standards, its value bound up in its apparent lack thereof. And thus does this scene flirt with the debasing qualities of entertainment only to theorize a jolly variety of musical nihilism, a pleasure to be had in cultural aporia that pervades *The Beautiful and Damned* and that Fitzgerald's soundtrack helps sustain through its frequent dares to find larger meanings in songs where there may not (or ought not) be any.

It is this feeling of uncertainty and this unanswered question of what, if anything, popular music ultimately stands for that most distinguishes Fitzgerald's soundtracked novel from the nonliterary media of the period that also aligned narrative and song in atypical or subversive ways. Musical disconnection had been common in the dramatic arts for years before *The Beautiful and Damned*, but it was usually much more obvious in its communication. Nineteenth-century stage productions often featured interludes between their acts that had as little connection to their larger plots as possible, so as to leave the impression that their audiences were getting their money's worth of varied entertainment. Silent film, meanwhile, had made musical-visual dissonance an everyday trope by 1922, much of it derived from the so-called funning that accompanists would indulge in by introducing humorously incongruous songs at key narrative moments.[50] While "funning" necessarily fell out of favor as cinema moved toward synchronization the late 1920s, it could still be heard from time to time in those films, stage works, and novels that used music to create sarcastic, even gruesome negative reinforcement: think, for example, of Theodore Dreiser's decision to have Roberta Alden sing "Oh, the sun shines bright in my old Kentucky home" just before she drowns in *An American Tragedy* (1925), or the alignment of James Cagney's corpse and the jolly recording of "I'm Forever Blowing Bubbles" in the final scene of *The Public Enemy* (1931).[51] By the time *The Beautiful and Damned* appeared, then, American audiences had become accustomed to narratives that existed in states of cross-aesthetic tension and demanded to be evaluated with varying degrees of irony, as though thumbing their noses at the idea of a unified, Wagnerian *Gesamtkunstwerk*.

As the years went by Fitzgerald became more and more adept at cinematic "funning," with his ability to create arresting, bitingly subversive contrasts between song and narrative especially evident in the many scenes of matrimonial despair in *Tender Is the Night* that have been punctuated by perky favorites from Dick and Nicole Diver's youth.[52] But more innovative was the musical uncertainty, anxiety, and eeriness that he was able to conjure in *The Beautiful and Damned*, whose soundtrack creates obvious aesthetic disconnections but seldom does so in the service of either humor or horror in their most obvious forms.[53] Indeed, the novel seems most modern in its willingness to play as many sides of the field as possible, inviting its readers both to identify with and condemn its frivolous consumers, to take pleasure in popular song even as they denigrate it, and to find its musically inflected scenes simultaneously amusing and off-putting. As in the case of Anthony, Gloria, and "Ring Ting-a-Ling," readers who can hear Fitzgerald's soundtrack are frequently asked to entertain more than one interpretation of its narrative significance, and the range of conclusions that they might reach can have profound implications for the novel's larger cultural commentary—especially if they decline to settle on any definitive ones.

Perhaps nowhere is the tuneful paradoxy of *The Beautiful and Damned* more audible than in its "Broken Lute" section, an attempt on Fitzgerald's part to write in scripted, dramatic form that has, as its title might indicate, a marked dissonance to it. Taken as a whole, the chapter reads as a quasi-musical comedy with a dis-orienting twist, accompanied by a soundtrack that is both humorously apropos and utterly cringe-inducing. The music in question is "Poor Butterfly," a song so inescapable in its day that it inspired a threatening response titled "If I Catch the Guy Who Wrote Poor Butterfly." The occasion for hearing it is a house party, with Anthony and his friends listening to a record while getting dangerously intoxi-cated. And while the ultimate message of this deeply unsettled literary moment is uncertain, this remarkable bit of soundtracking marks the beginning of a very long and painful end for Anthony, seeming to suggest that his failures to adapt to his cultural moment have now become irrevocable.◐

Considered on its own, "Poor Butterfly" is uncomfortably arrayed against itself. Its adaptation of Giacomo Puccini's well-worn tale of pining love, cultural submission, and suicide might read as melancholy on the page, but when one lis-tens to Elizabeth Spencer's 1917 recording of the song, the frequently upbeat, even sprightly delivery of Butterfly's story winds up sounding either childishly naïve or appallingly inappropriate. The musical flippancy with which this tragedy is presented grows still more perverse in Fitzgerald's literary context, as his stage directions indicate that Anthony and his friends are merrily singing along with the record: it takes but little imagination to hear a company of drunks imitat-ing Spencer's forced dialect and bellowing, at the song's extraordinarily operatic high point, that Butterfly has learned "to love with her soul" thanks to her having been exposed to "the 'Merican way." Fitzgerald was not always sensitive when he attended to race matters in his fiction, but here he seems to be condemning the song's cultural ideology and tarring his characters with it. Particularly repulsive are the ways in which his revelers make the song's chauvinism explicit in their own behavior, with one rousing Anthony's butler—significantly, a Japanese man named Tana—from his sleep and commanding him to accompany "Poor Butterfly" on flute. There is unmistakable cruelty in this increasingly surreal scene as Tana is placed atop a precariously balanced pile of furniture and made to add ethnic flavor to the song's exercise in exoticism, leaving the impression that Anthony and his circle are modern equivalents of Puccini's callous Pinkerton. And as the reader listens to the generically Oriental melodies of Spencer's record intertwining with the imagined sound of Tana's compulsory flute, the musical moment becomes, in the words of Fitzgerald's stage directions, "*one of those incidents in which life seems set upon the passionate imitation of the lowest forms of literature*" (*Damned* 230).

But if Fitzgerald intended to use "Poor Butterfly" as a means of casting his characters and the popular culture they enjoy in an exclusively unflattering light, then he failed for a simple reason: his scene and his musical selection are also quite funny, if not to the characters who actually experience them. Butterfly's story of bereavement and loss, so out of place in an often-peppy song and at a delirious party, turns out to be strangely appropriate when Anthony's grandfather, Adam Patch, appears suddenly in the room, his approach "*rendered inaudible by the pandemonium*" (*Damned* 230). Now Fitzgerald has entered the world of stock characters and theatrical cliché, for Adam Patch is significant primarily for being old, deeply conservative, and in control of Anthony's allowance—the last person in the world, of course, who ought to have stumbled upon such an affair. The elder Patch's timing is perfect in that it is so utterly imperfect, and it is a clever touch on Fitzgerald's part to have him arrive in the middle of a song whose protagonist yearns to be reunited with her "fine young American from the sea."[54] The song's Butterfly figure lives only for the moment when her lover will "come to me" and she will feel his embrace once more, but while she will presumably never enjoy such an experience, one of Anthony's out-of-control guests comes close: he "*begins to spin round and round, more and more dizzily—he staggers, recovers, staggers again and then falls in the direction of the hall . . . almost into the arms of old* ADAM PATCH" (*Damned* 230). As the phonograph sings of Butterfly's lovelorn hopes they are consummated by others in the most awkward manner imaginable, and with the near-collision comes a literary iteration of one of the all-time favorite "takes" of stage and film history: "*the phonograph gags*," the music grinds to a halt, and the party is left in silence, "*weighted with intolerably contagious apprehension*" (*Damned* 230). Thus does "The Broken Lute" become musical-literary slapstick: the dour, wealthy grandfather has dropped in not just at a bad time but at the worst possible one, a famous, melodramatic love scene has been burlesqued with undertones of homosexual panic, and an initially out-of-place song is revealed to be utterly, if grotesquely, appropriate.

The extraordinary quality of this scene is its musical equivocality, its uneasy combination of pitch-perfect comedic timing and deathly serious importance to the novel's larger narrative. On the one hand, it is probably the best bit of dramatic writing Fitzgerald ever produced, certainly funnier than anything he came up with in *The Vegetable*—his first and only proper play—and it works as well as it does because it is so hackneyed.[55] But if the incongruous "Poor Butterfly" makes such a scene all the more outlandish and humorous, it also, thanks to its racial insensitivity and its grim implication of mortality, casts a shadow that becomes darker and darker as Fitzgerald's narrative progresses. Adam Patch leaves the scene, writes his grandson out of his will, and dies three months later, and while in a Broadway musical such a development might kick off a series of madcap adventures (misplaced wills abound in Cohan's productions), here Anthony and Gloria are forced to sue for their inheritance and grow increasingly impoverished and self-abasing as the court case drags out. And when a judge finally rules in their favor, the sordidness of the "Poor Butterfly" affair and the morbidity lurking within the oddly upbeat song are intensified: in the novel's final chapter, Fitzgerald reveals that the assistant who escorted Adam Patch to the fateful party and managed the family fortune has shot himself dead in a Butterfly-like state of despair. The memorable music, if it is recalled at novel's end, lingers in both amusing and ominous ways, with Fitzgerald, a writer capable of simultaneously nailing and deflating pop conventions, aiming not to make readers laugh or blanch at "Poor Butterfly" in exclusivity but rather to do both, somewhat nervously, at once.

Much of the power of Fitzgerald's novel and its soundtrack lies in the uncertainty of each, with readers of *The Beautiful and Damned* invited to experience the cultural flux that Fitzgerald's characters must negotiate and to wrestle with the enigmatic commentary of an author who often drew his comedy and his tragedy from the same sources. At a historical moment when it was becoming increasingly common, even expected, for writers to weigh in on popular culture, Fitzgerald was one of the few to conclude contra the aloof satire of Lewis and the condemnation of Mencken that its literary merits often lay in its very badness, that one's attitude toward it could not but be one of constant and often paradoxical readjustment. His soundtrack, meanwhile, raises as many questions as it answers in relation to his narrative, provoking listeners with simultaneous cheer, bitterness, and irrelevance and seeming to suggest, in the words of one of Fitzgerald's more famous epigrams, that those who would contend with popular song must possess "the ability to hold two opposed ideas in the mind at the same time, and still retain the ability to function."[56] Ultimately it is hard to know whether Anthony's fate could have been happier had he been more flexible in his thinking and more attuned to the ambiguities of his cultural moment. But if his unenviable, catatonic end in the novel's final pages is any indication, the constant position-taking that such a moment demands is almost enough to drive one mad.

Never Again: *The Great Gatsby*

The question of how well music ever matches personal experience or the narratives that contain it would hang over the rest of Fitzgerald's novels, and most of the time he seems to have reached rather disappointed conclusions. The soundtracks of his later works tend toward either the depressing or the absurd: Dick Diver's favorite songs inspire torturous memories in *Tender Is the Night*, while the soprano of *The Last Tycoon* (1941) who sings a single lyric—"Come! Come! I love you only"—over and over again into a studio microphone seems positively mad, given that she is doing so in the middle of a jolting southern California earthquake.[57] *The Great Gatsby*, however, strikes a unique balance between harmony and dissonance, one that is particularly worth bearing in mind for the reader who would consider the larger problem of listening to long-outmoded but still audible musical literature. It presents a protagonist who seems determined, as Hugh Kenner has put it, to create a milieu in which "even when the words are wrong the music is right,"[58] with Gatsby's songs of courtship and nostalgia—"The Love Nest," "Ain't We Got Fun," and "Beale Street Blues"—seeming in many ways to be perfectly suited to the scenes, people, and actions they accompany. But so too does this novel's soundtrack point to music's inevitable sense of liminality, illustrating the impossibility of sustained, harmonious experience and reinforcing the sense of being out of tune that haunts so many of Fitzgerald's works.

On the one hand, the beguiling sound of music in *The Great Gatsby* involves the reader all the more intimately with Fitzgerald's ongoing search for what Milton Stern has called the "golden moment" in his fiction, the achievement of state of being so wondrous that it represents nothing less than a "release from the condition of time itself."[59] But on the other, Fitzgerald's soundtrack seems to indicate that musically inspired emotions are perfect only insofar as they are temporary and fleeting, escaping listeners even as they are possessed of them. Throughout his early writings, Fitzgerald shows himself to have been a born believer in the Keatsian notion that death is the mother of beauty, that moments of intense feeling are most poignant when just about to be extinguished. At the age of twenty-two he was already declaring, "God! How I miss my youth" in his letters, and at the start of his publishing career he observed through Amory Blaine that "the sentimental person thinks things will last—the romantic person has a desperate confidence that they won't."[60] But it was in *The Great Gatsby* that he was able to express this complex of happy melancholy and exquisite defeat most deftly, with his literary soundtrack allowing readers to share in the unique pleasure of fading emotion and possibility. Moreover, his soundtrack retains its ability to do this not in spite of but because of the fact that, as the years go by, it grows more and more unfamiliar. Whereas *This Side of Paradise* and *The Beautiful and Damned* tend to suffer when they lose their musical immediacy, *The Great Gatsby* seems to triumph all the more by its diminuendo.

Consumed in *The Great Gatsby* with the futility of attempting either to hold on to present moments or to repeat the past, Fitzgerald made his soundtrack something new: a musical accompaniment that can be heard clearly but that grows more compelling as it becomes less audible. All of the novel's songs function in this way, but the final party at Gatsby's mansion is the best single example of Fitzgerald's peculiarly explicit and distant melodiousness, one of the narrative's emotional breaking points and an illustration that its soundtrack can never be anything more than an echo of what it once was. A certain discord, a "pervading harshness," has settled upon the tense scene, but then Daisy Buchanan begins to sing, adding to the party's background music "a husky, rhythmic whisper, bringing out a meaning in each word that it had never had before and would never have again . . . and each change tipped out a little of her warm human magic upon the air" (*Gatsby* 81, 84). In some ways this is vintage Fitzgerald, a fleeting experience that cannot be repeated or even adequately described in words, one whose vitality fades at the very moment it becomes apparent. But it is not so ephemeral as that, for Fitzgerald also names the song that Daisy has performed, "a neat sad little waltz of that year" called "Three O'clock in the Morning" (*Gatsby* 85). This inspires musing from Nick Carraway: "What was it up there in the song that seemed to be calling her back inside? What would happen now in the dim incalculable hours?"

By way of finding out, the reader is encouraged to listen to the 1922 recording of "Three O'clock in the Morning" by the accomplished classical singer and popular recording artist John McCormack. ◐ Those who have never heard the song before are likely at first to feel somewhat cheated by it. Nick's uncertainty as to why "Three O'clock in the Morning" calls his cousin back to Gatsby seems positively baffling after its lyrics have been consulted, as their explicit preoccupation with courtship makes for painfully direct commentary on this scene:

> It's three o'clock in the morning,
> We've danced the whole night thru,
> And daylight soon will be dawning,

> Just one more waltz with you
> That melody so entrancing,
> Seems to be made for us two
> I could just keep right on dancing
> Forever dear, with you.[61]

So too does the song seem to find its own meaning to be utterly self-evident, enacting a kind of musical tautology by describing itself as a "melody so entrancing" and imagining that everything in the external world—whether a dancer's heart "beating in time" or an orchestra's ding-dong imitation of the Cambridge Quarters—moves to its 3/4 rhythm; to hear the song is to understand its significance instantly. But perhaps most striking is the grandiosity of "Three O'clock in the Morning," whose melody is comprised of heroic arpeggios, the occasional acrobatic leap (the words "be" and "dawning" are more than an octave apart), and other flamboyant touches that would be almost as appropriate in a circus as in Fitzgerald's dreamy setting. By the time McCormack delivers his full-throated, chivalric plea—"say that there soon will be a honeymoon"—the song has come in many ways to seem too flashy, too extravagant, and too literal for what is otherwise a brooding and ambiguous scene.

To a degree, then, Fitzgerald's soundtrack undercuts the emotional importance of this moment, leaving Daisy in the thrall of a rather cloying song and rendering Nick somewhat daft for not understanding why she is moved by it. Nor is there much reason to suppose that Fitzgerald's audience would have been any more forgiving than modern ones of such a cliché: the musicians who accompanied the silent films of his day were often warned not just against performing songs that seemed out of place in the larger story but also against ones that, like "Three O'clock in the Morning," were excessively obvious fits.[62] Music can distract from narrative even if it is in perfect synchronization with it, disappointing those audience members who might have expected something more creative or oblique. Reading this scene in conjunction with listening to McCormack's performance can therefore rob Daisy's singing of its mystery, no doubt leading some readers to decry, as did a sour William Butler Yeats after attending a McCormack concert in 1924, "the damnable clarity of the words."[63]

For quite some time, scholarship on Fitzgerald tended to keep a certain embarrassed silence about these and the other topical aspects of his fiction, whether the slang, the fads, or the celebrities. Instead, it concentrated on what were thought to be his timeless or universal themes for much the same reason that listeners are likely to recoil from "Three O'clock in the Morning"—the cultural detritus that

Fitzgerald chose to immortalize in his fiction can seem too slight, far from commensurate to the reader's capacity for wonder. But the fascinating quality of this song and so much of the music permeating *The Great Gatsby* is the extent to which its questionable, even dubious aesthetic worth is also the very thing that highlights Fitzgerald's almost transcendental sensitivity to what Emerson called the "evanescence and lubricity" of experience, his determination to record his impressions as they drifted away from him.[64] Even when it seems so harmonious as to be hackneyed, music makes Fitzgerald's point by negative rather than positive example, in this scene rendering Daisy increasingly unknowable even as it seems to lay bare her mood and mind, pulling readers into her performance at the same time that Fitzgerald points toward something in it that defies description. Just as one of Fitzgerald's great triumphs was to leave Gatsby "blurred and patchy" at novel's end in spite of all that has been revealed about him,[65] so too does the simultaneously audible and resistant presence of "Three O'clock in the Morning" draw attention toward an aspect of performance that cannot be understood except in its moment of creation, leaving readers all the more curious as to how Daisy transformed so straightforward and unexceptional a ditty into something that, at least to its auditory, was brimming with life.

The irony is that Fitzgerald could only have achieved these and other such effects in this novel with the much-abused mass entertainment of his day. As is the case with his allusions to cultural icons like the Broadway star Gilda Gray, the best-selling novel *Simon Called Peter*, and the Chicago "Black Sox," a song like "Three O'clock in the Morning" anchors Fitzgerald's mythic, imagined world in a specifically dated, eminently recognizable setting, reinforcing the novel's signature contrast of Platonic conception and persistent actuality. And no other variety of music would have allowed him so successfully to heed Joseph Conrad's famous call—which Fitzgerald named as a particular inspiration in his preface to the 1934 edition of *The Great Gatsby*—for a literature able "to make you hear, to make you feel" with palpable, physical intensity.[66] There is of course a great deal of vaguely described "yellow cocktail music" and other such aural abstraction in this text (*Gatsby* 34), but only a widely known song, one inextricably tied to its time and place and hopelessly dependent on the whims of fashion, can tantalize the reader with the sense that some crucial impression or revelation is near, as close as the melody of a famous tune, and yet also growing further out of reach with each passing year. Readers who are able hear "Three O'clock in the Morning" and the rest of Fitzgerald's soundtrack are thus obliged to share in the feelings of belatedness that haunt the novel, listening to the music that pervaded some of the most familiar scenes in American literature but left to conclude that they have missed something, that a crucial meaning has gone out of the songs.

Therein lies the ultimate problem for the critic or reader of soundtracked literature from ages past: it is not easy "musicking" to something that one must go to great lengths to hear at all, and those songs that can be recovered can seldom be listened to on the terms that they once were. Many of the old literary soundtracks are now available in ways unthinkable even twenty years ago, but delving into them often serves to illustrate just how remote so much of America's music has become and how unlikely it is ever to be otherwise. The novelty numbers can be too absurd, the sentimentality too extreme, the delivery too affected, the state of production too grating. When resurrected, such music can alienate audiences as much as interest them, making it difficult to imagine that the literary works that depend on it can be enlivened in any significant way by close listening. But in many of the most effectively soundtracked novels of the last hundred years, this difficulty often turns out to be less an obstacle than the point of writing about music in the first place. Returning to Powers and *The Time of Our Singing*, one finds that the problem of capturing a time-bound art—whether on a record or on the page—is no closer to being resolved in a new millennium of unprecedented inscription. Remembering a concert from his youth, Powers's narrator observes the following:

> I will look for this group throughout my life—on vinyl, then tape, then laser pit. I'll go to performances in hope of resurrection and come away empty. I'll search for these singers my whole life, and never come any closer than suspect memory. . . . I could look all the singers up: Every year we pass through is hidden away, if not in a cloistered scriptorium somewhere, then in a bank of steel filing cabinets and silicon chips. But anything I'd find would only kill that day. For what I thought I heard that day, there are no names. Who knows how good those singers really were? For me, they filled the sky.[67]

Now as then, the soundtracked novel maintains a fundamental tension between the archival and the evanescent, between the physical traces of the past and the futility of attempting to experience it in the present. Its music, when unfamiliar, ought not to be left cultural white noise when it is possible to make it audible, but neither can its recapitulation be assumed to bring a missing completeness to a text. Ever frozen in time and mechanically repeatable, such music and such literature must be heard anew on each encounter.

4. Make Them Black and Bid Them Sing

Musical Poetry, Racial Transformation, and the Harlem Renaissance

The Harlem Renaissance saw perhaps the most concerted and sustained attempt by American writers of any era, region, or race to establish a musical tradition of literature. The coterie of African American authors who achieved prominence in the 1920s brought music to bear on nearly everything they produced, creating a new variety of theater and a school of fiction rivaling F. Scott Fitzgerald's in its tunefulness. Their most significant innovation, however, was a poetics that emulated preexisting musical forms and that aspired to the condition of sacred and popular song. Here was poetry that, far from having a merely symbolic relation to music, could be and seemed in fact to demand that it be sung by its audiences. Resonant phrases from the spirituals appeared in poems, inviting readers to vocalize those classic expressions of slavery and transcendence in a literary context. Other poetic works emulated the spirituals rather than attempting to contain them, borrowing their lyrical metrics, patterns of dialect, imperative moods, and directness of imagery. Still others embraced the stark language and verse structures of the blues, presuming audience familiarity with a musical form that, as the folk music collector Alan Lomax has argued, was in the early years of the twentieth century on its way to becoming "the best-known tune humans have ever sung."[1] In all these cases, writers created poetry that makes for effective literature on the silent, printed page, but that also seems to derive much of its staying power from a beloved, sounding tradition of art—a tradition, moreover, that would continue to inform the African American canon for the rest of the century.[2]

By and large, the poets of the Harlem Renaissance wrote in musical forms for reasons related to the movement's overarching goal of creating a distinctively black literature. Some did so because African American music commanded wide respect for its aesthetic excellence, with many signaling their agreement with W. E. B. Du Bois's 1903 declaration that "the Negro folk-song" was nothing less than "the most beautiful expression of human experience born this side the seas."[3] Others believed, as James Weldon Johnson had claimed in 1921, that the ultimate measure of a people's greatness lay in "the amount and standard of the literature and art they have produced," and they therefore viewed their musical tradition as a symbol of black ingenuity, as a means of appealing to race pride, and as useful source material for progressive literary works.[4] But perhaps most compelling to these authors was music's unique ability to evoke a shared culture and to unite individuals in a larger, participatory community of song. As John F. Callahan and many other critics have shown, a constant aim in twentieth-century African American letters was to forge connections with readers through tropes of "call and response," to encourage audiences "to read and hear and, potentially, contribute to the still unfolding 'immense story' in our lives and voices beyond the solitary, private act of reading."[5] Authors might help expand the "solitary, private act of reading" in any number of ways, but one of the most effective in Harlem Renaissance verse was the deployment of unmistakable and inviting musical cues, ones that emanated from "calling" poets but could only be brought to life by singing, "responding" audiences. Readers could quite literally perform these poems and, in so doing, contribute their own music to the act of literary production.

In embracing black song and writing in musical forms, however, the poets of the Harlem Renaissance found themselves facing a paradoxical, sometimes disheartening, but ultimately productive conundrum: the music they drew upon in the service of racial self-expression and African American community-building was quite familiar and often deeply appealing to nonblack readers. Looking back from the vantage point of 1930, Johnson noted that spirituals, work songs, ragtime, blues, and jazz had over time received wide and enthusiastic attention from listeners of many races and countries, and he concluded that they had "gone into and, more or less, permeated our national life" to the point that "they are no longer racial, they are wholly national."[6] Somehow, in an era when basic civil rights for African Americans remained tenuous, a music that might once have been thought of as immutably black could be argued by the then-executive secretary of the NAACP to have become the common property of all citizens. And in evoking a music that, by dint of its popularity, could be referred to as "wholly national," the poetry of the Harlem Renaissance was capable of calling to and drawing responses from a much wider readership than might have at first appeared to have been the case. Indeed, one surprising aspect of this literary movement is the extent to which those poetic works that seem the most distinctively black in their musicality were also the ones most likely to invite a nonblack readership to sing them into audible life.

The poet Countee Cullen observed in his 1925 sonnet "Yet Do I Marvel" that it is a "curious thing" for God to "make a poet black, and bid him sing," and so too is it curious how much poetry of the Harlem Renaissance was capable of accomplishing something similar in its nonblack audiences—audiences that, as Charles Scruggs has argued, may have constituted the majority of the movement's first readers.[7] Verse in the styles of the spirituals and the blues might have been meant to appeal to a distinctively black sensibility, but its mobile musical forms also gave audiences of other races an opportunity to hear, participate in, and experience that sensibility (or at least to believe or pretend that they were doing so). Such musical poems were explicitly coded and obviously intended to be understood as "black," but because they could be sung by anyone familiar with their models they could inspire moments of racial emulation, ventriloquism, and role-playing as well as of self-expression, even raising the possibility that some readers could use them, in temporary and metaphorical ways, to sing their way into and occupy a different racial identity altogether. Some of the great questions surrounding this poetic tradition, then, are to what extent its authors were aware of the reach that their chosen music had; whether they set out to use musical forms in the service of racial transformation as well as of racial self-assertion; and whether their deployments of black song were meant, among other things, to demonstrate the fluidity of racial identity and to draw into question the very idea of racial distinction.

The pages that follow will discuss two writers of the Harlem Renaissance who more than any others used musical verse to complicate American notions of race: Jean Toomer and Langston Hughes. Taken together, their works demonstrate the extent to which musical forms governed the movement's poetry; the broad racial access and experiences that those musical forms offered to readers of any number of backgrounds; and the effects wrought on African American literary production by the possibility of multiracial musical responses to it. Toomer's *Cane* (1923) emulates the southern spirituals while Hughes's *The Weary Blues* (1926) and *Fine Clothes to the Jew* (1927) are suffused with the urban blues, but both rely on musical forms that were very much audible and in wide demand during the 1920s, available on the mass market to black and white listeners alike. Each poet asks readers to sing his poetry and deploys musical form to expedite its performance, and each does so in part to transcend the racial categories that his chosen music highlights. Toomer's participatory spirituals seek to accomplish a merging of the races into a state of ideality, Hughes's blues allow readers to adopt various racial personae, and in both cases, identity is rendered slippery in the moment and process of song. Theirs is a poetics of invitation and initiation that makes race at once palpable and elusive, and it depends on the broad popularity of racial music.

Before their stories are heard, however, one must pause and ask whether it is counterintuitive or strange to think of African American musical poetry—by Toomer, Hughes, or any other writer of the 1920s—as interracial in its construction and available to nonblack voices in its reception. Up to a point, the answer is no: critical approaches to the Harlem Renaissance as a movement have come increasingly to resist what Paul Gilroy has called "the continuing lure of ethnic absolutisms," instead arguing that *Cane*, *The Weary Blues*, and other texts of the time were products of a distinctively modern, "mongrel" cultural synthesis.[8] Certainly there have been eminent thinkers over the decades who have claimed that black writers were or should have been pursuing a separatist agenda in the 1920s, or that the effects of white participation on black cultural production in the period were generally damaging. But newer studies of the movement have tended instead to characterize it as an interracial nexus, defined by literary relations between blacks and whites that catalyzed expression both in American American culture and across a broadly defined modernism.[9] American American writing of the Harlem Renaissance is today more likely to be considered in expanded racial, aesthetic, and geographical contexts, with the movement's works shown to be calling and responding to audiences outside of the niches to which, far too often, their authors were sometimes consigned.

Yet unexamined assumptions remain in criticism of the Harlem Renaissance, particularly in regard to music and its influence on artists in other fields. While the movement as a whole is now understood to have been a vibrantly interracial one, its component strain of musical expression is seldom discussed in the same terms; the spirituals, the blues, and other musical forms are generally held up as wholly African American (and usually working-class African American) presences circulating within a multiethnic cultural network. As Gilroy has warned, modern paradigms of cultural diversity are often constructed in such a way that "right and left, racist and anti-racist, black and white tacitly share a view of it as little more than a collision between fully formed and mutually exclusive cultural communities."[10] In a similar vein, even the best historians of the Harlem Renaissance are sometimes inclined to hypothesize an uncomplicated strain of essentialized musical blackness within it: it remains common for critics of the movement—most of them primarily conversant in its literature—to describe it as an interracial meeting of the arts without noting the extent to which those arts were significantly interracial already. Black music is thus presumed to have been immutably so, even when it existed in a multiethnic historical moment; so too is the poetry that emulated it, even when it is studied by scholars explicitly committed to the multiethnic ideal.

If histories of the Harlem Renaissance have not always been as attuned to the interracial possibilities of racial music and musical poetry as they could be, it is in part because writers of the period often presented the relationship between verse structure and race in fairly rigid terms. Consider, for example, Hughes's ground-breaking 1926 essay "The Negro Artist and the Racial Mountain," in which he accused Countee Cullen of shamefully admitting that he "would like to be white" in obeying genteel models of prosody.[11] Against this formal cowardice Hughes arrayed an "honest American Negro literature" enriched by the spirituals, blues, and jazz,[12] and the relatively clear-cut distinction he articulated between an abject, essentially white poetics of assimilation and a confident, essentially black musicality was often in evidence during the 1920s, theorized by representatives of both races. Such divisions were further exacerbated by the broad intellectual framework of the Harlem Renaissance, whose leaders tended on the whole to assume, as Henry Louis Gates Jr. and Gene Andrew Jarrett have observed, that an "ahistorical, lower-class, and authentically black" folk culture underlay the movement's best works.[13]

A second obstacle to considering African American musical poetry as anything other than a self-explanatory, unambiguous expression of blackness lies in this nation's long, well-known history of exploiting the musics of its minority populations. White responses to black song in the 1920s—no matter how well meaning or sincerely felt in motivation—were marked so frequently by misunderstanding, condescension, and outright racism that it can be very difficult to think of the racial relationships they engendered as being ones of anything other than what Eric Lott has termed "love and theft."[14] The 1921 musical *Shuffle Along*, a landmark of African American theater, played to segregated houses and audiences that were close to 90 percent white; black social observers such as Wallace Thurman reported being "forced out of their own places" on the Harlem scene in favor of white cabaret-goers; and the plantation-themed décor and acts at such popular nightspots as the Cotton Club led the poet Sterling Brown to accuse whites who attended them of seeking "a 'jazzed-up' version" of "the contented slave . . . with cabarets supplanting cabins, and Harlemized 'blues,' instead of the spirituals and slave reels."[15] It was a time when even many outside of Harlem believed, as the white writer Carl Van Vechten dramatically argued in a 1925 issue of *Vanity Fair*, that much of the era's popular music had been "raped from the Negro," and the tensions that so often characterized musical relationships in that period can today add an ominous undertone to the question of black musical verse and interracial responses to it.[16]

Musical meaning, however, is not so easily located and fixed as this, with Gilroy and others arguing that it has a unique tendency to resist "categorisation as the practice of either legislators or interpreters," particularly in regard to race.[17] Readers of *Cane*, *The Weary Blues*, and other poetic works of the Harlem Renaissance would therefore do well to approach them from a musicological perspective as well as a literary one, for scholars in that field have come increasingly to argue that African American music, in the words of Christopher Small, represents a "brilliant tradition, which resulted from the collision in the Americas, during and after the times of slavery, between two great musical cultures" and which "partakes of the nature of both but is not the same as either."[18] The arguments of Gilroy, Small, and others presume that the flow of musical forms between African and European Americans in the United States and their constant adaptation along the way represent predictable and positive developments rather than causes for alarm, and moreover that it is in music that black and white Americans have most consistently enjoyed an intimacy that their nation, for much of its history, forbade in its laws and mores. Heard in such terms, the production, reception, and imitation of black music in the 1920s becomes part of an ongoing dynamic of communication and change, one whose allure lay in the opportunity it presented to performers and listeners alike to cross racial boundaries or to remake racial identities within an aesthetic space.[19] And such a musical dynamic, of course, has implications for the continuing study of the Harlem Renaissance poets, so many of whom called to their readers in song and sought to join in a far-flung musical conversation among diverse peoples.

When Johnson edited and published *The Book of American Negro Spirituals* in 1925, he found the music's fusion of "primitive" chant and Christian spirituality, its marriage of European melody and African rhythm, and its "fluid," simultaneously black and white language to be nothing less than a "miracle" of cultural amalgamation.[20] Similarly, in discussing the jazz of the 1920s, Zora Neale Hurston in 1934 described an ever-cycling racial flux, a spirit of collaboration that could be found there and in any number of that era's other, most distinctive cultural productions. "What we really mean by originality is the modification of ideas," she argued. "Thus has arisen a new art in the civilised world, and thus has our so-called civilisation come. The exchange and re-exchange of ideas between groups."[21] Few writers have so ably expressed the inclusive musical thinking that seems to have motivated Toomer and Hughes, and few have so effectively suggested the ways in which literary works by African Americans in the early twentieth century could use music to blur formal, generic, and racial boundaries while at the same time making race both palpable and elusive. As we shall hear, theirs is a musical poetics of broad invitation and initiation, and it represents a literary experiment that, as Hurston would observe a few years after their first works sounded, seems to be part of a fundamentally American story.

O Cant: *Cane*

Jean Toomer's thinking on race matters developed a great deal over his life, but when it came to the African American musics he encountered in 1921 while serving as a visiting teacher in Georgia, he never changed his tune. That sojourn, Toomer wrote years later, "was the first time I'd ever heard the folk-songs and spirituals. They were very rich and sad and joyous and beautiful. But I learned that the Negroes of the town objected to them. They called them "shouting." They had victrolas and player-pianos. So, I realized with deep regret, that the spirituals, meeting ridicule, would be certain to die out."[22] This was a crucial artistic awakening of Toomer's early life, and paying tribute to the music of Georgia thus came to be one of his central concerns in *Cane*, the diverse, enigmatic, and frequently southern-themed collection of poetry, prose sketches, and drama that he published two years later and upon which his reputation rests. Following Toomer's stated interest in song, several interpreters of *Cane* have over the years identified music as one of its unifying themes, likening the text to a performance of jazz, blues, or, as the advertising team at Boni and Liveright put it in 1923, "black vaudeville."[23] But it is perhaps best thought of as a field recording, an attempt on Toomer's part to catch a disappearing musical culture in words and to preserve it in literary form. Certainly this is how *Cane* was introduced to the public by Waldo Frank, the critic, novelist, and friend of Toomer who wrote the foreword to its first edition: "Reading this book, I had the vision of a land, heretofore sunk in the mists of muteness, suddenly rising up into the eminence of song. Innumerable books have been written about the South; some good books have been written in the South. This book *is* the South."[24]

If Toomer's attempt at capturing the South's musical essence was as successful as Frank suggests, it grows all the more impressive when one considers the many limitations—some self-imposed, some not—under which he worked. Though descended in part from southern blacks, he had grown up in Washington, DC, and claimed to have been entirely unfamiliar with the region's musical idiom before he encountered it in 1921. As a would-be preservationist, moreover, he had arrived on the scene rather late, for southern folk music and spirituals had already been in the process of being studied, gathered, published, recorded, and fretted over by collectors for some sixty years before *Cane*. Most significantly of all, Toomer's literary aesthetic and quasi-mystical sensibility impelled him to emphasize the fundamental mysteriousness of the music he had encountered rather than to document it in a straightforward manner. Evaluating, accounting for, or transcribing melodies, lyrics, and song structures in any precise way was, for Toomer, largely beside the point: in his autobiographical writings, he reports having been moved by the music of Georgia primarily because it expressed something greater than itself, a "folk-spirit" that was "walking in to die on the modern desert."[25] Unlike the exhaustively "soundtracked" fiction of Fitzgerald and Joyce, Toomer's text refers explicitly to a mere handful of independently verifiable folk pieces—"Deep River," "My Lord, What a Mornin'," and "Swing Low Sweet Chariot," and even then only in snippets. As a consequence, *Cane* can come to seem "musical" in an essentially abstract sense, more concerned with what one of its poems refers to as "soul sounds" than with anything that could be literally heard.[26] How, then, can the text be said to have achieved "the eminence of song" and captured the musicality of the South?

Cane grows more audible if one allows for the possibility that Toomer intended the South's music to resound not merely from his pages but also from another (if somewhat unexpected) source: his readers. The dearth of preexisting, classifiable, known music in *Cane* is counterbalanced by a great many original poems written in unmistakably musical forms, metered and arranged in such a way as to be easily recognized as spirituals or work songs in spite of the fact that they do not bring any particular, extra-literary melodies to mind. Music is seldom supplied but frequently suggested by Toomer's verse, and a crucial question in regard to *Cane* is how one is to interact with a text so insistently devoted to the signification of song but so lacking in clear indications for how it has been or is to be performed. Readers, having no conclusive sense of what these at once familiar and foreign airs are meant to sound like, may decide to read them as uninflected poetry, but a great deal of this text's enduring, incantatory power rests upon the fact that they are also free to sing Toomer's songs on their own and in whatever ways they like. Indeed, one could even go a step further and say that readers are in fact required to fashion their own melodies and aural interpretations of *Cane* if the South's music is to endure as what Toomer appears to have understood it to be: an artistic dynamic of ongoing, interpersonal relation. As shall be demonstrated, *Cane* memorializes a musical and social process of collaboration rather than a tradition of specific songs, and its central paradox is that it attempts to preserve the folk music and "spirit" of Georgia by asking its readers to make up a new folk music entirely.

By way of example, consider "Karintha," a prose sketch of rural life that opens *Cane* and is interwoven with some of Toomer's most singable verse. When published in *Broom* some months before *Cane* made its debut, "Karintha" had formally requested that its audience imagine it as an audibly accompanied performance, perhaps in the style of the poet Vachel Lindsay: in its first incarnation, it was to be read to "the humming of a Negro folk-song."[27] This instruction had disappeared by the time Toomer included the piece in *Cane*, but the redolent possibility of its being performed musically never did. The following is a stanza that arises or is alluded to at various points in the text:

> Her skin is like dusk on the eastern horizon,
> O cant you see it, O cant you see it,
> Her skin is like dusk on the eastern horizon
> . . . When the sun goes down.

(Cane 3)

Any number of melodies and musical interpretations might be supported by this poem's framework. "Karintha" aspires to the condition of the vernacular by including only two words of more than one syllable, making it especially adaptable; it is repetitive and thus easy for singers to take up as it continues to reverberate throughout the passage; and it deploys anapests in the first and third lines in the service of strong rhythmic flow. Even as Toomer provides musical prompts, however, he leaves a sense of open-ended mystery in regard to the poem's rendering that readers must improvise upon and resolve for themselves. The second line might either continue in the same rhythmical pattern as the first or begin with the double stress of a spondee, while the elision that precedes the final line negates one of the expected verbal stresses and creates a provisional space, one that is presumably to be filled with something other than words. But filled this poem must ultimately be, as its second line suggests in the phrase "O cant": in dropping the formal apostrophe and emphasizing the aural character of language over the visual, Toomer not only asks "can you not see it?" but also suggests the Latin *canto* and an imperative construction, thus calling on his readers to "cant" and sing even as they "hear."

In the context of Toomer's larger project of musical commemoration, the malleability on display in "Karintha" and elsewhere in *Cane* is meant to suggest several things, among them the fact that songs are often changed in the transmission from one person to another rather than simply absorbed and faithfully echoed. As his poem "Song of the Son" indicates in its resonant final stanza, the music of the folk and the "souls" expressed through it cannot be locked into static forms, with the "seed" of cultural heritage left for Toomer's generation by the elder one growing until it becomes

> An everlasting song, a singing tree,
> Caroling softly souls of slavery,
> What they were, and what they are to me,
> Caroling softly souls of slavery.

(Cane 14)

Here the question of what musical expressions "are" to their new singers and listeners is as important as what they "were" to their old ones, and the poem's emphasis on refashioning has implications not only for the preservationist credo of *Cane* but also for the ways in which a reader might go about interpreting Toomer's text. Scholars have often argued that the formally challenging modernism of *Cane* demands some kind of active collaboration on the part of its audience, as its sometimes bewildering shifts of perspective, setting, and genre presuppose a readership that can serve as "a coparticipant in the act of creation" and make sense of its avant-garde multiplicity.[28] Additionally, when it came to specifically musical practice Toomer believed, at least in his later years, that open and productive relations between artists and audiences essentially constituted the art: "What man, full of song, wants to keep it to himself?" he asked in 1937. "There are no misers in music. . . . The singer is not content to sing only for himself; by the law of his being his deepest urge is to share his song with others."[29] Music, by Toomer's definition, is fundamentally social, and it follows that an effective musical text would attempt to preserve songs not as recordings or as formal accounts of past performances— these are shown by *Cane* to be standardizations, even reifications—but rather as opportunities for audiences to participate in something new.

The musical openness of *Cane* also provides a rather ingenious way for the text to destabilize notions of racial classification, a subject about which Toomer—who claimed seven distinct bloodlines—was famously uneasy. In equating his verse with black folk song even as he makes it possible for audiences of many stripes to sing it, Toomer is able to emphasize difference and similitude, self and other, at the same time: his poetry asks readers to imagine an explicitly raced subject position and then to occupy it through the act of vocalization, demonstrating in the process what W. E. B. Du Bois had in 1921 called "the Universal in the Particular" in regard to racial categories.[30] During the performance of such poems, a black musical identity can be said to channel or command nonblack voices; so too can nonblack voices be said to assume or appropriate a black musical identity; and between these poles cycles a dialectic of racial specificity and musical collectivity that *Cane* never resolves and that appears to have consumed Toomer's thoughts while he wrote it. Corresponding in 1923 with Dubose Heyward, the white novelist whose *Porgy* would later achieve another sort of biracial musicality at the hands of George Gershwin, Toomer described his text thus: "Both black and white folk come into *Cane*'s pages. . . . But in no instance am I concerned primarily with race; always, I drive straight for my own spiritual reality, and for the spiritual truth of the South."[31] Here Toomer refers to the people and experiences that inspired *Cane*, but so too can his black and nonblack audiences both be said to "come into" his text on musical terms, contributors to an aesthetic that scholars have grown increasingly inclined over the years to identify as fundamentally interracial.[32]

Before delving into the folk songs that Toomer wrote for *Cane*, it will be useful to consider the tradition of musical letters from which he was distinguishing himself and the means by which he did so, as his text reads not just as an attempt at musical preservation but also as an extended criticism of various earlier approaches to African American musicality. In the years since Du Bois had adorned the chapter headings of *The Souls of Black Folk* (1903) with transcriptions of what he called the "Sorrow Songs" (204), writers had on several occasions turned to well-known African American music—the spirituals in particular—for literary effect. James Weldon Johnson's novel *The Autobiography of an Ex-Colored Man* (1912), anonymous upon publication, had been narrated by a composer who considers the "old slave songs" to be "material" for his own pieces, with the lyrics of "Swing Low Sweet Chariot" quoted at one point to give readers a more intimate sense of what his work might sound like.[33] Clement Wood's novel *Nigger* (1922), meanwhile, had chronicled the changing fortunes of a black family over several years and relied upon a soundtrack of sacred and popular tunes to reinforce the plot's passage of historical time, with his characters singing "I's Troubled in my Mind" and "Nobody Knows the Trouble I've Seen" at the story's beginning but listening to recordings of "My Old Kentucky Home" and "Snuggle Up a Little Closer" by the end.[34]

In these and other such cases, writers were aided in no small part by the fact that the songs they referred to had been broadly popular for decades and could therefore be presumed to be part of their readership's common fund of musical knowledge. The Fisk Jubilee Singers, a chorus of black undergraduates from Fisk University in Tennessee, had made the first national hit with the spirituals decades before when they began touring the United States (and eventually Europe) in the early 1870s, along the way raising $150,000 for their school, selling around

60,000 anthologies of their songs, and inspiring any number of imitation ensembles and vaudeville knockoffs throughout the land. The story repeated itself in 1909 when a quartet of Fisk singers began making phonograph records and cylinders for the three largest music labels (Victor, Edison, and Columbia), eventually becoming the second most-popular African American vocal act of the era and, as Tim Brooks has shown, selling some 2 million copies of their performances to a largely white, middle-class audience.[35] So too were the spirituals circulating widely in other settings in the early twentieth century, able to be found in preservationist book collections (including important volumes edited by Harry T. Burleigh, Natalie Curtis Burlin, Henry Edward Krehbiel, and John W. Work Jr. in the 1910s), in classical arrangements for recital or salon performance, and on the stage.

Perhaps the most important precursor to Toomer's musical verse, however, was Johnson's poem "O Black and Unknown Bards" (1908), an encomium à la Thomas Gray to the inglorious slaves who crafted the spirituals and a compelling model of how a writer might go about integrating song and prosody:

> Who heard great "Jordan roll"? Whose starward eye
> Saw chariot "swing low"? And who was he
> That breathed that comforting, melodic sigh,
> "Nobody knows de trouble I see"?
>
> What merely living clod, what captive thing,
> Could up toward God through all its darkness grope,
> And find within its deadened heart to sing
> These songs of sorrow, love, and faith, and hope?[36]

Few poems from the era so effectively demonstrate the power that an enduring song can have in a poetic context. Not every reader, of course, will be familiar with the spirituals Johnson refers to here, but if the poem is sung as well as recited by those who are, "O Black and Unknown Bards" becomes an exercise in multivocality, with a striking division emerging between musical language and the poetic kind. The dominant iambic pentameter is suspended temporarily by the snatches of song, with caesuras implied in the first and second lines and the fourth obeying a new rhythm entirely. The sound of the imported spirituals makes the contrast between the exalted art and degraded social position of the slave considerably more stark, with the cruel designation of "clod" falling with an uncomfortable thud after having followed the graceful melodic arc of "Nobody knows de trouble I see." And above all else, Johnson's invocation of music and his invitation to perform it (if accepted) guarantees the immortality of the bards, temporarily making the poem's interpreter a medium or instrument for the unknown artists it honors. For Johnson, these slaves still sing, and they sing through us.

Spirituals of the sort that Johnson praises (and would go on to publish in a collection of his own in 1925) can sometimes be found in *Cane*, but when Toomer traffics in familiar African American song he does so to very different and generally unsettling effect, as though arguing that known musics are obstructions to rather than facilitators of his text's larger aims. His first reference of this kind occurs in "Rhobert," an odd character sketch presenting a "banty-bowed, shaky, ricket-legged man" who, despite owning a home that affords him some degree of material comfort, is "way down" in his troubles (*Cane* 42). Toomer strikes an absurdist note throughout, likening Rhobert to a deep-sea explorer: his house is a "monstrous diver's helmet" that protects him from life's vicissitudes, but he is nevertheless a man in peril, one who "would sink in mud should the water be drawn off" and who has made the mistake of assuming the "practical infinity" of his metaphorical air supply. Rhobert's situation is perverse, and it grows yet more so when Toomer's piece concludes with an invocation of "Deep River," which the music historian Wayne Shirley has called "perhaps the best-known and best-loved spiritual of all among the general public."[37]

> Lets build a monument and set it in the ooze where he goes down. A monument of hewn oak, carved in nigger-heads. Lets open our throats, brother, and sing "Deep River" when he goes down.
>   Brother, Rhobert is sinking.
>   Lets open our throats, brother,
>   Lets sing Deep River when he goes down.
>
> (*Cane* 43)

If it is readers to whom Toomer refers when calling out for a "brother," then some of us can indeed "open our throats" and, up to a point, deliver these final three lines of verse in a Johnsonian manner. When sung according to what has come to be their standard melody, the words "Deep River" have something of a productive relationship to their literary context, creating a rare moment of calm and covering five distinct pitches that move progressively more "down" along with Rhobert. Yet much of "Deep River" is out of place here, with the song's stated desire for redemptive horizontal motion—"I want to cross over into Camp Ground"—markedly at odds with Rhobert's vertical sinking. Add to this Toomer's subsequent, impish description of God as "a Red Cross man with a dredge and a respiration-pump who's waiting for you at the opposite periphery" (*Cane* 42), and "Deep River" comes here to seem anachronistic, irrelevant, or amusing—anything, that is to say, but transcendent.

Toomer might have tweaked "Deep River" in this less than respectful manner for any number of reasons, but one was surely the widespread popularity that it and other spirituals enjoyed in the 1920s. As was seen in the previous chapter in relation to Fitzgerald, literary allusions to well-known pieces of music can have strikingly stimulative effects on readers, dredging up memories of specific performances that can then be brought to bear upon the text containing them—a process of automatic recognition that Toomer, with his distaste for "victrolas and player-pianos," would in all probability have regarded as mere ventriloquism rather than active participation of the sort required by the elusive "Karintha." Moreover, there is no predicting what might happen when readers are invited to access their musical memories in literary contexts, especially when the music in question exists in as many versions as the most famous spirituals did in 1923. "Deep River," for example, had been published in no fewer than twelve vocal settings by a single arranger in 1917 alone, precipitating a performance craze on the New York recital circuit and inspiring a 1921 hit called "Dear Old Southland" that, to some consternation, blatantly plagiarized the beloved melody. Indeed, there were dozens of contemporary versions of the song that Toomer's first readers might have heard before encountering it in *Cane*, thus making it difficult to say what an "appropriate" treatment of it in a literary context might actually entail.

Consider the stakes, for example, of Toomer's first readers aligning "Rhobert" with any of the three records of "Deep River" made by the white opera singer Frances Alda for the Victor company in 1917 and 1918.◑ The performances in question are characterized by lush orchestration, grandiose backup singing, and what can only be described as a virtuosic delivery on Alda's part, and while they might strike some modern listeners as excessive, they were nonetheless far from unusual at the time. Composers such as Antonín Dvořák and Harlem Renaissance thinkers such as Johnson and Alain Locke had long considered the spirituals worthy of classical settings, and by 1923 a sizable number of white musicians, concertgoers, and record buyers had come to agree. Thanks in large part to Burleigh's popular 1916 setting, "Deep River" made a bona fide hit in *lieder* circles in the years before *Cane* and became a staple of the repertoire for practically every male and female concert singer of note, with Shirley arguing that the song's "runaway popularity" was perhaps more responsible than anything else for making it "thinkable for spirituals to appear on a mainstream vocal recital."[38] By the time *Cane* was published, "Deep River" and other spirituals had gone from being marginal music to commanding a central place in America's classical canon, interpreted not just by singers but any number of instrumentalists as well. And if such performances are heard alongside Rhobert's predicament, Toomer's invocation of "Deep River" comes to seem even further out of place: it is of course all but impossible for most readers to open their throats and produce anything on the order of Alda's assured, expertly controlled rendering.

Even when *Cane* spells out how its allusions to black music are meant to be heard, it still causes the known spirituals to sound questionable or problematic. In the short story "Avey," for example, Toomer invokes "Deep River" for a second time and in a specific performance, with the song discussed in the context of an unsatisfying relationship between an anonymous narrator and the woman for whom the story is named. The setting is a park in Washington, DC, with the narrator—a college-educated artist with a somewhat romantic conception of himself—attempting a spiritual convergence with Avey and drawing upon music to facilitate it, hoping, as he puts it, "to find the truth that people bury in their hearts" (*Cane* 48). He begins to "hum a folk-tune," then recites some of his own works, and finally sings "a promise-song," but through it all an irritating sound in the background works against him: "A band in one of the buildings a fair distance off was playing a march. I wished they would stop. Their playing was like a tin spoon in one's mouth." Far better, the narrator says, would be something else: "I wanted the Howard Glee Club to sing 'Deep River,' from the road. To sing 'Deep River, Deep River,' from the road . . ." But all of his music and plans come to naught, with Avey falling asleep and the narrator left with little to do but shiver through the night and gaze upon the dome of the Capitol, a "gray ghost ship drifting in from sea" (*Cane* 49).

Once more does a reference to a spiritual exist in close proximity to a character's spiritual failure, and this time the discomfort Toomer creates cannot be blamed on readers' having divergent notions of what the song might be intended to sound like. Some critics have argued that the allusion to "Deep River" here is meant to indicate a folk heritage from which African Americans like Avey had grown alienated since the Civil War, but the narrator's stipulation that the song be sung by the Howard Glee Club raises a host of interpretive possibilities, among them that Toomer is using the music to cast his protagonist—and not his protagonist's paramour—as out of touch with this tradition. In mentioning one of the many celebrated choral groups from the nation's historically black colleges and universities, after all, Toomer could not help but wade into what was a widespread and controversial question among music collectors of his era, namely, whether trained singers were in fact capable of giving "legitimate" or "authentic" performances of the spirituals. Ensembles such as the Howard Glee Club had for decades been prominent on the national and international scene, but they had also been criticized in some quarters on the grounds that they used excessively elaborate vocal arrangements, thereby obscuring the spirituals' folk melodies under a weight of pretentious, quasi-classical harmonization. Thus do questions of the highbrow and lowbrow, of refinement and simplicity, and of the relation of race to all these categories accompany "Deep River" into Toomer's scene, drawing attention away from the narrator's pursuit of musical unification and fixing it on his implied desire for self-distinction instead.

Listening to a recording of "Deep River" by the aforementioned Fisk Jubilee Singers—dated from 1940, but in the same style as their extant 1920s performances—makes for a useful introduction to this debate, as their rendering of the song is even more formally complex than was Alda's.◐ Here the melody remains strong throughout, but the vocal lines that undergird it are in such constant and unpredictable harmonic flux that they suggest two very different idioms: on the one hand, the convoluted operatic choruses of Wagner, and on the other, the "overdone" style of "barber-shop" singing that Johnson believed had been derived from the spirituals many years before.[39] Depending on how this music strikes the reader's ear, then, Toomer's second, carefully specified invocation of "Deep River" in *Cane* can raise as many questions as it answers, among them whether the narrator, in having developed an urbane aesthetic sensibility and a taste for sophisticated music, has not become one of the snobbish, effete, "Dictie" blacks that Toomer's text sometimes satirizes (*Cane* 53). Avey's inability to comprehend the narrator and his musical overtures may mark her as cut off from a traditional folk heritage, but the musical signification implied by "Deep River" in a glee club setting may just as easily indicate something similar about the man who seems to view her as such. Though perhaps his tastes are not so elevated as he thinks? After all, the Fisk Singers' records were quite popular in the years before and after *Cane*, with the group moving as many as 100,000 units of their most acclaimed songs in an era when a record's selling 20,000 was considered a hit. Indeed, the narrator's sense for the musically appropriate would seem in many ways to align with that of the broader American public: as Brooks has shown, the records made by the Fisk Quartet (see Image 6) received relatively little attention in the black press but were the primary means by which "middle-class whites in the early twentieth century became familiar with this important aspect of African American culture."[40]

One might ask at this point why spirituals such as "Deep River" are contextualized so unfavorably by Toomer and why they fall short in accomplishing the musical entrancement and interpersonal reconciliation that *Cane* has been said to be pursuing more broadly. Toomer's treatment is surprising in many ways: a well-known song, after all, should be correspondingly inviting to audiences, and as the very existence of the Alda and Fisk records indicate, "Deep River" was the

JOHN WESLEY WORK   NOAH WALKER RYDER   ALFRED GARFIELD KING   JAMES ANDREW MYERS
JUBILEE QUARTETTE, 1900-1910

The "Jubilee Quartette" from Fisk University, whose recordings of the spirituals were instrumental in popularizing African American folk music. Used by permission, New York Public Library.

province of black, white, male, and female singers in the period. Moreover, other artists across the international modernist movement had been much more respectful than he in their deployment of folk materials. The composers Béla Bartók and Zoltán Kodály, for example, had made field recordings of Hungarian folk melodies and put them at the very center of their compositions, and many artists of the Harlem Renaissance had been inspired by the Celtic Revival and a corresponding rise of "folk theater" in Ireland, seeing it as a possible model for their own works. As we have already noted, however, Toomer was beset with anxieties about the passive consumption of song and the place of folk music in the commercial market. Even more problematic for him was the issue of freightedness, as preexisting pieces of music struck him as being too burdened with outside, sociopolitical associations to be capable of inspiring the sense of mystery and productive mutability that he was attempting in his text. The spirituals, after all, had long been at the center of discussions about the nature of race and, among other things, its role in musical expression—discussions that tended to draw attention to the very divisions of black and white that Toomer's art was largely intended to blur.

Most immediately, the field researchers who had collected and studied the folk culture of the former Confederate states in the years leading up to *Cane* had long sought to quantify or account for the "blackness" of the spirituals they had encountered, an anthropological project that resembled Toomer's literary one in more than one particular. The first three decades of the twentieth century saw more and more attention paid to the South's rural arts (which were widely believed to be imperiled by the spread of communication technology and mass entertainment), and in particular to African Americans (who were argued by black and white thinkers alike to represent the closest thing the nation had to a peasant class). In the United States, the chimerical goal was to locate musical and racial "authenticity," with the researchers who canvassed the region during the 1910s and 1920s dedicated to finding the purest, least "contaminated" examples of African American song and the best means of recording them. Here too was it presumed that the art's aesthetic validity depended on the racial identity of its performers, with collectors often expressing anxiety that the number of black singers capable of giving legitimate performances of the spirituals was dwindling by the day. In the years before Toomer visited Georgia, it was not at all unusual for preservationists to make melancholy pronouncements along the lines of this one from 1918:

> A recorder realizes, perhaps better than can another, how approximate only is any notation of music that was never conceived by the singers as a written thing. When one rereads the fixed transcription it seems to bear the same relation to the fluent original that the peep of a caged canary does to the free caroling of a bird on open wing. Would that some genius would add to our system of notation a gamut of more delicate symbols that would enable us better to express the unconscious voices of true folk-singers. Those of us who are now recording the old Negro melodies keenly realize that we come late to the harvesting, and that a generation and more have lived since the originators of the slave-songs passed from the plantations.[41]

Before and after *Cane*, collectors used a wide variety of techniques in attempting to leave the most precise and fullest possible account of their musical and racial specimens. Some opted for dialect over standard English in taking down lyrics; some used Western notation to transcribe melodies; some made audio recordings; and others tested a new process called phonophotography, which created a visual representation of a sound that accounted for pitch, time, and inflection and that was frequently accompanied by images of the singer's mouth in action. In almost all of these cases, however, collectors were united in the desire to discover and capture a quintessentially "old Negro" idiom, though most acknowledged that they were regrettably, even tragically "late to the harvesting" of "true" racial music.[42]

Moreover, Americans who were not privy to academic debates over the spirituals or to the concerns of anthropologists had nevertheless been fixated on the idea of racially "authentic" black music for quite some time as of 1923, thanks to purveyors of turn-of-the-century popular entertainment—the very institution, of course, blamed for desiccating the South's "authentic" musical idiom in the first place. Producers of African American stage reviews of the 1890s, for example, had frequently attempted to distinguish their acts from the long and tired tradition of blackface minstrelsy and *Uncle Tom's Cabin* adaptations by claiming direct connections to the musical culture that had developed in the South under slavery. The popular traveling extravaganza *The South before the War* (1891) featured, among other things, a chorus that sang spirituals, an on-stage cotton field, a camp meeting, and a grand cakewalk; *Black America* (1895) went one better and allowed its audiences to wander through its tableaux of cabins, farm animals, and cotton gins before the show started; and a host of imitators followed, all trumpeting their antebellum musical pedigrees and you-are-there verisimilitude. Authentic blackness was invariably the selling point of these and other such productions, and it was the yardstick by which they were usually measured by spectators: the *New York Times* review of *Black America* was typical in observing that its performers had been "selected from all the various sections of the South, and are well qualified to enlighten the Northern white man in relation to a life that will soon be extinct."[43] Race-based stage entertainment grew somewhat less anachronistic in the decades leading up to *Cane*, but an emphasis on rural, southern blackness as expressed in song was still to be found in the famous Bert Williams-George Walker comedies—notoriously marketed as the work of "Two Real Coons"—and in up-to-the-minute, sophisticated 1920s fare like *Shuffle Along*, *From Dixie to Broadway*, and the *Plantation Review*. As ever, these shows were judged to be hits insofar as they were believed to feature genuinely racial song, and their performers skillful insofar as they were perceived to bring audiences closer to some vital black actuality.[44]

All this is to say that *Cane* and its attempt at capturing the musical essence of the South had many antecedents in a variety of social contexts, and that in every previous case—whether aesthetic, anthropological, or commercial—to talk about the region's music was all but inevitably to talk about race as well. The universalist Toomer therefore took quite a risk in modeling his text on the African American musical idiom: it was very likely, both in his time and after, that his audiences would attend to the racial character of that idiom to the exclusion of all else. And in a great many cases this was in fact to be Toomer's fate, to see his poetry praised on the one hand for being "truly racial" by such luminaries as Hughes and on the other speculated to have been the work of a "racial opportunist" by such later readers as Alice Walker, with these opposing conclusions having little in common other than their concern for whether the race feeling and music of *Cane* is legitimately or sincerely felt.[45] Such categorization of art and identity alike came to irritate Toomer more and more over the course of his life, eventually leading him to deny that *Cane* or any of his other works were racial to any significant degree and to forbid their being reprinted in anthologies of African American verse. It should therefore come as no surprise that the best-known examples of the established African American musical tradition tend to be ironized in his literary treatment, and that the capacity of the most famous spirituals to ease or transcend racial division in the twentieth century is more or less dismissed in *Cane*.

Toomer's larger project of musical and racial merging is more likely to be enacted by poems that are free of specific referents and that are equally foreign to all his readers' ears, and those who would hear that project must therefore turn to the first section of *Cane*, where most of his poetry inspired by rural ways and black folk song is to be found. Toomer in fact suggested at one point that readers begin in the middle part of his text (which depicts urban life and features the failures of "Deep River" in "Rhobert" and "Avey") and only later turn to the beginning, with this jumbled itinerary in some ways confirming the popular interpretation of *Cane* as a search for and recovery of a lost, essential black heritage.[46] But Toomer's focus on black particularity and his use of black musical forms in the early poems of *Cane* are better thought of as access points rather than as final destinations, as a means of inviting readers to construct and participate in a musical idiom rather than to evaluate it from an outside perspective. The key is to avoid reductionism and not conclude that the musical pull of these poems is a direct and exclusive function of their blackness, of what the doomed young white man of Toomer's story "Blood-Burning Moon" insensitively and inadequately refers to as an ineffable, inherently racial "way": "What way was that? Damned if he knew. . . . Was there something about niggers that you couldnt know?" (*Cane* 33). For Toomer, the musical idiom as expressed in *Cane* was something that any number of readers could "know" through their own creation of it, with his invitation to participate in blackness meant to serve as a portal not only to racial experience but also to something beyond it.

The songs of this first section, that is to say, compel multiracial performances of ostensibly racial music, and many of them treat the unification of voices on a thematic level even as they make it possible on a formal one. Consider "Cotton Song," whose musicality is premised on the interplay of singers and depends upon an audible contrast of distinct, alternating sounds. There are at least two voices in this work song, the first of which begins by calling,

> Come, brother, come. Lets lift it;
> Come now, hewit! roll away!

> Shackles fall upon the Judgment Day
> But lets not wait for it.

(Cane 11)

As was the case in "Karintha," "Cotton Song" explicitly invites vocalization, with the singer's call to "lift it" in the first line not just implying that there is a job to be done but also striking a Johnsonian note, exhorting its audiences, as had the older poet in the so-called Negro National Anthem of 1900, to "lift every voice and sing."[47] Once again Toomer avoids formal punctuation, relying on homonyms to reinforce both the aurality of language and the inclusive aims of Toomer's verse: "hewit" sounds as "hew it," invoking that perplexing word that implies, as does "cleave," both a sharp separation and the tantalizing possibility of drawing close to a boundary. Finally, the voice's call to resist worldly "Shackles" reinforces the poem's emphasis on free expression, and then, in the following stanzas, Toomer makes a typographical decision that he repeats nowhere else in the Georgia poetry of *Cane*, with a second voice emerging and being set aside in quotation marks:

> God's body's got a soul,
> Bodies like to roll the soul,
> Cant blame God if we dont roll,
> Come, brother, roll, roll!
>
> Cotton bales are the fleecy way
> Weary sinner's bare feet trod,
> Softly, softly to the throne of God,
> "We aint agwine t wait until th Judgment Day!
>
> Nassur; nassur,
> Hump.
> Eoho, eoho, roll away!
> We aint agwine t wait until th Judgment Day!"
>
> God's body's got a soul,
> Bodies like to roll the soul,
> Cant blame God if we dont roll,
> Come, brother, roll, roll!

One voice is in an obviously marked dialect ("Nassur") while the other attempts a certain parable-like poetry ("Weary sinner's bare feet trod"), but common ground is as important as difference. The voices echo one another in referring to the

"Judgment Day," and their frequently repeated calls for the other to "roll" creates a sense of constant circularity, as if to demonstrate that this poem could roll on forever, cycling back and forth for as long as there is a new voice to respond to the last one.

Others of the Georgia poems suggest a Pythagorean conception of reality in which all supposedly discrete objects are revealed to be connected by some larger harmonic plan; their songlike lyricism reverberates in Toomer's surrounding prose passages and elides difference by working, as he would later put it in his autobiographical writings, to "lift facts, things, happenings to the planes of rhythm, feeling, and significance."[48] The story "Carma" demonstrates Toomer's almost cosmic sense of unity especially well, a tale of an assertive, adulterous woman whose life is said to be "the crudest melodrama"—or as the term's prefix, "melo," implies, the crudest musical drama (*Cane* 13). Her village of Dixie Pike is a place of constant singing, with the voices of neighbors ever in the air. Carma does not herself sing, but she is no less tuneful: indeed, "her body is a song" in and of itself (*Cane* 12). Lives are music, people are music, and it would seem that time is music as well, for at the beginning, middle, and end of "Carma," an imperative, chanting voice emerges both to invite the reader's participation and to mark key transition points in the narrative:

> Wind is in the cane. Come along.
> Cane leaves swaying, rusty with talk,
> Scratching choruses above the guinea's squawk,
> Wind is in the cane. Come along.

Sometimes it is cane, sometimes corn, that creates the sensation described in the first and fourth lines, but in either case the unifying effect is the same. The stalks suggest both the reeds that comprise the pipes of Pan and the wind-swept strings of the Aeolian Harp, with the "choruses" of the physical world echoing in their "Scratching" way the "crudest melodrama" of human affairs and thus merging the people of Georgia with the place itself. Even the fact that the sounds Toomer mentions are sometimes grating—scratching, squawking, and somehow "rusty"—only serves to highlight just how all-encompassing this musicality in fact is.

The song verses of *Cane* often interweave voices and depict the unification of humanity with the physical world, but perhaps most significant of all are the ways in which they seek to merge the races, with the story "Esther" serving as a fitting final symbol of the broad reconciliation that Toomer's text is so often devoted to. Here a black man named Barlo drops to his knees in a bar, claims to have fallen into a communion with Jesus, and relates the story of African enslavement at the hands of whites, with his words registering a transition into a musicalized state of being:

> "—but his head was caught up in th clouds. An while he was agazin at th heavens, heart filled up with th Lord, some little white-ant biddies came an tied his feet to chains. They led him t th coast, they led him t th sea, they led him across th ocean an they didnt set him free. The old coast didnt miss him, an th new coast wasnt free, he left the old-coast brothers, t give birth t you an me. O Lord, great God Almighty, t give birth t you an me."
>
> (*Cane* 23)

Read aloud, the rhythmical, even sing-song quality of Barlo's language becomes immediately audible, with a rhyme scheme emerging to connect the words "sea," "free," and "me," and his vision (beginning with "They led him t th coast" and ending with "birth t you an me") spontaneously organizing itself into ten lines of trimeter. As language shifts from prose-speak to verse the reader is called on to imagine and create the poem's musicality, and Toomer reinforces this openness by describing the ways in which the townspeople who surround Barlo contribute to his chant: "Old gray mothers are in tears. Fragments of melodies are being hummed." And strikingly, the revelatory, communally created space of song is shown to ease—if only temporarily—racial difference in Georgia, as "White folks are touched and curiously awed," preachers of both races "confer as to how best to rid themselves of the vagrant, usurping fellow," and even "old Limp Underwood, who hated niggers" seems to fall under Barlo's influence and wakes up the following morning "to find that he held a black man in his arms." In its moment of musicality, a tale of opposition also becomes the means by which opposition might be resolved, a fleeting echo of the at once racial and inclusive poetic project of *Cane*.

That Toomer hoped to use blackness as a means of expressing some broader spiritual understanding in his work is quite plain, as he revealed in a 1923 letter to Frank: "As an approach, as a constant element (part of a larger whole) of interest, Negro is good. But to try to tie me to one of my parts is surely to loose [*sic*] me. My own letters have taken Negro as a point, and from there have circled out."[49] But the circular quality of Toomer's text has frequently eluded his readers, largely because his most effective means of demonstrating the Du Boisian Universal in the Particular—the available and singable cadences of the black musical tradition— are so easy to associate exclusively with the latter. As Burlin, the aforementioned collector of southern folk culture, had declared some years before *Cane*, when an audience of Toomer's era heard African American song, it was not uncommon for them to "think of Emerson and ponder: The Negro 'Over-Soul'—is it Music?"[50] For Burlin and many like her, the music of the black South was to be sincerely admired, but so too was it understood to be the creation of a fundamentally different, possibly unknowable race. It was an art that could on the one hand be thought of as having achieved the heights of spiritual sublimity and yet on the other remain firmly segregated by what George M. Frederickson has termed "romantic racialism" on the part of whites, and so it was that Toomer could often be read, both in his time and since, as having gained access to a deep and particular race feeling through the songs of *Cane* but not gone further than this.[51]

The universalist Toomer, however, could at least have taken solace in knowing that he understood Transcendentalism better than had particularists like Burlin: race, after all, is precisely the sort of material concern that Emerson regarded as having distracted humanity from higher unities, with the very notion of a "Negro 'Over-Soul'" therefore being a contradiction in terms. Toward the end of his famous essay, Emerson writes, "the heart in thee is the heart of all; not a valve, not a wall, not an intersection is there anywhere in nature, but one blood rolls uninterruptedly an endless circulation through all men, as the water of the globe is all one sea, and, truly seen, its tide is one."[52] And if the Emersonian Over-Soul were to find its expression in music, it would not only sound black but would also achieve a vastness along the lines of the following passage from "The Blue Meridian," the most noteworthy poem that Toomer completed in his largely fallow years after *Cane*:

> Upon my phonograph are many records
> Played on sides in sacred and profane extremes;
> Sometimes I hear Gregorian chants
> Or Bach's "It Is Consummated";
> Sometimes I hear Duke Ellington
> Or Eddy Duchin sing popular contemporary;
> And some rare times
> I hear myself, the unrecorded,
> Sing the flow of I,
> The notes and language not of this experience,
> Sing I am,
> As the flow of I pauses,
> Then passes through my water-wheel—
> And those radiant others, the living real,
> The people identical in being.[53]

Each variety of music, "sacred and profane" and old and new alike, is an access point to that which is "not of this experience," and no one style is incompatible with any individual. It is the openness of the listener that matters, the ability in "rare times" to hear "the flow of I" even through a medium so ancient as the Gregorian monks or so unpromising as Eddy Duchin or so complex as Duke Ellington, the man lauded today for having achieved the Toomeresque ideal of creating a music that is unmistakably African American but is also, in the words of John Edward Hasse, "beyond category."[54] And while readers may not always have heard this expansiveness in the folk songs of *Cane*, the literary record that Toomer left behind is no less audible and its musical calls no less inviting for that.

Overtones, Undertones: *The Weary Blues* and *Fine Clothes to the Jew*

In his epochal essay "The Negro Artist and the Racial Mountain" of 1926, Langston Hughes recommends that the "younger Negro artists" embrace and contribute to a distinctively racial aesthetic "without fear or shame."[55] The best of the rising generation's works, he writes, will be those that aim to be as strident as "the blare of Negro Jazz bands and the bellowing voice of Bessie Smith," and Hughes's current standing as the most eminent poet of the Harlem Renaissance—perhaps of the entire African American literary canon—is in many ways a result of his having so effectively followed his own advice. A man of many talents and influences, Hughes distinguished himself over his long career in nearly every conceivable literary form, ranging from the libretto to the children's tale. But it was the song verse, and in particular the blues verse, that he wrote with the greatest consistency: the 1995 edition of Hughes's *Collected Poems* contains more than thirty titled blues and scores of poems besides that obey blues form, an output comparable to and in some cases larger than that of such pioneering early twentieth-century blues songwriters as Blind Lemon Jefferson, Charley Patton, and Robert Johnson.

There are several reasons the blues appealed to Hughes, among them the music's ability to express despair, stoicism, absurdity, and humor all in the same moment. In his 1941 essay "Songs Called the Blues," Hughes writes that the paradoxical spirit of the blues reflects the place and mind-set of the modern black American, with such music often marked by "the kind of humor that laughs to keep from crying" and therefore serving as a fitting art for a "beaten, but unbeatable" people, those "Loud-mouthed laughers in the hands/Of Fate" whom he praises in his poetry.[56]

He then offers the following stanza as an illustration of the emotional complexity that the best blues—and by extension his best poems—are capable of:

> Goin' down to de railroad,
> Lay ma head on de track.
> I'm goin' to de railroad,
> Lay ma head on the track—
> But if I see de train a-comin'
> I'm gonna jerk it back![57]

This verse and the prominence it enjoys in Hughes's essay point to a second reason for his attraction to the blues: they provided a preexisting canon of sorts for him to locate his poetry within and in relation to. As Adam Gussow has shown, Hughes alludes here to one of "the most representative stanzas in the blues lyric tradition," and in so doing he associates himself and his writings with a long cultural lineage.[58] Hughes most likely took the lines from "Trouble in Mind," a blues that had been published in 1926. But the words and analogues for them had existed long before and been taken up by artists in a variety of earlier contexts, among them Mamie Smith's "Crazy Blues" of 1920 (the record that first opened the studio door to black women vocalists); the spiritual "I'm a-Trouble in De Mind" (which had appeared in the landmark anthology *Slave Songs of the United States* in 1867); and the distant, all but lost folk practice that had predated and given rise to all of these. This blues verse thus expresses not just a singular instance of emotion but also encapsulates a more broadly felt sensibility, one that transcends generations, media, and circumstances. It is by extension easy to see why it would have been inspiring and useful to Hughes, whose first great poem, "The Negro Speaks of Rivers," had made the case that the peoples of the Euphrates, Congo, Nile, and Mississippi were all bound to one another by a trans-historical, unifying racial spirit.

There is, however, another contemporary echo of "Trouble in Mind" that could be added to this musical genealogy, one whose existence raises uncomfortable questions about Hughes's blues aesthetic and its connection to race: a vaudeville number with the insulting title of "Nigger Blues." Consider, for example, the white singer Al Bernard's 1919 recording of the piece ◐, in which he performs verse after verse of what could be called either blues conventions or blues clichés, culminating in a familiar image:

> I'm gonna lay my head, I'm gonna lay my head
> Down on some railroad line
> I'm gonna lay my head

Down on some railroad line
Let the Santa Fe
Pacify my mind.

Bernard's performance alters the lyrical content, humor, and fundamental aims of Hughes's representative blues verse in several important ways. The bluesman of "Trouble in Mind" is ultimately in control of his suicidal impulses and may only have been ribbing his listeners in discussing them, but the singer of "Nigger Blues" plans simply to die at song's end, with Bernard's jaunty, even smart-alecky delivery suggesting that the death of the song's protagonist is a matter of little consequence. Whereas the lyric Hughes invokes is meant to be indicative of the black tradition, it becomes associated with the blackface one when Bernard sings it, the conceit being that Bernard is engaged in burlesque and ventriloquism rather than anything like self-expression. And the larger, chilly function of "Nigger Blues" is to show just how easily one race's culture can be transposed into an explicitly racist framework. Indeed, if the sound of "Nigger Blues" is already in one's ear, it can be very hard to avoid reading a stanza of "Trouble in Mind"—or any other similarly patterned blues, for that matter—without involuntarily "hearing" it sung in Bernard's voice.

Bernard sings at one point that "you can call the blues any old thing you please" on his record, and the infinite adaptability that this lyric suggests leads to a peculiar yet frequently overlooked problem in discussions of both music history and Hughes's poetry: the blues, a music synonymous with blackness in the national imagination and perhaps the most recognizably African American song form ever created, was taken up by and made popular among whites almost from the moment it became commercially available. There is little indication that the blues had commanded much of an audience beyond southern blacks before W. C. Handy's first publications of them in 1912, but their subsequent entry into the mass market in that year irrevocably changed the music's profile. Long before the appearance of Hughes's essays, his earliest poems, and even the first significant blues records by black artists, the blues were performed incessantly by white musicians like Bernard, and by the end of the 1910s no less a fan than King George V had heard the "Characteristic Blues." Few Americans at the time believed, of course, that whites had invented the blues or that they enjoyed any kind of unique connection to them. As even so offensive a song as "Nigger Blues" makes plain, the blues were then presumed—much as they are today—to have grown out of the black experience, and they were usually discussed and marketed accordingly. Nevertheless, whites were very much involved in the form, whether in its production or consumption, for more than a decade before Hughes theorized a uniquely African American blues aesthetic in the mid-1920s. Then as now, there was debate over the merits of white participation in the blues, but the idea that such participation was widespread was never in dispute.[59]

On first gloss, the fact of the blues having had a wide and multiracial audience before the 1920s poses a problem for Hughes's art and the interpretation of it. He goes out of his way in his "Mountain" essay, after all, to claim the music as one of several "distinctly racial" art forms, thereby suggesting that his blues poetry is part of an "honest American Negro literature" that rejects white norms.[60] Moreover, virtually every critical study of Hughes since 1926 has been predicated on the unexamined assumption that the blues culture he invoked was essentially homogenous, with most scholars asserting that Hughes achieved a superior degree of racial "authenticity" in his poetry that was "guaranteed by the form, the rhythmic stresses, the rhyme scheme, and the tropes of the blues itself, a musical genre associated with African Americans."[61] Such a syllogism quickly breaks down, of course, if one takes into account the fact that the blues have long been among the more mobile musical forms in American life, available to any number of racial groups and able to impart a great many, often contradictory meanings that may or may not be "authentic." So too must Hughes's claim to have evaded "Caucasian patterns" and "the mold of American standardization" in his blues and jazz poetry be reevaluated in light of the blues' cosmopolitan character, its multiracial reception, and its far-flung, even global popularity.[62] What happens to the vital connection Hughes articulates between poetic form and racial self-assertion if, for example, white readers have an easier time identifying one of his verses as a blues than they do Countee Cullen's "Yet Do I Wonder" as an English sonnet? And what if they prefer the blues?

The answer is that the musical expression of race in Hughes's blues poetry becomes considerably more complex, and that his poetic project becomes even more interesting than it has traditionally been given credit for being. Hughes's blues works of the 1920s, far from being straightforward literary adaptations of an unambiguously black idiom, in fact meditate on the often-fluctuating degree of race feeling that musical forms can inspire, and they represent an extended attempt at ascertaining what sort of racial boundaries—if any—exist to delimit those feelings in listeners. As shall be seen in the pages that follow, Hughes invokes the blues to different effects in his first two volumes of poetry, *The Weary Blues* of 1926 and *Fine Clothes to the Jew* of 1927, but in both cases his musical aesthetic accounts for and is made more resonant by the possibility of multiracial responses to it. *The Weary Blues* reflects the expansive cultural and racial framework that the blues had long existed in, with Hughes calling on his readers to participate in an open, shared musical form and, in so doing, to experience Toomeresque sensations of indeterminacy. *Fine Clothes to the Jew*, conversely, is inflected by and helps enact a larger movement of racial and musical authentication that was redefining what the "real" blues entailed during the 1920s, with Hughes now presenting the music as uniquely black and inviting readers to empathize with specifically African American subjects. In both cases and over the rest of his career, however, Hughes appears to have understood that blues form could never be entirely owned by a particular race, and he seems to have written his poems with this flexibility in mind. At some points in his life he celebrated the universality of the blues and at others despaired over their appropriation, but he was always attuned to the ambiguities at the heart of this "distinctly racial" music.

The protean character that Hughes heard in the blues is most immediately evident in his affinity for the phrase "Weary Blues," which provided the title for his first collection of poems, for a subsection of fifteen poems within that collection, and for the first poem within that subsection. "The Weary Blues" poem, an account of a late-night encounter with a Harlem blues musician and the song he sings, helped launch Hughes's career when it won a 1925 literary contest sponsored by *Opportunity*, and it has since proven one of Hughes's most enduring works. It also doubles as a model for how one might go about interacting with Hughes's musical pieces more generally, as it both questions what it means for music to be adapted into poetic form and suggests the ways in which readers of such poetry can take part in its production. The action of the poem cleverly echoes the act of reading it, for just as one might turn a page and encounter "The Weary Blues" in written form, so too does the poem's speaker wander Harlem and stumble upon a pianist playing a song referred to, of course, as "those Weary Blues":

> In a deep song voice with a melancholy tone
> I heard that Negro sing, that old piano moan—
> > "Ain't got nobody in all this world,
> > Ain't got nobody but ma self.
> > I's gwine to quit ma frownin'
> > And put ma troubles on the shelf."
> Thump, thump, thump, went his foot on the floor.
> He played a few chords then he sang some more—
> > "I got the Weary Blues
> > And I can't be satisfied.
> > Got the Weary Blues

And can't be satisfied—
I ain't happy no mo'
And I wish that I had died."
And far into the night he crooned that tune.
The stars went out and so did the moon.
The singer stopped playing and went to bed
While the Weary Blues echoed through his head.
He slept like a rock or a man that's dead.

(*Poems* 23–24)

In later life, Hughes would claim that "The Weary Blues" was a relatively simple piece "about a working man who sang the blues all night and then went to bed and slept like a rock. That was all."[63] But it has generated more critical commentary than perhaps anything else he ever wrote, in large part because its obvious musicality raises a host of questions about the intersection of the written and the spoken word, of the relationship of performers to audiences, and of the appropriateness of calling "The Weary Blues" a "poem" at all.

Houston A. Baker has compellingly argued that blues and blues-inspired literature tend to dissolve the boundaries that separate musicians from their listeners and authors from their readers, with blues texts creating a liberating aesthetic space in which all manner of people may "freely improvise their own distinctive tropes for cultural explanation."[64] Granting this, "The Weary Blues" emerges as an exemplary blues text, as it seems motivated primarily by a desire for inclusivity and satisfies that desire by giving readers the opportunity to participate, quite literally, in the performance that the poem describes. "The Weary Blues," after all, can be sung almost as easily as it can be read, and its musical accessibility lies in its use of what has come to be known as the classic "AAB" blues verse pattern: an idea is introduced ("I got the Weary Blues/And I can't be satisfied"), then repeated a single time in slightly altered form, and then responded to with a final rejoinder ("I ain't happy no mo'/And I wish that I had died"). As a great many readers no doubt know already, this structure is by far the most famous of all blues forms today, and it was similarly familiar to audiences in the years before Hughes wrote. The question thus becomes whether Hughes's poem, because it can be sung by readers, in fact ought to be, and if anything is lost when it is allowed to remain silent on the page.

"The Weary Blues" is of course an effective piece of writing whether it is sung out loud or not, but Hughes, a frequent performer of his works, seems to have had an especially keen sense for how vocalization and nonlinguistic sound can energize poetics.⁶⁵ And if Hughes in fact hoped that readers would make his musical poems audible, then his choice of blues form was particularly appropriate, for it has long been considered a uniquely inviting and singable music. As has often been noted, much of the blues stanza's appeal lies in its combination of familiar regularity and adventurous unpredictability, in its set parameters on the one hand and the possibilities it allows for departing from those parameters on the other. At least in its popular AAB form, the blues is regularly plotted and intensely repetitive. Yet this structure contains a great deal of room for improvisation, with the seeming simplicity of the blues having given rise to an extraordinarily diverse range of melodic, lyrical, and timbral expression over the last century. Indeed, in the year that Hughes's first volume of poetry was published, W. C. Handy and Abbe Niles's seminal anthology *Blues* praised the music on precisely these grounds, with Niles citing the music's seemingly limitless accessibility: "Anyone who understands the form can compose a blues tune; try it on your piano. If you are merely 'anyone,' it will be worthless, but it will be blues. . . . [T]he blues [are] essentially a mold, filled, emptied and refilled, like a child's seashore toy."⁶⁶ Few popular forms, according to Niles, offer so much helpful direction to the would-be musician and yet give such free rein for imaginative performance, and while one might say that all of Hughes's musical poetry of the 1920s—whether jazzy, folksy, or simply lyrical—is singable in one way or another, his blues works are especially so.

At least by Niles's definition, any blues poem in AAB form would be easy for a reader to perform, but Hughes goes even further out of his way to involve his audience in "The Weary Blues" by placing an actual song at its center. One of the most surprising oversights in Hughes scholarship over the years has been its lack of attention to the fact that, more than a decade before Hughes's first volume of poetry was published, the phrase "Weary Blues" had also served as the title of a popular composition by Artie Matthews, published as sheet music in 1915. Having appeared just after Handy's first blues works captivated the nation, "Weary Blues" had enough of a profile by the 1920s that many of Hughes's first readers would have had some version of it, and perhaps more than one, in mind before encountering it in a literary context: in the years between its publication and the appearance of Hughes's first poems, the "Weary Blues" had been performed by such luminaries as Jelly Roll Morton, Bessie Smith, Louis Armstrong, and many more besides. Obviously, the existence of Matthews's prefabricated "Weary Blues" melody and the many preexisting interpretations of it would have had made Hughes's "Weary Blues" all the easier for his 1920s audiences to vocalize, providing them with any number of models for their own performances.

But while the presence of an actual "Weary Blues" analogue inflects Hughes's poem in certain ways, it does not limit the improvisatory possibilities of his literary blues, as Matthews's composition had already been much adapted, even radically so, by musicians in the years before Hughes took it up. If the Morton recording is any indication, interpreters often ignored Matthews's suggestion that his piece be played at a "slow" tempo.[67] ◓ Even more significantly, the incursion of language— any language at all—into Matthews's "Weary Blues" necessarily makes a new song of the old one, as it had originally been published as a purely instrumental work, a blues without words. For his part, Hughes said that his lyrics for the "Weary Blues" had been lifted from a musician he had once heard "way back in Lawrence, Kansas, when I was a kid," but his verse was but one of many to be attached to the "Weary Blues" during the period.[68] And just as myriad verses had already been associated with the "Weary Blues" before Hughes took it up in poetry, so too had the song's title already traveled far beyond any songwriter's attempts at claiming it. Allusions to the "Weary Blues" were so widespread in Hughes's day that Niles thought the phrase was a broadly generic term,[69] evident throughout the folk and popular traditions: consider, for example, Handy's novelty of the first world war, "The Kaiser's Got the Blues (He's Got Those Weary Blues)," published in 1917. As was the case with "Trouble in Mind," a single, resonant blues phrase in Hughes's poem inevitably draws it into a preexisting and ever-expanding network of musical forms and ideas, allowing him to make a new contribution to the blues tradition and to present readers with the opportunity of doing the same.

The possibility, even the imperative of the reader's working in concert with Hughes and vocalizing his "Weary Blues" is further reinforced by the other parts of his poem, many of which serve to elide difference in various ways and suggest an overall aesthetic of collaboration. As has been frequently noted by critics, "The Weary Blues" begins with what a grammar stickler might identify as a misplaced modifier but the student of Hughes would call a crucial and productive moment of poetic ambiguity:

> Droning a drowsy syncopated tune,
> Rocking back and forth to a mellow croon,
>   I heard a Negro play.
> Down on Lenox Avenue the other night
> By the pale dull pallor of an old gas light
>   He did a lazy sway . . . .
>   He did a lazy sway . . . .
> To the tune o' those Weary Blues.

> (*Poems* 23)

Situationally it seems obvious that it is the "Negro" musician—identified as a pianist in a later line—who performs the "syncopated tune," but the subject of Hughes's first sentence is in fact the roving "I," with this slippage raising the possibility that the poem's speaker is in fact "Droning" and "Rocking" rather than just bearing witness to these actions. The distinction between performer and audience, "Negro" and "I," is thus collapsed, and as the poem progresses, Hughes's treatment of the musicking act only grows more ambiguous. Even as the voice that sings "those Weary Blues" is set off in quotation marks, for example, the speaker's description of the performance slips into a jingly, anapestic rhythm that is itself musical: "Thump, thump, thump, went his foot on the floor./He played a few chords then he sang some more" (*Poems* 23). The overall effect is one of addition and accumulation, as though Hughes is suggesting that the "Weary Blues" not only constitutes the AAB verse that announces itself as such ("I got the Weary Blues") but also includes the observations and reactions of the poetic consciousness—hence, the appropriateness of the larger poem's also bearing the subsuming title of "The Weary Blues." Indeed, by poem's end all boundaries between audience and performer appear to have been erased, with Hughes's final lines achieving a heretofore unapparent omniscience in describing "the singer," his interior state, and the ways in which "the Weary Blues echoed through his head" before he nods off to sleep (*Poems* 24). And one might further ask: which "singer," exactly? The reference could by this point be to the "Negro" pianist, the speaker, or the reader, each a plausible participant in the creation of the "Weary Blues." Ultimately, it is the impossibility of definitively answering this question that shows just how attuned Hughes's poem is to the improvisatory, inclusive possibilities so often associated with his chosen music.

As one might expect, Hughes's studied vagueness in this and others of his blues poems has attracted considerable scholarly interest over the years, with most critics taking Hughes's larger authorial project to be the consideration and resolution of cultural dualities. "The Weary Blues" and its musical ilk have been variously found to be merging the literary tradition with the oral one, the cosmopolitan with the folk, and, in a popular strain of recent scholarship, normative categories of sexuality with ostensibly transgressive ones.[70] But even in the case of so inclusive and flexible a poet, there is one duality in the critical conversation on Hughes that has been allowed to stand more or less unchallenged, namely, the opposition of blackness and whiteness as expressed in musical form. In nearly every study of Hughes ever undertaken, the blues are invariably held up as a distinctly African American music that presents a stark racial contrast to some fundamentally different literary mode of expression, usually coded as white. *The Weary Blues*, because it contains both blues and Western lyric forms, is therefore said to function as a kind of staging ground for various, contending racial aesthetics. The mistake here is the assumption that the blues represent an entirely "black" ingredient in the mixed cultural milieu that Hughes's volume represents and depicts, as the blues—at least as Hughes had encountered them in 1910s and 1920s America—could be said to have been a mixed cultural form already. Indeed, even if Hughes had wanted to present the blues as a distinctively and exclusively African American music in his works, the music's multiracial reception in the decade leading up to his first blues poems would have rendered his hope a practical impossibility.

Close attention to a poem such as "The Weary Blues," however, illustrates that Hughes seems to have believed at this early point in his career that sensations of racial indeterminacy were key functions of the blues, perhaps even the primary source of their allure. The speaker of Hughes's poem identifies the "Weary Blues" as emanating "from a black man's soul" (*Poems* 23), yet the poem as a whole is designed to distribute the music of that "soul" as broadly as possible. The poem's speaker—whose race and gender Hughes quite deliberately declines to identify— mirrors the actions of the "Negro" and may be a participant in his act of song; so

Miguel Covarrubias's cover art for the early editions of *The Weary Blues*, emphasizing the blackness of Hughes's imagined blues musician. Copyright 1926 by Alfred A. Knopf, a division of Random House, Inc., from *The Weary Blues* by Langston Hughes. Used by permission of Alfred A. Knopf, a division of Random House, Inc.; and The Henry Ransom Center at the University of Texas at Austin.

too does the poem's accessible AAB form allow the reader to mirror the speaker's mirroring, to add a third voice to an already layered performance. The effect of all this is that "The Weary Blues" universalizes a racially specific music, allowing an audience of persons similar only in musical awareness to access the song, and therefore the "soul," of the poem's black subject (see Images 7 and 8). An action, a mood, and a perspective are thus shared by a "Negro," a poetic consciousness, and a reader in a musical-literary moment, with Hughes's poem presenting this uni-fication as both exhilarating (witness the speaker's ejaculation of "O Blues!") and invasive, even sinister (see the speaker's eerie final description of the pianist as "a man that's dead") (*Poems* 23–24). Crucially, however, the blues do not represent a single, homogeneous half of a black-and-white duality, one that awaits resolution through Hughes's poetry. As they function here, the blues effectively create and contain duality in and of themselves.

Hughes's treatment of the blues is wider ranging than scholars have tradition-ally recognized, but in depicting the blues as a malleable and potentially interra-cial art, Hughes was in many ways simply being faithful to his historical moment.

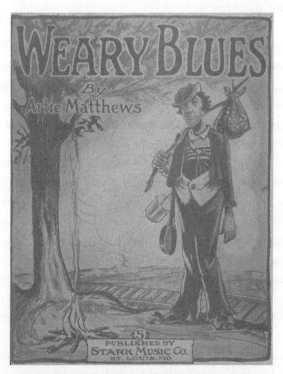

The cover art for Artie Matthews's "Weary Blues" sheet music, which appears to depict a down-and-out Caucasian. Used by permission, Crouch Fine Arts Library, Baylor University, Waco, Texas.

Racial ambiguity of the sort found in his version of the "Weary Blues" was in fact central to blues culture at the time, or at least the blues culture that most Americans were conversant with during Hughes's early life. Many of the most popular blues compositions relied only partially on the famous AAB verse structure, sometimes surrounding it with musical idioms associated with other nationalities: the "St. Louis Blues," a Handy piece of 1914 that Hughes considered to be one of America's greatest songs, used a tango to preface what Handy referred to as a "low-down blues,"[71] as can be heard in a version by the white singer Marion Harris from 1920.◐ Moreover, white artists who crossed the blues color line were objects of considerable interest during the 1920s: Niles praised Harris in his *Blues* anthology for having convinced thousands of African American record buyers that she was "one of them," and he made an epigraph for the volume out of F. Scott Fitzgerald's reference to the "Beale Street Blues" in *The Great Gatsby*.[72] Nor was Fitzgerald the only white literary figure to engage with the blues in these years, for writers such as Carl Sandburg, Clement Wood, and Dorothy Parker also penned what have been identified as blues verses around the same time that Hughes did.

Perhaps most significant of all, a great many blues recordings of the period became popular precisely because they were so obviously and explicitly "inauthentic" when it came to the issue of racial identity, so determined—as Hughes seems also to have been—to make the blues a music of interracial possibility. In 1917, for example, the white singer Marie Cahill had a hit with "The Dallas Blues," a song distinctive not so much for its relatively conventional music and lyrics as for the minute-long anecdote Cahill tells as an introduction, recounting the "Weary Blues"-like circumstances under which she allegedly discovered and learned what she identifies as a specifically black tune.◐ According to Cahill's testimony on her recording, "The Dallas Blues" was originally a ditty that she "heard a darky sing down in Dallas, Texas," which she then "repeats" in a peppy, even chirpy vaudeville style, with the obvious limitations of race and gender posing no obstacle to her assuming the bluesman's persona. This deliberately absurd song is, of course, deeply rooted and complicit in a long history of racist caricature and cultural exploitation, and yet it and other such pieces from the period are also oddly suggestive on the subject of race as expressed in song, at least from a musicological perspective. According to Richard Middleton, early twentieth-century performances of the blues by whites such as Cahill can create something like a musical, racial, and historical palimpsest: listeners are obliged simultaneously to attend to "the voice we actually hear, the voice [the performer] wants us to imagine, and the voice blotted out but that we know is there, somewhere, could we but find it."[73] Cahill's performance, that is to say, is able to evoke multiple and otherwise irreconcilable voices within a famously flexible musical format, and while her "Dallas Blues" unquestionably differs from Hughes's "Weary Blues" in its intentions and motivations, the peculiarly fluid effect she aims to have on audiences is not altogether dissimilar from the one that his poem accomplishes.

The problem with this musical and racial open-endedness, however, is that Hughes's control over his poem is much diminished as a result. As has already been demonstrated in regard to Toomer's use of the spirituals in *Cane*, literary invocations of racial music are inevitably shaped by readers for their own purposes, and so the possibility of Hughes's blues being vocalized in what might be thought of as "white" styles—and perhaps in explicitly racist ones—cannot be altogether ignored. A musical rendering of "The Weary Blues" that respected Hughes's tastes and intentions during the 1920s would in all likelihood sound something like a performance by Bessie Smith, the singer who, as Steven C. Tracy's study of Hughes and the blues makes clear, was a particular favorite of his at the time. But as disheartening as it may be to imagine Hughes's 1920s readers setting his poem to the tune of "The Dallas Blues" or the execrable "Nigger Blues," it is impossible to say that such a thing never occurred, or even that it was unlikely.

There is every reason to believe, however, that from the beginning Hughes was aware of the broad reach that his blues poetry would have; that he was not troubled by the possibility of its being embraced, even co-opted, by whites; and that he wrote with this musical-literary adaptability in mind. Turning to the other musical poems in *The Weary Blues* volume—usually classified as jazz works, but still included under the sectional heading of "The Weary Blues"—one finds unusual sensitivity on Hughes's part to the polysemic quality of song and the ways in which the same sound can impart different meanings to different listeners at any given moment. Indeed, a significant number of these pieces seem concerned primarily with depicting the multiply-voiced quality of music, the vital role that audiences play in constructing its meaning, and the degree to which a piece like "The Weary Blues" must change whenever it finds a new reader, listener, or singer.

Consider, for example, "Negro Dancers," a poem whose tone depends almost entirely on its readers' preexisting assumptions about race and its relation to musical performance. It begins with the following exhortation, presumably sung or chanted by one of the eponymous dancers:

> "Me an' ma baby's
> Got two mo' ways,
> Two mo' ways to do de buck!

> Da, da,
> Da, da, da!
> Two mo' ways to do de buck!"

(Poems 25)

The message here is fairly simple, a revelation that what has been seen and heard in this performance is only a hint of a larger array of possibilities and "ways." The tone of these lines, however, is difficult to fix, with the poem able to be interpreted either as an excited promise of further showmanship or a mocking, insider's declaration that there will always be aspects of "de buck" that will elude the reader. The dancer's scat-sung declaration of "Da, da,/Da da da!" is similarly inscrutable, presenting an object for interpretation only to suggest the ultimate futility of the task, not unlike the intonations of "DA" at the conclusion of T. S. Eliot's *The Waste Land*.[74] Nor is the problem of fixing the poem's meaning made any easier when the next stanzas bring Hughes's "Negro Dancers" into racial relief by introducing a cohort of whites:

> Soft light on the tables,
> Music gay,
> Brown-skin steppers
> In a cabaret.
>
> White folks, laugh!
> White folks, pray!

Why the command that whites "laugh" and "pray" in this context? Is it an invitation to a musically inspired, racially inclusive ecstasy? Or does it point to feelings of detachment and condescension, for which these pleasure-seeking whites are to be damned? Critics have reached both conclusions in discussing this poem, but the point seems to be that no one explanation is any more likely than the other, and that the poem's overall mood hinges on how much credence the reader is willing to give to the idea that African American song can meaningfully unite the races.

Hughes traffics in musical and racial irony in "Negro Dancers," and others of his jazz poems in *The Weary Blues* seem to delight in being similarly slippery: "Harlem Night Club," for example, is both alluring and ominous in describing the manner in which "White girls' eyes/Call gay black boys./Black boys' lips/Grin jungle joys" (*Poems* 28). But Hughes's musical ambiguity is also deployed in the service of melancholy, as in "Cabaret" and its fleeting sense of a meaning just missed in song:

> Does a jazz-band ever sob?
> They say a jazz-band's gay.
> Yet as the vulgar dancers whirled
> And the wan night wore away,
> One said she heard the jazz-band sob
> When the little dawn was grey.
>
> *(Poems* 27)

That which is "gay" to one listener can also "sob" to this woman, and while it is impossible to verify whether the emotion she heard was in fact communicated by the music, it is the jazz-band's ability to signify in multiple registers that provides the occasion for the poem. And by the end of "The Weary Blues" section of *The Weary Blues* volume, the open-ended pursuit of musical meaning has come to be of greater interest than the actual acquisition of it, as in "Lenox Avenue: Midnight" and its suggestion that music both expresses the world and is a world unto itself:

> The rhythm of life
> Is a jazz rhythm,
> Honey.
>
> The gods are laughing at us.
> The broken heart of love,
> The weary, weary heart of pain,—
>   Overtones,
>   Undertones,
> To the rumble of street cars,
> To the swish of rain.
>
> *(Poems* 32)

Years before Ralph Ellison's famous notion that a musical black voice could speak for all of America on the "lower frequencies,"[75] Hughes finds life to be a "jazz rhythm" that provides unification even as it suggests multitudinous possibility. Especially significant is Hughes's evocation of the "Overtones" and "Undertones" of musical existence, which from one perspective alludes to the complex physical properties of sound: as Robert Jourdain has explained, a musical tone is not a single, vibrating frequency but rather a stacked collection of several mathematically related ones called "overtones," and while most of us "pass our entire lives without realizing that we're hearing many sounds" in apparently isolated ones, those who listen closely enough can hear them nonetheless.[76] So too does Hughes's choice of terminology inevitably connect the composition of sound with the task of locating meaning within the "jazz rhythm": fully experiencing life requires that one be attuned to its overtones and undertones, to its elusive particularities and shadings. "Lenox Avenue: Midnight" celebrates unity and diversity in music and life alike, and it should therefore come as no surprise that the blues emerges in Hughes's early poetry as a malleable musical form, one that black and white readers can populate with overtones and undertones of their own choosing. As he would put it in his "Racial Mountain" essay a few months after *The Weary Blues* was published, "the relations between Negroes and whites" in 1920s America were themselves characterized by "innumerable overtones and undertones" that made them a worthy subject for literature,[77] and it therefore stands to reason that such relations would need a capacious, inclusive music for their expression.

Hughes's flexibility on the subject of the blues would be quickly tested, however, because he wrote his first poems in the same historical moment that the blues—or at least what were coming to be thought of as the "authentic" blues—were being redefined as southern in origin, folksy in sensibility, and above all else, specifically African American in performance. It was a pronounced, even revolutionary shift in musical understanding that was then under way, and not simply because the racial boundaries of the blues were being shored up. Those who sought in this period to re-brand the blues as a distinctively black folk music faced skepticism on several fronts, including from some of the most prominent advocates for African American culture. *The New Negro* anthology of 1925, for example, had dedicated itself to finding "the very heart of the folk-spirit" of black Americans and yet had rather conspicuously declined to locate it in the blues, with Alain Locke and many others of the period believing such songs to have been shaped by Tin Pan Alley and the mass market instead.[78] Another sticking point was the problem of the historical record: then as now, there was very little reliable testimony indicating that the blues existed in their familiar AAB form before 1912, the year, inconveniently, of Handy's first blues publication. Abundant evidence existed to prove that the spirituals had been born of the black experience under slavery and thus had been a "folk" music long before achieving national popularity, but the same could not be shown of the blues. For much of the 1920s, then, blues promoters found themselves in the position of having to locate or plausibly theorize a past for a music that struck many as being essentially modern.

Advocates for the blues were eventually successful, however, in arguing that the music's cosmopolitan profile in the 1910s and 1920s had been an aberration, the result of white popularization and commercial exploitation. The movement reached something of an apex in 1930 with Sterling Brown's essay "The Blues as Folk Poetry," which defined the "real" rural blues in stark opposition to the "urbanized fake folk things" and "cabaret appetizers" that had been the rage in earlier decades.[79] Brown's aim was to redefine the blues in such a way as to cast musicians such as Bernard, Harris, and Cahill as illegitimate interlopers to the idiom, and it is a testament to his persuasiveness that he and others were ultimately so successful in changing the terms under which the music would be and is now discussed. As Francis Davis has observed, when modern audiences imagine a blues singer of the 1920s, the image they now see tends to be "that of a man in overalls holding a guitar within shouting distance of a cotton plantation, not the confusing image of a woman in sequins fronting an entourage of jazz musicians under a tent or a proscenium arch."[80] Practically speaking, decades of popular blues history and performance have been all but erased from the nation's collective memory, largely because the folk blues narrative delineated by Brown and others of the period has become the standard one for most musically minded Americans.

As the eminent blues historian Paul Oliver has put it, the search for the "real" blues and its "true" roots was and remains inevitably self-defeating: "When, or indeed how, the blues emerged is a question which has provoked much speculation but, not surprisingly, no incontestable evidence," he observes.[81] In the 1920s, however, the urge to define the blues as folk music and to locate their primal origins was fueled by the same anxieties about modernization and the influence of popular culture on American life that had shadowed Toomer and *Cane*, anxieties that once again were shared by a remarkably eclectic group of social observers. Aesthetic primitivists lamented, as did D. H. Lawrence in an overview of Jazz Age novels, that "the eternal Negroid soul, black and glistening and touched with awfulness and with mystery," was in fact a chimera, with "a gramophone grinding over the old records" in its place.[82] Anthropologists such as Zora Neale Hurston worried that southern blacks were in the process of having their "Negroness . . . rubbed off by close contact with white culture" and watered down by "the phonograph and its blues."[83] White collectors of folk blues such as John and Alan Lomax visited prisons in the hopes of finding songwriters who had been shielded from the pernicious influence of "canned music."[84] And as ever, record companies proved remarkably adept at addressing the very problem that they were accused of creating, sending more teams of field recorders to the South than any other institution once it became clear that there was a public hunger for (and corresponding willingness to purchase) the blues in archaic-sounding styles.

As was also the case in regard to the spirituals during this decade, definitions of racial "authenticity" were always at stake in discussions of the folk blues, and

Hughes was inevitably swept up in the conversation. In a 1927 essay he showed himself to be up on the latest anthropological blues studies and expressed particular admiration for Dorothy Scarborough's *On the Trail of Negro Folk Songs* (1925), which had dubbed the blues "authentic folk-music" in spite of the fact that their popularity had in earlier years made them "seem to have little relation" to rural black culture.[85] Hughes's friendship with Carl Van Vechten, meanwhile, drew him away from the cabarets of Harlem and what Van Vechten called their mere "transcribed versions of folksongs," with the men's letters to one another in this period replete with verses and titles of what they thought to be more genuine blues works.[86] Perhaps most significant of all, however, was the sense of dissatisfaction, even embarrassment, that Hughes appears to have begun to feel about the musical inclusiveness of his earlier poetry and the musical liberties that his literary blues had allowed audiences to take. Particularly galling was a Washington, DC, reading he gave under Locke's stewardship shortly after the publication of *The Weary Blues*, which a Hughes biography describes in telling language:

> In a daring move, [Hughes] had selected a Seventh Street bluesman, funky and unfettered, to howl during the intermission. Locke, however, had thought of all the respectable black folk and the whites who would come, then sneaked in—to Hughes' intense annoyance—a housebroken Negro. The man played, according to Langston, "nice music, but nothing grotesque and sad at the same time, nothing primitive, nothing very 'different.'"[87]

Hughes, it would seem, was coming to believe that there was a limit to how much the blues ought to be adapted or changed to suit other people's tastes, and his musical allegiances were becoming more fixed. No more the cosmopolitan blues that he had heard in the clubs of Harlem and Paris; it was the "primitive" music of "the ordinary Negroes," the "folks who work hard for a living with their hands," that was beginning to interest him.[88]

Thus came an emphatic musical shift in Hughes's next volume of poetry, *Fine Clothes to the Jew*, published the year after *The Weary Blues*. This second collection features considerably more blues verses than did the first, which is perhaps to be expected in a work whose title refers to a man reduced to pawning his valuables. Equally noteworthy is Hughes's attempt to define the blues as well as deploy them, as is illustrated by the text's curatorial introductory paragraph:

> The first eight and the last nine poems in this book are written after the manner of the Negro folk-songs known as *Blues*. The *Blues*, unlike the

Spirituals, have a strict poetic pattern: one long line repeated and a third line to rhyme with the first two. Sometimes the second line in repetition is slightly changed and sometimes, but very seldom, it is omitted. The mood of the *Blues* is almost always despondency, but when they are sung people laugh.

(*Poems* 73)

Few likely readers of Hughes's book would have needed this primer, especially if they were the aforementioned "ordinary Negroes" to whom he believed the music most legitimately belonged. But if one bears in mind the years of popularity the blues had enjoyed and the multivalence Hughes had previously attributed to them, his explanation comes to seem less strange. In its 1920s context, this paragraph can be read as part of a concerted attempt to establish a music's pedigree, with Hughes introducing a set of standards and criteria that can distinguish the authentic blues—crucially, "Negro folk-songs"—from the other kind. So too does Hughes's preface serve as a self-correction, as his 1927 definition of the blues excludes the very sorts of verse that he had featured in "The Weary Blues" the year before: by the new standard of *Fine Clothes to the Jew,* the "Negro" bluesman of Hughes's earlier poem strays into non-folk territory by deploying a stanza not in AAB form ("Ain't got nobody in all this world/Ain't got nobody but ma self . . ."). A blues that aspires to formal complexity beyond a certain "strict poetic pattern"—a blues in the style of Handy, for example—is now argued to lie outside of the folk tradition, and it does not take much of an imaginative leap to conclude that Hughes might have been second-guessing his own, earlier stabs at blues writing.

With Hughes's turn toward a more rigidly defined blues form also came a turn away from the racial ambiguity enacted by "The Weary Blues," with the musical works of *Fine Clothes to the Jew* written so as to be obviously African American in origin, language, and delivery. Also gone are the framing devices, layers of mediation, and perspectival multiplicity of the earlier poems, with Hughes purporting here to transcribe the songs of singular people as sung by them and no one else. (In this, his blues now resemble poetic forms of direct address like the dramatic monologue.) See, for example, this verse from "Gal's Cry for a Dying Lover," whose third line goes out of its way to clarify any lingering doubts about whether the singer is, in fact, black:

> Black an' ugly
> But he sho do treat me kind.
> I'm black an' ugly

But he sho do treat me kind.
High-in-heaben Jesus,
Please don't take this man o' mine.

(*Poetry* 110)

Fine Clothes to the Jew also has a new grimness of tone and contains an implicit rebuke to those who might think of the blues as a frivolous, merely entertaining music. Hughes does not entirely abandon the emotional complexity—the mixture of optimism and melancholy—that had characterized his earlier "Weary Blues," and neither is he entirely bereft of humor. But the volume is markedly stark nonetheless, as in this blues verse from "Suicide":

Ma sweet good man has
Packed his trunk and left.
Ma sweet good man has
Packed his trunk and left.
Nobody to love me:
I'm gonna kill ma self.

(*Poetry* 76)

Finally, Hughes often works to prevent the possibility of a reader's identifying with his singers, with some of them so blatantly offensive in their behaviors as to be positively repulsive. See, for example, the singer of "Bad Man," whose blues response to having the blues is enough to make the reader want to avoid the music entirely:

I beats ma wife an'
I beats ma side gal too.
Beats ma wife an'
Beats ma side gal too.
Don't know why I do it but
It keeps me from feelin' blue.

(*Poetry* 77)

Hughes wrote at one point that he considered *Fine Clothes to the Jew* "a better book than my first, because it was more impersonal, more about other people than myself," and to a very real degree he was correct: in these and others of his 1927 blues works, Hughes emphasizes separation, idiosyncrasy, and difference rather than commonality.[89]

Yet the old possibilities of musical participation and unification remain, as Hughes's decision to pare his verses down to a simpler AAB form and strip them of extraneous, more sophisticated structures makes his poetry easier to perform rather than harder. Granted, Hughes's reliance on gritty subject matter and salt-of-the-earth voices serves in many ways to eliminate or at least problematize the possibility of their being set to jaunty melodies, or sung in the manner of such white novelties as "The Dallas Blues" and "Nigger Blues." But in spite of their insistent singularity and their limiting formal patterns, Hughes's new blues still invite readerly involvement, with a great many his blues singers asking for or encouraging recognition and empathy. The singer of "Young Gal's Blues," for example, is admirable precisely insofar as she is able to imagine occupying the position of another person:

> I'm gonna walk to de graveyard
> 'Hind ma friend Miss Cora Lee.
> Gonna walk to de graveyard
> 'Hind ma dear friend Cora Lee
> Cause when I'm dead some
> Body'll have to walk behind me.

(Poems 110)

The singer of "Listen Here Blues," on the other hand, attempts to bring about a moral change in her listeners—she is addressing a company of "sweet girls"—by asking them to imagine her in a situation resembling their own:

> I used to be a good chile,
> Lawd, in Sunday School.
> Used to be a good chile,—
> Always in Sunday School,
> Till these licker-headed rounders
> Made me everybody's fool.

(Poems 112)

One's capacity for empathy, moreover, is shown to be closely related to the ability to channel the voice of another, as in the blues of "Hard Daddy." Here, an unsympathetic male figure's callousness is made even more apparent by the female singer's willingness to adopt his way of speaking, to take up his language without the distancing effects of punctuation or objective pronouns:

> I cried on his shoulder but
> He turned his back on me.

Cried on his shoulder but
He turned his back on me.
He said a woman's cryin's
Never gonna bother me.

(*Poems* 113)

If anything, the "impersonality" that Hughes believed he had achieved in these and others of his blues poems seems closer to the doctrine of "depersonalization" famously propounded by Eliot, in which poetry forces the "continual surrender" of the self and allows for the assumption of new identities.[90] Hughes's blues singers often ask for understanding, and blues form offers one way for readers to give it to them: one can sing the song of another and, in a sense, momentarily become that other. The speakers, roles, and racial character of Hughes's blues poems have become more sharply delineated, but the possibilities for musical performances by all manner of readers have not; the form of Hughes's starker blues may be more "authentically" African American, but the opportunity for vocalization remains available to diverse audiences.

One of the great ironies in Hughes's early blues writing is that his poetry in *Fine Clothes to the Jew*, explicitly intended to be a faithful reflection of the black experience and a contribution to a distinctively African American literary aesthetic, fell short with the very readers it was addressed to. Reviews in the black press were famously harsh, far more negative than had been the case for *The Weary Blues*, and they tended to focus their ire on Hughes's insistent racial specificity: Hughes was said to have cast African Americans in an unflattering light, to have fallen under the sway of voyeuristic whites like Van Vechten, and to have damaged the race in purporting to show its "true" colors. Others argued that, in laboring to produce the most "authentic" possible blues, Hughes had in fact hobbled his poetics and made an unnecessary fetish of form. Wallace Thurman, for one, faulted him with mechanically obeying a "strait-laced" blues structure, with treating song conventions as "an end in themselves rather than as a means to an end" and thus producing "some of the most banal poetry of the age."[91] Still others questioned Hughes's motivation in embracing the "folk" blues, suggesting that his supposedly "low-down" poetics was as faddish as the Harlem nightlife poetry of his first volume. As Robert Bone put it in later years, the embrace of folk culture by such Harlem Renaissance authors as Hughes was frequently understood to be self-serving, a means by which they might "assuage their guilt for outdistancing the black community; resolve their ambivalence toward the black masses; and in brief, keep them true to themselves as they faced the temptations of upward mobility."[92]

From a twenty-first century perspective, however, Hughes's greatest oversight in his turn toward the "folk" blues was his simplification of an extraordinarily varied musical idiom and his desire to locate it within a circumscribed racial experience and past. With the theorization of "folk" blues by Hughes and many others in the 1920s came a hope that musical connections still existed to a vanishing culture, one that predated phonograph records, sheet music, and white involvement with the form. The now-pervasive notion of a naïve, distinctively African American blues tradition was coming into being, and the musicians who eventually came to seem the best exemplars of that tradition—Jefferson, Patton, Johnson, Leadbelly, and others—have for decades been revered as folk heroes. But history is only now starting to recognize, as Benjamin Filene has put it, that no musician of the period was ever "as isolated as the entrepreneurs of the folk revival wished," and that the sounds that have for so long symbolized the provincial, the archaic, and the distinctively black may in fact have been among the most sophisticated, modern, and inter-traditional arts of the period.[93] Listen, for example, to Jefferson's "Stocking Feet Blues" of 1926 and note its deliberately ramshackle organization, its casual lack of concern for temporal regularity, and its ceaseless variation of its line lengths, all of it an off-kilter exercise in disorientation made still more strange by Jefferson's unflappable, almost bored-sounding voice.◐ Songs like this were once pointed to as proof of Jefferson's rural limitations and his folk authenticity. But the irregular, even experimental "Stocking Feet Blues" is more likely today to be discussed in concert with the very trends of cultural modernity that he and other musicians like him were long assumed to have been immune to: the preponderance of racial musics on the open market, the various mediations of commercial entertainment, and the briccolage of high and low that was coming to define early twentieth-century cultural life. Jefferson's musical world was much larger than AAB verses, rhythmic regularity, and a singular racial existence. Indeed, as Ted Gioia has put it, it now seems more appropriate to compare him with "the avant-garde artists dazzling audiences in other genres in the 1920s—Joyce, Picasso, Eliot, and the like" than with those unknown bards of the simple, imagined, and racially homogeneous past.[94]

In fairness to Hughes, however, he seldom held himself up as an authority on folk culture and always recognized the cosmopolitan possibilities of his art: as he famously puts it toward the end of his autobiography *The Big Sea*,

"I was Chicago and Kansas City and Broadway and Harlem."[95] So too was he clear-eyed and fair on the subject of the blues and its interracial appeal, willing to acknowledge over the rest of his career that African American music—and by extension his poetry—held important meanings for nonblacks, even as he criticized white exploitation of it. At points he sounded notes of anger, as in this poem of 1959:

> You've done taken my blues and gone—
> Sure have! You sing 'em on Broadway,
> And you sing 'em in Hollywood Bowl.
> You mixed 'em up with symphonies,
> And you fixed 'em so they don't sound like me.
> Yep, you done taken my blues and gone!
> You also took my spirituals and gone.
> Now you've rocked-and-rolled 'em to death![96]

At others, he sardonically argued that black music was like religion, in that "both can cross physical color lines with ease, but neither seems to have much effect on most white people's hearts and souls."[97] But in his extraordinary essay "Jazz as Communication" of 1959, he penned as ecumenical a love letter to African American song as has ever been written, making the case that the blackest of blues, the whitest of rock 'n' roll, and every music in between is unified on some fundamental level by the "steady beat of the drums of Congo Square—that going-on beat—and the Marching Bands' loud and blatant *yes!!*"[98] Invoking one of his favorite metaphors, he goes on to declare that jazz "is a great big sea," with the many popular musics that came before and all those that would come after—including the songs of Elvis—representing

> kinds of water. There's salt water and Saratoga water and Vichy water, Quinine water and Pluto water—and Newport rain. And it's all water. Throw it all in the sea, and the sea'll keep on rolling along toward shore and crashing and booming back into itself again. The sun pulls the moon. The moon pulls the sea. They also pull jazz and me. Beyond Kai to Count to Lonnie to Texas Red, beyond June to Sarah to Billy to Bessie to Ma Rainey. And the Most is the It—the all of it.

The poet of 1926 who wrote that his works, too, sang America in the broadest possible sense never stopped believing it, and the expansive racial music capable of enveloping him, others, and us never stopped rolling along.

Many-Colored Variations: The Legacy of the Harlem Renaissance

In the decades after the Harlem Renaissance, Toomer became ever more convinced that Americans were either unable or unwilling to abandon what he considered to be an arbitrary, shortsighted preoccupation with racial distinction. "In point of fact all of the main races are mixed races—and so mixed that no one can unravel them in all of their blended complexity," he wrote in a memoir that went unpublished in his lifetime. "What I have said above is known to almost everyone who has experienced the people of this country. Yet most of us play a game and agree not to see what we cannot help but see and know."[99] Toomer could just as easily have changed his phrasing and said that Americans of his period ought have been able to "hear" the fact of interracialism in their lives, as well: in retrospect, it is positively striking how often artists of the early twentieth century suggested that music had brought the nation closest to accomplishing, however unconsciously, its stated ideals of racial pluralism and fusion.

Sometimes the mood was unabashedly optimistic, with such narratives as Edna Ferber's *Show Boat* of 1926—and the landmark 1927 musical of the same name—theorizing that racial melodies might be able to eliminate racial difference altogether: in one scene Ferber's white heroine, raised on "plaintive, wistful Negro plantation songs," sings some of them to herself in a hotel room and then opens the door to find an audience of appreciative black workers gathered outside, paying her "as flattering and sincere a compliment as ever a singer received."[100] Others, such as Wallace Thurman, detected something false and even sinister in music's unique ability to draw—or seem to draw—the races together, as in his 1932 novel *Infants of the Spring* and one character's observation of a hedonistic Harlem dance:

> Whites and blacks clung passionately together as if trying to effect a permanent merger. Liquor, jazz music, and close physical contact had achieved what decades of propaganda had advocated with little success. . . . Raymond felt nauseated. The music, the noise, the indiscriminate love-making, the drunken revelry began to sicken him. The insanity of the party, the insanity of its implications, threatened his own sanity. It is going to be necessary, he thought, to have another emancipation to deliver the emancipated Negro from a new kind of slavery.[101]

Sometimes a benevolent, natural force and other times a dangerous compulsion, music was said again and again in this period to be the art most likely to bring about racial commonality and to express a fundamental human unity that, according to thinkers like Toomer, Americans should have accepted long before.

For those Harlem Renaissance writers who attempted to harness the power of song in their literary works, there must have been something mystifying, perhaps even frustrating, about music's almost effortless ability to cross racial boundaries. Toomer wrote at one point that the lyricism of *Cane* was born out of "an agony of internal tightness, conflict, and chaos," and his difficulties in creating an inclusive musical poetics must have felt all the more painful when compared to the matter-of-fact, almost quotidian ease with which actual songs spread across the races.[102] Consider, for example, the long and diverse legacy of Papa Charlie Jackson's "Shake That Thing," as representative a "racial" song as the 1920s ever heard. Marketed in 1925 as a black country blues, it quickly took on a life of its own. It was recorded on at least three occasions by vaudeville singers. Ethel Waters covered it the same year it was published and sang a more elegant and stately version for the Columbia label. Waters's record became a particular favorite of Carl Van Vechten, who quoted some of its lyrics in his risqué novel *Nigger Heaven* (1926) only to be accused of copyright infringement. Hughes came to Van Vechten's rescue and wrote a clutch of new, replacement blues verses for the novel, but he turned to "Shake That Thing" himself in 1931 when he needed a dance number for a folk play, *Mule Bone*, that he and Hurston were collaborating on. And it is hard even to begin counting the number of times that the catchy tune of "Shake That Thing" was echoed by singers of other races, in a variety of styles. (When Jackson sings "I'm getting sick and tired of telling you to shake that thing," for example, he anticipates the strikingly similar melody of Hank Williams's 1947 country hit "Move It On Over.") Black or white, male or female, urban or rural, musical or literary— such divisions ultimately appear irrelevant in the case of this popular number, and it was but one song of many that was able to reach a broad cross-section of American society in these years.

How to channel the seemingly unlimited capacity of songs to dissolve the nation's most persistent boundaries? For some writers, doing so seemed all but impossible, with evocations of music on the printed page often bearing but a scant resemblance to the real, audible thing. Moreover, the immediately recognizable, formally musical poetics of Toomer and Hughes represented but one path to be taken in this period; others aimed to use language in the service of musical abstraction rather than bend language to fit the preexisting structures of popular or sacred song. Claude McKay's novel *Banjo* of 1929, for example, is every bit as intriguing a musical text as *Cane* or *The Weary Blues*, but it needs little more than the title of a popular tune—as it happens, "Shake That Thing"—to stimulate it to dizzying heights of expression. McKay's protagonist, an itinerant musician, has a limited repertoire and tends mainly to play "Shake That Thing" again and again, and yet the novel shows the ways in which even a familiar, repetitive song can create vast sensations of ecstasy in those who are able to hear and participate in it:

> Shake to the loud music of life playing to the primeval round of life. Rough rhythm of darkly-carnal life. Strong surging flux of profound currents forced into shallow channels. Play that thing! One movement of the thousand movements of the eternal life-flow. Shake that thing! In the face of the shadow of Death. Treacherous hand of murderous Death, lurking in sinister alleys, where the shadows of life dance, nevertheless, to their music of life. Death over there! Life over here! Shake down Death and forget his commerce, his purpose, his haunting presence in a great shaking orgy. Dance down the Death of these days, the Death of these ways in shaking that thing. Jungle jazzing, Orient wriggling, civilized stepping. Shake that thing! Sweet dancing thing of primitive joy, perverse pleasure, prostitute ways, many-colored variations of the rhythm, savage, barbaric, refined—eternal rhythm of the mysterious, magical, magnificent—the dance divine of life. . . . Oh, Shake That Thing![103]

McKay's maximalist prose on the one hand creates a sense of musically inspired transcendence—of race, of class, of time, of the body, of mortality—and on the other draws attention to the gap that must always separate literary expression from the aural kind. Here and elsewhere, McKay's exuberant prose excites the reader but also seems out of proportion to the humble musical selection that provides the occasion for it. It is therefore a fitting reminder of the challenges faced by any artist, then or now, who attempts to reach across aesthetic boundaries.

In the end, however, it is the challenges that these artists encountered in attempting to bridge racial and formal divides—and not so much their success or failure at doing so—that makes the Harlem Renaissance so interesting to the modern observer. Whatever shortcomings Toomer, Hughes, and others may have detected in their own works, their cultural broad-mindedness remains instructive and helps reveal the fact that important, progressive acts of artistry are often accomplished in unexpected places and ways. As the writer Rudolph Fisher put it in his essay "The Caucasian Storms Harlem" of 1927, for example, America's racial future could often be seen and heard most clearly in the realms of entertainment, as opposed to in such lofty forms as the novel, the poetic stanza, or the prose essay.

Declining to dismiss whites who patronized Harlem's 1920s nightspots as faddish exploiters, Fisher suggests that the consumption of popular culture can sometimes be nothing short of revolutionary:

> Is this interest akin to that of the Virginians on the veranda of a planta-tion's big-house—sitting genuinely spellbound as they hear the lugubri-ous strains floating up from the Negro quarters? Is it akin to that of the African explorer, Stanley, leaving a village far behind, but halting in spite of himself to catch the boom of its distant drum? Is it significant of basic human responses, the effect of which, once admitted, will extend far beyond cabarets? Maybe these Nordics at last have tuned in on our wave-length. Maybe they are at last learning to speak our language.[104]

If music is, as Fisher suggests, a language unto itself, then the literature of the Harlem Renaissance must be approached in a new, more generically expansive way. Its poems must be sung; its music must be read; and its racial subject matter must be understood as a "wave-length" that any number of peoples might be able to tune in to. As the study of American literature in general and of modernism in particular comes to be ever more interdisciplinary, multisensory, and attentive to the ambiguities of race, it seems all but certain that this literary movement and its musical poetics will occupy a central place in the canon.

5. "Got Over"
The Chorus Girl Novel and the Musical Stage

The novelist Bradford Ropes wrote in 1932 that America was still waiting for "the *Uncle Tom's Cabin* of the chorus girl," a comment that the present-day reader would be forgiven for finding something of a non sequitur.[1] The chorus girl, so often thought of as an essentially decorative background performer on the American stage, obviously did not present anything like the moral and political dilemma for the nation that chattel slavery had eighty years before. But Ropes was correct that she was a worthy subject for literature: for all her anonymity, she had nevertheless been among the most prominent figures of American popular culture for several decades, a feminine archetype and theatrical fixture who exerted such a powerful hold on the public imagination that some contemporary observers believed she was "more talked about than the president."[2] And because Ropes was discussing the prospects for "the *Uncle Tom's Cabin* of the chorus girl" toward the beginning of his own novel *42nd Street*, a tale of backstage life and intrigue on Broadway, it is fair to assume that he thought he had finally written it.

Ropes was right to sense that he had a hit on his hands. His narrative of aspiring chorines, autocratic producers, and egotistical stars was quickly made into a movie musical by the director Busby Berkeley, and the spectacular fusion of story, song, dance, cinematography, and architectural design that is the *42nd Street* film stands today as an intriguing illustration of popular culture's capacity for self-reflection; as a textbook example of Berkeley's famously excessive, pop-Wagnerian aesthetic; and as the best-known crystallization of the many discourses that surrounded musical theater and the iconic chorus girl in the first half of the twentieth century. The nature of feminine beauty and the politics of its display, the fate of sexual relations in an environment where women are both wage earners and capital, the tension between the individual and the group in a hierarchy of talent, the social function and value of entertainment, the question of celebrity and the price of fame—all of these themes run through *42nd Street* in its novelistic and filmic forms.

The *42nd Street* phenomenon is a milestone of American popular culture, but Ropes's success does not make him correct about the supposed uniqueness of his novel. If we grant his claim that no "*Uncle Tom's Cabin* of the chorus girl" existed in 1932, it was certainly not because Ropes was the first writer to take the theater and its legions of performing women seriously. Rather, he had been beaten to the punch on the subject so many times by so many other authors that the literary field he negotiated could only have struck him as uncomfortably crowded, with so much jostling among contenders for Harriet Beecher Stowe's mantle that no lead had yet been able to emerge. It scarcely matters what Ropes was attempting to imply by invoking Stowe, or which aspects of her famous work he had in mind when he envisioned a chorus girl novel built on its model. If he meant that it would reveal dimensions of a social institution that readers had been hitherto unaware of, then Theodore Dreiser's *Sister Carrie* (1900) and its hardscrabble chorus girl heroine could be offered as an easy retort. If he meant that it would expose the brutality that underlay the feminine economy of the American stage, then the traumatized chorine at the center of John Dos Passos's *Manhattan Transfer* (1925) could counter him. If he meant that it would use the chorus as a prism through which to engage with race, then Paul Lawrence Dunbar's *Sport of the Gods* (1902) and Jean Toomer's *Cane* (1923) could be said to have done so already. And if he meant that it simply needed to achieve the sort of popular, multimedia success that the frequently adapted *Uncle Tom's Cabin* had, then a great many other chorus girl narratives that had previously appeared both on the page and in performance could be argued to have cleared the way.[3] Indeed, a survey of American literature in the first three decades of the twentieth century finds so many writers attempting something like Ropes's study of the chorus girl that they form a chorus in their own right.

The following chapter will consider why American writers turned to the chorus girl, her theatrical milieu, and the Broadway musical so frequently in the early twentieth century. The chorus girl was, first and foremost, a figure of access to and an occasion for raising questions about popular culture, and the chorus girl novel is as often as not an allegory of cultural discernment, reflecting a desire on the part of American audiences not just to be amused by entertainment but also to be sophisticated and knowing in regard to it. Chorus girl novels presuppose curiosity about institutions of popular culture, and their plots tend to revolve around acts of evaluation and distinction: their heroines are aspiring actresses who tend to be possessed of a certain, unique quality that will allow them to attain fame and leave choral obscurity behind, and yet they cannot shine as brightly as they otherwise might unless they are first noticed by a director, choreographer, spectator, or some other outside observer. And because such novels generally purport to grant unusual, even omniscient insight into a theatrical world where insight is especially prized, they in a sense flatter their readers, allowing them to enjoy an authoritative, quasi-Jamesian understanding of the cultural landscape. The chorus girl novel creates readers on whom nothing in regard to entertainment is lost, and because it is as concerned with the evaluation of the popular arts as it is with their production, the result is a subgenre of American letters that theorizes what might be called an aesthetics of pop cultural reception, an art of spectatorship.

Two important formal features define the chorus girl novel as a genre: its striking resemblance to turn-of-the-century Broadway musicals, and its "backstage," "behind-the-scenes" point of view. In regard to the former, the chorus girl novel borrows its standard plot and many of its narrative conventions from the musical stage, to the point that it might even be considered a literary adaptation of it. More specifically, it draws on the so-called Cinderella musical, which as a rule tells the story of an impoverished, working-class, or otherwise humble woman who rises in the world thanks to her unimpeachable virtue, her can-do attitude, and, of course, her well-timed singing performances. The Cinderella figure in such a musical might be anything from a dishwasher to an actress; the protagonist of a chorus girl novel, on the other hand, is always a chorus girl, but she too tends to be on an upward trajectory, and in a clever bit of doubling her pursuit of a theatrical career is conflated with the very stories of professional mobility that she might one day be asked to star in. The specifics and tone of Broadway's Cinderella stories varied over the decades, beginning as optimistic, feminine Horatio Alger tales at the century's turn and becoming more hard-edged and ironic in the 1920s and 1930s. But in all cases they were fundamentally musical narratives, imbued with a sense of harmony and balance that lent them a certain mythic quality, and the novels that emulate them tend also to carry a hint of musical, even utopian possibility. Just as the musical stage blurs the line that separates speech from song, movement from dance, and the everyday from the fantastical, so too does the chorus girl novel invoke musical associations in order to create an atmosphere of narrative liminality, merging the realistic and the romantic.

The chorus girl novel's second distinguishing characteristic is its titillating, even transgressive suggestion that the reader is crossing an important boundary by entering Broadway's backstages. Such novels promise intimacy with a rising star and a behind-the-scenes realm, and in doing so they adapt another concept from the musical stage: the notion of "getting over." For the turn-of-the-century actress, this phrase referred to the process by which she might make a connection with spectators beyond the footlights or the theater's "fourth wall," projecting herself with such singularity across the barrier that separates performers from spectators that she was assured of being noticed and remembered. In the chorus girl novel, however, this dynamic becomes reciprocal, with the text allowing readers to "get over" to a stage performer and into her private life, which constitutes a show going on behind the show. Moreover, the act of "getting over" is a useful metaphor for a great many other features of the chorus girl novel, whose plots are often replete with instances of boundaries being overleaped, bypassed, or penetrated. "Getting over" can be classed in such works, with the chorus girl heroine moving from one socioeconomic level to the next; so too can it take on connotations of celebrity as she makes the transition from anonymity to fame; and so too can it be understood to describe the considerable success that this particular narrative has enjoyed across various media, told as it has been on the page, stage, and screen. The chorus girl novel is founded on oppositions and divisions, and much of its intrigue arises from the ways in which those oppositions and divisions are bridged or elided.

Such novels are usually less audible than the varieties of musical texts that have been discussed in this book thus far. They tend not to be so thoroughly sound-tracked as Fitzgerald's works, and in spite of their Broadway settings, they seldom break into musical numbers. Neither does narrative fiction have the capacity to be modeled on singable musical forms, as poetry can be. The chorus girl novel is instead a kind of second-order hybrid: it is a blend of fiction and musical-theatrical plotting, with musical theater of course representing a blending of the arts already. Yet it is important to bear in mind that musical theater cannot ever be disentangled from sound, and that the nonmusical, narrative element of the Broadway shows discussed here usually held the least amount of interest for their audiences. The plots of Cinderella musicals, after all, tended to be more or less the same from show to show and iteration to iteration. What did change each time was the cast, the staging, and the tunes, with the same story told again and again in a profusion of keys and settings. Consequently, the invocation of a Cinderella plot in fiction invites readerly participation in much the same way that other musical texts do, necessarily reminding in-the-know audiences of any number of songs, dance numbers, and stage personalities that they associate with this well-known plot. As is the case with soundtracked fiction or sung poetry, chorus girl novelists cannot entirely control the associations or responses that they inspire, or the ways that those associations and responses might change the reception of their works.

But by setting such a process in motion, they require their readers to reflect upon the larger problem of cultural apprehension, whether in regard to music, drama, literature, or the arts writ large.

This chapter sketches the lineage and significance of the chorus girl novel by focusing on Dreiser's *Sister Carrie* and Dos Passos's *Manhattan Transfer*. Both men adapted the musical stage in their fiction and promised access to hidden realms of popular culture through the iconic chorus girl, but they reached very different conclusions about what they found. In the case of Dreiser, exploring the theater's backstages and dispelling its artifice leads, somewhat paradoxically, to a transcendence far beyond the emotional experiences that entertainment promises, with the observer's ability to see the hidden, gritty, and sordid backstory of a chorus girl's otherwise charmed life revealing not just harsh truths but also a higher music. A quarter century later, however, Dos Passos saw Broadway encouraging invasive and aggressive behavior on the part of both performers and audiences, and he cast his chorines as victims and victimizers in a system of cheap, alienating cultural commerce. Taken together, Dreiser and Dos Passos chronicle a pronounced shift in attitude toward entertainment, with *Sister Carrie* presenting an art that nurtures the individuality of performers but *Manhattan Transfer* finding American popular culture to have become essentially mechanical and standardized. But even in these two, almost diametrically opposed commentaries, the chorus girl novel remains what it almost always has been: an induction into the secrets of the theater, a meditation on what it might mean to be the best possible consumer of entertainment, and an implicit compliment to the reader who is able to grasp and make sense of the entire cultural landscape.

The Belle of New York: *Sister Carrie*

Few American novels offer their readers so privileged a perspective on popular culture as does the Broadway insider's tale that is *Sister Carrie*. As Carrie Meeber graduates from the community theater of Chicago to the chorus lines of New York and finally to the promise of international celebrity, readers are assured at several points along the way that they are, in fact, watching a success story unfold: in one representative moment Carrie, stuck in the lower rungs of the chorus and comparing herself to the featured performers, tells herself that "I could do better than that," to which Dreiser's oracular narrative voice adds, "she was right."[4] Carrie's pursuit of stardom has a seemingly inevitable outcome, and the novel's tension therefore arises from the question of whether Dreiser's other characters will be as discerning in regard to her as his readers are allowed to be, whether they will be sharp enough to recognize, support, or avail themselves of her talent before she passes them by. The novel is suffused with a knowing, dramatic irony, one that inflects such exchanges as the following—featuring a stage manager who has just declined to hire Carrie—with a certain austere humor:

> "She was good-looking, wasn't she?" said the manager's companion, who had not caught all the details of the game he had played.
> "Yes, in a way," said the other, sore to think the game had been lost. "She'd never make an actress, though. Just another chorus girl—that's all."
>
> (*Carrie* 177)

Readers sit in judgment in this moment as two men miss a remarkable opportunity, pigeonholing what is in fact a rising star. Theirs has been a failure of cultural interpretation in a text that celebrates the ability to distinguish the individual from the mass, the subtly incongruous from the uniform, the talented from the mediocre. And it is a mistake that readers are seldom likely to make themselves.

Sister Carrie is the prototypical chorus girl novel, the first significant literary adaptation of the musical Cinderella narrative and one of the earliest American novels to "get over" into Broadway's backstages. Much of its plot would have struck the theatergoing reader of 1900 as familiar, and many of its devices would become standard conventions, even clichés, as the chorus girl genre developed in later years.[5] But in spite of its indebtedness to the past, and for all the familiarity of its twentieth-century legacy, *Sister Carrie* is unique in its attention to the inner workings of entertainment, its curiosity about the nature of performance, and its almost awestruck respect for the power of popular culture. Much of what makes the novel so distinctive grows out of Dreiser's frequently bleak worldview, with *Sister Carrie* utilizing an unblinking, even pitiless observational mode that gives its exposé of the theater a too-full, sometimes repulsive completeness. Dreiser quite literally shows where the bodies are hidden along Carrie's path to celebrity, less interested in revealing the gossipy, behind-the-scenes intrigue so often associated with the chorus girl novel than he is in depicting the miseries that his heroine leaves in her wake. Yet in doing so Dreiser does not dispel the pleasures associated with the popular stage so much as he intensifies them, aiming not to undercut the theater but to create a vast, existential variety of it. For Dreiser, drawing back the curtain on the theater, the chorus, and the business of entertainment is a means of dramatizing the play of yet-larger forces, forces that, when apprehended, move according to a universal, musical harmony. Consequently, readers of *Sister Carrie* are invited not just to see through the popular stage but also to see it transposed into a higher form, with the omniscience it grants them in relation to entertainment producing a kind of cosmic flattery.

Consider first the matter of Dreiser's plot, much of which revolves around a single question: who can interpret Carrie correctly? She has a talent that is obvious to the reader and will eventually make her famous, but it also seems, like Poe's purloined letter, to have been hidden in plain view, such that only those of superior perception are initially able to detect it. Carrie is therefore left "waiting to be noticed" through most of the novel (263), and before she makes a hit on Broadway she must endure the indignity of being ignored or dismissed outright by blinkered characters who, as Dreiser makes plain, commit grave errors in doing so. Most egregious of all is Carrie's erstwhile husband, Hurstwood, whose fatal series of misjudgments begins when he draws the "peculiar conclusion" that his wife is "of the thoroughly domestic type of mind" and reaches its apex when he presumes that, even if she were to gain employment on the stage, she would only be able to act "in some cheap way" (*Carrie* 213, 261). He does not realize, as the reader does, that Carrie has what Dreiser calls "emotional greatness" and is therefore capable of becoming "one of the big guns" (*Carrie* 261), and while the abandonment, indigence, and death he suffers as a result is the harshest punishment meted out in the text, Hurstwood is far from alone in failing to recognize that she has theatrical zeal in the veins. Carrie's professional odyssey in New York begins with rejection after rejection as she visits its theaters looking for work, and Dreiser makes something of a wry joke out of this by having her turned away at one point by a "placid, indifferent" representative of the Broadway impresario Augustin Daly, a man whom Dreiser understood at the time to be among the very best in the business (*Carrie* 266).[6] The interest and the flattery for readers here should be obvious: the novel has allowed them to discover a talent that even the captains of the entertainment industry have difficulty seeing.

Carrie finds work in a chorus line in spite of these obstacles and from there her stardom is all but fated, a fact that Dreiser goes out of his way to emphasize by having her professional successes arise from the slightest of coincidences and the most trivial of incidents, as though her abilities had only just been held in check before. An improvised response to a comedian's tossed-off line ("I am yours truly") catapults her into the company of speaking actresses, and a single frown so delights her audience one night that her facial expression becomes "the chief feature of the play" and is described as "one of the most delightful bits of character work ever seen" in a newspaper review (*Carrie* 301, 313). The almost surreal speed and ease with which Carrie becomes famous serves to heighten the satisfaction that readers take in having known her talent in advance, and while they might pity Hurstwood for his miscalculation or chuckle over Daly's oversight, they also have proxies in those rarer characters who notice something special in her early on. June Howard has theorized that readers of literary naturalism tend to identify with authors because both have "a kind of control over forces and events through their power to comprehend them,"[7] but in *Sister Carrie* such comprehension is also on display in Lola Osborne, another member of Carrie's chorus who from the first recognizes her talent, offers her professional advice, and is instrumental in advancing her career. In assuring Carrie, "Oh, you'll get up" (*Carrie* 303), Lola reveals herself to be farsighted where Hurstwood is myopic, and she is thus able, in one of many acts of symmetrical counterbalancing in this novel, to take his place, becoming Carrie's new apartment-mate and living with her in domestic comfort for the foreseeable future. Lola is as attuned to the rhythms of popular culture and Carrie's place in it as Dreiser's readers are, and she is handsomely rewarded for her discernment.

The insight and flattery that *Sister Carrie* offers readers in regard to entertainment would be relatively trivial were it not for the fact that Dreiser freights the institution of the theater—and the chorus in particular—with considerable symbolic significance, thereby rendering the ability to recognize a star in the making something more than mere connoisseurship. In its theatrical context, the chorus that Carrie starts out in is simply ornamental, a company of women who are paraded about and given very little to do other than sing in unison and be on display. But in Dreiser's treatment the chorus becomes a microcosm for larger social conditions, the testing ground on which a woman's worth is to be measured and the crowd out of which a unique individual might emerge. To begin, the chorus is explicitly classed, with Dreiser remarking early in Carrie's career that women "who can stand in a line and look pretty are as numerous as labourers who can swing a pick" (*Carrie* 265). And for Carrie, the question of class is also one of identity: she figures the solo performers as "high and mighties" while she as a chorine is "absolutely nothing at all," a face in a crowd and a body in a slot, "that fourth girl there on the right" until allowed to be otherwise (*Carrie* 271, 278). Before long, however, Carrie is promoted and put at the head of one of the chorus's columns because of her "chic way of tossing her head to one side, and holding her arms as if for action," and her advancement represents something more than a lucky break to her: "she thought that the heretofore leader must be ill; but when she saw her in the line, with a distinct expression of something unfavourable in her eye, she began to think that perhaps it was merit" (*Carrie* 278). The precise nature of Carrie's "merit" is left vague in this moment, but the foreordained quality of Dreiser's plot nevertheless makes it clear that she has at last been evaluated correctly and her trajectory allowed to continue on its proper course.

So it goes for the rest of the novel, with Carrie climbing a professional lad-der whose regularly demarcated rungs allow her to emerge from the chorus with ever-increasing singularity, first winning leadership of a line and then a snatch of dialogue, a song, and finally her name in lights. Most immediately Carrie is being rewarded for her skill as an entertainer, but Dreiser implies throughout that there is something more profound at work in her progress, with Carrie figured as a symbolic individual who exists in greater and greater contrast to the collective hierarchy that the chorus represents.[8] Particularly significant is the fact that this dialectical tension between chorus and star, group and individual, is in some ways embodied by Carrie herself: her two most frequently emphasized talents, imita-tion and feeling, make her ideally suited for either sphere, which in turn seems to indicate that the reader is privy not just to a narrative of professional advance-ment but also to a larger meditation on the formation of selfhood as expressed in a cultural idiom. Certainly this is how Carrie chooses to interpret her success, as her wounded, intensely personal reaction makes plain when a drama critic damns her with faint praise in an interview piece, describing her as being "merely pretty, good-natured, and lucky" (*Carrie* 321). None of these adjectives is offensive on its own, but together they "cut like a knife" because they create the impression that she is a beneficiary of chance, a pleasing but ultimately passive vessel who is not markedly different from the other members of her chorus, those women who lack agency and therefore remain "nothing." Simply being picked out of a line is not enough: Carrie, who has a somewhat Whitmanesque habit of watching crowds pass by and speculating about the individuals in them, needs to believe that an act of selection is also an act of deeper recognition.

The broad outlines of Dreiser's plot, his theme of individual distinction, and his implied flattery of his reading audience would be echoed by nearly every chorus girl novel that followed in the ensuing decades, but it is important to note that *Sis-ter Carrie* itself echoes the stage works that constitute so much of its subject matter. Attention to the theatrical context of *Sister Carrie* shows the novel in many ways to be a product of its era: some of Dreiser's first readers would have immediately recognized it as a version of the Cinderella musicals that had captivated British theatergoers during the 1890s and subsequently been imported to America, where they had enjoyed such success that Dreiser felt compelled in 1897 to mention the fad in an issue of the arts and entertainment publication he was then editing.[9] Time and again during this decade, such theaters as the Gaiety in London, the Casino in New York, and the Daly in both cities presented rising heroines who start out as working girls or women of lowly birth, their modest social designations often announced by the names of the shows they appeared in: *The Shop Girl* (1894),

The Circus Girl (1896), *The Runaway Girl* (1898), *An Artist's Model* (1895). Drama historians now tend to credit this storyline with laying the foundations for modern musical theater, and audiences—especially American ones—became increasingly enamored of it over the years: by the early 1920s, after a wave of such box office hits as *Irene* (1919), *Mary* (1920), and *Sally* (1920), almost half of all musicals on Broadway could have been classified as variations on the Cinderella formula.[10]

Additionally compelling for Dreiser would have been the stage's tendency to figure the female chorus as a meritocratic social crucible out of which a few unique individuals might emerge, with a number of period musicals going so far as to make theatrical success on the order of what Carrie accomplishes central to their plots. Musicals from this era sometimes concluded not just with the heroine marrying a wealthy or titled man, but also with her being deemed talented enough to join a chorus line or, better yet, to leave the chorus behind and become an artist in her own right; perhaps the most famous was the Gaiety's self-referential production of *A Gaiety Girl* (1893), in which the Cinderella figure's triumph comes when she joins the very chorus that the audience has spent the last few hours watching. The pleasure of seeing feminine worth thus rewarded by the popular stage was made even richer on those occasions—great favorites in Broadway lore—when life imitated art and lead roles were filled by actresses who had themselves graduated from obscure choruses: *The Belle of New York*, an international favorite in 1897, was all the more beloved for the fact that its lead actress, Edna May, had been promoted on the show's second night out of the Casino chorus, the same chorus, as it happens, that gives Carrie her first paying job in the theater (see Image 9). Whether by narrative design, casting, or some combination of the two, the figure of the plucky chorine who makes a better life for herself delighted turn-of-the-century audiences, a fact that Dreiser's text registers when a newspaper review singles Carrie out but still associates her with the multitude, dubbing her "one of the cleverest members of the chorus" (*Carrie* 309).

The popularity of such productions had everything to do with the fact that they, like *Sister Carrie*, rely heavily on dramatic irony and implicitly flatter their audiences. Spectators of a Cinderella drama are allowed a certain measure of self-congratulation because they are never in danger of misjudging the woman whom they know all along to be a worthy heroine, in spite of the discrimination, snobbery, and misidentification that the other characters in such plots generally engage in. This flattery, of course, was especially effective in America, a country in which tales of class fluidity had resonated at least since the days of Benjamin Franklin. And on those occasions when the musical theater merged the story of the rising woman with that of the rising chorus girl or actress (as the chorus girl

Miss Edna May
1897
Casino Theatre.

Edna May as "The Belle of New York," a possible inspiration for Carrie Meeber and her up-from-the-chorus theatrical success. Used by permission, The Billy Rose Theater Collection at the New York Public Library.

novel does), its flattery of audiences became more specifically related to cultural discernment. Musicals about musicals compliment their viewers not just for being insightful, class-blind judges of character but also for having good taste: the heroine is almost always on her way to becoming a star, and viewers are granted the satisfaction of having understood her talent before her onstage peers do.

Even the "backstage" authorial perspective of *Sister Carrie* has its antecedents on Broadway, where the institutional voyeurism associated with modern celebrity culture reached new heights in the years when Dreiser was honing his craft. The century's turn saw a florescence of publications—*Billboard* (founded 1894) and *Variety* (founded 1905) being the most remembered today—that covered the stage world, with the private lives of chorus girls providing a great deal of copy. (One, *Munsey's Weekly*, published some of Dreiser's journalism before he became a novelist.) An equally popular topic was the theoretical possibility of smitten audience members quite literally getting over into backstage realms and wooing their favorite chorines: during a run of *A Gaiety Girl* as many as eighteen members of the chorus were said to have left to get married, while the entire sextet of *Florodora*—the most famous chorus in America during the first decade of the twentieth century—did the same shortly after the show premiered in 1900. The idea that a viewer might thus breach the barrier between chorus and audience was, according to the critic George Jean Nathan in a retrospective view from 1942, more than just fodder for the scandal sheets; stage musicals in fact depended on "the spectator's positive awareness . . . that he is in the immediate presence of living, appetizing and inviting femininity and that, if he had money in his pocket, if his hair were not getting thin, if his wife were away, and if the gods were just, he could go around to the stage-door and take a prime sample of it out to supper."[11] If Nathan's language seems disconcerting, what with the impression it leaves that the "appetizing," "prime sample" of femininity is herself going to be consumed at supper, it is nevertheless representative of an access-hungry era in which the "Stage Door Johnny"— a man who lingered at the back entrances to theaters in the hopes of meeting the actress of his fancy—was a favorite stock figure.

In many ways, then, *Sister Carrie* and the various truths it purports to reveal about a rising chorus girl and the business of entertainment can be situated in an established tradition of popular theater and mass media.[12] Dreiser's point of departure, however, lies in the unusual lengths he goes to in revealing Carrie's emotional resources and the nature of her artistry: *Sister Carrie* offers access not only to an upwardly mobile chorus girl and her offstage life, but also to her interiority and the wellsprings of her talent. Like the Cinderella musical, it establishes that its heroine can and will rise in her profession, but it goes further in exploring the perennially intriguing question of why certain performers are able to accomplish great feats of artistry while others are not. What, exactly, does it take to make a bona fide hit in entertainment, what is the nature of the gift that allows an actress to get over, and what are the criteria by which one might discern a successful artist in his or her earliest developmental stages? In posing these questions Dreiser is simultaneously imitating, critiquing, and outdoing the popular stage by creating an all-encompassing Cinderella tale, one that grants readers comprehensive, even omniscient awareness of its theatrical heroine, of the unusually powerful effect she has on her audiences, and of the abilities that set her apart and mark her as more than just "another chorus girl."

As presented by Dreiser, Carrie's artistry seems rooted in an ability to decode, translate, or see beyond immediate experience and to discover an otherwise hidden realm of it: she is a conduit to an alternate, musical existence, and is in a sense able to achieve a state of fundamental musicality like the one Whitman had called for half a century earlier. For all his reputation for literal-mindedness and journalistic plainness in his novels, the Dreiser of *Sister Carrie* is almost a Transcendentalist in his supposition—expressed as early as the novel's third paragraph—of a Pythagorean universe whose underlying, "large forces" obey an ineluctable, musical harmony (*Carrie* 1). And Carrie is shown to be an artist insofar as she is able to register those forces, echo them in her being, and communicate them to others, a talent that begins to reveal itself in her profoundly emotional reactions to literally audible music in the novel's first half. On one such occasion, a piano being played in a nearby room affects her "as certain strings of a harp vibrate when a correspond-ing key of a piano is struck," and though she is moved to tears she nevertheless spends much of the rest of the novel attempting to recapture this melancholy yet pleasurable sensation (*Carrie* 74). Other characters hear music, but Carrie, in her ability to enact something like what the groundbreaking nineteenth-century theo-rist Hermann L. F. Helmholtz had termed "sympathetic resonance," is able quite literally to become it.[13] Her sensitivity to the music that surrounds her is a function of both a scientific principle of physics and an abstract, Romantic notion of natural harmony, and her theatrical talent is rooted in each.

Carrie's ability to achieve and communicate a musical condition is very much bound up in what has struck many readers as her most distinctive fea-ture: her intense and seemingly insatiable longing. Walter Benn Michaels's reading of the novel finds Carrie's desire—so powerful, Michaels writes, that it "outstrips its object" and often has no object at all—to be symbolic of the self-perpetuating commodity appetites that systems of capitalism tend to inculcate in consumers.[14] But it should be noted that desire is also one of the fundamental underpinnings of musical composition, an art that devel-ops in time; whose formal organization keeps listeners suspended in states of anticipation for future moments; and whose most sophisticated practitioners tend, as Robert Jourdain has shown, to delay gratification for extraordinary lengths in the service of ecstatic effect. Indeed, music is distinct among the arts insofar as anticipation actually creates significance: a single tone can rarely communicate anything when it is removed from its larger, unfolding musical framework, while a standalone word or image can always denote something outside of an overarching narrative context. Carrie herself seems to under-stand this and invites the reader to understand her longing as somehow aes-theticized when she attempts to explain the power that music has over her, saying that it "always makes me feel as if I wanted something" (*Carrie* 340). And at various points in the novel, Dreiser conflates her longing with her desire to recapture musical experience: in one such instance she becomes "too wrought up to care to go down to eat, too pensive to do aught but rock and sing. Some old tunes crept to her lips, and, as she sang them, her heart sank.

She longed and longed and longed" (*Carrie* 83). Because it has no fixed object, Carrie's longing promises to be never-ending, as repetitive as Dreiser's prose. Yet paradoxically, to achieve a condition of ceaseless, irresolvable yearning is also to find a certain satisfaction, as Dreiser asserts that Carrie is in this moment "as happy, though she did not perceive it, as she ever would be," a claim that the novel's famous final image—Carrie in her rocking chair, "still waiting" for a "halcyon day" in spite of her Broadway success—bears out (*Carrie* 83, 354).

Carrie's longing serves her well as an actress and puts her in a position to have a musical effect on her audiences, a point that her friend Ames—often identified by critics as a stand-in for Dreiser—articulates toward novel's end in stating that, like a "pathetic song," she is "representative of all desire" and therefore "a thing the world likes to see," and presumably hear, on stage (*Carrie* 341–342). Certainly this is the case in Carrie's debut in the melodrama *Under the Gaslight*, in which she achieves her signature musicalization by "putting herself even more in harmony with the plaintive melody now issuing from the orchestra" and by entrancing her audience with "that quality of voice and manner which, like a pathetic strain of music, seems ever a personal and intimate thing" (*Carrie* 134, 131). Her tuneful performance is remarkable, and it is all the more so given that she is not actually singing in this moment, able to forge a musical connection with her audience through her carriage and speaking voice alone. Ultimately, it is this embodied musicality that gets her out of the chorus and over on Broadway, with her famous pout inducing an echo of her own desire in the men who watch her: "The portly gentlemen in the front rows began to feel that she was a delicious little morsel. It was the kind of frown they would have loved to force away with kisses. All the gentlemen yearned toward her. She was capital" (*Carrie* 313). The aestheticized longing that Carrie projects and gives rise to seems in some ways to create the possibility of her being exploited in this and other such scenes, as the men who "yearn toward" her appear almost aggressive in their acquisitiveness—she is a "capital" performer to them, and she also represents "capital" itself.[15] But Dreiser's narrative indicates more broadly that her musicalized state of being makes her as independent in her upward mobility as she is desirable, with her contact with men lessening even as their attraction to her increases—Carrie is implied to have a robust sex life while in Chicago, but it evaporates after she achieves professional success in New York.

One of the problems that *Sister Carrie* has encountered over the years, however, has been the difficulty some readers have had in taking Carrie's artistry seriously and in recognizing it as the achievement that Dreiser presents. Part of the problem lies in her material, which Dreiser can seem at times to belittle, as when he describes Carrie's part in *Under the Gaslight* as a "little thing which, to an ordinary observer, had no importance at all" and asserts that her audience, in admiring her, detects "power where it was not" (*Carrie* 115, 131). Additionally problematic is the fact that Carrie first makes her mark in melodrama, a genre whose excessiveness would represent something of an embarrassment to later generations of theatergoers: as the noted drama critic Brooks Atkinson has put it, acting styles are historically contingent, and it is today difficult to "sit comfortably in judgment on the broad, swaggering, sentimental acting of 1900 because our society is wary, self-conscious, and squeamish, and reluctant to suspend the capacity for disbelief."[16] Worst of all, Carrie is described as a singularly passive performer who is prone to outside suggestion and who seems not so much to act as to channel the larger forces she perceives, the Aeolian "harp in the wind" invoked by Dreiser's final chapter title.[17] For these and other reasons, it is easy to conclude—as Carrie's dismissive reviewer does—that her emergence from the chorus is a matter of luck rather than accomplishment, a case of the public's having capricious taste rather than of worth being discerned and rewarded. And if readers interpret the novel in this way, they do not "get over" to Carrie and understand her artistry to the extent that Dreiser seems to have intended.

To a degree, these problems can be addressed by considering Carrie in the light of turn-of-the-century theatrical practice, which reveals her passivity and near-total lack of professional expertise in fact to be a rather extraordinary talent. A melodramatist of the sort that Carrie represented in her debut would have in all likelihood followed the then-popular Delsarte method of acting, a highly gestural technique designed, in the words of its American practitioner Anna Morgan, to grant actors a "Harmonic Poise" that would render motion a form of intensified, nonverbal communication and suggest "universality" and the fundamental essence of "Being."[18] An actor might have an innate sense for "Harmonic Poise" or achieve it through practice, but in either case the goal of Delsartian performance was to extinguish self-consciousness, break "the stiffness of individuality," and communicate a quasi-primordial naturalness that would in turn generate the heightened, musical associations that melodrama sought to convey (as is implied by the word's prefix, taken from the ancient Greek *melos*, meaning a song, melody, or musical phrase).[19] And as any reader of Dreiser's text is likely to have noticed, Carrie's somewhat oxymoronic talent is an ability to act naturally. As early as the first chapter she is described as being unaware of "the many little affectations with which women conceal their true feelings," possessed of the Wordsworthian simplicity that "the child, the genius with imagination" has and that, according to the Delsarte method, is at the heart of evocative theatrical performance (*Carrie* 5, 6). If Carrie is indeed a successful thespian, then, it is in all likelihood because of the fact that she has received no formal instruction and has very little sense for what acting even entails, which therefore allows her to communicate instinctually the harmonic naturalness that other performers must labor to create.[20]

The more adept an actress is at the harmonic Delsarte method, the more efficient she can be in suggesting musical universality in her physical being. As Morgan goes on to explain, a great performer is able to "keep constantly narrowing the plane over which his efforts are dispersed; from the universal and general going to the specific and particular," to the point that even the smallest gestures—such as Carrie's frown—carry the weight of something considerably more profound.[21] This, it would seem, is Carrie's great, and great because unconscious, gift: she is able to create multilayered and musicalized complexes of word, sound, image, and ethos in her actions, practicing a fused and broadly readable aesthetic of the body that bears some resemblance to the concept of operatic *Gestus* theorized by Bertolt Brecht and Kurt Weill some decades later.[22] The reader's ability to interpret Carrie's performance is of course hampered by its being rendered in prose, and it is easy to dismiss a play like *Under the Gaslight* as a mere diversion, especially in those moments when Dreiser inserts quotations of its inflated dialogue into the text.[23] But it is a mistake to judge Carrie's artistry by her lines alone or even by Dreiser's description of it, as the reader is warned throughout the novel that words are fickle and slippery signifiers, "the vague shadows of the volumes we mean" (*Carrie* 6). Moreover, a follower of Delsarte would argue that it is the force of and proximity to an actress's personality, and not the theatrical work that is her occasion for displaying it, that ultimately gives pleasure. Indeed, it is precisely the text's failure to render Carrie's artistry in convincing terms that signals just how extraordinary it is, implying that her musicalized performance exists in another aesthetic dimension entirely.

In revealing the desire and musicality at the heart of Carrie's stage presence, Dreiser shows that her promotion from the chorus is more than mere happenstance, and he obliges readers to get past even his own lapses of narrative judgment, as his interior view of her belies his description of an audience that sees "power where it was not." Such errors serve to heighten the text's concern over discernment and the proper reading of popular culture, its implicit question of who will realize and uncover—as the reader already has—this formidable and yet somehow inscrutable talent. And in presenting the problem of how one might know a star before she actually becomes one, Dreiser once more weighs in on a subject that frequently came up in the popular press, as illustrated by Nathan's amazed appreciation of George Lederer, the prescient Broadway producer who elevated Edna May out of the chorus of *The Belle of New York* and cast the celebrated *Florodora* sextet:

> Lederer started them all on their careers of beauty. He dug them out of obscure choruses; his alert eye detected them in out-of-the-way restaurants, in the auditoriums of provincial theatres, in the crowded waiting-room outside his office. He found them in strange corners, in strange nooks, here, there, everywhere; and he took them and led them into spotlights that were soon to flash the news of their beauty across America, and across the seas to London.[24]

But even Broadway insiders sometimes fail to detect talent that in retrospect seems readily apparent, and the mystery of how this could be is of considerable interest to Carrie's fictional observers. One review notes in regard to her extraordinary frown that "[e]vidently the part was not intended to take precedence, as [she] is not often on the stage, but the audience, with the characteristic perversity of such bodies, selected for itself. . . . The vagaries of fortune are indeed curious" (*Carrie* 313). As is hopefully plain by now, however, the audience's response is not "perversity" but rather a flash of recognition, Carrie's success is something more than "fortune," and this reviewer is incompletely discerning in thinking otherwise.

To an extent, the comprehensive understanding that Dreiser offers readers of Carrie's artistry and career functions as an extended in-joke, an opportunity to be amused by unsophisticated characters like her abandoned beau Drouet, who, after Carrie has made her name on the stage, rather pathetically tells her, "I knew you would, though. I always said you could act—didn't I?" (*Carrie* 335) But in this novel Dreiser also illustrates—and for this reason seems recognizably modern from a twenty-first century view—that commercial entertainment in general and the chorus in particular can for all their artificiality and deliberate frivolity be objects of real importance for audiences; that they have value beyond their commodity status; and that to study them is to gain insight into something very significant indeed. This was in part a matter of biography, as Dreiser was unusually susceptible as a young man to the "super-cosmic realm" that the theater purported to represent, thrilling to the sorts of performances that Carrie excels in and later admitting that as "unbelievable as it may be—my reading, experiences and other things considered—I still took stage drama, or rather stage melodrama, for practically what it represented itself to be."[25] Some of the most persuasive readings of *Sister Carrie* over the years have therefore noted hints of the young Dreiser's sympathy for audiences of popular productions, of his sense that the "escapism" offered by the stage in fact has a vital social function.[26]

Dreiser goes yet further, however, casting the theatrical chorus as a symbol of nearly universal import that does not simply offer a means of coping with the world's "large forces" but also reflects and obeys them, with the ability to comprehend its rhythms having vast implications for the most discerning viewers. This can be attributed in part to the fact that Dreiser seems to have understood talent as a raw and transposable quantity, such that accomplishment in one venue could be thought of as being analogous to most other varieties of it; the protagonist of his later novel *The "Genius"* (1915), for example, proves himself to be as great an advertiser as he is a scenic painter when given the opportunity. Dreiser was especially attuned to what he regarded as the tragedy of misapplied or undiscovered talent, which he believed he had seen typified by his brother Paul Dresser, a composer of popular songs who had achieved considerable fame but eventually ceased to please the public and died young, his body consigned to a pauper's grave until Dreiser could afford something better. In later writings Dreiser sometimes appears embarrassed by the "exceedingly middle-class" sentimentality of his brother's tunes, and yet he also concludes that they were such superior examples of their genre that, had Paul "been conventionally educated in music, he might have composed operas and symphonies."[27] The question of talent is one of context and how it is deployed, such that a commercial artist could just as easily be another sort of one: "When I think of my brother Paul," Dreiser reflects in one of his memoirs, "I often think of Gray's thought in regard to unknown Miltons and Caesars walking obscure ways in obscure places."[28] It is therefore hard to avoid hearing echoes of Paul in Dreiser's description of Carrie before her stage debut, and not just because he had, at an early stage, planned to center his novel around a songwriter rather than an actress. "There is nothing so inspiring in life as the sight of a legitimate ambition, no matter how incipient," he writes. "It gives colour, force, and beauty to the possessor" (*Carrie* 115). Carrie may be a melodramatist and a chorus girl, but because she has force of talent she resembles Dreiser's other heroes, his artists, financiers, and titans.[29]

Carrie's abilities on the stage must be understood, then, to have relevance off of it as well, but not just because talent can be redirected. As Ellen Moers has pointed out, Dreiser takes pains throughout the novel to establish parallels—often eerily precise ones—between the stories his characters see at the theater and the narrative that Dreiser makes out of their lives, creating the impression that stage romance and everyday reality are not at odds so much as they flow in and out of one another. Dreiser illustrates this point with particular directness in an early scene when Drouet, unaware of the fact that Hurstwood has begun to woo Carrie behind his back, fails to realize the "ironical situation" that arises when they take in a play about a cuckolding, further confirming his obliviousness by declaring that "I haven't any pity for a man who would be such a chump as that" (*Carrie* 98). In this moment, the spectator is not naïve if, like the young Dreiser, he takes the "super-cosmic realm" of the theater seriously, but rather if he fails to recognize himself in the mirror that the stage represents. Indeed, Dreiser describes so many of his characters' interactions in explicitly theatrical terms that waking life seems a performance without end: Carrie's love triangle makes for a "peculiarly involved comedy," while Hurstwood's spoken words and deeper feelings of ardor are often aligned but seldom unified, having the same relation to one another that "the low music of the orchestra does to the dramatic incident which it is used to cover" (*Carrie* 77, 85). In such an environment the ability to interpret the theater and see what lies behind it has practical consequences, and it appears, significantly, to be the near-exclusive domain of Dreiser's readers.

If the world of *Sister Carrie* is to be understood as broadly theatrical, then fin-de-siècle New York is distinguished by being inherently choral, obeying the same rhythms of rising and falling, evincing the same tension of groups and individuals, and demanding the same powers of discernment that a Casino production does. The city at first strikes Carrie as a place of "peculiar indifference," but when she visits Broadway and sees its promenading, well-dressed crowds for the first time, she finds a place of "showy parade" where the unabashed observation of others seems "the proper and natural thing" (*Carrie* 211, 218). This scene has long been a favorite for analysis by scholars, who have found it to comment upon conspicuous consumption, panoptics, and the performative nature of identity.[30] Less apparent, however, has been Dreiser's sense that selfhood is defined in an essentially relational manner, knowable only in comparison with others. Carrie, who is at this point in the company of her friend Mrs. Vance, feels shame over her clothes, believing that "any one looking at the two would pick Mrs. Vance for her raiment alone," with the question of just what is meant by the word "pick"— picked for what, exactly?—left suggestively ambiguous (*Carrie* 217). She therefore resolves to purchase "more and better clothes to compare with this woman" and achieve a new standard of appearance, which will allow her to blend in with the crowd more effectively and then, somewhat paradoxically, put her in a better position to be picked out of it. Mrs. Vance, on the other hand, is more assured but nevertheless needs a group to impress herself upon, "going purposely to see and be seen, to create a stir with her beauty and dispel any tendency to fall short in dressiness by contrasting herself with the beauty and fashion of the town" (*Carrie* 218). Ultimately, it is this notion of contrast, of individuality expressed against and drawn out of collectivity, that provides an underlying logic not just for the New York promenade and Carrie's emergence from the chorus but also, as Dreiser would argue in Blakean language some years later, for any novel or other work of art that would seek to capture social realities: "Without contrast there is no life."[31]

It should come as no surprise that life for the Broadway elite makes for a grand show,[32] but positively striking is Dreiser's extension of the chorus dynamic and its attendant associations of getting over and contrast into the realm of urban poverty. This he dramatizes in the person of Hurstwood, whose lengthy and pitiful decline parallels Carrie's rise with an unnerving exactness. In facing New York he, too, finds it a place of indifference and competition: "The sea was already full of whales. A common fish must needs disappear wholly from view—remain unseen. In other words, Hurstwood was nothing"—the very same sort of comparative "nothing," of course, that Carrie finds herself to be in her first days onstage (*Carrie* 205). Some time after he fails to realize his wife's talent, the abandoned and increasingly penurious Hurstwood encounters an advertisement featuring her image—she is dressed as a "demure and dainty" Quaker—and her beauty makes his indigence stand out all the more, as Mrs. Vance's once did to Carrie's: "His clothes were shabby, and he presented a marked contrast to all that she now seemed to be" (*Carrie* 322). And their trajectories become almost inversely proportional when he is taken under the wing of a man known only as "captain" and who drums up charitable donations for the homeless by publicly arranging them in a formation that resembles nothing so much as a grotesque chorus:

> They fell into a sort of broken, ragged line. One might see, now, some of the chief characteristics by contrast. There was a wooden leg in the line. Hats were all drooping, a group that would ill become a second-hand Hester Street basement collection. Trousers were all warped and frayed at the bottom and coats worn and faded. In the glare of the store lights, some of the faces looked dry and chalky. . . . A few spectators came near, drawn by the seemingly conferring group, then more and more, and quickly there was a pushing, gaping crowd.
>
> (*Carrie* 330)

In this way are the men assembled, presented to an audience in both singular and collective terms (sometimes "these men," sometimes "this man"), and auctioned off, with the "captain" securing, cent by cent, the alms they will need for beds that night and presenting them to the "gaping crowd" in a way that they cannot do for themselves.

With even his beggars obeying the dynamics of the chorus, Dreiser seems to suggest that the world perpetually organizes itself into hierarchies and subjects those who find themselves within them to the pressure of climbing out in one way or another, an ongoing and competitive performance that is played out on every conceivable stage. For every success such as Carrie's, there must also be a great many counterbalancing cases of mediocrity and outright failure such as Hurstwood's, with the individual in a sense rising at the expense or on the backs of the collective. Yet one of the stranger aspects of Dreiser's text is that for all the sympathy that Hurstwood's fate might command, the arresting symmetry of his scene in the charity line and its almost choreographed harmonization with Carrie's ascendance has struck a great many readers as pleasing even in its abjection. Donald Pizer, for example, has theorized an "aesthetic of 'thrashing'" in this novel, an authorial perspective that not only finds poetry in accomplishment but also detects "an awesome beauty in the collapse of a man who had failed to hold his place," with that beauty being in part a function of the reader's ability to comprehend both the depth of Hurstwood's fall and the relief it puts Carrie's rise into.[33] Hurstwood is obliterated by the same forces that Carrie channels and is lifted by, but there is nevertheless a certain grandeur in his being a temporary instrument and then a victim of her talent, with his oddly satisfying decline connecting Dreiser's novel to other literary works of the period that treat feminine theatrical accomplishment as simultaneously appealing and destructive. She is not a chorus girl, but Miriam Rooth, the actress of Henry James's *The Tragic Muse* (1890), nevertheless seems to anticipate Carrie in casting her adoring audiences "in the blinding light of a comparison by which it would be presumptuous even to be annihilated," while Thea Kronborg, the opera star of Willa Cather's *The Song of the Lark* (1915), seems similarly elemental when visiting the ruined city of a long-departed race of Cliff Dwellers and absorbing an ancient and "sensuous" music from it, her artistry rather uncomfortably associated with the extinction of a people's way of life.[34]

A character in Cather's novel observes at one point that "there are a lot of halfway people in this world who help the winners win. . . . They may hate to, worse than blazes, and they may do a lot of cussin' about it, but they have to help the winners and they can't dodge it. It's a natural law."[35] He might well be thinking in this moment of such "halfway people" as Hurstwood or Carrie's fellow chorines: few writers, after all, have the reputation for being as interested in "natural law" as was Dreiser, and few literary characters seem to illustrate its workings so completely as do those of *Sister Carrie*. It would be a mistake, however, to conclude that Dreiser, in offering a backstage view of the popular theater and revealing the pitiless competition that underlies its surface artificiality, is sounding a gloomy note of the sort often associated with literary naturalism. All too frequently, *Sister Carrie* has been read as a text that engages with the romance of popular culture only to undercut it with a cruel realism, its larger project symbolized by the sometimes jarring tonal disjunctions between its metrical, musical chapter titles and its starker prose passages. As Lionel Trilling has noted, there is a long tradition of Dreiser's florid language and readily apparent sentimentalism being overlooked by those who deem him most relevant when trafficking in "material reality, hard, resistant, unformed, impenetrable, and unpleasant," a mode of interpretation that in many ways reached its apogee with the heavily edited and markedly sterner Pennsylvania edition of the novel that appeared in 1981.[36] And as far as the text's theatrical content is concerned, it has generally been the "reality" and accuracy of Dreiser's treatment that has been most important to readers, as was the case when the Broadway insider Will A. Page, in his 1926 memoir *Behind the Curtains of the Broadway Beauty Trust*, quibbled with Dreiser's factual errors and dubbed them "child-like to the experienced manager or player."[37]

Certainly Dreiser's text, fluctuating as it does between journalistic plainness and Daly-like melodrama, presents interpretive challenges for the reader, and the Darwinian qualities of the *Sister Carrie* plot—which on occasion reads as a choral illustration of the doctrine of survival of the fittest—can seem in conflict with its fairy tale, Cinderella aspects. But there appears to be a growing critical consensus that it is necessary, as Jennifer L. Fleissner has argued, "to consider Dreiser as not finally a realist or a sentimentalist but as genuinely engaged with both idioms."[38] Turning to Dreiser's self-evaluation, one finds that, for him, the investigatory imperatives of realism could be entirely consistent with the spiritual transport of romance, and were in fact prerequisites for it:

> I have since thought that for all my modest repute as a realist, I seem, to my self-analyzing eyes, somewhat more of a romanticist than a realist. . . . [L]ife, true life, by whomsoever set forth or discussed, cannot want utterly of romance or drama, and realism in its most artistic and forceful form is the very substance of both. It is only the ignorant or insensitive who fail to perceive it.[39]

Within the context of *Sister Carrie*, Dreiser's self-analysis helps to explain why even the darkest behind-the-scenes revelations do not disrupt the musical harmoniousness of his heroine's theatrical career and why the "curious shifts of the poor" that he depicts so bluntly can nevertheless suggest what Christophe Den Tandt has termed the "urban sublime."[40] Indeed, by Dreiser's formulation, the works of fantasy peddled by Broadway and depicted in *Sister Carrie* are not excessively romantic but rather insufficiently so, as they are obviously and flagrantly untrue when taken on their own terms. But when their backstages, their inner workings, their secrets, and even their horrors are exposed and their chorus girls are presented to the reader in an unflattering but honest light, the theater can then attain "the very substance" of the romance it purports to offer, at last becoming drama on an expanded scale. In laying the mechanism of the stage bare and granting full access to a rising star, Dreiser asks readers to understand his novel as registering something much larger, even transcendent—his setting becomes a theater of forces and velocities, his chorus girl a leitmotif in an ongoing and universal music.

Dreiser's novel not only established a standard plot for writers in the years to come, but also suggested that getting over into private realms of entertainment would be a worthy, even vital undertaking for Americans in the new century. Indeed, Dreiser had been encouraging audiences for some time to investigate the popular arts actively rather than merely consume them, most touchingly in "Whence the Song," a short vignette of Broadway published one year before *Sister Carrie*. At points seeming to echo Abraham Lincoln's first inaugural address, the essay expresses amazement at the ability of certain songs to be heard everywhere from the "mansion and hovel" to the "blazing furnace of the factory" to the "farm-land cottage."[41] But even more poetic to Dreiser—because tragic—is the capacity of songs to linger in the nation's collective memory long after their composers have died, and he argues that only those who know the history of such music in the most immediate possible terms, who know from "whence" it came and have encountered the people who created it, can grasp it in its fullness. "Only those who venture here in merry Broadway shall witness the contrast," he writes. "Only they who meet these radiant presences shall know the marvel of the common song."[42] That sense of "contrast," of course, would provide the fundamental dynamic of Dreiser's seminal chorus girl novel the following year, but he could not have anticipated in 1900 just how frequently audiences in later years would "know the marvel" of the Broadway backstages that *Sister Carrie* had revealed.

A Birrd in a Geelded Cage: *Manhattan Transfer*

Decades after *Sister Carrie* went behind the scenes on Broadway and became the first in a long line of American chorus girl novels, John Dos Passos sent a copy of his *U.S.A.* trilogy to Dreiser with the following inscription:

> Dear Dreiser:
> I just want you to know that I still feel that if it hadn't been for your pioneer work none of us would have gotten our stuff written or published.[43]

In calling Dreiser's novels "pioneer work," Dos Passos was expressing the then-common belief that they had challenged a conservative American reader-ship and cleared the way for later writers to take up once-taboo subject matter. But he might also have been acknowledging the fact that *Manhattan Transfer*—Dos Passos's 1925 novel of New York City and his first successful deployment of a fractured, formally modernist aesthetic—represented another step forward in the chorus girl tradition that *Sister Carrie* had inaugurated. Dos Passos's plot picks up where Dreiser's leaves off, retelling the archetypal Cinderella story for the next generation: his heroine Ellen Thatcher, whose path to Broadway fame will eventually be said to have "started in the cradle," is presented as "a regular little balletdancer" of a child in 1896, the year in which Carrie makes her first great impressions onstage.[44] The novel then jumps forward in time, returning to Ellen after she has finished a two-year stint in a chorus and been granted "one of these tiny exquisite bits everybody makes such a fuss over," a role on the order of Carrie's frowning episode (*Manhattan* 597). Before long, producers are clamoring for her to take a part in "an absolute knockout" of a show called *The Zinnia Girl*, and she appears to be on an upward trajectory that would have been familiar to any reader of Dreiser's novel (*Manhattan* 657).

But if *Manhattan Transfer* resembles *Sister Carrie* in its plot, it is almost unrecognizably different in its grim, despairing tone. When this star is born in a hospital off Third Avenue she is likened, in one of Dos Passos's most vivid and unpleasant images, to a squirming "knot of earthworms," and after she is removed from a quasi-choral collection of infants in the nursery—"How can you tell them apart nurse?" asks her father—she is greeted by her hysterical mother shrieking, "It's not mine. It's not mine. Take it away. . . . That woman's stolen my baby" (*Manhattan* 481, 484). Some years later, an actor helps Ellen out of the chorus and she marries him to return the favor, but when she departs on her honeymoon the reader is privy to this interior monologue: "Oh I want to die. I want to die. All the tight coldness of her body was clenching in her stomach.

Oh I'm going to be sick" (*Manhattan* 583). And as the author of *The Zinnia Girl* attempts to convince Ellen to take the part he is writing for her, she is figured as nothing less than a victim of sexual assault, feeling "his words press against her body, nudge in the hollows where her dress clings; she can hardly breathe for fear of listening to him" (*Manhattan* 657). *Manhattan Transfer* is unquestionably a chorus girl novel and it pays lip service to many conventions of the Cinderella tradition in musical theater, but the dreamy qualities of its stage antecedents have become the stuff of nightmares. Dos Passos's text also follows Dreiser's in purporting to illuminate the "real" stories that go on behind the curtains of Broadway, but the sense of sublimity that *Sister Carrie* imparts has been replaced with a pervasive sordidness.

Manhattan Transfer is an exposé that asks its readers to scrutinize and then recoil from a rising chorus girl and the culture of entertainment she typifies. It borrows a familiar, well-worn tale from the musical stage and creates a dark, shattered version of it, turning Broadway romance into horror and transforming the Cinderella of the popular imagination into something considerably less inspiring. It caters to the public's interest in peeking behind the scenes of pop cultural institutions but then shows more than even the most dedicated Stage Door Johnny could possibly desire, invading the famous Ellen Thatcher's private experience and revealing her abjection with such ruthlessness that, at times, the text seems bent on making readers choke on the too-abundant "dirt" it dishes them. And it turns the notion of "getting over," of performers and spectators forging intimate relationships with one another, into a pathological dynamic, with the public obsessing over, stalking, and forcing itself upon popular artists even as those artists intrude upon the public with an almost aggressive persistence. Ultimately, this jarring transposition of an otherwise familiar popular narrative frames a larger argument on Dos Passos's part about the place, function, and reception of commercial entertainment in America, with *Manhattan Transfer* examining the deleterious effects it has on both producers and consumers of it and questioning whether anyone who comprehends it in its totality could allow it to continue in its present form.

The difference between Dos Passos's polemical treatment of musical theater and Dreiser's awestruck one is due in part to the fact that their subject had become a considerably larger and more consolidated business enterprise between 1900 and 1925. The Cinderella heroines of the 1890s—and in particular the figure of the rising chorine—were brought up to date and paraded on the stage again and again in subsequent decades, their stories told with an ever-increasing frequency and polish to a consistently interested public. With this came an intensification of the attention, curiosity, and desire for access that had always surrounded the iconic chorus girl, making her an ever-more potent cultural symbol for the American writer. But in presenting Ellen as a representative figure of American entertainment Dos Passos suggests that performers have grown dramatically and unhealthily disconnected from their audiences in the years since Dreiser took up this theme, with the relationship having become a peculiar amalgam of isolation and rampant overexposure. The chorus girl heroine and Broadway audiences of *Manhattan Transfer* are therefore presented as victims in a system of cultural commerce that is at once alienating and inescapable, but while Dos Passos's subversive take on the Cinderella musical is unprecedented in its grimness, it is not entirely without hope, nor is it opposed to popular culture as such. For in revealing the inner workings of the stage to his readers in this novel and allowing them, as Dreiser had put it, to "witness the contrast" between entertainment's seductive promises and actual perniciousness, Dos Passos attempts to educate by productive shock, to compel audiences to turn away from one variety of popular culture and toward a new, better, even revolutionary one.

Identifying *Manhattan Transfer* as a chorus girl novel—or any other kind of novel, for that matter—can make for a somewhat dicey proposition, as its fragmented narrative structure, its multitudinous, even overwhelming number of story arcs, and its polyphonic argumentative mode all tend to resist neat classification; it is not easy to locate what Bud Korpenning, the indigent wanderer introduced in Dos Passos's first chapter, memorably refers to as "the center of things" in this text (*Manhattan* 482).[45] But there is a powerful case to be made for Ellen's being the protagonist, with the popular culture she works in and represents providing a kind of thematic glue that holds the sometimes chaotic narrative together. Ellen is a vortex, a body around which others swirl: she provides a common point of reference between the novel's otherwise unconnected characters, and she seems in tune even with the trajectories of Dos Passos's most oblique storylines. Ellen's almost spooky interconnectivity is further reinforced by her omnipresence as a stage icon, as she seems quite literally to be everywhere in her capacity as an entertainer: she is the item in a newspaper gossip section, the face emblazoned on an advertisement, the name on the public's lips. The sounds, imagery, and figures of American popular culture are as pervasive in this novel as is the clattering motif of the city's L-trains, and Ellen is that culture's most prominent symbol.

Manhattan Transfer implies, as does *Sister Carrie*, that to gain an informed and comprehensive understanding of America's entertainment and the women who provide it is also to grasp the play of larger social forces. It is no accident that Bud, when asking where "the center of things" is to be found, more immediately wants to know how to "get to Broadway," the place most closely identified with the centripetal Ellen (*Manhattan* 482). But in bringing readers behind the scenes on Broadway in 1925 and providing access to both a star and the inner workings of the popular culture she embodies, Dos Passos's revelation to readers is less in Dreiser's vein than Gertrude Stein's, as there is, so to speak, no there there. Entertainment is a largely empty affair and the people who work in it are almost without exception hypocrites, aware that "actors and actresses are put on the market like patent medicines" but inclined to blame the public—not themselves—for a culture that "has sadly degenerated since the old days" (*Manhattan* 694–695). Harry Goldweiser, author of *The Zinnia Girl*, claims that there is "no art like the stage that soars so high moldin the passions of men," but he freely admits to Ellen that his own works are nothing more than something to invest in:

> "If I could only do what I wanted we'd be the greatest people in the world. You'd be the greatest actress. . . . I'd be the great producer, the unseen builder, d'you understand? But the public dont want art, the people of this country wont let you do anythin for em. All they want's a detective melodrama or a rotten French farce with the kick left out or a lot of pretty girls and music. Well a showman's business is to give the public what they want."
>
> (*Manhattan* 711)

Ellen, who has not yet reached the pinnacle of her fame, does not want to believe this, responding that "I think that this city is full of people wanting inconceivable things." There is even, Dos Passos reveals, a crusading, idealistic streak in his heroine; at one point she fantasizes about an entirely new variety of theatrical "getting over," one that would entail running "down to the foots" in the middle of a performance and informing her audience that Broadway doles out "a rotten show and a lot of fake acting and you ought to know it" (*Manhattan* 666). But in the end she sacrifices principle for money just as so many other figures of entertainment in the novel do and commits to *The Zinnia Girl*, a show whose very title—reminiscent as it is of the various girl-themed musicals of the Gaiety era—seems to imply that it is yet another iteration of a stale but still lucrative storyline.

The "backstage" view of *Manhattan Transfer* functions primarily to illustrate that the commercial theater is at its heart a fraud, and it makes its case most powerfully by juxtaposing the sunny fantasies of Broadway with its heroine's unremittingly miserable existence. The novel presents Ellen as being somewhat like the Cinderella figures of the popular imagination but then deconstructs her mercilessly, placing her on a trajectory toward wealth and fame but also showing her to be traumatized, isolated, and emotionally exhausted. In this Dos Passos is both emulating and mocking the stage musicals of his era, in which the figure of the rising actress was even more popular than she had been in the 1890s. Broadway routinely complimented itself in these years for being a quintessentially American meritocracy in which dreams of feminine advancement could be realized: one of the biggest hits of the period was the stridently egalitarian *Sally* (1920), the tale of a dishwasher who pursues a singing career in spite of "bein' right at the bottom of the ladder" and who is "made for life" when a talent scout offers her a spot in the *Follies*.[46] The show launched the career of Marilyn Miller and was imitated countless times on Broadway during the 1920s, but its beloved, oft-repeated story also became grist for the dour *Manhattan Transfer*, which goes through many of the same motions as its generic model but conspicuously rejects its optimism. Ellen is an outwardly shining but inwardly devastated Sally, and in thus deflating one of the theater's favorite narratives Dos Passos questions its glorification of what he later referred to as "Success, that mythic tabloid crown that hovers over the bright lights and skysigns of Manhattan."[47]

Dos Passos's suspicions about Broadway's "mythic tabloid crown" in *Manhattan Transfer* are particularly evident in his decision to make explicit what had in Dreiser's novel only been implied—namely, that a willingness to sleep with powerful men is as likely to help a chorus girl rise in the world as theatrical talent is. Like Carrie, Ellen accepts suitors only to reject them when a better prospect appears, first marrying the aforementioned actor John Oglethorpe but then moving on to the dissipated gadabout Stan Emery, the journalist Jimmy Herf, and finally—and most promising—the politician George Baldwin. But this novel's abandoned men are considerably more forceful than Drouet or Hurstwood, willing to accuse the onetime chorine of being "no better than a common prostitute" when she leaves them; a fellow actress is only slightly more polite in quipping, "Why that girl'd marry a trolleycar if she thought she could get anything by it" (*Manhattan* 682, 616). And Dos Passos appears on many occasions to confirm such accusations by revealing, in one of the novel's bleakest touches, an arresting disjuncture between Ellen's willingness to indulge men and her visceral dislike for them. John is a homosexual, and his mere proximity horrifies her: "When she had vomited she felt better. Then she climbed into bed again careful not to touch John. If she touched him she would die" (*Manhattan* 583–584). George, on the other hand, is positively inflamed with desire for her, and yet on the evening they become engaged Ellen feels "a gradual icy coldness stealing through her like novocaine" and wearily tells him, "I guess I can stand it if you can George" in accepting his proposal (*Manhattan* 811–812). Her body might revolt but she gives herself nonetheless, suppressing her instincts as often as she effaces her name—it is alternately Ellen, Elaine, Ellie, and Helena—in exchange for whatever it is that these men have to offer.

In deploying the language and imagery of prostitution in *Manhattan Transfer*, Dos Passos further turns the Cinderella narrative on its head and aligns it with a very different but no less familiar Broadway tale, one of smut and sexual exploitation in Times Square. At century's turn one could find three houses of prostitution for each block in and around New York's theater district, making for a mix of glamour and degradation that had been registered in literature as far back as Stephen Crane's *Maggie: A Girl of the Streets* (1893). In taking this step and directly equating a chorine's "Stage Door Johnnies" with a streetwalker's "Johns," Dos Passos thus taps into a long-standing popular association between actresses and prostitutes, one that David Graham Phillips's *Susan Lennox: Her Fall and Rise* (1917) had acknowledged some years before in presenting a protagonist who works both jobs. But *Manhattan Transfer* is no exercise in easy sexual moralizing, no simplistic portrait of a ruined chorine who, in the words of a popular turn-of-the-century ballad quoted in the novel, has traded her beauty for money and therefore become "a birrd in a geelded cage" (*Manhattan* 532).[48] Ellen may in fact be selling herself, but Dos Passos uses her debased condition to represent and indict the larger system of cultural commerce that she is obliged to participate in, one in which very little has value and yet nearly everything is for sale. The dynamic of prostitution seems to touch all aspects of Ellen's personal and professional life, with the simultaneous ease and disgust with which she surrenders herself to men resembling her uneasy willingness to mortgage her artistic integrity for *The Zinnia Girl*. Further, Ellen's unhappy compromises between emotional desire and material comfort are mirrored over and over again by Dos Passos's other characters, with the novel so fixated on the ways that capitalist exchange impinges upon private experience that, in the words of Michael Trask, it "renders everyone with a job into a prostitute" of one sort or another.[49]

If many of the characters in this text are prostitutes, a great many more are shoppers, with *Manhattan Transfer* leaving a sense that those who are for sale—particularly those who sell themselves on stage—are condemned to live with the world's lecherous, acquisitive gaze ever upon them. The theatrical milieu of *Manhattan Transfer* is, as it was in *Sister Carrie*, a place of perpetual observation, but with the specter of prostitution looming it is also suffused with paranoia and an ever-present threat of sexual violence. In an early Broadway scene, the novel's narrator sets an unsettled mood by trailing an unnamed man who is himself trailing two girls, one of whom has eyes "like the thrust of a knife" and may or may not be a sex worker: "He passed them again. Her face was turned away. Maybe she was. . . . No he couldn't tell. Good luck he had fifty dollars on him. He sat on a bench and let them pass him. Wouldnt do to make a mistake and get arrested" (*Manhattan* 533). Women are available for purchase but are also killing instruments here, while the man who pursues them so doggedly is at once pathetic and menacing in his breathless, somewhat manic desire.

This scene of commingled eroticism and aggression in many ways prefigures Ellen's experience as a stage icon, which Dos Passos depicts as an ongoing defense against ever-clustering men who seem to attack her even as they slavishly adore her. Stan Emery—here being introduced to Ellen—may not mean anything sinister in saying, "I saw you last night, but you didn't see me. . . . I almost jumped over the foots I thought you were so wonderful" (*Manhattan* 602). But when he waits outside the hotel where she is having a drink, watches the door until she leaves, and suddenly emerges from the crowd to catch her alone, the novel questions where admiration ends and pathology begins, and at other points it shows that the surveillance Ellen lives under has induced a sense of perpetual panic in her:

> Ellen sits in the armchair drowsily listening, coolness of powder on her face and arms, fatness of rouge on her lips, her body just bathed fresh as a violet under the silk dress, under the silk underclothes; she sits dreamily, drowsily listening. A sudden twinge of men's voices knotting about her. She sits up cold white out of reach like a lighthouse. Men's hands crawl like bugs on the unbreakable glass. Men's looks blunder and flutter against it helpless as moths. But in the deep pitblackness inside something clangs like a fire engine.
>
> (*Manhattan* 640)

Here Ellen is assaulted and yet also shielded from harm, with men—quite literally moths to a flame—at once terrifying and pitifully ineffectual in their swarming persistence. The woman who courts the world's attention is also haunted by it, the men who want access to her are at once brutal and powerless, and from every angle the relationship between a female performer and male audience is shown to have gone perversely wrong.

In both its insider's view of Broadway and its vivid depiction of Ellen being smothered by her fame, *Manhattan Transfer* reflects and critiques the public's ever-increasing interest in the private lives of chorines and actresses, an interest that in some ways came to define 1920s celebrity culture. Audience hunger for gossip about these performing women had grown to the point that Broadway sometimes incorporated behind-the-scenes perspectives into its own productions, most effectively in a self-referential dramatic genre known as the "backstage play" in which plots were centered on the process of putting on a show, actors played actors, and intrigue arose from the same nexus of sex, money, and theater business that *Manhattan Transfer* sets out to expose. As far back as James Forbes's *The Chorus Lady* of 1908, audiences had enjoyed seeing the stage reveal its seedier side, particularly when actress-protagonists were in danger of being sexually compromised; the key line of Forbes's production arrives when his heroine, facing down a lothario who is blackmailing a chorus girl, declares, "I suppose you think your measly money pays. Pays for the homes you ruin, the mothers' hearts you break, the girls you send to hell. *You* pay! No, it's the woman that pays, and pays and pays."[50] In contrast, by 1925 audiences had grown so accustomed to the idea that Broadway was a den of vice and feminine corruption that plays could be matter-of-fact, even glib about the topic. Nowhere was this more apparent than in Avery Hopwood's smash hit *The Gold Diggers* (1919), which ran for ninety weeks, spawned five film adaptations, and did more than any other narrative to establish the popular image of the chorus girl as a calculating "chiseler." The play features a company of chorines who extract money and gifts from admirers in their off-stage hours, with most of its humor coming from its supposition that Broadway's most dangerous sexual predators are, in fact, female. As one of Hopwood's male victims complains in an obvious riposte to *The Chorus Lady*, "I often think of those dramas that you see, where, at the end of the third act the heroine exclaims, 'And the woman pays, and pays, and pays!' My dear fellow—from what I've seen and experienced—it's the man, God help him!, who pays—and pays and pays!"[51]

To a degree, the chorus girl novel and the backstage play as genres operate in the same manner, most obviously in their behind-the-scenes viewpoints, their implied flattery of audiences, and their reliance on dramatic irony. Plays like *The Gold Diggers*—with their wink-and-nudge promises to let viewers in on the "real" stories that Broadway's "artificial" offerings tend to obscure—responded to the public's curiosity by providing a glimpse of their own, often scandalous inner workings, and while *Manhattan Transfer* is quite different in mood, it also imparts a privileged understanding of entertainment and its mechanics to an elite audience. But in deploying the insider perspective that the chorus girl novel and the backstage play both depend on, Dos Passos appears also to be attempting a kind of bait-and-switch, promising intimacy with a famous chorine but then pushing so far into her traumatized interior that he induces discomfort, even revulsion, in readers. Janet Casey's convincing reading of the novel puts it thus: "While the 'private' moments revealing Ellen's misery and loneliness effect for the reader her transformation from mere image into the subject of a story, the novel's structure allows Dos Passos literally to show, rather than simply relate, Ellen's objectification within the culture at large."[52] In making his mode of narration actively participate in such objectification rather than simply describe it, Dos Passos obliges readers to intrude upon Ellen in much the same way that her fictional audiences do, a maneuver that makes them complicit in the spectatorial assault that she is suffering under.

Dos Passos's revelation of deeply unpleasant private truths about his celebrity heroine is a crucial innovation in regard to the chorus girl novel, and in the process he makes an implicit case for limits on the public's scrutiny of Broadway stars. He accomplishes this in part by inspiring pity for a woman so harried that she is, paradoxically, utterly alone: nearly every male character who enters her presence fairly drools with desire and one goes so far as to make an attempt on her life, all of which invests her statement that "It's not so easy never to be able to have friends" with a weary pathos (*Manhattan* 678). But the reader's sympathy for Ellen is not so easy, either, as Dos Passos's warts-and-all presentation not only reveals her victimization but also causes her to emerge as a person of extraordinary, off-putting cruelty. Particularly striking is her treatment of Cassie Wilkins, a dancer who resembles Dreiser's Lola Osborne in her almost childlike admiration for Ellen but who receives nothing but contempt in return. At one point Cassie—pregnant and petrified by a carnal horror that she feels "cweeping up on me, killing me"—reaches out for help, but Ellen responds by airily discussing her apartment decor, her divorce, and the difficulties of hotel life before hustling Cassie off for an abortion, concluding with the quip, "My dear child it's the only thing to do" (*Manhattan* 645–646). One might expect Ellen, who is herself subject to a knotting, crawling strain of sexual panic, to see a kindred spirit in Cassie, but the case is quite the opposite: "Ellen walked up and down the room with clenched teeth. I hate women. I hate women" (*Manhattan* 645). Indeed, Ellen seems determined in this scene to exacerbate and prolong Cassie's "cweeping, killing" terrors rather than abate them, almost as though she wishes another to be as traumatized as she.

Dos Passos goes out of his way in such moments to emphasize the most unflattering aspects of his heroine's character and drive a wedge between her and the reader, but any disgust Ellen might inspire pales next to her own, often pitiless self-judgment. One of the more lurid aspects of *Manhattan Transfer* is its channeling of Ellen's subjectivity, which is riven by masochism and a deep-seated desire for death. Her thoughts, when presented in stream-of-consciousness form, are often jumbled and paranoid: "It's such a hellish nuisance, I'd like to cut it all off . . . spreads apace. The shadow of white Death. . . . Oughtnt to stay up so late, those dark circles under my eyes. . . . And at the door, Invisible Corruption. . . . If I could only cry; there are people who can cry their eyes out, really cry themselves blind" (*Manhattan* 709). Yet she is determined to maintain a perennially icy composure, one that she achieves by deny- ing herself emotional release and treating herself with much the same cruelty she has shown to Cassie. Before long Ellen must also endure an abortion, and when she arrives at the clinic she "hates the quaver in her voice," tamping down her fears and taking a businesslike tone in asking, "It wont take very long will it? If I can pull myself together I have an engagement for tea at five" (*Manhattan* 716). After the operation Ellen is "a shell of throbbing agony," but she will not allow herself to betray vulnera- bility: "Taxi!" she calls, "Drive to the Ritz" (*Manhattan* 717). In thus revealing the vast gap that exists between his heroine's fractured mind and insouciant exterior, Dos Passos is drawing uncomfortably close to her, suffusing his novel with what Philip Fisher has called an "element of *National Enquirer* tabloid voyeurism" and inducing a kind of guilt in the reader for knowing—and perhaps for wanting to know—such intimate truths about her.[53] That which is being revealed is that which Ellen is des- perately attempting to suppress, and readers are inclined to flinch because they are granted a fuller understanding of her than even she wants for herself.

The woman at the heart of New York popular culture, then, is shown to be alter- nately terrified, callous, and suicidal, with her emotional instability driving her to attempt a radical disconnection from herself. She affects coldness as a means of escape and forgetting, such that scholars tend to refer to her using terminol- ogy of automatonism and the machine; Phillip Arrington is representative, and correct, in arguing that Dos Passos links Ellen with "those other synecdoches for the Metropolis: revolving doors, squirrel cages, steamrollers, rollercoasters, nick- elodeons, and fire engines."[54] Less emphasized in the critical study of *Manhattan Transfer*, however, has been the sense that Ellen's calcification is a result of and per- haps even demanded by the entertainment she produces. The sensations of Jimmy Herf toward novel's end are particularly revealing on this subject:

> Typewriters rain continual nickelplated confetti in his ears. Faces of Follies girls, glorified by Ziegfeld, smile and beckon to him from the windows. Ellie in a gold dress, Ellie made of thin gold foil absolutely lifelike beckon- ing from every window. And he walks round blocks and blocks looking for the door of the humming tinselwindowed skyscraper, round blocks and blocks and still no door.
>
> (*Manhattan* 803)

Ellen eventually leaves the stage to work as the editor of a magazine, but this passage captures her as she will in all probability be remembered by the public: a frozen, infinitely reproducible image, a doll that perpetually invites the world's attention. Dos Passos's prose mirrors the endlessly repetitive quality of the entertainment that Ellen quite literally represents, a continual procession of smiling girls and narrative clichés. And as was the case with Dreiser, the stage and the larger social order blend into one another, with women and skyscrapers alike figured as metallic, ever-reflecting surfaces from which there is little hope of escape. Here it is Jimmy, recently abandoned by Ellen, who is tormented by this imagery, but *Manhattan Transfer* makes it plain that life is no better for the "gold foil absolutely lifelike" woman who constitutes it.

Perhaps the most significant of Jimmy's fleeting observations in this passage, however, is his association of Ellen with Florenz Ziegfeld, the legendary showman whose female choruses were thought by many to be the sine qua non of American stage entertainment in the 1920s and who adds additional thematic depth to Ellen's unenviable fate. As historians of the stage have repeatedly pointed out, it was Ziegfeld who did more than anyone else to bring the chorus to the forefront of the national consciousness in the early twentieth century, with his yearly *Follies* having become one of the most widely known of Broadway's attractions by 1925. The secret of his success lay in far-reaching standardization: every component of a Ziegfeld show, human or otherwise, was a cog in what Joel Dinerstein has dubbed an "American pleasure machine."[55] Ziegfeld's women were convention-setters in regard to beauty and fashion; his choreography cast them as either living statuary or drilled marchers in a stately parade; and his variety format absorbed the most successful acts from New York's dying vaudeville scene into a single, streamlined production. Edmund Wilson was one of many to grasp Ziegfeld's symbolic importance in this decade:

> He tries . . . to represent, in the maneuvers of his well-trained choruses, not the movement and abandon of emotion, but what the American male really regards as beautiful: the efficiency of mechanical movement. The ballet at the Ziegfeld Follies is becoming more and more like military drill: to watch a row of well-grown girls descend a high flight of stairs in a deliberate and rigid goose-step is far from my idea of what ballet ought to be; it is too much like watching setting-up exercises.[56]

Gilbert Seldes made much the same point in praising Ziegfeld's "mania for perfection" (see Image 10), asserting that the *Follies* and the "steady, incorruptible purr of the dynamo" that drove them appealed to an Apollonian quality in America's taste.[57] So too did Siegfried Kracauer, writing on the other side of the Atlantic, see something similar in John Tiller's choruses, those "indissoluble girl clusters whose

Florenz Ziegfeld directing one of his famous choruses, which were among the biggest theatrical attractions of the 1910s and 1920s and which symbolize commercial entertainment itself in *Manhattan Transfer*. Used by permission, The Billy Rose Theater Collection at the New York Public Library.

movements are demonstrations of mathematics" and whose legs were potent symbols, just as "the hands in the factory" were, of capitalism.[58] Consequently, Jimmy's association of Ellen with the famed Ziegfeld Girls imbues her with much larger associations of mass production, marketing, and mediation, situating her within a nationwide system of cultural exchange.

Dos Passos would later argue that "people are formed by their trades and occupations much more than by their opinions," and if this is indeed the case, Ellen is a fitting representative of a Broadway institution whose favorite feminine product was, as Ziegfeld's choreographer put it in 1920, "a creation as completely thought out, moved about, wired and flounced, beribboned and set dancing, as any automaton designed to please, to delight, to excite an audience."[59] But if the name of Ziegfeld's game was the mass display of mechanical femininity, Dos Passos does him one better in *Manhattan Transfer*, rendering his chorine a literally dehumanized object and, in one of the novel's most tragic touches, allowing her to understand precisely what it is that she is becoming: "It seemed as if she had set the photo-graph of herself in her own place, forever frozen into a single gesture. . . . Ellen felt herself sitting with her ankles crossed, rigid as a porcelain figure under her clothes, everything about her seemed to be growing hard and enameled, the air blues-treaked with cigarettesmoke, was turning to glass" (*Manhattan* 811). In the novel's final view of its heroine, moreover, this process of hardening seems to be irrevers-ible. After witnessing a shopgirl being hideously burned in a workplace accident, Ellen teeters on the verge of sympathy, almost able to breach the boundary that has separated her from virtually every other person in the text and ever so briefly imagining what it might mean to be "like that girl, disfigured for life" (*Manhattan* 833). She allows herself a flash of self-criticism as she pulls away in a cab: "It's like a busted mechanical toy the way my mind goes brrr all the time" (*Manhattan* 834). But then she arrives at the Algonquin, and before she can investigate her "sudden pang of something forgotten" she has surrendered once more, "advancing smiling towards two gray men in black and white shirtfronts getting to their feet, smiling, holding out their hands." Once more Ellen's churning interior is suppressed, her self-presentation is made polished and perfect, and the show—automatic, repeti-tive, painfully artificial—goes on.

The backstage view of *Manhattan Transfer* reveals Ellen to have paid a terrible price in becoming an instrument of popular culture, but when Dos Passos changes focus and depicts the ways in which American audiences consume entertainment, a sad irony emerges: she has endured trauma and isolation in order to give the pub-lic something it seems in many cases not even to want. Popular culture is at best an irritating distraction and at worst a variety of torture for most of Dos Passos's New Yorkers, a production that scarcely merits her suffering. The tale of the celeb-rity architect Stanford White, murdered in a dispute over the chorus girl Evelyn Nesbit, infuriates one man because of its obscene pointlessness; the "querulous Sunday grinding" of an apartment building full of simultaneously playing phono-graphs puts "It's a Bear" and *Lucia di Lammermoor* into absurd juxtaposition while a man reads the newspaper (*Manhattan* 653); and in one of the novel's most dis-turbing scenes, the strains of George Gershwin's melancholy but still utterly incon-gruous "Somebody Loves Me" flit through a woman's head after a sexual encounter that reads very much like a rape. Indeed, it would no doubt surprise Ellen to know that, for one anonymous man on the street, it is chorines like her who impinge upon the public and not the other way around: "Aint it a croime? Aint it a croime?" he asks. "Them young actresses all dressed naked like that. . . . Why cant they let you alone. . . . If you aint got no work and you aint got no money, what's the good of em I say?" (*Manhattan* 606) Popular culture has little to no meaningful relation to this man's life, and its fantasies, far from lifting him out the problems of the everyday, seem only to highlight and reinforce them. As a result, one of the novel's most potent images is that of an unnamed bum on Broadway who, like Hurstwood in the presence of Carrie's advertisement, brings its glorification of wealth and success into stark, accusatory relief by his very existence: *"He took a newspaper out of his pocket and unwrapped a hunk of bread and a slice of gristly meat.... 'The Gay White Way,' he said aloud in a croaking voice. 'The Gay White Way'"* (*Manhattan* 548, emphasis original).

In allowing readers to comprehend the cultural system in all its social registers and contrasts, *Manhattan Transfer* shows that everyone loses in an environment of ubiquitous entertainment, all-pervading access, and paradoxically crowded alienation. This impasse is most vividly illustrated in the novel's many instances of abjection, but it is also underscored in its fleeting but nonetheless significant nostalgia, its sense that the nation's popular arts were not always this way. Harry Goldweiser looks back fondly on the days of "Boirnhardt, Rachel, Dusc, Mrs. Siddons" even as he sells out his artistic ambitions for *The Zinnia Girl*, while Ellen wishes she could return to her earlier days in musical shows, ones in which "you could be sincere" (*Manhattan* 711, 666). The problem is less that Ellen and Harry are entertainers as such and more that they have allowed entertainment to become a perversion of its former self: the actress and writer have consented, as do a great many characters in Dos Passos's fiction, to become what Michael Denning has termed "word-slingers," cynics who muddy the nation's discourse with the cant of Tin Pan Alley, advertising, and the yellow press.[60] The musical stage may have once been a vibrant art, but in the twentieth century it is little more than feedback in the cacophony that Dos Passos memorably conjures in the opening of *U.S.A.*: "NOISE GREETS NEW CENTURY ... GAIETY GIRLS MOBBED IN NEW JERSEY."[61]

In illustrating the unfortunate turn he understood the American musical stage to have taken in *Manhattan Transfer*, Dos Passos criticizes its commercialization, overproduction, and standardization, but perhaps his greatest concern is for the fissure he had come to perceive between its performers and audiences. Dos Passos often complained in other venues that the theater, once an exemplar of what he called "the arts of direct contact," had retreated too far behind an "invisible fourth wall" during the 1920s and come to resemble "the movies and radio and subsequent mechanical means of broadcasting entertainment and propaganda."[62] To him, the advent of "mechanical" entertainment represented an historic change, a movement away from arts of active collaboration between actors and spectators—vaudeville, cabaret, and the like—and toward ones that required only passive consumption. Dos Passos was not alone among the American modernists in detecting such polarization in the popular arts; T. S. Eliot had mourned the death of the music hall star Marie Lloyd in much the same terms in 1922, predicting that she would take with her a tradition of theater in which the "working man . . . joined in the chorus" and was able to be "part of the act."[63] But *Manhattan Transfer* illustrates, perhaps more vividly than any other novel before Nathaniel West's *The Day of the Locust* (1939), how desperate Americans on both sides of entertainment's isolating divide could become in attempting to reassert their agency. In an environment where the old channels of "getting over" have dried up and the stage's vital dynamic of interplay has been disrupted, audiences will seek access to their performers in unforeseen and unhealthy ways; so too will performers feel themselves drawn, even compulsively so, to their audiences, no matter how dangerous or repellent doing so might feel.

Considered in such a light, Dos Passos's grim exposé of Broadway seems less an argument for audiences to abandon popular culture wholesale and more a spur for them to demand something better from it. Certainly he understood that commercial entertainment could be usefully redirected in the service of literature. Many scholars have shown the ways in which the quick-cutting *Manhattan Transfer* and Dos Passos's other novels are indebted to film; John Trombold finds him deploying the lyrics of popular song in inventive, sometimes politically subversive ways; and the author would himself argue a decade later that when "the American mass myth changes . . . the change is much more likely to find expression on Tin Pan Alley and in the syncopating feet of a musical-comedy chorus than in the lugubrious world of drama leaguers, Pulitzer Prize Committees and students of Professor Baker's courses."[64] Dos Passos was also, in rarer times, convinced that something of the stage's old intimacy survived in the 1920s and could be rehabilitated:

> What we have in American theaters today is a great uncöordinated swirl of individual energy and mechanical skill, that if it could only be got into motion towards an end would produce something inconceivable. There is in the extraordinary skill with which vaudeville performers put themselves over individually to the audience in the short time allotted to them, in the satire and construction you get occasionally in burlesque shows and musical comedies, in the brilliant acting and producing it takes to get across trick melodramas and mystery plays, raw material for anything one wants to make.[65]

This "inconceivable" art that Dos Passos thinks possible here—one that resurrects the old possibilities of "getting over"—could no doubt satisfy the desire for anti-commercial, "inconceivable things" that Ellen also detects in her audiences. The question is who will give it to them, and how.

Dos Passos himself tried to get the stage "into motion" in the years after *Manhattan Transfer* with his own forays into playwriting, and the result was *The Garbage Man,* a work that he called "an attempt to bridge the horrible chasm between the 'serious' play that takes itself seriously and thinks that it's ART and the regular Broadway show that everybody is ashamed of, but that manages to keep a houseful of people sitting straight up in their seats from eight-thirty to eleven-thirty six nights a week."[66] It is in many ways an expression of Dos Passos's belief that America's popular culture could best be changed not through highbrow condemnation but from within itself,[67] and it should therefore come as no surprise that the play once more takes up the Cinderella story at the heart of *Sister Carrie, Manhattan Transfer,* and the Broadway musical as a genre. Two young lovers are driven apart, she rises to stardom, and he falls into homelessness, with everything accompanied by popular songs. But as the protagonists work their way back to one another the familiar story grows increasingly surreal, with the final act building to a spectacular climax in which squawking phonographs and radio voices make a clamorous din, a mob of actors rushes the audience, and a gong hidden in the back of the theater is struck with thunderous force. It as though Dos Passos, after assaying Broadway's wreckage, has seen a way to invigorate its exhausted forms and use them to reestablish contact—a chaotic and yet exhilarating one—between the prisoners on either side of the footlights.

Dos Passos's chorus girl heroine never suggests the universal, musicalized forces that Carrie does, nor is she ever shown connecting with anyone else in a meaningful, productive way. But there is the slightest of hints in this novel that, if given the opportunity, she could. At one point the man who casts her in *The Zinnia Girl* temporarily abandons his cynicism and argues that marketing and commercial calculation can never achieve the wholesale standardization of American entertainment: "If you could do it with advertising every producer in New York'd be a millionaire," he says with a flash of his all but buried idealism. "It's the mysterious occult force that grips the crowds on the street. . . . Advertising wont do it, good criticism wont do it, maybe it's genius maybe it's luck but if you can give the public what it wants at that time and at that place you have a hit" (*Manhattan* 694–695). The popular arts, for all their fixation on the bottom line, still possess an "occult" magic that transcends the circumstances of their making, and if there is anyone who proves this, he says, it is Ellen: "Now that's what [Ellen] gave us in this last show. . . . She established contact with the audience. . . . And I dont know how you do it, nobody dont know how you do it" (*Manhattan* 695). If only for an instant, a chorus girl represents the best that popular culture has to offer, its ability to break the mold, and its potential for the unification of unhappily disparate spheres. The problem, as ever, is in uncovering what has been buried.

The Same Old Hokum: *U.S.A.* and Beyond

For all its sense of grim finality, *Manhattan Transfer* was not the end of the chorus girl novel, nor did its deep reservations about behind-the-scenes spectatorship prevent future novelists from using the Cinderella story to satisfy the public's desire for access. Dos Passos would tell much the same tale in *U.S.A.*, putting the actress Margo Dowling on a path toward ever-greater fame that functions as an allegory of American cultural development in the first three decades of the twentieth century. She is the consummate rising star, beginning as a child in a theatrical family and performing vaudeville, then being discovered by Ziegfeld and cast in his chorus, and finally making the jump to Hollywood. The backstage view of her success is, once again, a lurid one that finds her sexually assaulted, toyed with, or exploited at every step along the way: her mother's beau rapes her, one of Ziegfeld's casting agents enlists her for a dubious "real test" on his farm, a businessman makes her a kept woman, and the movies transform her into an image to be consumed by men in celluloid perpetuity.[68] As her director puts it to the male lead who romances her on camera: "They all feel they are you, you are loving her for them, the millions who want love and beauty and excitement, but forget them . . . you are alone except for your two beating hearts, you and the most beautiful girl in the world, the nation's newest sweetheart."[69] Once more has Dos Passos told a tale of classic American success through the classic American figure of the chorus girl, and once more has he undercut it.

But even though Dos Passos is repeating himself in this novel of the 1930s, his revelations about the dark underbelly of entertainment wind up seeming somewhat redundant when considered in the context of the many other chorus girl novels, plays, and films that had shown much the same thing to American audiences since 1925. Beth Brown's *Applause* of 1928—as well as its 1929 film adaptation—had told the story of a rising chorus girl in similarly nightmarish terms, complete with a would-be rapist stepfather, the exchange of sex for money and gifts, a ghoulish audience, and, for good measure, a dramatic suicide. So confident was Brown's novel of its audience's sophistication in regard Cinderella stories that it could make fun not just of dramatic conventions but even of the ironization of them:

> "All these musical comedy plots are alike. Eight o'clock rags-eleven o'clock royal raiment! Hero comes on in hobo clothes and walks out in full-dress. That's me. Heroine comes on in an apron and goes out in an ermine wrap. The same old hokum, Kitty."
>
> "Some stories go the other way, Jo! It's rags for the final curtain!"[70]

In the event that American readers or moviegoers had missed *Applause*, they might have instead caught such darkened "backstage" narratives as the 1926 play *Broadway* (featuring gangland intrigue and a murder); the 1926 play or 1928 novel *Burlesque* (whose chorine protagonist falls in love with a dangerously alcoholic actor and is stalked by a fan); or the aforementioned Bradford Ropes novel *42nd Street*, which exposes the theater's mechanical heart with much the same pitilessness that *Manhattan Transfer* does. "But the machine could not pause to brood over the destinies of the human beings that were caught up in its motion," Ropes writes of the Ziegfeldian show at the center of his text. "Machines are impersonal things not given to introspect and retrospect. All that driving force was pounding relentlessly toward one goal—a successful première on Forty-Second Street. The unwanted cogs . . . were cast aside."[71]

Seeing through the clichés of Broadway and muddying the myth of the Cinderella chorus girl, in other words, had become clichés themselves in the years since *Manhattan Transfer*. And perhaps nowhere is this turn more evident than in the very blockbuster spectacles that Dos Passos had attempted in his novels to subvert. Some of the biggest productions of the 1920s echoed the chorus girl novel at its most investigatory, mocking their own artificiality and making shows of their inner workings. At the beginning of the decade such critics as George Jean Nathan were already decrying "the now long stale and manifest evasion of having one character stop suddenly toward the conclusion of the show and ask what has become of the libretto,"[72] and Ziegfeld was still at it in 1929 with *Show Girl*, which begins as a plantation drama but then strikes its own sets after a telegram complaining about the acting arrives from Ziegfeld himself. Nor did the biggest names in show business balk at including touches of the coldness that gives *Manhattan Transfer* its power. Ziegfeld's chorine film of 1929, *Glorifying the American Girl*, is in many ways astonishingly bleak, opening with an eerie montage of women striding, zombie-like, across a map of the United States and concluding with its heroine achieving fame but left broken-hearted by her lover (after, it should be noted, he runs over her best friend with his automobile). Even the film musical of *42nd Street*, which smoothes away nearly every rough edge of Ropes's novel, features a woman being pursued and stabbed in its final dance number, a reminder of Broadway's seediness brought into choreographed, musical harmony. Here and elsewhere, American popular culture proves its boundless capacity for absorption, for making even the most biting critiques of a show part and parcel of the show itself.

The chorus girl novel's adeptness at detecting, reflecting, manipulating, and catering to the public's desire for cultural knowingness was perhaps its most lasting legacy. But it was Dreiser's sense that the view behind the curtains was an essentially rewarding one—and not Dos Passos's desire to expose the fraudulence of entertainment—that seems most familiar when looking back on the twentieth century, the most obvious thread connecting the many backstage musicals, making-of specials, and reality television programs that America has seen over the years. Perhaps the capstone of the chorus girl tradition, then, is the 1941 film *Ziegfeld Girl*, whose three chorine protagonists represent nothing less than Hollywood's prehistory and self-construction. Judy Garland's onetime vaudevillian abandons her novelty songs and outdated jokes to join the sophisticated *Follies*; Hedy Lamarr and her husband, a classically trained violinist, bring high art to what would become America's globally dominant entertainment industry; and Lana Turner, who fades and appears to have died by the film's end, suggests the fate of the stage in the era of the screen. The message of *Ziegfeld Girl* seems to be that while some forms of entertainment must pass so that others may survive, there is nevertheless a certain pleasure to be had in watching this struggle play itself out, with the act of looking behind the scenes of entertainment in many ways being just as entertaining as the actual product. The ever-resonant symbol of the female chorus thus illustrates the boundless capacity of popular culture to perpetuate itself by puncturing itself, and it is perhaps this ironic dynamic of productive self-consumption that Peter Gay, in his recent history of modernism, is referring to when he writes that twenty-first century Americans can expect "the marginalization of future avant-gardes" because they live "in an age of musical comedies."[73] If this is indeed such an age, and if the musical comedy's happy adaptation of the chorus girl novel's investigatory perspective is any indication, then it will indeed be challenging for literary artists to see through a culture of entertainment that is only too delighted to see through itself.

Coda. The Bridge
Motifs in Contemporary Musical Fiction

This book's study of musical literature ends in the 1930s, but the beat went on and, if anything, grew ever more insistent over the rest of the century. Indeed, the musical methods pioneered by the writers of Tin Pan Alley's heyday and modernism's moment are now so common as to seem inevitable in hindsight. It is all but impossible to imagine the literature of the 1960s, for example, without the righteous singing of the civil rights movement or the anthems of youth culture: James Baldwin's *Another Country* (1962) would lose much of its political and sexual edge without its soundtrack of blues records, while the historical currents of Thomas Pynchon's *The Crying of Lot 49* (1966) might spin out of control without its here-and-now grounding in rock and psychedelia. So too is the music of more recent decades a conspicuous presence in contemporary literature, amplified in no small part by our age's steady evolutions in sound media, the ease of access we enjoy to seemingly infinite digital collections, and our everyday saturation in song. For today's authors, music is yet more available and immediate than it was for those of a century ago, and it remains just as useful an instrument for transcending boundaries and spanning divisions on the printed page.

The interplay of music and poetry is still a fascinating dynamic, whether heard in the recent meditations on Beethoven and blackness in Rita Dove's *Sonata Mulattica* (2009) or amid the controversies generated by transcription errors in the Yale University Press's *Anthology of Rap* (2010). It is in fiction, however, that readers can most frequently hear the "silent" art of literature becoming audible. One might begin by consulting the sheer number of titles that have become attached to both narrative and musical works over the years, thereby merging print with sound

before a book cover is even cracked. There is the "33 1/3" series from the Continuum Publishing Group, which as of this writing boasts eighty-six appreciations
of classic albums in a variety of forms: in *Master of Reality* (2008), John Darnielle
channels the voice of a fifteen-year-old boy to discuss Black Sabbath's eponymous
LP, while in *Meat Is Murder* (2003) Joe Pernice presents a novella about the Smiths
record of the same name. Speaking of The Smiths, their fans can also consult the
short story collection *Please* (2010), which contains a few dozen pieces inspired
by and sharing titles with some of the band's best-known songs; there are similar
volumes devoted to The Fall and Sonic Youth, as well. And in his internationally
celebrated novel *Norwegian Wood* (1987), Haruki Murakami invites constant comparison between his narrator's wistful remembrance of lost love and John Lennon's opaque, sardonic "Norwegian Wood (This Bird Has Flown)," to distinctively
suggestive and elusive effect. In all of these cases, the reader is asked to navigate
a literary plot with a musical accompaniment in mind, and much of the pleasure
lies in experiencing points of confluence and moments of tension between two
aesthetic planes.

   Music has long been understood to be a uniquely powerful stimulant to memory, and so contemporary fiction often deploys song in an attempt at manipulating the flow of time or mingling the past with the present. Sometimes the aim is
nostalgic: in Jennifer Egan's *A Visit from the Goon Squad* (2010)—note the Elvis
Costello reference—a jaded record producer grouses that twenty-first-century artists strike him as "Too clear, too clean. The problem was precision, perfection; the
problem was *digitization*, which sucked the life out of everything that got smeared
through its microscopic mesh."[1] It is only when listening to the analogue punk rock
of his younger days that he can feel "the rapturous surges of sixteen-year-old-ness"
again, and the greatest strength of Egan's musical novel is its ability to become
similarly unstuck in time, its plot skipping between decades and characters with
the ease of a multidirectional, ahistorical, and all too digital playlist of mp3s. In
other cases, music's importance to fiction lies less in escaping temporality than
in reinforcing it, as in the many novels that deploy the songs of the past to resur-
rect that past in the reading present. Though concerned with the lives of classical
musicians, Richard Powers's *The Time of Our Singing* (2003) relies on such popular touchstones as Miles Davis's *Sketches of Spain* and The Beatles's *Sgt. Pepper's
Lonely Hearts Club Band* to make the novel's epic, sixty-year plot more audible.
Zachary Lazar's *Sway* (2008) uses the Luciferian music of the Rolling Stones to
summon Charles Manson's California, ending with the observation that even forty
years later "you'll hear a snatch of it through a car window, the sound of it still a
surprise over a stranger's radio, the old song sent around the planet in waves that

never end."² And while Toni Morrison's *Jazz* (1992) contains little in the way of actual song references, its title creates a pervasive, formally musical atmosphere that invites readers to listen for connections and echoes among her polyphonic tales of 1920s Harlem.

Just as cultural critics in the early twentieth century often marveled at the speed and ease with which American music traveled the globe, so too do contemporary authors sometimes deploy popular song in order to demonstrate the porousness of geographic boundaries and to serve what we now call a transnational aesthetic. Salman Rushdie's *The Ground Beneath Her Feet* (2000), an alternate history of the 1960s, not only finds John F. Kennedy surviving an assassination attempt in Dallas but also presents an Indian musician with telepathic access to as-yet-unwritten American rock 'n' roll. As "Da Doo Ron Ron," "Eve of Destruction," "I Got You Babe," and "Like a Rolling Stone" are performed by Rushdie's protagonist years before they would appear on our timeline, the reader is presented with the challenge of reimagining these most Western of songs in an Eastern context (to say nothing of envisioning a world in which Bob Dylan and Barry McGuire enjoy such undeserved equivalence). So too does Roddy Doyle's *The Commitments* (1987) take pleasure in removing music from its national contexts, following the brief rise and fall of a "Dublin soul" band with a taste for retro, African American styles. Doyle's pages resound with bellowed lyrics that can be assigned to familiar recordings—"THAT'S THE SOUND O' THE MEN—/WORKIN' ON THE CHAIN—/ GA—EE—ANG"—and the interest of such moments lies in the reader's attempts at contrasting a familiar black voice with an unfamiliar Irish one.³ Discomforting suggestions of musical and cultural imperialism, however, are never far away in such novels. Particularly ghastly is Ryu Murakami's *Popular Hits of the Showa Era* (1994), a grim, violent portrait of a postwar Japan hollowed out by global capitalism's insidious culture industry. Murakami presents two karaoke-obsessed groups of same-sex friends who get into a motiveless feud and proceed to stab, shoot, blow apart, and finally incinerate one another, all to a soundtrack of saccharine pop. When not occupied with killing, the men dress in drag and perform songs on a deserted beach, while the women compare themselves to The Beatles and The Rolling Stones, depending on how many of them have been left alive in the carnage.

Much of the pathology in Murakami's novel grows out of music's much-noted ability to violate boundaries of consciousness, to overwhelm the individual will, and to compel participation in mass culture. But for other contemporary writers, music's coercive power redounds upon those who have mastered it and offers a unique kind freedom, with the musical novel sometimes serving as an account of the artist's triumph over category. Matthew Specktor's *That Summertime Sound* (2009) revisits the Columbus rock scene of 1986 and begins by rehearsing typical Generation X anxieties about historical belatedness and the emptiness of pastiche: watching a musician perform, the narrator detects "a gesture I'd seen somewhere before, what Brian Jones did on the original 'Jumpin' Jack Flash' 45's picture-sleeve. Was everything a quotation with him?"[4] Eventually, however, he reaches the Eliotic conclusion that music's allure lies precisely in its invitation to consume and deploy that which came before, with the authentically new talent always one of "strange and stolen originality, the originality that was his because it was borrowed, the only kind of originality that counts."[5] A similar but more exhilarating conviction can be found in Paul Beatty's *Slumberland* (2008), whose DJ protagonist is crafting a collage of sound that seems to encompass not just all of music but a great deal of the world, as well:

> Brando's creaking leather jacket in *The Wild One*, a shopping cart tumbling down the concrete banks of the L.A. River, Mothers of Invention, a stone skimming across Diamond Lake, the flutter of Paul Newman's eyelashes amplified ten thousand times, some smelly kid named Beck who was playing guitar in front of the Church of Scientology, early, early, early Ray Charles, Etta James, Sonic Youth, the Millennium Falcon going into hyperdrive, Foghorn Leghorn, Foghat, Melvin Tormé, aka 'The Velvet Fog,' Issa Bagayogo, the sizzle of an Al's Sandwich Shop cheesesteak at the exact moment Ms. Tseng adds the onions . . .[6]

For Eliot, the poet's absorption in other texts and his ability to channel other voices was valuable in part because it allowed for an escape from the strictures of personality. For Beatty, on the other hand, the DJ's command of sonic miscellany allows for an escape from suffocating racial categories: his narrator seeks a sound "so perfect as to render musical labels null and void. A melody so transcendental that blackness has officially been declared passé. . . . [W]hat we threw down was the content not of character, but *out* of character. It just happened to be of indeterminate blackness and funkier than a motherfucker."[7] Here and elsewhere in contemporary fiction, it is in music that difference can finally be dissolved.

Perhaps the most enduring division that today's musical literature explores, however, is the one separating artists from their audiences: like Dreiser and Dos Passos before them, contemporary authors are very much attuned to the desire of listeners and readers alike to "get over," to draw nearer to artists and their wellsprings of creativity. Generally speaking, their novels treat such hopes with skepticism. Especially uncomfortable is Arthur Phillips's *The Song Is You* (2009), in which a middle-aged commercial director is impressed by an up-and-coming musician at a concert and asks the club's bartender to pass her a list of suggestions; she follows most of her unknown benefactor's advice (to great success), even as he begins tailing her and periodically breaking in to her apartment. Thus does a fan make a real, gratifying contribution to an artist's craft, but so too does Phillips show that fan crossing over into something like obsession, with one character speculating that he may in fact be the Mark David Chapman to her Lennon. Jonathan Lethem's *You Don't Love Me Yet* (2007) is similarly uneasy, the story of an anonymous man who suggests lyrics to a female musician over a complaint hotline; eventually he joins her band, which promptly falls apart and seems to illustrate the wisdom of keeping artists and audiences separated. For a rare, optimistic take, however, one can turn to the fiction of Nick Hornby, whose *High Fidelity* (1995)—perhaps the most determinedly soundtracked novel ever written—ends with its neurotic, record-collecting protagonist vowing to start his own music label, no longer simply consuming music but actively producing it. So too does Hornby's *Juliet, Naked* (2009) find artist and fan coming to a more complete understanding of one another, with a reclusive, Dylanesque musician named Tucker Crowe drawn into the orbit of a devoted "Crowologist."[8] And in a subtle defense of musical fiction, *Juliet, Naked* suggests that authors are ultimately better equipped than most to "get over" and understand the true nature of musical talent: it is the character who writes the most eloquent, witty, and perceptive online review of Crowe's new album who inspires him to break his decades-long public silence, and not the ponderous exegetes and ungrammatical commenters on his fan website.

Yet how effective, ultimately, can any writer be at evoking music in a nonmusical form? Let us conclude with Geoff Dyer, whose *But Beautiful: A Book about Jazz* (1996) is perhaps the most explicit and creative response to this question of the last few decades. *But Beautiful* is a text of indeterminate genre, a series of portraits of actual jazz musicians that are grounded in reality but veer into imaginative, lyrical realms when describing private lives and experiences. Attempting something neither fictional nor biographical but both, Dyer describes his authorial method as a performance of "standards," insofar as he is "stating the identifying facts more or less briefly and then improvising around them, departing from them completely in some cases."[9] The bassist and bandleader Charles Mingus is uniquely well suited to such an approach, a man who united worldly experiences with musical ones and who allows today's listeners—and surely today's writers—to make their own contributions to his art:

> He packed his music so full of life, so full of the noise of the city, that thirty years in the future someone listening to "Pithecanthropus Erectus"

or "Hog-Calling Blues" or any of those other wild steamrolling things wouldn't be sure whether that wail and scream was a horn on the record or the red-and-white siren of a prowl car shrieking past the window. Just listening to the music would be a way of joining in with it, adding to it.

(111)

Many other parts of *But Beautiful* are similarly inclusive, but at points the distance between writer and musician seems impossible to overcome. Laboring to capture the pianist Bud Powell, Dyer seems finally to throw up his hands, addressing his subject directly: "Bud? Have you even heard what I've been saying? Was any of it like that, was any of it the way I've imagined it? Maybe it's all wrong but I tried" (79). He hopes Powell will recognize that he "didn't have much to go on" when writing and will therefore forgive the necessarily limited, partial nature of his work, but it is still Dyer's uncertainty that resonates most powerfully here.

The limitations of the literary and the elusiveness of the musical are painfully obvious in such moments, and yet Dyer's inspired writing is still a testament to the possibility of aesthetic synthesis, particularly in his demonstration that what might initially sound like a failure can in fact be the greatest success of all. Perhaps nowhere have the simultaneous pitfalls and triumphs of musical literature been on better display than in his description of Thelonious Monk, specifically Monk's idiosyncratic habit of structuring pieces around known melodies without ever actually playing those melodies straight:

> If Monk had built a bridge he'd have taken away the bits that are considered essential until all that was left were the decorative parts—but somehow he would have made the ornamentation absorb the strength of the supporting spars so it was like everything was built around what wasn't there. It shouldn't have held together but it did and the excitement came from the way that it looked like it might collapse at any moment just as Monk's music always sounded like it might get wrapped up in itself.

(41)

To add a final written improvisation to Dyer's, we might say that the case of Monk is also the case of musical literature more broadly. We must acknowledge the persistent fact that texts, whether today or a hundred years ago, contain no actual sound: the "bits that are considered essential" to listening are indubitably missing, and nothing on the printed page is truly, physically detectible to the ear. Insofar as literature aspires to the condition of music, then, it can do so only by suggestion, with those who write such books sometimes consumed by the impossibility of their task. And yet we have seen and heard many times that, like a composition that "shouldn't have held together" but improbably does, music in literature remains somehow present in its absence, audible in its silence, vivid in its ineffability. When we read, hear, and sing the Great American Songbooks, we walk upon and build the bridge.

Appendix: Audio Guide

Excerpts from the following recordings can be found in an online audio guide hosted by Oxford University Press (at www.oup.com/us/thegreatamericansongbooks/, by using the username Music1 and password Book5983). Complete recordings can be found at the locations indicated.

1) Maria Callas, "Dormono Etrambi," from *Norma* (1952). The complete recording is available on CD (EMI, 1995), and for download at www.itunes.com.

2) Montserrat Caballé, "Il Dolce Suono," from *Lucia di Lammermoor* (1976). The complete recording is available on CD (Decca, 2002), and for download at www.itunes.com.

3) Plácido Domingo and Raina Kabaivanska, "Cessaro I Suoni," *Ernani* (1969). The complete recording is available on CD (Oper d'oro, 2007), and for download at www.itunes.com

4) Seiji Ozawa, Maurice Peress, and Leonard Bernstein, *Central Park in the Dark* (1962). The complete recording is available on CD (Sony, 2005), and for download at www.itunes.com.

5) Harry MacDonough and Lucy Isabelle Marsh, "Babes in the Wood" (Victor, 1917). The complete recording can be found at www.archive.org.

6) Marie Tiffany, "Kiss Me Again" (Edison, 1919). The complete recording can be found at cylinders.library.ucsb.edu.

7) Elizabeth Spencer, "My Beautiful Lady" (Edison, 1913). The complete recording can be found at cylinders.library.ucsb.edu.

8) Ada Jones, "Ring Ting-a-Ling" (Columbia, 1912). The complete recording can be found at www.archive.org.

9) Elizabeth Spencer, "Poor Butterfly" (Edison 1917). The complete recording can be found at cylinders.library.ucsb.edu.

10) John McCormack, "Three O'clock in the Morning" (Victrola, 1922). The complete recording can be found at www.archive.org.

11) Frances Alda and the Orpheus Quartet, "Deep River" (Victor, 1917). The complete recording can be found at www.collectionscanada.gc.ca/gramophone.

12) The Fisk Jubilee Singers, "Deep River" (1940). The complete recording is available on CD, *Fisk Jubilee Singers in Chronological Order* (Document, 1997), and for download at www.itunes.com.

13) Al Bernard, "Nigger Blues" (Edison, 1919). The complete recording can be found at cylinders.library.ucsb.edu.

14) The New Orleans Rhythm Kings and Jelly Roll Morton, "Weary Blues" (Gennett 1923). The complete recording is available on CD, *New Orleans Rhythm Kings and Jelly Roll Morton* (Milestone, 1992), and for download at www.itunes.com.

15) Marion Harris, "St. Louis Blues" (Columbia, 1920). The complete recording is available at www.archive.org.

16) Marie Cahill, "The Dallas Blues" (Victor, 1917). The complete recording is available at www.archive.org.

17) Blind Lemon Jefferson, "Stocking Feet Blues" (Paramount, 1926). The complete recording is available on CD, *Blind Lemon Jefferson* (Milestone 1991), and for download at www.itunes.com.

18) Papa Charlie Jackson, "Shake That Thing" (Paramount, 1925). The complete recording is available on CD, *Complete Recorded Works* (Document, 1994), and for download at www.itunes.com.

Notes

CHAPTER 1

1. Walter Pater, *The Renaissance: Studies in Art and Poetry* (1888; rpt. Oxford: Oxford University Press, 2010), 124. Emphasis original. Further references to this edition will appear parenthetically in the text.

2. Ezra Pound, "Vortex," *Blast* 1 (London: John Land, 1914), 154.

3. William Carlos Williams, *Spring and All* (1923; rpt. New York: New Directions, 1986), 235.

4. T. S. Eliot, *The Waste Land: A Facsimile and Transcript of the Original Drafts Including the Annotations of Ezra Pound* (New York: Harcourt Brace Jovanovich, 1971), 40–41; T. S. Eliot, *The Use of Poetry and the Use of Criticism: Studies in the Relation of Criticism to Poetry in England* (1933; rpt. Cambridge: Harvard University Press, 1986), 22.

5. F. Scott Fitzgerald, *This Side of Paradise* (1920; Cambridge: Cambridge University Press, 1995), 103.

6. See especially Daniel Albright, *Untwisting the Serpent: Modernism in Music, Literature, and Other Arts* (Chicago: University of Chicago Press, 2000); and Brad Bucknell, *Literary Modernism and Musical Aesthetics: Pater, Pound, Joyce, and Stein* (Cambridge: Cambridge University Press, 2001). For more on modernism as an essentially interdisciplinary practice, see Jay Bochner and Justin D. Edwards, eds., *American Modernism across the Arts* (New York: Peter Lang, 1999); Douglas Mao and Rebecca L. Walkowitz, eds., *Bad Modernisms* (Durham: Duke University Press, 2006); and Julian Murphet, *Multimedia Modernism: Literature and the Anglo-American Avant-Garde* (Cambridge: Cambridge University Press, 2009). Other studies of modernism that consider Pater an important intellectual precursor include Tim Armstrong, *Modernism: A Cultural History* (Cambridge: Polity, 2005); Anthony Cuda, *The Passions of Modernism: Eliot, Yeats, Woolf, and Mann* (Columbia: University of South Carolina Press, 2010); Hugh Kenner, *The Pound Era* (Berkeley: University of California Press, 1971); Michael H. Levenson, *A Genealogy of Modernism: A Study of English Literary Doctrine, 1908–1922* (Cambridge: Cambridge University Press, 1984); Pericles Lewis, *The Cambridge Introduction to Modernism* (Cambridge: Cambridge University Press, 2007); James Longenbach, *Modernist Poetics of History: Pound, Eliot, and the Sense of the Past* (Princeton: Princeton University Press, 1987); Louis Menand, *Discovering*

Modernism: T. S. Eliot and His Context (Oxford: Oxford University Press, 1987); and Peter Nicholls, *Modernisms: A Literary Guide* (Berkeley: University of California Press, 1995).

7. Christopher Small, *Musicking: The Meanings of Performing and Listening* (Hanover: Wesleyan University Press, 1998), 8.

8. The recent critical collection *Phrase and Subject: Studies in Literature and Music*, ed. Delia da Sousa Correa (London: LEGENDA, 2006), is generally representative of this subfield, containing as it does only two essays on American artists, no studies of black ones, and scarcely a word on music outside of the classical canon.

9. Christopher Small, *Music of the Common Tongue: Survival and Celebration in Afro-American Music* (Hanover: Wesleyan University Press, 1998), 53–54.

10. Amazon.com, "Inherent Vice." Accessed September 11, 2011. http://www.amazon.com/Inherent-Vice-Novel-Thomas-Pynchon/dp/0143117564/ref=sr_1_1?s=books&ie=UTF 8&qid=1315760137&sr=1-1.

11. Julie Bosman, "Bells and Whistles for a Few E-Books," *New York Times*, August 23, 2011. Accessed August 23, 2011. www.nytimes.com/2011/08/24/books/booktrack-introduces-e-books-with-soundtracks.html?ref=arts.

12. Walt Whitman, *Complete Poetry and Collected Prose* (New York: Library of America, 1982), 1252. Emphasis original.

13. Henry David Thoreau, *Journal IX (August 16, 1856–August 7, 1857)* (Cambridge: Riverside Press, 1906), 218. Emphasis original.

14. On this subject, see Jamie James, *The Music of the Spheres: Music, Science, and the Natural Order of the Universe* (New York: Grove Press, 1993); and Kathi Meyer-Baer, *The Music of the Spheres and the Dance of Death: Studies in Musical Iconology* (Princeton: Princeton University Press, 1970). Nineteenth-century conceptions of musical ideality and the scholarship devoted to them are taken up in the second chapter of this book.

15. Ralph Waldo Emerson, *Essays and Lectures* (New York: Library of America, 1983), 484.

16. Thoreau, *Journal IX*, 222.

17. James Fenimore Cooper, *The Last of the Mohicans* (1826; rpt. New York: Modern Library, 2001), 169; Herman Melville, *Pierre; or, The Ambiguities* (1852; rpt. New York: Library of America, 1984), 151; Kate Chopin, *The Awakening* (1899; rpt. New York: W.W. Norton, 1976), 80.

18. Paul Verlaine, *Jadis et Naguére* (1885; rpt. Paris: Le Club du meilleur livre, 1959), 513.

19. On the musical character of Symbolism, see Nicholls, *Modernisms*; and David Michael Hertz, *The Tuning of the Word: The Musico-Literary Poetics of the Symbolist Movement* (Carbondale: Southern Illinois University Press, 1987). On music's influence on the visual arts in the late nineteenth and early twentieth centuries, see Kerry Brougher et al., *Visual Music: Synaesthesia in Art and Music since 1900* (New York: Thames and Hudson, 2005); Christopher Butler, *Early Modernism: Literature, Music, and Painting in Europe, 1900–1916* (Oxford: Clarendon Press, 1994); James Leggio, ed., *Music and Modern Art* (New York: Routledge, 2002); Richard Leppert, *The Sight of Sound: Music, Representation, and the History of the Body* (Berkeley: University of California Press, 1993); and Peter Vergo, *The Music of Painting: Music, Modernism, and the Visual Arts from the Romantics to John Cage* (London: Phaidon Press, 2012). On the musicality of the Futurists and others of the twentieth century avant-garde, see Douglas Kahn, *Noise Water Meat: A History of Sound in the Arts* (Cambridge: MIT Press, 1999). See also Vincent Sherry's *Ezra Pound, Wyndham Lewis,*

and Radical Modernism (Oxford: Oxford University Press, 1993), which contrasts visual and musical approaches to literary modernism.

20. Albright, *Untwisting the Serpent*, 5.

21. Pater, *The Renaissance*, 120; Ezra Pound, *Literary Essays* (1918; rpt: New York: New Directions, 1968), 4.

22. Eric Prieto, *Listening In: Music, Mind, and the Modernist Narrative* (Lincoln: University of Nebraska Press, 2002), 8. Other studies of music and literature include Alex Aronson, *Music and the Novel: A Study in Twentieth-Century Fiction* (Totowa: Rowman and Littlefield, 1980); Calvin S. Brown, *Music and Literature: A Comparison of the Arts* (Athens: University of Georgia Press, 1948); Correa, *Phrase and Subject*; Steven Paul Scher, ed., *Music and Text: Critical Inquiries* (Cambridge: Cambridge University Press, 1992); and Werner Wolf, *The Musicalization of Fiction: A Study in the Theory and History of Intermediality* (Amsterdam: Rodopi, 1999). Scholarship on intersections of music and poetry more specifically will be taken up in this book's second chapter. Anthologies of musical fiction and poetry include Sascha Feinstein and Yusef Komunyakaa, eds., *The Jazz Poetry Anthology* (Bloomington: Indiana University Press, 1999); Feinstein and Komunyakaa, eds., *The Second Set: The Jazz Poetry Anthology* (Bloomington: Indiana University Press, 1996); Art Lange and Nathaniel Mackey, eds., *Moment's Notice: Jazz in Poetry and Prose* (Minneapolis: Coffee House Press, 1993); and Murray J. Levith, ed., *Musical Masterpieces in Prose* (Neptune: Paganiniana Publications, 1981).

23. LeRoi Jones, *Blues People: Negro Music in White America* (New York: Morrow Quill, 1963), x.

24. Paul Gilroy, *The Black Atlantic: Modernity and Double Consciousness* (Cambridge: Harvard University Press, 1993), 73–74. Criticism on African American literature and music is taken up in this book's fourth chapter.

25. Rita Felski, *The Gender of Modernity* (Cambridge: Harvard University Press, 1995), 22; Virginia Woolf, *A Room of One's Own* (1929; rpt. Oxford: Oxford University Press, 2008), 136. Much of the recent scholarly conversation on gender and modernism in America has sought to emphasize points of commonality as well as points of departure between male and female artists. It was once common to argue, as do Sandra M. Gilbert and Susan Gubar in their monumental *No Man's Land: The Place of the Woman Writer in the Twentieth Century*, that the relationship between modernism's men and women was fundamentally oppositional and part of an ongoing "sexual battle" in literature (I: xiv). More recent studies, however, have sought to show how each gender's literary tradition was significantly intertwined with the other's, even as critics recover neglected works by women and deepen the scholarly sense of female modernism. Recent studies have also been profitably attuned to the ways in which women's writing of the period was significantly interdisciplinary and committed to complicating the boundaries of high and low art. Exemplary in this vein are Suzanne Clark, *Sentimental Modernism: Women Writers and the Revolution of the Word* (Bloomington: Indiana University Press, 1991); Marianne DeKoven, *Rich and Strange: Gender, History, Modernism* (Princeton: Princeton University Press, 1991); Rachel Blau DuPlessis, *Genders, Races, and Religious Cultures in Modern American Poetry, 1908–1934* (Cambridge: Cambridge University Press, 2001); Jessica R. Feldman, *Gender on the Divide: The Dandy in Modernist Literature* (Ithica: Cornell University Press, 1993); and Felski, *The Gender of Modernity*. For collections of critical essays, see Ann L. Ardis and Leslie W. Lewis, eds., *Women's Experience of Modernity, 1875–1945* (Baltimore: Johns Hopkins University

Press, 2003); Lisa Botshon and Meredith Goldsmith, eds., *Middlebrow Moderns: Popular American Women Writers of the 1920s* (Boston: Northeastern University Press, 2003); Bridget Elliott and Jo-Ann Wallace, *Women Artists and Writers: Modernist (im)positionings* (London: Routledge, 1994); Maren Tova Linett, ed., *The Cambridge Companion to Modernist Women Writers* (Cambridge: Cambridge University Press, 2010); Lisa Rado, ed., *Modernism, Gender, and Culture: A Cultural Studies Approach* (New York: Garland, 1997); and Rado, ed., *Rereading Modernism: New Directions in Feminist Criticism* (New York: Garland, 1994). For anthologies, see Bonnie Kime Scott, ed., *The Gender of Modernism: A Critical Anthology* (Bloomington: Indiana University Press, 1990); and Scott, ed., *Gender in Modernism: New Geographies, Complex Intersections* (Urbana: University of Illinois Press, 2007).

26. R. Murray Schafer, *The Tuning of the World* (New York: Alfred A. Knopf, 1977), 3.

27. The standard history of American popular music is Russell Sanjek's three-volume *American Popular Music and Its Business: The First Four Hundred Years* (Oxford: Oxford University Press, 1988). See also Richard Crawford, *America's Musical Life: A History* (New York: W.W. Norton, 2001); Philip Furia, *The Poets of Tin Pan Alley: A History of America's Great Lyricists* (Oxford: Oxford University Press, 1990); Reebee Garofalo, *Rockin' Out: Popular Music in the USA* (Boston: Allyn and Bacon, 1997); Charles Hamm, *Yesterdays: Popular Song in America* (New York: W. W. Norton, 1979); Russel Nye, *The Unembarrassed Muse: The Popular Arts in America* (New York: Dial Press, 1970); Derek B. Scott, *Sounds of the Metropolis: The Nineteenth-Century Popular Music Revolution in London, New York, Paris, and Vienna* (Oxford: Oxford University Press, 2008); David Suisman, *Selling Sounds: The Commercial Revolution in American Music* (Cambridge: Harvard University Press, 2009); Nicholas E. Tawa, *The Way to Tin Pan Alley: American Popular Song, 1866–1910* (New York: Schirmer Books, 1990); and Ian Whitcomb, *After the Ball: Pop Music from Rag to Rock* (Baltimore: Penguin, 1972).

28. Burnet Hershey, "Jazz Latitude," *New York Times*, June 25, 1922, 5.

29. Emily Thompson, *The Soundscape of Modernity: Architectural Acoustics and the Culture of Listening in America, 1900–1933* (Cambridge: MIT Press, 2002), 2.

30. George M. Beard, *American Nervousness: Its Causes and Consequences; A Supplement to Nervous Exhaustion (Neurasthenia)* (New York: G.P. Putnam's Sons, 1881), 114.

31. John Philip Sousa, "The Menace of Mechanical Music," *Appleton's Magazine* 8 (August 1906), 281.

32. Willa Cather, *Willa Cather in Person: Interviews, Speeches, and Letters* (Lincoln: University of Nebraska Press, 1986), 148.

33. Anonymous, "How Popular Song Factories Manufacture a Hit," *New York Times*, September 18, 1910, SM11.

34. Charles K. Harris, *After the Ball: Forty Years of Melody, An Autobiography* (New York: Frank-Maurice Inc., 1926), 40.

35. Frank Norris, *McTeague: A Story of San Francisco* (1899; rpt. New York: W.W. Norton, 1997), 5.

36. Deems Taylor, "Music," in *Civilization in the United States: An Inquiry by Thirty Americans* (New York: Harcourt, Brace, 1922), 212.

37. Theodore Dreiser, *A Hoosier Holiday* (New York: John Lane, 1916), 359–360.

38. Ronald Schleifer, *Modernism and Popular Music* (Cambridge: Cambridge University Press, 2011); Alfred Appel Jr., *Jazz Modernism: From Ellington and Armstrong to Matisse and Joyce* (New York: Alfred A. Knopf, 2002), 13.

39. F. Scott Fitzgerald, *My Lost City: Personal Essays, 1920–1940* (Cambridge: Cambridge University Press, 2005), 132.

40. For a consideration of how the retrospective sense of "authentic" jazz has blinkered modernist criticism, see Ryan Jerving, "Early Jazz Literature (And Why You Didn't Know)," *American Literary History* 16:4 (2004), 648–674. See also Jed Rasula, "Jazz and American Modernism," in *The Cambridge Companion to American Modernism*, ed. Walter Kalaidjian (Cambridge: Cambridge University Press, 2005), 157–176. Scholarship on jazz and African American literature is taken up in this book's fourth chapter.

41. John Dos Passos, *Manhattan Transfer* (1925; rpt. New York: Library of America, 2003), 653.

42. Alan Lomax, *Mister Jelly Roll: The Fortunes of Jelly Roll Morton, New Orleans Creole and "Inventor of Jazz"* (1950; rpt. Berkeley: University of California Press, 1973), 66.

43. Studies of the phonograph and its effects on American cultural life are legion. See Michael Chanan, *Repeated Takes: A Short History of Recording and Its Effect on Music* (New York: Verso, 1995); Timothy Day, *A Century of Recorded Music: Listening to Musical History* (New Haven: Yale University Press, 2000); Evan Eisenberg, *The Recording Angel: Music, Records and Culture from Aristotle to Zappa* (New Haven: Yale University Press, 2005); Reebee Garofalo, *Rockin' Out*; Lisa Gitelman, *Always Already New: Media, History, and the Data of Culture* (Cambridge: MIT Press, 2006); Gitelman, *Scripts, Grooves, and Writing Machines: Representing Technology in the Edison Era* (Stanford: Stanford University Press, 1999); Mark Katz, *Capturing Sound: How Technology Has Changed Music* (Berkeley: University of California Press, 2004); William Howland Kenney, *Recorded Music in American Life: The Phonograph and Popular Memory, 1890–1945* (Oxford: Oxford University Press, 1999); Marshall McLuhan, *Understanding Media: The Extensions of Man* (New York: McGraw-Hill, 1964); Andre Millard, *America on Record: A History of Recorded Sound* (Cambridge: Cambridge University Press, 2005); Greg Milner, *Perfecting Sound Forever: An Aural History of Recorded Music* (New York: Faber and Faber, 2009); Robert Philip, *Performing Music in the Age of Recording* (New Haven: Yale University Press, 2004); Jonathan Sterne, *The Audible Past: Cultural Origins of Sound Reproduction* (Durham: Duke University Press, 2003); and Suisman, *Selling Sounds*. For one of the more famous meditations on music's alleged degradation in the mass market, see Jacques Attali, *Noise: The Political Economy of Music* (1977; rpt. Minneapolis: University of Minnesota Press, 1985).

44. Irving Babbitt, *The New Laokoon: An Essay on the Confusion of the Arts* (Boston: Houghton Mifflin, 1910), 112. Further references to this edition will appear parenthetically in the text.

45. Joseph Conrad, *The Nigger of the "Narcissus"* (1897; rpt. New York: Dover, 1999), vii. Emphasis original.

46. T. S. Eliot, *Selected Prose* (New York: Harcourt Brace Jovanovich, 1975), 64, 66. Note also the corporeality of Eliot's poem "Whispers of Immortality" from the same period, which praises Donne as a writer "Who found no substitute for sense,/To seize and clutch and penetrate;/Expert beyond experience,/He knew the anguish of the marrow/The ague of the skeleton;/No contact possible to flesh/Allayed the fever of the bone." See Eliot, *The Complete Poems and Plays, 1909–1950* (New York: Harcourt Brace, 1980), 32–33.

47. Gertrude Stein, *Selected Writings* (New York: Vintage, 1962), 516.

48. Kahn, *Noise Water Meat*, 4–5.

49. See the following "sound studies" approaches to the humanities in the nineteenth and twentieth centuries: Charles Bernstein, ed., *Close Listening: Poetry and the Performed Word*

(Oxford: Oxford University Press, 1988); Michael Bull and Les Black, eds., *The Auditory Culture Reader* (Oxford: Berg, 2003); Veit Erlmann, ed., *Hearing Cultures: Essays on Sound, Listening, and Modernity* (Oxford: Berg, 2004); Douglas Kahn and Gregory Whitehead, eds., *Wireless Imagination: Sound, Radio, and the Avant-Garde* (Cambridge: MIT Press, 1992); Adalaide Morris, ed., *Sound States: Innovative Poetics and Acoustical Technologies* (Chapel Hill: University of North Carolina Press, 1997); Fred Moten, *In the Break: The Aesthetics of the Black Radical Tradition* (Minneapolis: University of Minnesota Press, 2003); Marjorie Perloff and Craig Dworkin, eds., *The Sound of Poetry/The Poetry of Sound* (Chicago: University of Chicago Press, 2009); John M. Picker, *Victorian Soundscapes* (Oxford: Oxford University Press, 2003); Mark M. Smith, ed., *Hearing History: A Reader* (Athens: University of Georgia Press, 2004); Susan Stewart, *Poetry and the Fate of the Senses* (Chicago: University of Chicago Press, 2002); and Alexander G. Weheliye, *Phonographies: Grooves in Sonic Afro-Modernity* (Durham: Duke University Press, 2005). For an overview of various sensory approaches to reading that include listening, see David Howes, ed., *Empire of the Senses: The Sensual Culture Reader* (Oxford: Berg, 2005); and Michael Syrotinski and Ian Maclachlan, eds., *Sensual Reading: New Approaches to Reading in Its Relation to the Senses* (Lewisburg: Bucknell University Press, 2001).

50. See especially Eric A. Havelock, *The Muse Learns to Write: Reflections on Orality and Literacy from Antiquity to the Present* (New Haven: Yale University Press, 1986); Walter J. Ong, *Orality and Literacy* (1982; rpt. New York: Methuen, 1988); Marshall McLuhan, *The Gutenberg Galaxy: The Making of Typographic Man* (Toronto: University of Toronto Press, 1962); and McLuhan, *Understanding Media*. See also John Barth's 1968 story collection *Lost in the Funhouse* (rpt. New York: Anchor, 1988), whose pieces are said by its author to be variously intended for "Print, Tape, Live Voice" mediation (vii).

51. Ong, *Orality and Literacy*, 8.

52. On the oral dimension of African American literature, see the fourth chapter of this book.

53. Roland Barthes, *S/Z: An Essay* (New York: Hill and Wang, 1970), 5.

54. Garrett Stewart, *Reading Voices: Literature and the Phonotext* (Berkeley: University of California Press, 1990), 2, 11.

55. William R. Paulson, *The Noise of Culture: Literary Texts in a World of Information* (Ithaca: Cornell University Press, 1988), ix.

56. Juan A. Suárez, *Pop Modernism: Noise and the Reinvention of the Everyday* (Urbana: University of Illinois Press, 2007), 8–9.

57. Philipp Schweighauser, *The Noises of American Literature, 1890–1985: Toward a History of Literary Acoustics* (Gainesville: University Press of Florida, 2006), 24, 3. Emphasis original.

58. Lisa Gitelman, *Scripts, Grooves, and Writing Machines*, 11; Michael North, "Visual Culture," in *The Cambridge Companion to American Modernism* (Cambridge: Cambridge University Press, 2005), 185.

59. Friedrich A. Kittler, *Gramophone, Film, Typewriter* (1986; rpt. Stanford: Stanford University Press, 1999), 4.

60. Kittler, *Gramophone, Film, Typewriter*, 10.

61. Friedrich A. Kittler, *Discourse Networks, 1800/1900* (1985; rpt. Stanford: Stanford University Press, 1990), 229–264.

62. Sterne, *The Audible Past*, 6.

63. McLuhan, *Understanding Media*, 54. On the effects of technology on literary modernism, see Tim Armstrong, *Modernism, Technology, and the Body: A Cultural Study* (Cambridge: Cambridge University Press, 1998); Nicholas Daly, *Literature, Technology, and Modernity, 1860–2000* (Cambridge: Cambridge University Press, 2004); Sara Danius, *The Senses of Modernism: Technology, Perception, and Aesthetics* (Ithaca: Cornell University Press, 2002); Frederick J. Hoffman, *The Twenties: American Writing in the Postwar Decade* (New York: Collier, 1962); Hugh Kenner, *The Mechanic Muse* (Oxford: Oxford University Press, 1987); Murphet, *Multimedia Modernism*; Miles Orvell, *The Real Thing: Authenticity and Imitation in American Culture, 1880–1940* (Chapel Hill: University of North Carolina Press, 1989); Lisa M. Steinman, *Made in America: Science, Technology, and American Modernist Poets* (New Haven: Yale University Press, 1987); Suárez, *Pop Modernism*; and Cecelia Tichi, *Shifting Gears: Technology, Literature, Culture in Modernist America* (Chapel Hill: University of North Carolina Press, 1987). On literature that depicts early sound recording technology, see Kahn, *Noise Water Meat*; Sebastian D. G. Knowles, "Death by Gramophone," *Journal of Modern Literature* 27:1 (2003), 1–14; and Colin Symes, "From *Tomorrow's Eve* to *High Fidelity*: Novel Responses to the Gramophone in Twentieth Century Literature," *Popular Music* 24:2 (2005), 193–206.

64. Danius, *The Senses of Modernism*, 20.

65. F. T. Marinetti, "Destruction of Syntax—Radio Imagination—Words-in-Freedom," in *Futurism: An Anthology* (New Haven: Yale University Press, 2009), 143.

66. Hart Crane, *Complete Poems and Selected Letters and Prose* (New York: Liveright, 1966), 219.

67. Ford Madox Ford, *Henry James: A Critical Study* (1913; rpt. New York: Octagon Books Inc., 1964), 174.

68. Walter Benjamin, in *The Work of Art in the Age of Its Technological Reproducibility, and Other Writings on Media* (Cambridge: Harvard University Press, 2008), 22, 40.

69. Kittler, *Gramophone, Film, Typewriter*, 80.

70. Fitzgerald, *This Side of Paradise*, 82. Emphasis original.

71. As Richard Middleton has pointed out, it was in the late nineteenth century that the word "popular" in its relation to music came to be associated with the mass market, as opposed to the "traditional" or "peasant" arts. See *Studying Popular Music* (Philadelphia: Open University Press, 1990), 3–4. On the development of taste hierarchies in America, see Michael Kammen, *American Culture, American Tastes: Social Change and the 20th Century* (New York: Alfred A. Knopf, 2000); Kammen, *The Lively Arts: Gilbert Seldes and the Transformation of Cultural Criticism in the United States* (Oxford: Oxford University Press, 1996); and Lawrence W. Levine, *Highbrow/Lowbrow: The Emergence of Cultural Hierarchy in America* (Cambridge: Harvard University Press, 1990).

72. See, for example, Malcolm Bradbury and James McFarlane, "The Name and Practice of Modernism," in *Modernism: A Guide to European Literature, 1890–1930* (1976; rpt. London: Penguin Books, 1991), 21.

73. Peter Bürger, *Theory of the Avant-Garde* (Minneapolis: University of Minnesota Press, 1984), 22.

74. Andreas Huyssen, *After the Great Divide: Modernism, Mass Culture, Postmodernism* (Bloomington: Indiana University Press, 1986), 60.

75. Terry Eagleton, *Against the Grain: Essays 1975–1985* (London: Verso, 1986), 140.

76. Van Wyck Brooks, *America's Coming-of-Age* (1915; rpt. New York: Viking, 1930), 9. Further references to this edition will appear parenthetically in the text.

77. On politically engaged American modernism, see Kevin Bell, *Ashes Taken for Fire: Aesthetic Modernism and the Critique of Identity* (Minneapolis: University of Minnesota Press, 2007); Laura Browder, *Rousing the Nation: Radical Culture in Depression America* (Amherst: University of Massachusetts Press, 1998); Susan Hegeman, *Patterns for America: Modernism and the Concept of Culture* (Princeton: Princeton University Press, 1999); Michael Denning, *The Cultural Front: The Laboring of American Culture in the Twentieth Century* (New York: Verso, 1996); Adele Heller and Lois Rudnick, eds., *1915, The Cultural Moment: The New Politics, the New Woman, the New Psychology, the New Art and the New Theatre in America* (New Brunswick: Rutgers University Press, 1991); Hoffman, *The Twenties*; David Kadlec, *Mosaic Modernism: Anarchism, Pragmatism, Culture* (Baltimore: Johns Hopkins University Press, 2000); Walter Kalaidjian, *American Culture between the Wars: Revisionary Modernism and Postmodern Critique* (New York: Columbia University Press, 1993); Cary Nelson, *Repression and Recovery: Modern American Poetry and the Politics of Cultural Memory, 1910–1945* (Madison: University of Wisconsin Press, 1989); and Steve Watson, *Strange Bedfellows: The First American Avant-Garde* (New York: Abbeville Press, 1991). Criticism on the Harlem Renaissance and African American writers more specifically will be taken up in the fourth chapter of this book.

78. Michael North, *Reading 1922: A Return to the Scene of the Modern* (Oxford: Oxford University Press, 1999), 30; Lawrence Rainey, *Institutions of Modernism: Literary Elites and Public Culture* (New Haven: Yale University Press, 1998); Suárez, *Pop Modernism*, 5.

79. On the intersections of modernist practice with popular culture across various arts, see Appel, *Jazz Modernism*; Nancy Bentley, *Frantic Panoramas: American Literature and Mass Culture, 1870–1920* (Philadelphia: University of Pennsylvania Press, 2009); Clark, *Sentimental Modernism*; Robert M. Crunden, *Body and Soul: The Making of American Modernism* (New York: Basic Books, 2000); Bernard Gendron, *Between Montmartre and the Mudd Club: Popular Music and the Avant-Garde* (Chicago: University of Chicago Press, 2002); North, *Reading 1922*; Allison Pease, *Modernism, Mass Culture, and the Aesthetics of Obscenity* (Cambridge: Cambridge University Press, 2000); Nancy Lynn Perloff, *Art and the Everyday: Popular Entertainment and the Circle of Erik Satie* (Oxford: Clarendon Press, 1991); Schleifer, *Modernism and Popular Music*; Robert Scholes, *Paradoxy of Modernism* (New Haven: Yale University Press, 2006); Suárez, *Pop Modernism*; and Jeffery Weiss, *The Popular Culture of Modern Art: Picasso, Duchamp, and Avant-Gardism* (New Haven: Yale University Press, 1994). A particularly robust strain of criticism takes up modernism's relationship to the popular press and the publishing industry; see Mark McGurl, *The Novel Art: Elevations of American Fiction after Henry James* (Princeton: Princeton University Press, 2001); Mark S. Morrisson, *The Public Face of Modernism: Little Magazines, Audiences, and Reception, 1905–1920* (Madison: University of Wisconsin Press, 2001); Rainey, *Institutions of Modernism*; Thomas Strychacz, *Modernism, Mass Culture, and Professionalism* (Cambridge: Cambridge University Press, 1993); and Catherine Turner, *Marketing Modernism: Between the Two World Wars* (Amherst: University of Massachusetts Press, 2003). Collections of essays include Kevin J. H. Dettmar, ed., *Rereading the New: A Backward Glance at Modernism* (Ann Arbor: University of Michigan Press, 1992); Dettmar and Stephen Watt, eds., *Marketing Modernisms: Self-Promotion, Canonization, Rereading* (Ann Arbor: University of Michigan Press, 1996); Maria DiBattista and Lucy McDiarmid, eds., *High and*

Low Moderns: Literature and Culture, 1889–1939 (Oxford: Oxford University Press, 1996); Walter Kalaidjian, ed., *The Cambridge Companion to American Modernism* (Cambridge: Cambridge University Press, 2005); Jani Scandura and Michael Thurston, eds., *Modernism, Inc.: Body, Memory, Capital* (New York: New York University Press, 2001); and Kirk Varnedoe and Adam Gopnik, eds., *Modern Art and Popular Culture: Readings in High and Low* (New York: Harry N. Abrams, 1990).

80. Paul Whiteman and Mary Margaret McBride, *Jazz* (New York: J. H. Shears, 1926), 181.

81. Hershey, "Jazz Latitude," 5.

82. Harold Stearns, *America and the Young Intellectual* (New York: George H. Doran, 1921), 159.

83. James Weldon Johnson, *Writings* (New York: Library of America, 2004), 62. Emphasis original.

84. Johnson, *Writings*, 71.

85. Middleton, *Studying Popular Music*, 7.

86. Kammen, *American Culture, American Tastes*, 22.

87. Theodor W. Adorno, *Essays on Music* (Berkeley: University of California Press, 2002), 458.

88. See Barry J. Faulk, *Music Hall and Modernity: The Late-Victorian Discovery of Popular Culture* (Athens: Ohio University Press, 2004).

89. Edmund Wilson, *The Shores of Light: A Literary Chronicle of the Twenties and Thirties* (New York: Farrar, Straus and Young, 1952), 246–247.

90. Eliot, *The Use of Poetry and the Use of Criticism*, 152–154.

91. Peter Swirski, *From Lowbrow to Nobrow* (Montreal: McGill-Queen's University Press, 2005), 10. For more on "nobrow" culture, see Richard A. Peterson, "Understanding Audience Segmentation: From Elite and Mass to Omnivore and Univore," *Poetics* 21:4 (August 1992), 243–258; John Seabrook, *Nobrow: The Culture of Marketing, the Marketing of Culture* (New York: Vintage, 2001); and Carl Wilson, *Let's Talk about Love: A Journey to the End of Taste* (New York: Continuum, 2007).

92. On subversive popular music, see especially Dick Hebdige, *Subculture: The Meaning of Style* (1979; rpt. London: Routledge, 1991).

93. See John Edward Hasse, *Beyond Category: The Life and Genius of Duke Ellington* (New York: Da Capo Press, 1993); and Christopher B. Ricks, *Dylan's Visions of Sin* (London: Viking, 2003).

94. Gilbert Seldes, *The Seven Lively Arts* (New York: Harper & Brothers, 1924), 203.

95. Seldes, *The Seven Lively Arts*, 204.

CHAPTER 2

1. James William Johnson, "Lyric," in *The New Princeton Encyclopedia of Poetry and Poetics* (Princeton: Princeton University Press, 1993), 720.

2. On the intersections of music and poetry, see Daniel Albright, *Untwisting the Serpent: Modernism in Music, Literature, and Other Arts* (Chicago: University of Chicago Press, 2000); Jean-Pierre Barricelli, *Melopoiesis: Approaches to the Study of Literature and Music* (New York: New York University Press, 1988); Marc Berley, *After the Heavenly Tune: English Poetry and the Aspiration to Song* (Pittsburgh: Duquesne University Press, 2000); Charles Bernstein, ed., *Close Listening: Poetry and the Performed Word* (Oxford: Oxford University Press, 1988); Calvin Brown, *Tones into Words: Musical Compositions as Subjects of Poetry*

(Athens: University of Georgia Press, 1953); Lars Eckstein, *Reading Song Lyrics* (New York: Rodopi, 2010); David Michael Hertz, *The Tuning of the Word: The Musico-Literary Poetics of the Symbolist Movement* (Carbondale: Southern Illinois University Press, 1987); John Hollander, *Images of Voice: Music and Sound in Romantic Poetry* (Cambridge: Heffer, 1970); Hollander, *Poetry and Music* (London: Routledge, 2007); Hollander, *The Untuning of the Sky: Ideas of Music in English Poetry, 1500–1700* (Princeton: Princeton University Press, 1961); Lawrence Kramer, *Music and Poetry: The Nineteenth Century and After* (Berkeley: University of California Press, 1984); Charmenz S. Lenhart, *Musical Influence on American Poetry* (Athens: University of Georgia Press, 1956); James S. Malek, *The Arts Compared: An Aspect of Eighteenth-Century British Aesthetics* (Detroit: Wayne State University Press, 1974); Marjorie Perloff and Criag Dworkin, eds., *The Sound of Poetry/The Poetry of Sound* (Chicago: University of Chicago Press, 2009); Jahan Ramazani, "'Sing to Me Now': Contemporary American Poetry and Song," *Contemporary Literature* 52:4 (2011), 716–755; Monroe K. Spears, *Dionysus and the City: Modernism in Twentieth-Century Poetry* (Oxford: Oxford University Press, 1970); Susan Stewart, *Poetry and the Fate of the Senses* (Chicago: University of Chicago Press, 2002); and James Anderson Winn, *Unsuspected Eloquence: A History of the Relations between Poetry and Music* (New Haven: Yale University Press, 1981).

3. Perloff and Dworkin, *The Sound of Poetry*, 1.

4. Sidney Lanier, *The Centennial Edition of the Works of Sidney Lanier,* Volume II: *The Science of English Verse and Essays on Music* (Baltimore: Johns Hopkins University Press, 1945), 31.

5. Leonard Bernstein, *The Unanswered Question: Six Talks at Harvard* (Cambridge: Harvard University Press, 1976), 76.

6. F. O. Matthiessen, *American Renaissance: Art and Expression in the Age of Emerson and Whitman* (1941; rpt. Oxford: Oxford University Press, 1968), 137.

7. Arthur Hobson Quinn, *Edgar Allan Poe: A Critical Biography* (1941; rpt. Baltimore: Johns Hopkins University Press, 1998), 429. Emphasis original.

8. Ezra Pound, *Literary Essays* (1918; rpt: New York: New Directions, 1968), 3.

9. Exceptions include Robert Crawford, *Devolving English Literature* (Oxford: Oxford University Press, 1992); Philip Hobsbaum, "Eliot, Whitman and American Tradition," *Journal of American Studies* 3:2 (December 1969), 239–264; Gregory S. Jay, *T. S. Eliot and the Poetics of Literary History* (Baton Rouge: Louisiana State University Press, 1983); James E. Miller Jr., *The American Quest for a Supreme Fiction: Whitman's Legacy in the Personal Epic* (Chicago: University of Chicago Press, 1979); S. Musgrove, *T. S. Eliot and Walt Whitman* (Wellington: New Zealand University Press, 1952); and Roy Harvey Pearce, *The Continuity of American Poetry* (Princeton: Princeton University Press, 1961).

10. Walt Whitman, *Complete Poetry and Collected Prose* (New York: Library of America, 1982), 1021. Further references to this edition will appear parenthetically in the text.

11. T. S. Eliot, *Selected Prose* (New York: Harcourt Brace Jovanovich, 1975), 114.

12. Horace Traubel, *With Walt Whitman in Camden, Vol. II* (New York: Michell Kennerley, 1915), 174.

13. So too have Whitman's words been adapted by various composers, including Frederick Delius, Howard Hanson, Paul Hindemith, Kurt Weill, Ralph Vaughn Williams, and many others. Studies of Whitman and his use of music are voluminous. On Whitman and Italian opera, see especially Robert D. Faner, *Walt Whitman and Opera* (1951; rpt. Carbondale: Southern Illinois University Press, 1972); David Reynolds, *Walt Whitman's*

America: A Cultural Biography (1995; rpt. New York: Vintage, 1996); and Carmen Trammell Skaggs, *Overtones of Opera in American Literature from Whitman to Wharton* (Baton Rouge: Louisiana State University Press, 2010). Other studies of Whitman's variously defined musicality include Calvin S. Brown, *Music and Literature: A Comparison of the Arts* (Athens: University of Georgia Press, 1948); Bryan K. Carman, *A Race of Singers: Whitman's Working-Class Hero from Guthrie to Springsteen* (Chapel Hill: University of North Carolina Press, 2000); Alice L. Cooke, "Notes on Whitman's Musical Background," *New England Quarterly* 19.2 (June 1946), 224–235; Deniz Ertan, "When Men and Mountains Meet: Ruggles, Whitman, and Their Landscapes," *American Music* (Summer 2009), 227–253; John T. Irwin, *American Hieroglyphics: The Symbol of the Egyptian Hieroglyphics in the American Renaissance* (New Haven: Yale University Press, 1980); Jack Kerkering, "'Of Me and Mine': The Music of Racial Identity in Whitman and Lanier, Dvorak and Du Bois," *American Literature* 73:1 (March 2001), 147–184; Lawrence Kramer, *After the Lovedeath: Sexual Violence and the Making of Culture* (Berkeley: University of California Press, 1997); Lawrence Kramer, ed., *Walt Whitman and Modern Music: War, Desire, and the Trials of Nationhood* (New York: Garland, 2000); Sydney J. Krause, "Whitman, Music, and Proud Music of the Storm," *Publications of the Modern Language Association (PMLA)* 72.4 (September 1957), 705–721; Lenhart, *Musical Influence on American Poetry*; Günter Leypoldt, "Democracy's 'Lawless Music': The Whitmanian Moment in the U.S. Construction of Representative Literariness," *New Literary History* 38 (2007), 333–352; F. O. Matthiessen, *American Renaissance*; Richard Pascal, "Walt Whitman and Woody Guthrie: American Prophet-Singers and Their People," *Journal of American Studies* 24:1 (April 1990), 41–59; Manuel Villar Raso, "Musical Structure of Whitman's Poems," in *Utopia in the Present Tense: Walt Whitman and the Language of the New World*, ed. Marina Camboni (Rome: Università degli Studi di Macerata, 1994), 189–202; Ned Rorem, "Words without Song," in *The Artistic Legacy of Walt Whitman: A Tribute to Gay Wilson Allen*, ed. Edwin Haviland Miller (New York: New York University Press, 1970); W. D. Snodgrass, "The Rhythm That Rocks Walt's Cradle," *Sewanee Review* 116:3 (Summer 2008), 398–410; William C. Spengemann, *Three American Poets: Walt Whitman, Emily Dickinson, and Herman Melville* (Notre Dame: University of Notre Dame Press, 2010); Floyd Stovall, *The Foreground of Leaves of Grass* (Charlottesville: University of Virginia Press, 1974); and C. K. Williams, *On Whitman* (Princeton: Princeton University Press, 2010).

14. Walt Whitman, "All about a Mocking-Bird," in *Walt Whitman: The Contemporary Reviews* (Cambridge: Cambridge University Press, 1996), 75; John Townsend Towbridge, "Reminiscences of Walt Whitman," *Atlantic Monthly* (February 1902), 166.

15. Walt Whitman, *The Journalism: Volume I, 1834–1846* (New York: Peter Lang, 1998), 202.

16. Lawrence Kramer, *After the Lovedeath*, 55.

17. On the reception of Italian opera in nineteenth-century America, see Karen Ahlquist, *Democracy at the Opera: Music, Theater, and Culture in New York City, 1815–60* (Urbana: University of Illinois Press, 1997); Ahlquist, "Mrs. Potiphar at the Opera: Satire, Idealism, and Cultural Authority in Post-Civil War New York," in *Music and Culture in America, 1861–1918*, ed. Michael Saffle (New York: Garland, 1998); Richard Crawford, *America's Musical Life: A History* (2001; rpt. New York: W.W. Norton, 2005); John Dizikes, *Opera in America: A Cultural History* (New Haven: Yale University Press, 1993); Joseph Horowitz, *Classical Music in America: A History of Its Rise and Fall* (New York: W.W. Norton, 2005); Elise K. Kirk, *American Opera* (Urbana: University of Illinois Press, 2001); Lawrence W. Levine,

Highbrow/Lowbrow: The Emergence of Cultural Hierarchy in America (Cambridge: Harvard University Press, 1988); June C. Ottenberg, *Opera Odyssey: Toward a History of Opera in Nineteenth-Century America* (Westport: Greenwood Press, 1994); and Derek B. Scott, *Sounds of the Metropolis: The Nineteenth-Century Popular Music Revolution in London, New York, Paris, and Vienna* (Oxford: Oxford University Press, 2008). See also Max Maretzek's *Crotchets and Quavers, or Revelations of an Opera Manager in America* (rpt. New York: Da Capo Press, 1966), published in the same year as the first edition of *Leaves of Grass* and detailing the often-amusing story of Marezek's attempts at establishing a taste for Italian opera "not amongst the 'Upper Ten,' but in the public heart of New York" (171).

18. Dizikes, *Opera in America*, 95–96.

19. Walt Whitman, *Notes and Fragments: Left by Walt Whitman* (London: Talbot, 1899), 74.

20. William Weber, *The Great Transformation of Musical Taste: Concert Programming from Haydn to Brahms* (Cambridge: Cambridge University Press, 2008), 86. On musical idealism, the relation of music and language, and the influence of instrumental music on concert programming, see also Carolyn Abbate, *Unsung Voices: Opera and Musical Narrative in the Nineteenth Century* (Princeton: Princeton University Press, 1991); Daniel Albright, *Music Speaks: On the Language of Opera, Dance, and Song* (Rochester: University of Rochester Press, 2009); Bernstein, *The Unanswered Question;* Tim Blanning, *The Triumph of Music: The Rise of Composers, Musicians, and Their Art* (Cambridge: Harvard University Press, 2008); Mark Evan Bonds, *Music as Thought: Listening to the Symphony in the Age of Beethoven* (Princeton: Princeton University Press, 2006); Wayne D. Bowman, *Philosophical Perspectives on Music* (Oxford: Oxford University Press, 1998); Michael Broyles, *"Music of the Highest Class": Elitism and Populism in Antebellum Boston* (New Haven: Yale University Press, 1992); Daniel K. L. Chua, *Absolute Music and the Construction of Meaning* (Cambridge: Cambridge University Press, 1999); Deryck Cooke, *The Language of Music* (Oxford: Oxford University Press, 1959); Carl Dahlhaus, *The Idea of Absolute Music* (Chicago: University of Chicago Press, 1989); Jamie James, *The Music of the Spheres: Music, Science, and the Natural Order of the Universe* (New York: Grove Press, 1993); Peter Kivy, *Antithetical Arts: On the Ancient Quarrel between Literature and Music* (Oxford: Clarendon Press, 2009); Kivy, *The Fine Art of Repetition: Essays in the Philosophy of Music* (Cambridge: Cambridge University Press, 1993); Kivy, *New Essays on Musical Understanding* (Oxford: Clarendon Press, 2001); Kivy, *Osmin's Rage: Philosophical Reflections on Opera, Drama, and Text* (Princeton: Princeton University Press, 1988); Kivy, *Philosophies of Arts: An Essay in Differences* (Cambridge: Cambridge University Press, 1997); Kivy, *Sound and Semblance: Reflections on Musical Representation* (Princeton: Princeton University Press, 1984); and Kivy, *Sound Sentiment: An Essay on the Musical Emotions* (Philadelphia: Temple University Press, 1989).

21. Bonds, *Music as Thought*, xiv.

22. Arthur Schopenhauer, *The World as Will and Representation, Volume II* (1818; rpt. Mineola: Dover, 1969), 257. Emphasis original.

23. Walt Whitman, *The Uncollected Poetry and Prose of Walt Whitman, Much of Which Has Been but Recently Discovered with Various Early Manuscripts Now First Published, Volume I* (New York: Peter Smith, 1932), 256.

24. Broyles, *"Music of the Highest Class,"* 231.

25. Ralph Waldo Emerson, *The Early Lectures of Ralph Waldo Emerson, 1833–1836* (Cambridge: Harvard University Press, 1959), 49.

26. Carl Dahlhaus, *The Idea of Absolute Music* (1978; rpt. Chicago: University of Chicago Press, 1989), 60, 63.

27. Schopenhauer, *The World as Will and Representation, Volume II*, 261.

28. Eduard Hanslick, *The Beautiful in Music* (1854; rpt. New York: Liberal Arts Press, 1957), 67.

29. Whitman, *Uncollected Poetry and Prose*, I 258–259.

30. In his semi-historical novel *Specimen Days* (New York: Picador, 2005), the contemporary author Michael Cunningham depicts Whitman's New York City (and, for a few pages, Whitman himself) with a similar sense of all-encompassing musicality: "Carriages rolled by bearing their mistresses home, and the newsboys called out, 'Woman murdered in Five Points, read all about it!' Red curtains billowed in the windows of the hotels, under a sky going a deeper red with the night. Somewhere someone played 'Lilith' on a calliope, though it seemed that the street itself emanated music, as if by walking with such certainty, such satisfaction, the people summoned music out of the pavement. . . . If Simon was in heaven, it might be this. Lucas could imagine the souls of the departed walking eternally, with music rising from the cobblestones and curtains putting out their light" (8).

31. Walt Whitman, *Notebooks and Unpublished Prose Manuscripts, Volume 1* (New York: New York University Press, 1984), 127.

32. On Whitman and reader response, see Vincent J. Bertolini, "'Hinting' and 'Reminding': The Rhetoric of Performative Embodiment in *Leaves of Grass*," *English Literary History (ELH)* 69 (2002), 1047–1082; Ezra Greenspan, *Walt Whitman and the American Reader* (Cambridge: Cambridge University Press, 1990); C. Carroll Hollis, *Language and Style in Leaves of Grass* (Baton Rouge: Louisiana State University Press, 1983); M. Jimmie Killingsworth, "Whitman's Physical Eloquence," in *Walt Whitman: The Centennial Essays* (Iowa City: University of Iowa Press, 1994), 68–78; Michael Moon, *Disseminating Whitman: Revision and Corporeality in Leaves of Grass* (Cambridge: Harvard University Press, 1991); Tenney Nathanson, *Whitman's Presence: Body, Voice, and Writing in Leaves of Grass* (New York: New York University Press, 1992); Stephen Railton, "'As If I Were with You': The Performance of Whitman's Poetry," *The Cambridge Companion to Walt Whitman* (Cambridge: Cambridge University Press, 1995), 7–26; and William Waters, *Poetry's Touch: On Lyric Address* (Ithaca: Cornell University Press, 2003).

33. Leypoldt, "Democracy's 'Lawless Music,'" 94; Weber, *The Great Transformation of Musical Taste*, 274.

34. Horowitz, *Classical Music in America*, 124; Crawford, *America's Musical Life*, 181.

35. Walt Whitman, *New York Dissected: A Sheaf of Recently Discovered Newspaper Articles by the Author of Leaves of Grass* (New York: Rufus Rockwell Wilson, 1936), 19.

36. Levine, *Highbrow/Lowbrow*, 86. Emphasis original.

37. Christopher Beach, *The Politics of Distinction: Whitman and the Discourses of Nineteenth-Century America* (Athens: University of Georgia Press, 1996), 3. Emphasis original.

38. Dizikes, *Opera in America*, 52.

39. Walt Whitman, *Faint Clews and Indirections: Manuscripts of Walt Whitman and His Family* (Durham: Duke University Press, 1949), 19.

40. Whitman, *New York Dissected*, 22.

41. For studies that situate Whitman in the context of popular culture, see Beach, *The Politics of Distinction*; David Haven Blake, *Walt Whitman and the Culture of American Celebrity* (New Haven: Yale University Press, 2006); David S. Reynolds, *Beneath the*

American Renaissance: The Subversive Imagination in the Age of Emerson and Melville (Cambridge: Harvard University Press, 1988); Reynolds, *Walt Whitman's America*; and Joseph Jay Rubin, *The Historic Whitman* (University Park: Pennsylvania State University Press, 1973).

42. Howard J. Waskow, *Whitman: Explorations in Form* (Chicago: University of Chicago Press, 1966), 16–17.

43. Whitman, "All about a Mocking-Bird," 75.

44. Vincenzo Bellini, *Norma* (1831; Achivio R.A.I., 1983), 7.

45. Walt Whitman, *Prose Works 1892, Volume I* (New York: New York University Press, 1963), 235.

46. "Walt Whitman as Musical Prophet," *Musical America* (July 3, 1915), 18.

47. Waldo Frank, *The Re-Discovery of America: An Introduction to a Philosophy of American Life* (New York: Charles Scribner's Sons, 1929), 208.

48. For studies of Whitman's reputation after his death and his influence on subsequent artists, see Bryan K. Carman, *A Race of Singers*; Miller, *The American Quest for a Supreme Fiction*; Timothy Morris, *Becoming Canonical in American Poetry* (Urbana: University of Illinois Press, 1995); Kenneth M. Price, *Whitman and Tradition: The Poet in His Century* (New Haven: Yale University Press, 1990); Patrick Redding, "Whitman Unbound: Democracy and Poetic Form, 1912–1931," *New Literary History* 41:3 (Summer 2011), 669–690; Michael Robertson, *Worshipping Walt: The Whitman Disciples* (Princeton: Princeton University Press, 2008); and Charles B. Willard, *Whitman's American Fame: The Growth of His Reputation after 1892* (Menasha: George Banta, 1950). Poems saluting Whitman have been collected in Sheila Coghill and Thom Tammaro, eds., *Visiting Walt: Poems Inspired by the Life and Work of Walt Whitman* (Iowa City: University of Iowa Press, 2003).

49. Horace Traubel, *With Walt Whitman in Camden, Vol. III* (New York: Michell Kennerley, 1914), 423; Esther Shephard, *Walt Whitman's Pose* (New York: Harcourt, Brace, 1938), 260.

50. George Sand, *Consuelo, Volume II* (1842–43; rpt. Boston: Estes and Lauriat, 1897), 216.

51. Frank, *The Re-Discovery of America*, 130.

52. Louis Untermeyer, "Disillusion vs. Dogma," in *T. S. Eliot: The Contemporary Reviews* (Cambridge: Cambridge University Press, 2004), 94.

53. Clive Bell, *Since Cézanne* (New York: Harcourt, Brace, 1922), 222.

54. Alfred Appel Jr., *Jazz Modernism: From Ellington and Armstrong to Matisse and Joyce* (New York: Alfred A. Knopf, 2002), 13–14.

55. On Eliot and popular culture, see especially the work of David. E. Chinitz, including "A Jazz-Banjorine, not a Lute: Eliot and Popular Music before *The Waste Land*," in *T. S. Eliot's Orchestra: Critical Essays on Poetry and Music* (New York: Garland, 2000), 3–24; "A Vast Wasteland? Eliot and Popular Culture," in *A Companion to T.S. Eliot* (Oxford: Wiley-Blackwell, 2009), 66–78; "In the Shadows: Popular Song and Eliot's Construction of Emotion," *Modernism/Modernity* 11:3 (2004), 449–467; "The Problem of Dullness: T. S. Eliot and the 'Lively Arts' in the 1920s," in *T. S. Eliot and Our Turning World* (London: Macmillan, 2001), 127–140; *T. S. Eliot and the Cultural Divide* (Chicago: University of Chicago Press, 2003); and "T. S. Eliot's Blue Verses and Their Sources in the Folk Tradition," *Journal of Modern Literature* 23 (1999), 329–333. Other studies that situate Eliot in the contexts of popular culture and popular music include John Xiros Cooper, ed., *T. S. Eliot's Orchestra: Critical Essays on Poetry and Music* (New York: Garland, 2000); Barry J. Faulk, "Modernism and the Popular: Eliot's Music Halls," *Modernism/Modernity* 8:4 (2001), 603–621; Faulk,

"T. S. Eliot and the Symbolist City," in *A Companion to T. S. Eliot*, 27–39; Herbert Howarth, *Notes on Some Figures behind T. S. Eliot* (Boston: Houghton Mifflin, 1964); Manju Jaidka, *T. S. Eliot's Use of Popular Sources* (Lewiston: Edwin Mellen Press, 1997); Sebastian D. G. Knowles, "'Then You Wink the Other Eye': T. S. Eliot and the Music Hall," *American Notes and Queries* 11:4 (Fall 1998), 20–32; Amy Koritz, *Gendering Bodies/Performing Art: Dance and Literature in Early Twentieth-Century British Culture* (Ann Arbor: University of Michigan Press, 1995); Michael North, *The Dialect of Modernism: Race, Voice, and Twentieth Century Literature* (Oxford: Oxford University Press, 1994); North, *Reading 1922: A Return to the Scene of the Modern* (Oxford: Oxford University Press, 1999); Allison Pease, *Modernism, Mass Culture, and the Aesthetics of Obscenity* (Cambridge: Cambridge University Press, 2000); Lawrence Rainey, *Revisiting* The Waste Land (New Haven: Yale University Press, 2005); Ronald Schuchard, *Eliot's Dark Angel: Intersections of Life and Art* (Oxford: Oxford University Press, 1999); Eric Sigg, "Eliot as a Product of America" in *The Cambridge Companion to T. S. Eliot*, ed. A. David Moody, (Cambridge: Cambridge University Press, 1994), 14–30; Juan A. Suárez, *Pop Modernism: Noise and the Reinvention of the Everyday* (Urbana: University of Illinois Press, 2007); and David Yaffe, *Fascinating Rhythm: Reading Jazz in American Writing* (Princeton: Princeton University Press, 2006).

56. T. S. Eliot, "Marianne Moore," *The Dial* 75:6 (December 1923), 595. Emphasis original.

57. T. S. Eliot, *Inventions of the March Hare: Poems 1909–1917* (New York: Harcourt Brace, 1996), 64. Further references to this edition will appear parenthetically in the text.

58. Lyndall Gordon, *T. S. Eliot: An Imperfect Life* (New York: W.W. Norton, 1998), 7.

59. Levine, *Highbrow/Lowbrow*, 134.

60. James Weldon Johnson, *Writings* (New York: Library of America, 2004), 690, 61.

61. Robert Crawford, *The Savage and the City in the Work of T. S. Eliot* (Oxford: Clarendon Press, 1987), 53.

62. T. S. Eliot, *The Complete Poems and Plays, 1909–1950* (New York: Harcourt Brace, 1980), 8. Further references to this edition will appear parenthetically in the text.

63. A discussion of the phonograph in American life and an overview of scholarship on this subject can be found in this book's first chapter.

64. Reebee Garofalo, *Rockin' Out: Popular Music in the USA* (Boston: Allyn and Bacon, 1997), 22.

65. Constant Lambert, *Music Ho! A Study of Music in Decline* (1934; rpt. London: Hogarth, 1985), 200.

66. Richard Middleton, *Voicing the Popular: On the Subjects of Popular Music* (New York: Routledge, 2006), 175. Emphasis original.

67. Walter Benjamin, *The Work of Art in the Age of Its Technological Reproducibility, and Other Writings on Media* (Cambridge: Harvard University Press, 2008), 22.

68. Benjamin, *The Work of Art in the Age of Its Technological Reproducibility*, 40.

69. Chinitz, *T. S. Eliot and the Cultural Divide*, 47.

70. Oliver Sacks, *Musicophilia: Tales of Music and the Brain* (New York: Alfred A. Knopf, 2007), 48.

71. Gene Buck and Herman Ruby, "That Shakespearian Rag," in T. S. Eliot, *The Waste Land* (New York: W. W. Norton, 2001), 52.

72. Eliot, *Selected Prose*, 48. Emphasis original.

73. Indeed, so familiar was this sensation of involuntary listening to well-known popular songs among the American public that it had already been the subject of, what else,

well-known popular songs. Perhaps the most famous had been Irving Berlin's self-referential "That Mysterious Rag" of 1911, which had provocatively asked, "Did you hear it? Were you near it?/If you weren't then you've yet to fear it;/Once you've met it you'll regret it,/Just because you never will forget it." See Irving Berlin and Ted Snyder, "That Mysterious Rag" (New York: Ted Snyder Co. 1911), 2–3.

74. Friedrich A Kittler, *Gramophone, Film, Typewriter* (1986; rpt. Stanford: Stanford University Press, 1999), 80.

75. Sinclair Lewis, *Main Street* (1920; rpt. New York: Library of America, 1992), 304; John Dos Passos, *Three Soldiers* (1921; rpt. New York: Library of America, 2003), 316–317.

76. Recent research on the human brain suggests that in the post-phonographic era, many musical memories are in fact copies of preexisting recordings. As Daniel J. Levitin has noted his aptly titled *This Is Your Brain on Music* (New York: Dutton, 2006), testing has shown that when subjects are asked to perform songs that they have previously heard on records, they are generally quite faithful to the originals, "singing along with the memory representation" in their heads to an "astonishingly accurate" degree. Brain imaging also suggests that imagining music and listening to musical recordings creates "virtually indistinguishable" brain activity (150).

77. T. S. Eliot, "London Letter," *The Dial* 73: 6 (December 1922), 663. Further references to this edition will appear parenthetically in the text.

78. Oliver Goldsmith, *Poems and Essays* (New York: William A. Barrow, 1824), 108.

79. T. S. Eliot, *The Sacred Wood: Essays on Poetry and Criticism* (1920. Rpt. London: Methuen, 1934), 70; T. S. Eliot, *The Use of Poetry and the Use of Criticism: Studies in the Relation of Criticism to Poetry in England* (1933; rpt. Cambridge: Harvard University Press, 1986), 22.

80. Eliot, *The Use of Poetry*, 122. Readings of *The Waste Land* that emphasize its polyphonic, multiply-voiced quality include Michael Levenson, *A Genealogy of Modernism: A Study of English Literary Doctrine, 1908–1922* (Cambridge: Cambridge University Press, 1984); Marc Manganaro, *Myth, Rhetoric, and the Voice of Authority: A Critique of Frazer, Eliot, Frye, and Campbell* (New Haven: Yale University Press, 1992); and John T. Mayer, *T. S. Eliot's Silent Voices* (Oxford: Oxford University Press, 1989). For opposed readings arguing that the poem employs a unitary perspective or protagonist, see Calvin Bedient, *He Do the Police in Different Voices: The Waste Land and Its Protagonist* (Chicago: University of Chicago Press, 1986); Cleanth Brooks, *Modern Poetry and the Tradition* (Chapel Hill: University of North Carolina Press, 1939); James E. Miller Jr., *T. S. Eliot's Personal Waste Land: Exorcism of the Demons* (University Park: Pennsylvania State University Press, 1977); and Grover Smith, *T. S. Eliot's Poetry and Plays: A Study in Sources and Meaning* (1950; rpt. Chicago: University of Chicago Press, 1968).

81. Eliot, *The Use of Poetry*, 111. In keeping with Eliot's aural metaphor, Peter Schwenger has called this practice of associative reading "The Obbligato Effect"; see his essay of the same name in *New Literary History* 42:1 (Winter 2011), 115–128. For reader-response studies of Eliot's poetry, see Anne C. Bolgan, *What the Thunder Really Said: A Retrospective Essay on the Making of* The Waste Land (Montreal: McGill-Queen's University Press, 1973); Jewel Spears Brooker and Joseph Bentley, *Reading* The Waste Land: *Modernism and the Limits of Interpretation* (Amherst: University of Massachusetts Press, 1990); John Xiros Cooper, *T. S. Eliot and the Politics of Voice: The Argument of* The Waste Land (Ann Arbor: UMI Research Press, 1987); Steve Ellis, "*The Waste Land* and the Reader's Response," in *The Waste Land*, ed. Tony Davies and Nigel Wood (Buckingham: Open University Press, 1994), 83–104;

and Maud Ellmann, *The Poetics of Impersonality: T. S. Eliot and Ezra Pound* (Cambridge: Harvard University Press, 1987).

82. I. A. Richards, *Principles of Literary Criticism* (1934; rpt. New York: Routledge, 2001), 276.

83. For other arguments that *The Waste Land* follows an abstractly musical model of composition, see Paul Chancellor, "The Music of 'The Waste Land,'" *Comparative Literature Studies* 6:1 (1969), 21–32; Helen Gardner, *The Art of T. S. Eliot* (London: Cresset Press, 1949); F. R. Leavis, *New Bearings in English Poetry: A Study of the Contemporary Situation* (1932; rpt. London: Chatto and Windus, 1938); F. O. Matthiessen, *The Achievement of T. S. Eliot* (New York: Houghton Mifflin, 1935); Marshall McLuhan, "Pound, Eliot, and the Rhetoric of *The Waste Land*," *New Literary History* 10:3 (Spring, 1979), 557–580; Grover Smith, *The Waste Land* (London: George Allen and Unwin, 1983); C. K. Stead, *The New Poetic: Yeats to Eliot* (1964; rpt. Philadelphia: University of Pennsylvania Press, 1987); and Stead, *Pound, Eliot and the Modernist Movement* (London: Macmillan, 1986).

84. On Wagner's relation to *The Waste Land*, see William Blissett, "Wagner in *The Waste Land*," in *The Practical Vision: Essays in English Literature in Honour of Flora Ray*, ed. James Campbell and James Doyle (Waterloo: Wilfred Laurier University Press, 1978), 71–85; Margaret E. Dana, "Orchestrating *The Waste Land*: Wagner, Leitmotiv, and the Play of Passion," in *T. S. Eliot's Orchestra: Critical Essays on Poetry and Music*, ed. John Xiros Cooper (New York: Garland, 2000), 267–295; Bernard Harris, "'This music crept by me': Shakespeare and Wagner," in *"The Waste Land" in Different Voices*, ed. A. D. Moody (London: Edward Arnold), 105–116; Martin Stoddard, *Wagner to "The Waste Land": A Study of the Relationship of Wagner to English Literature* (London: Macmillan, 1982); Leon Surette, *The Birth of Modernism: Ezra Pound, T. S. Eliot, W. B. Yeats, and the Occult* (Montreal: McGill-Queen's University Press, 1993); and Philip Waldron, "The Music of Poetry: Wagner in *The Waste Land*," *Journal of Modern Literature* 18:4 (Fall 1993), 421–434.

85. Ralph Ellison, *Shadow and Act* (1964; rpt. New York: Vintage, 1995), 159–160.

86. Pound, *Literary Essays*, 9.

87. Ezra Pound, *The Cantos of Ezra Pound* (New York: New Directions, 1996), 26.

88. Pound, *The Cantos*, 143.

89. Hart Crane, *Complete Poems and Selected Letters and Prose* (New York: Liveright, 1966), 261. Further references to this edition will appear parenthetically in the text.

CHAPTER 3

1. According to Alex Ross, possible coiners of the phrase include Martin Mull, Steve Martin, and Elvis Costello. See *Listen to This* (New York: Farrar, Straus and Giroux, 2010), xi.

2. Richard Powers, *The Time of Our Singing* (New York: Picador, 2003), 431.

3. McCartney himself noted the mutability that his works are subject to several decades in advance of Powers, telling an interviewer, "We write songs. We know what we mean by them. But in a week someone else says something about it, says that it means that as well, and you can't deny it. Things take on millions of meanings." Quoted in Nicholas Knowles Bromell, *Tomorrow Never Knows: Rock and Psychedelics in the 1960s* (Chicago: University of Chicago Press, 2002), 32.

4. Pamela Robertson Wojcik and Arthur Knight, eds., *Soundtrack Available: Essays on Film and Popular Music* (Durham: Duke University Press, 2001), 1.

5. Indeed, there are entire subgenres of fiction that would be difficult to imagine without it, such as the contemporary rock 'n' roll novel (including such titles as Roddy Doyle's

The Commitments, Nick Hornby's *High Fidelity,* Salman Rushdie's *The Ground beneath Her Feet,* Jonathan Lethem's *You Don't Love Me Yet,* and Zachary Lazar's *Sway,* to name but a few). This is not to say, however, that a rock novel presupposes an audible soundtrack: most of the songs referred to in Don DeLillo's *Great Jones Street*—with the notable exception of "Good King Wenceslas"—are decidedly fictional.

6. E. L. Doctorow, *Ragtime* (1975; rpt. New York: Modern Library, 1997), 110, 160.

7. On James Joyce and music, see Ruth H. Baurle, ed., *The James Joyce Songbook* (New York: Garland, 1982); Baurle, ed., *Picking Up Airs: Hearing the Music in Joyce's Text* (Urbana: University of Illinois Press, 1993); and Zack Bowen, *Musical Allusions in the Works of James Joyce: Early Poetry through Ulysses* (Albany: State University of New York Press, 1974).

8. Matthew J. Bruccoli, ed., *New Essays on The Great Gatsby.* Cambridge: Cambridge University Press, 1985), 9.

9. F. Scott Fitzgerald, *The Beautiful and Damned* (1922; rpt. Cambridge: Cambridge University Press, 2008), 160. Further references to this edition will appear parenthetically in the text.

10. Michael Bull, *Sounding Out the City: Personal Stereos and the Management of Everyday Life* (New York: Berg, 2000), 181.

11. Matthew J. Bruccoli, *Some Sort of Epic Grandeur: The Life of F. Scott Fitzgerald* (Columbia: University of South Carolina Press, 2002), 296–297.

12. Zelda Fitzgerald, *Save Me the Waltz* (1932; rpt. Carbondale: Southern Illinois University Press, 1974), 146. Emphasis original.

13. John Dos Passos, *The Best Times: An Informal Memoir* (New York: New American Library, 1966), 129.

14. Ruth Prigozy's pioneering essay "'Poor Butterfly': F. Scott Fitzgerald and Popular Music" (*Prospects* 2, 1976), for example, is a valuable catalogue of the song titles that appear in the Fitzgerald oeuvre and a sensitive analysis of both the lyrics he quotes and the scenes he includes them in, but she treats music in almost exclusively linguistic terms and not as a sonic art that unfolds in time. More recently, Mitchell Breitwieser's "Jazz Fractures: F. Scott Fitzgerald and Epochal Representation" (*American Literary History* 12:3, 2000) offers what is perhaps the most seductive articulation of Fitzgerald's debt to 1920s jazz and African American musical expression, but much of his argument hinges upon an imaginary song ("Vladimir Tostoff's Jazz History of the World"), a scene that its author at one point judged to be "rotten," and an early draft of the novel that he would significantly revise later. See Fitzgerald, *The Great Gatsby* (1925; rpt. Cambridge: Cambridge University Press, 1991), 41; and Fitzgerald, *F. Scott Fitzgerald: A Life in Letters* (New York: Scribner's, 1994), 92. Moreover, Breitwieser's argument leaves untouched the novel's many real and literally audible songs, very few of which are likely to strike the contemporary listener as signifying blackness in any meaningful way. On Fitzgerald, music, and jazz, see also Bruce Bawer, "'I Could Still Hear the Music': Jay Gatsby and the Musical Metaphor," *Notes on Modern American Literature* 5:4 (1981) 6–10; Ronald Berman, *The Great Gatsby and Modern Times* (Urbana: University of Illinois Press, 1994); Gene Bluestein, "The Blues as a Literary Type," *Massachusetts Review* 8:4 (1967) 593–617; Breitwieser, "*The Great Gatsby*: Grief, Jazz and the Eye-Witness," *Arizona Quarterly* 47:3 (1991), 17–70; Robert M. Crunden, *Body and Soul: The Making of American Modernism* (New York: Basic Books, 2000); Gerald Early, "The Lives of Jazz," *American Literary History* 5:1 (1993), 129–146; Nicholas M. Evans, *Writing Jazz: Race, Nationalism, and Modern Culture in the 1920s* (New York: Garland, 2000); Ryan Jerving, "Early Jazz Literature (And Why You Didn't Know)," *American Literary History*

16:4 (2004), 648–674; Darrel Mansell, "*The Jazz History of the World* in *The Great Gatsby*," *English Language Notes* 25:2 (1987), 57–62; and Paul McCann, *Race, Music, and National Identity: Images of Jazz in American Fiction, 1920–1960* (Madison: Farleigh Dickinson University Press, 2008).

15. On the problem of how to approach lyrics on the printed page, see Mark W. Booth, *The Experience of Songs* (New Haven: Yale University Press, 1981); Lars Eckstein, *Reading Song Lyrics* (New York: Rodopi, 2010); and Robert Gottlieb and Robert Kimball, "Introduction," *Reading Lyrics* (New York: Pantheon, 2000) xxiii–xxvi.

16. Christopher Small, *Musicking: The Meanings of Performing and Listening* (Hanover: Wesleyan University Press, 1998), 2. In addition to Small, useful theorizations of the role audiences play in the construction of meaning in popular music include Simon Frith, *Performing Rites: On the Value of Popular Music* (Cambridge: Harvard University Press, 1996); Brian Longhurst, *Popular Music and Society* (Cambridge: Polity, 1995); and Keith Negus, *Popular Music in Theory: An Introduction* (Hanover: Wesleyan University Press, 1996).

17. Fitzgerald, *The Great Gatsby*, 86. Further references to this edition will appear parenthetically in the text.

18. F. Scott Fitzgerald, *The Letters of F. Scott Fitzgerald* (New York: Charles Scribner's Sons, 1963), 63.

19. F. Scott Fitzgerald, *This Side of Paradise* (1920; rpt. Cambridge: Cambridge University Press, 1996), 35–36. Emphasis original. Further references to this edition will appear parenthetically in the text.

20. The song as published by Jerome Kern and Schuyler Greene in sheet music form is "Babes in the Wood," but Fitzgerald refers it to it as "Babes in the Woods," as does the Victor recording company. This chapter uses the sheet music title.

21. Jerome Kern and Schuyler Green, "Babes in the Wood" (New York: T. B. Harms and Francis, Day and Hunter, 1915), 2–5.

22. Certainly this was the song's message in its original context, which Fitzgerald may or may not have been intending to evoke. "Babes in the Wood" had first appeared toward the end of the musical comedy *Very Good Eddie* (1915), in which a man and a woman, both separated from their spouses, are forced into close proximity with one another in a hotel but remain true to their marriage vows. In novel, play, and song, the much-discussed kiss never arrives, with the musical message being that anticipation is as powerful a source of poetic experience as its fruits are.

23. Pearl James, "History and Masculinity in F. Scott Fitzgerald's *This Side of Paradise*," *Modern Fiction Studies* 51:1 (2005), 2.

24. John Keats, *The Major Works* (Oxford: Oxford World's Classics, 2008), 288.

25. Looking back more than a decade after his departure from Princeton, Fitzgerald lamented—but not without a sense of humor—the anti-romantic turn that his undergraduate literary magazine had taken in a short review titled "F. Scott Fitzgerald Is Bored by Efforts at Realism in 'Lit'" (1927): "In my days stories in the *Lit* were about starving artists, dying poilus, the plague in Florence and the soul of the Great Khan. They took place, chiefly, behind the moon and a thousand years ago. Now they all take place on Nassau Street, no longer back than yesterday." See Fitzgerald, *F. Scott Fitzgerald in His Own Time: A Miscellany* (New York: Popular Library, 1971), 150.

26. F. Scott Fitzgerald, *The Basil and Josephine Stories* (New York: Charles Scribner's Sons, 1973), 103.

27. F. Scott Fitzgerald, *F. Scott Fitzgerald's Ledger: A Facsimile* (Washington, DC: NCR/ Microcard Editions, 1972), 167.

28. Rick Altman, *Silent Film Sound* (New York: Columbia University Press, 2004), 35.

29. Brett Page, *Writing for Vaudeville* (Springfield: Home Correspondence School, 1915), 299.

30. Fitzgerald, *A Life in Letters*, 17.

31. Fitzgerald, *A Life in Letters*, 15, 17, 28, 30.

32. John Kuehl, in F. Scott Fitzgerald, *The Apprentice Fiction of F. Scott Fitzgerald, 1909–1917* (New Brunswick: Rutgers University Press, 1965), 89. Fitzgerald would later assert that formlessness in first novels "is permissible, perhaps even to be encouraged, as the lack of a pattern gives the young novelist more of a chance to assert his or her individuality, which is the principal thing." See Fitzgerald, *F. Scott Fitzgerald in His Own Time*, 137.

33. Raymond Knapp, *The American Musical and the Formation of National Identity* (Princeton: Princeton University Press, 2005), 13.

34. George M. Cohan, "We Do All the Dirty Work" (New York: Cohan and Harris Publishing, 1911), 2–3.

35. Another analogue for Fitzgerald's musical-theatrical aesthetic is stage melodrama, an anti-realist mode that aims for the more abstract variety of "truth" associated with allegory or myth. Ben Singer is instructive on this point: "even though its characters lack psychological depth, melodrama has been championed for its capacity to reveal the reality of the psyche. Melodrama overcomes repression, giving full expression to the magnified passions, the intensities of love and hate residing deep (or not so deep) within us all." See Singer, *Melodrama and Modernity: Early Sensational Cinema and Its Contexts* (New York: Columbia University Press, 2001), 51.

36. Victor Herbert and Henry Blossom, "Kiss Me Again" (New York: M. Witmark and Sons, 1915), 2.

37. Herbert and Blossom, "Kiss Me Again," 3.

38. Whether he knew it or not, Fitzgerald could not have picked a better song with which to make this point, as the history of "Kiss Me Again" is in many ways illustrative of music's mutability, the power of audiences, and the vagary of taste. As first written in 1905, "Kiss Me Again" was a parody of overwrought waltz tunes, appearing toward the end of "If I Were on the Stage," a song suite designed to illustrate an actress's versatility. It begins with the singer impersonating a "simple maiden" with a gavotte, then portraying a "prima donna" with a polonaise, and finally singing "Kiss Me Again" after delivering these lines: "But best of all the parts I'd play/If I could only have my way/Would be a strong romantic role/Emotional and full of soul/And I believe for such a thing/A dreamy sensuous waltz I'd sing." See Victor Herbert and Henry Blossom, "If I Were on the Stage" (New York: M. Witmark, 1905), 6. The supposedly exaggerated waltz, however, became so popular with the public that it was eventually released as a stand-alone song, with its original, ironic qualities having grown considerably less audible by the time Fitzgerald included it in *This Side of Paradise*.

39. Fitzgerald, *A Life in Letters*, 15.

40. Edmund Wilson, "F. Scott Fitzgerald," in *F. Scott Fitzgerald in His Own Time* (New York: Popular Library, 1971), 405.

41. Bruccoli, *Some Sort of Epic Grandeur*, 119.

42. Ivan Caryll and C. M. S. McLellan, "My Beautiful Lady" (New York: Chappell, 1910), 3.

43. Caryll and McLellan, "My Beautiful Lady," 3.

44. Caryll and McLellan, "My Beautiful Lady," 3.

45. Caryll and McLellan, "My Beautiful Lady," 2.

46. Fitzgerald, *F. Scott Fitzgerald in His Own Time*, 139.

47. Gilbert Seldes, *The Seven Lively Arts* (New York: Harper and Brothers, 1924), 353.

48. Fitzgerald, *The Beautiful and Damned*, 347; Seldes, *The Seven Lively Arts*, 3.

49. Jean Schwartz and William Jerome, "Ring Ting-a-Ling" (New York: Jerome and Schwartz, 1912), 3–4.

50. For more on the history of asynchronous musical accompaniment in turn-of-the-century film and theater, see Rick Altman, *Silent Film Sound* (New York: Columbia University Press, 2004); Scott Eyman, *The Speed of Sound: Hollywood and the Talkie Revolution* (New York: Simon and Schuster, 1997); James Lastra, *Sound Technology and the America Cinema: Perception, Representation, Modernity* (New York: Columbia University Press, 2000); and David Mayer and Helen Day-Mayer, "A 'Secondary Action' or Musical Highlight? Melodic Interludes in Early Film Melodrama Reconsidered," in *The Sounds of Early Cinema* (Bloomington: Indiana University Press, 2001).

51. Theodore Dreiser, *An American Tragedy* (1925; rpt. New York: Dell, 1959), 521. This practice on the part of authors as well as filmmakers serves to confirm Michel Chion's sense that the "juxtaposition of scene with indifferent music has the effect not of freezing emotion but rather of intensifying it." See Chion, *Audio-Vision: Sound on Screen* (New York: Columbia University Press, 1994), 8.

52. There is a great deal of "funning" in Fitzgerald's stories, as well. For two particularly good examples of action juxtaposed with music at its most obviously inappropriate, see "Three Acts of Music" (1936) in *The Lost Decade: Short Stories from Esquire, 1936–1941* (Cambridge: Cambridge University Press, 2008); and "That Kind of Party" (1937) in *The Basil and Josephine Stories*.

53. In this Fitzgerald might be profitably compared with those modernists of film and opera who felt that the creation of discontinuity across the arts and senses could be an aesthetic end in and of itself rather than merely a means of disrupting or enlivening linear narrative. Perhaps the most obvious counterpart to Fitzgerald's musical experimentalism is Sergei Eisenstein's 1928 "Statement" on sound recording technology, which argued for the "contrapuntal" relation of visuality and aurality in the avant-garde cinema and against the clearer, easily explained varieties of synchronicity and asynchronicity that characterize most film today. See Eisenstein, *Film Form: Essays in Film Theory* (New York: Harcourt, Brace and World, 1949), 258. For an overview of musical asynchronicity in modernism across the arts, see Daniel Albright, *Untwisting the Serpent: Modernism in Music, Literature, and Other Arts* (Chicago: University of Chicago Press, 2000).

54. Raymond Hubbell and John L. Golden, "Poor Butterfly" (New York: T. B. Harms and Francis, Day and Hunter, 1916), 3.

55. George Jean Nathan, the famously demanding theater critic to whom *The Beautiful and Damned* is dedicated, might as well have been describing the "Poor Butterfly" scene when he dryly observed some years before that on the often-conventional musical stage, it is all but guaranteed that "[w]hen a character observes: 'When I see that fellow So-and-So again, you *bet* I'll tell him what I think of him!' the character must presently turn around, see that the man against whom he has just lodged the threat has been standing there all the while, and, beholding him, must slink meekly away." See Nathan, *Another Book on the Theatre* (New York: B. W. Heuebsch, 1915), 34–35.

56. F. Scott Fitzgerald, *My Lost City: Personal Essays, 1920–1940* (Cambridge: Cambridge University Press, 2005), 139.

57. F. Scott Fitzgerald, *The Last Tycoon: An Unfinished Novel* (1941; rpt. New York: Scribner's, 1970) 21.

58. Hugh Kenner, *A Homemade World: The American Modernist Writers* (Baltimore: Johns Hopkins University Press, 1989), 42.

59. Milton R. Stern, *The Golden Moment: The Novels of F. Scott Fitzgerald* (Urbana: University of Illinois Press, 1970), 57.

60. Fitzgerald, *A Life in Letters*, 18; Fitzgerald, *This Side of Paradise*, 212.

61. Julian Robledo and Dorothy Terriss, "Three O'clock in the Morning" (London: West's Limited, 1921), 3–4.

62. James Lastra, *Sound Technology and the America Cinema*, 112–113.

63. Yeats made this comment to Compton Mackenzie—the founder of *Gramophone* magazine—who repeated it several years later in a memoir. See Mackenzie, *My Record of Music* (London: Hutchinson, 1955), 53. Mackenzie, as it happens, was one of Fitzgerald's first literary idols, with his novel *Sinister Street*—the tale of a young man's personal and intellectual development at Oxford University—frequently named as a major influence on *This Side of Paradise*.

64. Ralph Waldo Emerson, *Essays and Lectures* (New York: Library of America, 1983), 473.

65. Fitzgerald, *A Life in Letters*, 126.

66. Joseph Conrad, *The Nigger of the "Narcissus"* (1897; rpt. New York: Dover, 1999), vii.

67. Powers, *The Time of Our Singing*, 160.

CHAPTER 4

1. Alan Lomax, *The Land Where the Blues Began* (New York: New Press, 1993), ix.

2. On African American musical poetics and narrative since the Harlem Renaissance, see T. J. Anderson III, *Notes to Make the Sound Come Right: Four Innovators of Jazz Poetry* (Fayetteville: University of Arkansas Press, 2004); Tony Bolden, *Afro-Blue: Improvisations in African American Poetry and Culture* (Urbana: University of Illinois Press, 2004); Michael Borshuk, *Swinging the Vernacular: Jazz and African American Modernist Literature* (New York: Routledge, 2006); Sascha Feinstein, *Jazz Poetry: From the 1920s to the Present* (Westport: Greenwood Press, 1997); Jürgen E. Grandt, *Kinds of Blue: The Jazz Aesthetic in African American Narrative* (Columbus: Ohio State University Press, 2004); Charles O. Hartman: *Jazz Text: Voice and Improvisation in Poetry, Jazz, and Song* (Princeton: Princeton University Press, 1991); Stephen Henderson, *Understanding the New Black Poetry: Black Speech and Black Music as Poetic References* (New York: William Morrow, 1973); Meta DuEwa Jones, *The Muse Is Music: Jazz Poetry from the Harlem Renaissance to Spoken Word* (Urbana: University of Illinois Press, 2011); Graham Lock and David Murray, *Thriving on a Riff: Jazz and Blues Influences* (Oxford: Oxford University Press, 2009); Paul McCann, *Race, Music, and National Identity: Images of Jazz in American Fiction, 1920–1960* (Madison: Fairleigh Dickinson University Press, 2008); Fred Moten, *In the Break: The Aesthetics of the Black Radical Tradition* (Minneapolis: University of Minnesota Press, 2003); Aldon Lynn Nielsen, *Black Chant: Languages of African-American Postmodernism* (Cambridge: Cambridge University Press, 1997); Keren Omry, *Cross-Rhythms: Jazz Aesthetics in African-American Literature* (New York: Continuum, 2008); Wilfried Raussert, *Negotiating Temporal Differences: Blues, Jazz and Narrativity in African American Culture* (Heidelberg: Universitätsverlag

C. Winter Heidelberg, 2000); Jennifer D. Ryan, *Post-Jazz Poetics: A Social History* (New York: Palgrave Macmillan, 2010); Michael Soto, *The Modernist Nation: Generation, Renaissance, and Twentieth-Century American Literature* (Tuscaloosa: University of Alabama Press, 2004); Craig Hansen Werner, *Playing the Changes: From Afro-Modernism to the Jazz Impulse* (Urbana: University of Illinois Press, 1994); and David Yaffe, *Fascinating Rhythm: Reading Jazz in American Writing* (Princeton: Princeton University Press, 2006).

3. W. E. B. Du Bois, *The Souls of Black Folk* (1903; rpt. New York: Penguin, 1996), 205.

4. James Weldon Johnson, *Writings* (New York: Library of America, 2004), 688. On music's symbolic importance in and during the Harlem Renaissance, see Paul Allen Anderson, *Deep River: Music and Memory in Harlem Renaissance Thought* (Durham: Duke University Press, 2001); Brent Hayes Edwards, *The Practice of Diaspora: Literature, Translation, and the Rise of Black Internationalism* (Cambridge: Harvard University Press, 2003); Samuel A. Floyd Jr., ed., *Black Music in the Harlem Renaissance: A Collection of Essays* (Westport: Greenwood Press, 1990); Kathy J. Ogren, *The Jazz Revolution: Twenties America and the Meaning of Jazz* (Oxford: Oxford University Press, 1989); Eric Porter, *What Is This Thing Called Jazz? African American Musicians as Artists, Critics, and Activists* (Berkeley: University of California Press, 2002); and Jon Michael Spencer, *The New Negroes and Their Music: The Success of the Harlem Renaissance* (Knoxville: University of Tennessee Press, 1997).

5. John F. Callahan, *In the African-American Grain: The Pursuit of Voice in Twentieth-Century Black Fiction* (Urbana: University of Illinois Press, 1988), 21. On spoken language, dialect, and the dynamic of call and response in relation to African American literature (and American literature more broadly), see also Fahamisha Patricia Brown, *Performing the Word: African-American Poetry as Vernacular Culture* (New Brunswick: Rutgers University Press, 1999); Henry Louis Gates Jr., *Figures in Black: Words, Signs, and the "Racial" Self* (Oxford: Oxford University Press, 1987); Gates, *The Signifying Monkey: A Theory of African-American Literary Criticism* (Oxford: Oxford University Press, 1988); Sylvia Wallace Holton, *Down Home and Uptown: The Representation of Black Speech in American Fiction* (Cranbury: Associated University Presses, 1984); Gavin Jones, *Strange Talk: The Politics of Dialect Literature in Gilded Age America* (Berkeley: University of California Press, 1999); Gayl Jones, *Liberating Voices: Oral Tradition in African American Literature* (Cambridge: Harvard University Press, 1991); Lisa Cohen Minnick, *Dialect and Dichotomy: Literary Representations of African American Speech* (Tuscaloosa: University of Alabama Press, 2004); Aldon L. Nielsen, *Writing between the Lines: Race and Intertextuality* (Athens: University of Georgia Press, 1994); Michael North, *The Dialect of Modernism: Race, Voice, and Twentieth Century Literature* (Oxford: Oxford University Press, 1994); Ben Sidran, *Black Talk* (New York: Holt, Rinehart and Winston, 1971); Robert Stepto, *From behind the Veil: A Study of Afro-American Narrative* (Urbana: University of Illinois Press, 1979); Eric J. Sundquist, *The Hammers of Creation: Folk Culture in Modern African-American Fiction* (Athens: University of Georgia Press, 1992); and Sundquist, *To Wake the Nations: Race in the Making of American Literature* (Cambridge: Harvard University Press, 1993).

6. James Weldon Johnson, *Black Manhattan* (1930; rpt. New York: Arno Press, 1968), 260–261.

7. Countee Cullen, *Color* (1925; rpt. New York, Arno Press, 1969), 3; Charles Scruggs, "'All Dressed Up but No Place to Go': The Black Writer and His Audience during the Harlem Renaissance," *American Literature* 48: 4 (1977), 543.

8. Paul Gilroy, *The Black Atlantic: Modernity and Double Consciousness* (Cambridge: Harvard University Press, 1993), 3.

9. Interracial approaches to the Harlem Renaissance, its literary context, and modernism include Houston A. Baker Jr., *Modernism and the Harlem Renaissance* (Chicago: University of Chicago Press, 1987); Ann Douglas, *Terrible Honesty: Mongrel Manhattan in the 1920s* (New York: Farrar, Straus and Giroux, 1995); Rachel Blau DuPlessis, *Genders, Races, and Religious Cultures in Modern American Poetry, 1908–1934* (Cambridge: Cambridge University Press, 2001); Susan Gubar, *Racechanges: White Skin, Black Face in American Culture* (Oxford: Oxford University Press, 1997); George Hutchinson, *The Harlem Renaissance in Black and White* (Cambridge: Harvard University Press, 1995); Sieglinde Lemke, *Primitivist Modernism: Black Culture and the Origins of Transatlantic Modernism* (Oxford: Oxford University Press, 1998); Walter Benn Michaels, *Our America: Nativism, Modernism, and Pluralism* (Durham: Duke University Press, 1995); Nielsen, *Reading Race: White American Poets and the Racial Discourse in the Twentieth Century* (Athens: University of Georgia Press, 1988); Nielsen, ed., *Reading Race in American Poetry: "An Area of Act"* (Urbana: University of Illinois Press, 2000); North, *The Dialect of Modernism*; Werner Sollors, *Ethnic Modernism* (2002; rpt. Cambridge: Harvard University Press, 2008); and Glenn Willmott, *Modernist Goods: Primitivism, the Market, and the Gift* (Toronto: University of Toronto Press, 2008).

10. Gilroy, *The Black Atlantic,* 7.

11. Langston Hughes, *The Collected Works of Langston Hughes,* Volume 9: *Essays on Art, Race, Politics, and World Affairs* (Columbia: University of Missouri Press, 2002), 31.

12. Hughes, *Essays,* 34.

13. Henry Louis Gates Jr., and Gene Andrew Jarrett, "Introduction," *The New Negro: Readings on Race, Representation, and African American Culture, 1892–1938* (Princeton: Princeton University Press, 2007), 9.

14. Eric Lott, *Love and Theft: Blackface Minstrelsy and the American Working Class* (Oxford: Oxford University Press, 1993), 38.

15. Wallace Thurman, *The Collected Writings of Wallace Thurman: A Harlem Renaissance Reader* (New Brunswick: Rutgers University Press, 2003), 37; Sterling A. Brown, *A Son's Return: Selected Essays of Sterling A. Brown* (Boston: Northeastern University Press, 1996), 176.

16. Carl Van Vechten, *"Keep A-Inchin' Along": Selected Writings of Carl Van Vechten about Black Art and Letters* (Westport: Greenwood, 1979), 34.

17. Gilroy, *The Black Atlantic,* 76.

18. Christopher Small, *Music of the Common Tongue: Survival and Celebration in Afro-American Music* (Hanover: Wesleyan University Press, 1998), 3.

19. Particularly compelling or well-known overviews of black-white influence and its role in creating a distinctively American musical tradition (in addition to Gilroy's and Small's) include Greil Marcus, *Mystery Train: Images of America in Rock 'n' Roll Music* (1975; rpt. New York: Plume, 1990); Karl Hagstrom Miller, *Segregating Sound: Inventing Folk and Pop Music in the Age of Jim Crow* (Durham: Duke University Press, 2010); Ronald Radano, *Lying Up a Nation: Race and Black Music* (Chicago: University of Chicago Press, 2003); and Nick Tosches, *Where Dead Voices Gather* (Boston: Little, Brown, 2001).

20. James Weldon Johnson and J. Rosamond Johnson, *The Book of American Negro Spirituals* (1925; rpt. New York: Viking, 1964), 19, 43, 21.

21. Zora Neale Hurston, *Folklore, Memoirs, and Other Writings* (New York: Library of America, 1995), 838.

22. Jean Toomer, *The Wayward and the Seeking: A Collection of Writings by Jean Toomer* (Washington, DC: Howard University Press, 1980), 123.

23. Michael Soto, "Jean Toomer and Horace Liveright; or, A New Negro Gets 'into the Swing of It,'" in *Jean Toomer and the Harlem Renaissance* (New Brunswick: Rutgers University Press, 2001), 170. On the musical and vocal structures of *Cane*, see Barbara E. Bowen, "Untroubled Voice: Call and Response in *Cane*," in *Black Literature and Literary Theory*, ed. Henry Louis Gates Jr. (New York: Methuen, 1984), 187–203; Callahan, *In the African-American Grain*; Geneviève Fabre, "Dramatic and Musical Structures in 'Harvest Song' and 'Kabnis': Toomer's *Cane* and the Harlem Renaissance," in *Jean Toomer and the Harlem Renaissance*, ed. Geneviève Fabre and Michel Feith (New Brunswick: Rutgers University Press, 2001), 109–127; Karen Jackson Ford, *Split-Gut Song: Jean Toomer and the Poetics of Modernity* (Tuscaloosa: University of Alabama Press, 2005); Farah Jasmine Griffin, "*Who Set You Flowin'?*": *The African-American Migration Narrative* (Oxford: Oxford University Press, 1995); B. F. McKeever, "*Cane* as Blues," *Negro American Literature Forum* 4 (July 1970), 61–64; and Philipp Schweighauser, *The Noises of American Literature, 1890–1985: Toward a History of Literary Acoustics* (Gainesville: University Press of Florida, 2006).

24. Waldo Frank, "Foreword," in Jean Toomer, *Cane: Norton Critical Edition* (1923; rpt., New York: W. W. Norton, 1988), 138.

25. Toomer, *The Wayward and the Seeking*, 123.

26. Jean Toomer, *Cane* (1923; rpt. New York: W. W. Norton, 1988), 15. Further references to this edition will appear parenthetically in the text.

27. Jean Toomer, "Karintha," *Broom* (January 1923), 83.

28. Joel B. Peckham, "Jean Toomer's Cane: Self as Montage and the Drive toward Integration," *American Literature* 72 (June 2000), 279. For more on Cane and modernist technique, see Maria Isabel Caldiera, "Jean Toomer's *Cane*: The Anxiety of the Modern Artist," *Callaloo* 25 (Autumn 1985), 544–550; Rachel Farebrother, "'Adventuring through the Pieces of a Still Unorganized Mosaic': Reading Jean Toomer's Collage Aesthetic in *Cane*," *Journal of American Studies* 40 (December 2006), 503–521; Catherine Gunther Kodat, "To 'Flash White Light from Ebony': The Problem of Modernism in Jean Toomer's *Cane*," *Twentieth Century Literature* 46 (Spring 2000), 1–19; North, *The Dialect of Modernism*; Frederik L. Rusch, "Form, Function, and Creative Tension in *Cane*: Jean Toomer and the Need for the Avant-Garde," *MELUS* 17 (Winter, 1991–1992), 15–28; and Werner Sollors, "Jean Toomer's *Cane*: Modernism and Race in Interwar America," in *Jean Toomer and the Harlem Renaissance*, ed. Geneviève Fabre and Michel Feith (New Brunswick: Rutgers University Press, 2001), 1–37.

29. Jean Toomer, *A Jean Toomer Reader: Selected Unpublished Writings* (New York: Oxford University Press, 1993), 276.

30. W. E. B. Du Bois, *Essays and Articles* (New York: Library of America, 1987), 1194.

31. Cynthia Earl Kerman and Richard Eldridge, *The Lives of Jean Toomer: A Hunger for Wholeness* (Baton Rouge: Louisiana State University Press, 1987), 95.

32. On the interracialism of *Cane*, see Robert Bone, *Down Home: A History of Afro-American Short Fiction from Its Beginnings to the End of the Harlem Renaissance* (New York: G. P. Putnam's Sons, 1975); Gates, *Figures in Black*; Matthew Pratt Guterl, *The Color of Race in America, 1900–1940* (Cambridge: Harvard University Press, 2001); Charles Harmon, "*Cane*, Race, and 'Neither/Norism,'" *Southern Literary Journal* 32 (Spring 2000), 90–101; George Hutchinson, "Jean Toomer and American Racial Discourse," *Texas Studies in*

Literature and Language 35 (Summer 1993), 226–250; Ross Posnock, *Color and Culture: Black Writers and the Making of the Modern Intellectual* (Cambridge: Harvard University Press, 1998); and Jeff Webb, "Literature and Lynching: Identity in Jean Toomer's *Cane*," *English Literary History* 67 (Spring 2000), 205–228.

33. Johnson, *Writings*, 86, 108.

34. Clement Wood, *Nigger: A Novel* (New York: E. P. Dutton, 1922), 45, 147.

35. Tim Brooks, *Lost Sounds: Blacks and the Birth of the Recording Industry, 1890–1919* (Urbana: University of Illinois Press, 2004), 192.

36. Johnson, *Writings*, 817.

37. Wayne D. Shirley, "The Coming of 'Deep River,'" *American Music* 15 (Winter 1997), 493.

38. Shirley, "The Coming of 'Deep River,'" 515.

39. Johnson and Johnson, *The Book of American Negro Spirituals*, 36.

40. Brooks, *Lost Sounds*, 192.

41. Natalie Curtis Burlin, *Negro Folk-Songs* (New York: G. Schirmer, 1918), II: 10.

42. On anthropology, folklore, and the spirituals, see Regina Bendix, *In Search of Authenticity: The Formation of Folklore Studies* (Madison: University of Wisconsin Press, 1997); Gene Bluestein, *Poplore* (Amherst: University of Massachusetts Press, 1994); Erika Brady, *A Spiral Way: How the Phonograph Changed Ethnography* (Jackson: University of Mississippi Press, 1999); Robert Cantwell, *When We Were Good: The Folk Revival* (Cambridge: Harvard University Press, 1996); Jon Cruz, *Culture on the Margins: The Black Spiritual and the Rise of American Cultural Interpretation* (Princeton: Princeton University Press, 1999); Dena J. Epstein, *Sinful Tunes and Spirituals: Black Folk Music to the Civil War* (1977; rpt. Urbana: University of Illinois Press, 1981); Benjamin Filene, *Romancing the Folk: Public Memory and American Roots Music* (Chapel Hill: University of North Carolina Press, 2000); Lawrence W. Levine, *Black Culture and Black Consciousness: Afro-American Folk Thought from Slavery to Freedom* (Oxford: Oxford University Press, 1977); John Lovell Jr., *Black Song: The Forge and the Flame: The Story of How the Afro-American Spiritual Was Hammered Out* (New York: Paragon House, 1972); Radano, *Lying Up a Nation*; Lauri Ramey, *Slave Songs and the Birth of African American Poetry* (New York: Palgrave Macmillan, 2008); and Eileen Southern, *The Music of Black Americans: A History* (1971; rpt. New York: W.W. Norton, 1983). Readings of *Cane* that connect it to the theory and practice of African American folklore collection include Bone, *Down Home*; J. Martin Favor, *Authentic Blackness: The Folk in the New Negro Renaissance* (Durham: Duke University Press, 1999); and David G. Nicholls, *Conjuring the Folk: Forms of Modernity in African America* (Ann Arbor: University of Michigan Press, 2000).

43. Anonymous, "Scenes in 'Black America,'" *New York Times*, May 26, 1895, 16.

44. Useful histories and theorizations of African American musical theater include Daphne Brooks, *Bodies in Dissent: Spectacular Performances of Race and Freedom, 1850–1910* (Durham: Duke University Press, 2006); Errol G. Hill and James V. Hatch, *A History of African American Theatre* (Cambridge: Cambridge University Press, 2003); David Krasner, *A Beautiful Pageant: African American Theatre, Drama, and Performance in the Harlem Renaissance, 1910–1927* (New York: Palgrave Macmillan, 2002); Krasner, *Resistance, Parody, and Double Consciousness in African American Theatre, 1895–1910* (New York: St. Martin's Press, 1997); Southern, *The Music of Black Americans*; and Allen Woll, *Black Musical Theatre: From Coontown to Dreamgirls* (Baton Rouge: Louisiana State University Press, 1989).

45. Langston Hughes, *Essays*, 34; Alice Walker, *In Search of Our Mothers' Gardens* (New York: Harcourt Brace Jovanovich, 1983), 63.

46. Jean Toomer, *The Letters of Jean Toomer, 1919–1924* (Knoxville: University of Tennessee Press, 2006), 101.

47. Johnson, *Writings*, 874.

48. Toomer, *The Wayward and the Seeking*, 20.

49. Toomer, *The Letters of Jean Toomer*, 113.

50. Burlin, *Negro Folk-Songs*, IV:5.

51. George M. Fredrickson, *The Black Image in the White Mind: The Debate on Afro-American Character and Destiny, 1817–1914* (New York: Harper and Row, 1971), 108.

52. Ralph Waldo Emerson, *Essays and Lectures* (New York: Library of America, 1983), 399.

53. Toomer, *The Wayward and the Seeking*, 228.

54. John Edward Hasse, *Beyond Category: The Life and Genius of Duke Ellington* (New York: Da Capo Press, 1993), 19.

55. Hughes, *Essays*, 36.

56. Hughes, *Essays*, 213; Langston Hughes, *The Collected Works of Langston Hughes*, Volume 1: *The Poems, 1921–1940* (Columbia: University of Missouri Press, 2001), 108. Subsequent references to the latter edition will appear parenthetically in the text.

57. Hughes, *Essays*, 213.

58. Adam Gussow, *Seems Like Murder Here: Southern Violence and the Blues Tradition* (Chicago: University of Chicago Press, 2002), 1.

59. In keeping with their centrality in American popular music, the blues have inspired abundant commentary over the last century. Any survey of the literature ought to begin with the numerous works of Paul Oliver, including *Aspects of the Blues Tradition* (1968; rpt. New York: Oak, 1970); *The Meaning of the Blues* (1960; rpt. New York: Collier Books, 1963); *Songsters and Saints: Vocal Traditions on Race Records* (Cambridge: Cambridge University Press, 1984); and *The Story of the Blues* (Philadelphia: Chilton, 1969). Other useful histories and theorizations of the blues include William Barlow, *"Looking Up at Down": The Emergence of Blues Culture* (Philadelphia: Temple University Press); Samuel B. Charters, *The Country Blues* (London: Michael Joseph, 1959); Lawrence Cohn, *Nothing but the Blues: The Music and the Musicians* (New York: Abbeville Press, 1993); Francis Davis, *The History of the Blues* (1995; rpt. Cambridge: Da Capo Press, 2003); Robert M.W. Dixon and John Godrich, *Recording the Blues* (London: Studio Vista, 1970); David Evans, *Big Road Blues: Tradition and Creativity in the Folk Blues* (Berkeley: University of California Press, 1982); Benjamin Filene, *Romancing the Folk*; Ted Gioia, *Delta Blues: The Life and Times of the Mississippi Masters Who Revolutionized American Music* (New York: W.W. Norton, 2008); Marybeth Hamilton, *In Search of the Blues* (New York: Basic Books, 2008); LeRoi Jones, *Blues People: The Negro Experience in White America and the Music That Developed from It* (New York: Morrow Quill, 1963); Miller, *Segregating Sound*; Albert Murray, *Stomping the Blues* (New York: McGraw-Hill, 1976); Robert Palmer, *Deep Blues* (New York: Viking, 1981); Tony Russell, *Blacks, Whites, and Blues* (1970; rpt. in *Yonder Come the Blues*, Cambridge: Cambridge University Press, 2001); Southern, *The Music of Black Americans*; Robert Springer, ed. *Nobody Knows Where the Blues Come From: Lyrics and History* (Jackson: University of Mississippi Press, 2006); Jeff Todd Titon, *Early Downhome Blues: A Musical and Cultural Analysis* (1977; rpt. Chapel Hill: University of North Carolina Press, 1994); and Elijah Wald, *Escaping the Delta: Robert Johnson and the Invention of the Blues* (New York: HarperCollins, 2004).

60. Hughes, *Essays*, 34–35.

61. Brian Smethurst, "Lyric Stars: Countee Cullen and Langston Hughes," in *The Cambridge Companion to the Harlem Renaissance* (Cambridge: Cambridge University Press, 2007), 121. For traditional studies of Hughes that argue the link between the blues and blackness, see Richard K. Barksdale, *Langston Hughes: The Poet and His Critics* (Chicago: American Library Association, 1977); Patricia E. Bonner, "Cryin' the Jazzy Blues and Livin' Blue Jazz: Analyzing the Blues and Jazz Poetry of Langston Hughes," *West Georgia College Review* 20 (1990), 15–29; Peter Booker, "Modernism Deferred: Langston Hughes, Harlem and Jazz Montage," *Locations of Literary Modernism: Region and Nation in British and American Modernist Poetry*, ed. Alex Davis and Lee M. Jenkins (Cambridge: Cambridge University Press, 2000), 231–248; David Chinitz, "Literacy and Authenticity: The Blues Poems of Langston Hughes," *Callaloo* 19:1 (1996) 177–192; William H. Hansell, "Black Music in the Poetry of Langston Hughes: Roots, Race, Release," *Obsidian* 4:3 (1978), 16–38; Onwuchekwa Jemie, *Langston Hughes: An Introduction to the Poetry* (New York: Columbia University Press, 1976); Patricia Johnson and Walter C. Farrell Jr., "How Langston Hughes Used the Blues," *MELUS* 6:1 (Spring 1979), 55–63; Monica Michlin, "Langston Hughes's Blues," *Temples for Tomorrow: Looking Back at the Harlem Renaissance*, ed. Geneviève Fabre and Michel Feith (Bloomington: Indiana University Press, 2001), 236–253; Omry, *Cross-Rhythms*; and Edward E. Waldron, "The Blues Poetry of Langston Hughes," *Negro American Literature Forum* 5:4 (Winter 1971), 140–149.

62. Hughes, *Essays*, 32.

63. Langston Hughes, *The Collected Works of Langston Hughes*, Volume 13: *Autobiography: The Big Sea* (Columbia: University of Missouri Press, 2002), 171.

64. Houston A. Baker Jr., *Blues, Ideology, and Afro-American Literature: A Vernacular Theory* (Chicago: University of Chicago Press, 1984), 14.

65. For more on the spoken or sung word and its relation to Hughes's poetry, see Herman Beavers, "Dead Rocks and Sleeping Men: Aurality in the Aesthetic of Langston Hughes," *Langston Hughes Review* 11:1 (1992), 1–5; Karen J. Ford, "These Old Writing Paper Blues: The Blues Stanza and Literary Poetry," *College Literature* 24:3 (October 1997), 84–103; Gayl Jones, *Liberating Voices*; Meta DuEwa Jones, "Listening to What the Ear Demands: Langston Hughes and His Critics," *Callaloo* 25:4 (Autumn 2002), 1145–1175; and Sherley A. Williams, "The Blues Roots of Contemporary Afro-American Poetry," in *Chant of Saints: A Gathering of Afro-American Literature, Art, and Scholarship* (Urbana: University of Illinois Press, 1979), 123–135.

66. Abbe Niles, "Introduction: Sad Horns," in *Blues: An Anthology* (New York: Albert and Charles Boni, 1926), 10.

67. Artie Matthews, *Weary Blues* (St. Louis: Stark Music, 1915), 1.

68. Hughes, *The Big Sea*, 171.

69. Niles, "Introduction: Sad Horns," 9.

70. For readings of Hughes's variously defined project of merging in his musical and blues poetry, see Borshuk, *Swinging the Vernacular*; Edwards, *The Practice of Diaspora*; Hartmut Grandel, "The Role of Music in the Self-Reflexive Poetry of the Harlem Renaissance," in *Poetics in the Poem: Critical Essays on American Self-Reflexive Poetry*, ed. Dorothy Z. Baker (New York: Peter Lang, 1997), 119–131; Jahan Ramazani, *Poetry of Mourning: The Modern Elegy from Hardy to Heaney* (Chicago: University of Chicago Press, 1994); and Arnold Rampersad, *The Life of Langston Hughes*, Volume I: *1902–1941: I, Too, Sing*

America (Oxford: Oxford University Press, 1986). For queer readings of Hughes's blues poetry, see Nicholas M. Evans, *Writing Jazz: Race, Nationalism, and Modern Culture in the 1920s* (New York: Garland, 2000); Martin Joseph Ponce, "Langston Hughes's Queer Blues," *Modern Language Quarterly* 66:4 (December 2005), 505–537; Sam See, "'Spectacles in Color': The Primitive Drag of Langston Hughes," *PMLA* 124:3 (Winter 2009), 798–816; and Shane Vogel, *The Scene of Harlem Cabaret: Race, Sexuality, Performance* (Chicago: University of Chicago Press, 2009).

71. W. C. Handy, *Father of the Blues* (1941; rpt. New York, Collier, 1970), 127.

72. Niles, "Introduction: Sad Horns," 24, 1.

73. Richard Middleton, *Voicing the Popular: On the Subjects of Popular Music* (New York: Routledge, 2006), 43.

74. T. S. Eliot, *The Complete Poems and Plays, 1909–1950* (New York: Harcourt Brace, 1980), 49.

75. Ralph Ellison, *Invisible Man* (1952; rpt. New York: Vintage, 1995), 581.

76. Robert Jourdain, *Music, the Brain, and Ecstasy: How Music Captures Our Imagination* (New York: Quill, 1997), 35.

77. Hughes, *Essays*, 33.

78. Alain Locke, ed., *The New Negro* (1925; rpt. New York: Simon and Schuster, 1992), xxv.

79. Sterling A. Brown, "The Blues as Folk Poetry," in *Folk-Say: A Regional Miscellany* (Norman: University of Oklahoma Press, 1930), 324, 339.

80. Francis Davis, *The History of the Blues*, 84.

81. Oliver, *Songsters and Saints*, 260. The elusiveness of the blues and the impossibility of definitively locating their early, pre-1912 forms provides much of their allure, at least if the titles of such recent studies as Hamilton's *In Search of the Blues* and Springer's *Nobody Knows Where the Blues Come From* are any indication.

82. D. H. Lawrence, *Phoenix: The Posthumous Papers of D. H. Lawrence* (New York: Viking, 1936), 362.

83. Robert E. Hemenway, *Zora Neale Hurston: A Literary Biography* (Champaign: University of Illinois Press, 1980), 91–92.

84. Alan Lomax, *Selected Writings, 1934–1997* (New York: Routledge, 2003), 21–22.

85. Dorothy Scarborough, *On the Trail of Negro Folk-Songs* (Cambridge: Harvard University Press, 1925), 264.

86. Van Vechten, "Keep A-Inchin' Along," 47.

87. Arnold Rampersad, *The Life of Langston Hughes,* Volume I, 123.

88. Hughes, *The Big Sea*, 166.

89. Hughes, *The Big Sea*, 202.

90. Eliot, *Selected Prose* (New York: Harcourt Brace Jovanovich, 1975), 40.

91. Thurman, *The Collected Writings of Wallace Thurman*, 214–215.

92. Bone, *Down Home*, 122.

93. Filene, *Romancing the Folk*, 71.

94. Gioia, *Delta Blues*, 73.

95. Hughes, *The Big Sea*, 243.

96. Hughes, *Essays*, 381.

97. Hughes, *Essays*, 265.

98. Hughes, *Essays*, 369. Emphasis original.

99. Toomer, *The Wayward and the Seeking*, 92.

100. Edna Ferber, *Show Boat* (Garden City: Doubleday, Page, 1926), 291–292.

101. Wallace Thurman, *Infants of the Spring* (1932; rpt. Boston: Northeastern University Press, 1992), 186–187.

102. Kerman and Eldridge, *The Lives of Jean Toomer*, 100.

103. Claude McKay, *Banjo: A Story without a Plot* (New York: Harper and Brothers, 1929), 57–58.

104. Rudolph Fisher, "The Caucasian Storms Harlem," *American Mercury* 11:44 (August 1927), 398.

CHAPTER 5

1. Bradford Ropes, *42nd Street* (New York: Grosset and Dunlap, 1932), 22.

2. Lois W. Banner, *American Beauty* (New York: Alfred A. Knopf, 1983), 180. Other useful histories and theorizations of the chorus girl and actresses include Robert C. Allen, *Horrible Prettiness: Burlesque and American Culture* (Chapel Hill: University of North Carolina Press, 1991); Martha Banta, *Imaging American Women: Ideas and Ideals in Cultural History* (New York: Columbia University Press, 1987); Faye E. Dudden, *Women in the American Theatre: Actresses and Audiences, 1790–1870* (New Haven: Yale University Press, 1994); Susan A. Glenn, *Female Spectacle: The Theatrical Roots of Modern Feminism* (Cambridge: Harvard University Press, 2000); Angela J. Latham, *Posing a Threat: Flappers, Chorus Girls, and Other Brazen Performers of the American 1920s* (Hanover: Wesleyan University Press, 2000); Linda Mizejewski, *Ziegfeld Girl: Image and Icon in Culture and Cinema* (Durham: Duke University Press, 1999); Derek Parker and Julia Parker, *The Natural History of the Chorus Girl* (Indianapolis: Bobbs-Merrill, 1975); and Rachel Shteir, *Striptease: The Untold History of the Girlie Show* (Oxford: Oxford University Press, 2004).

3. See F. Scott Fitzgerald's story "Head and Shoulders" and its film adaptation *The Chorus Girl's Romance* (both in 1920), George Manker Watters's and Arthur Hopkins's novel *Burlesque* and its stage version (1926 and 1928), Beth Brown's novel *Applause* and its film adaptation (1928 and 1929), and J. P. McEvoy's novel *Show Girl* and its stage version (1928 and 1929), to name a few.

4. Theodore Dreiser, *Sister Carrie* (1900; rpt. New York: W. W. Norton, 2006), 272. Further references to this edition will appear parenthetically in the text. Because this chapter argues that *Sister Carrie* had a formative and specifically historical influence on the chorus girl novel as it developed in subsequent decades, it refers to the Donald Pizer edition of the novel—based on the published text of 1900—rather than the later, significantly revised University of Pennsylvania edition of 1981.

5. As Philip Fisher has argued, *Sister Carrie* is one of a handful of American novels that "colonized so quickly the national mind" upon publication and became such integral parts of the American cultural imagination that their insights are today more or less taken for granted. See Fisher, *Hard Facts: Setting and Form in the American Novel* (Oxford: Oxford University Press, 1985), 21.

6. Beyond having an international reputation as one of the great showmen of his era, Daly was a suggestive figure to Dreiser because of his extraordinary attention to and ability to work with theatrical talent. In his memoir of his early days in New York, Dreiser recalls being told the following in regard to him: "Now here, my boy, is a manager. He makes actors—he doesn't hire them." Daly was also the author of *Under the Gaslight* (1867), the play in which Carrie makes her debut. See Dreiser, *Newspaper Days* (Philadelphia: University of Pennsylvania Press, 1991), 582.

7. June Howard, *Form and History in American Literary Naturalism* (Chapel Hill: University of North Carolina Press, 1985), x.

8. In this, the turn-of-the-century female chorus resembles the chorus of classical drama, in which actors are not singular entities so much as manifestations of the state, the will of the people, or something comparably broad. Indeed, little else other than an emphasis on collectivity can be said to connect the many varieties of choruses that the American stage has seen over the years, as they have taken the form of everything from companies of bystanders to dance troupes that move with a well-drilled, almost military precision; Parker and Parker define the chorus girl as "any young lady who, unnamed, has trod the boards in the company of her friends, providing a picture of feminine beauty for the delight of an audience of admiring men," with the operative word being "unnamed" (Parker and Parker, *The Natural History of the Chorus Girl*, 6). In the musical theater and chorus girl novel alike, the chorus is generally to be understood as an institution of mass anonymity, providing a contrast to the unique women who exist apart or emerge from it.

9. Theodore Dreiser, *Theodore Dreiser's Ev'ry Month* (Athens: University of Georgia Press, 1996), 299.

10. Useful histories of the Broadway musical include Rick Altman, *The American Film Musical* (Bloomington: University of Indiana Press, 1987); Geoffrey Block, *Enchanted Evenings: The Broadway Musical from Show Boat to Sondheim* (Oxford: Oxford University Press, 1997); Gerald Bordman, *American Musical Comedy: From Adonis to Dreamgirls* (Oxford: Oxford University Press, 1982); William A. Everett and Paul R. Laird, eds., *The Cambridge Companion to the Musical* (Cambridge: Cambridge University Press, 2002); David Ewen, *The Complete Book of the American Musical Theater* (New York: Holt, Rinehart and Winston, 1958); Mark N. Grant, *The Rise and Fall of the Broadway Musical* (Boston: Northeastern University Press, 2004); Alan Hyman, *The Gaiety Years* (London: Cassell, 1975); Raymond Knapp, *The American Musical and the Formation of National Identity* (Princeton: Princeton University Press, 2005); Knapp, *The American Musical and the Performance of Personal Identity* (Princeton: Princeton University Press, 2006); and Ethan Mordden, *Make Believe: The Broadway Musical in the 1920s* (Oxford: Oxford University Press, 1997).

11. George Jean Nathan, *The Entertainment of a Nation, or, Three-Sheets in the Wind* (New York: Alfred A. Knopf, 1942), 107.

12. On *Sister Carrie* in relation to the "working girl" novel, see Cathy N. Davidson and Arnold E. Davidson, "Carrie's Sisters: The Popular Prototypes for Dreiser's Heroine," *Modern Fiction Studies* 23:3 (Autumn 1977), 395–408. On *Sister Carrie* and popular novels, see M. H. Dunlop, "Carrie's Library: Reading the Boundaries between Popular and Serious Fiction," in *Theodore Dreiser: Beyond Naturalism*, ed. Mariam Gogol (New York: New York University Press, 1995), 201–215.

13. Hermann L.F. Helmholtz, *On the Sensations of Tone as a Physiological Basis for the Theory of Music* (1885; rpt. New York: Dover, 1954), 36.

14. Walter Benn Michaels, *The Gold Standard and the Logic of Naturalism: American Literature at the Turn of the Century* (Berkeley: University of California Press, 1987), 44.

15. On the subject of gender economics, Carrie has been argued to be everything from an investment opportunity for men to a manipulative speculator in them. Blanche H. Gelfant reads her as in a sense shopping for male companionship, with her rise in the world driven by her tendency to "reject one man for another with superior taste," while Kevin R. McNamara sees her as a passive commodity to be directed toward certain ends, "a speculum—a mirror

reflecting desires (ultimately, male desire) and social ideals." But as Susan Glenn has per-suasively shown, the turn-of-the-century stage often demanded that actresses occupy both roles at once, giving women the opportunity for liberating self-display even as it left them obliged to the men who employed, directed, or paid to see them. See also Charles Harmon, who argues that Carrie's performance in this scene offers men a temporary respite from capitalistic endeavor by inviting them to "assume emotions that are commonly associated with powerless women." See Gelfant, "What More Can Carrie Want? Naturalistic Ways of Consuming Women," in *The Cambridge Companion to American Realism and Naturalism: Howells to London* (Cambridge: Cambridge University Press, 1995), 183; McNamara, *Urban Verbs: Arts and Discourses of American Cities* (Stanford: Stanford University Press, 1996), 61; Glenn, *Female Spectacle*; and Harmon, "Cuteness and Capitalism in *Sister Carrie*," *American Literary Realism* 32:2 (Winter 2000), 132.

16. Brooks Atkinson, *Broadway* (New York: Macmillan, 1974), 23.

17. Dreiser, *Sister Carrie*, 342. On Carrie's passivity, see McNamara, *Urban Verbs*; Rachel Bowlby, *Just Looking: Consumer Culture in Dreiser, Gissing, and Zola* (New York: Meth-uen, 1985); Barbara Hochman, "A Portrait of the Artist as a Young Actress: The Rewards of Representation in *Sister Carrie*," in *New Essays on Sister Carrie* (Cambridge: Cambridge University Press, 1991), 43–64; David Minter, *A Cultural History of the American Novel: Henry James to William Faulkner* (Cambridge: Cambridge University Press, 1994); and Cris-tina Ruotolo, "'Whence the Song:' Voice and Audience in Dreiser's *Sister Carrie*," in *Sister Carrie* (New York: W. W. Norton, 2006), 584–603.

18. Anna Morgan, *An Hour with Delsarte: A Study of Expression* (1889; rpt. Boston: Lee and Shepard, 1895), 83, 15, 37.

19. Morgan, *An Hour with Delsarte*, 15.

20. For an overview of melodrama and its influence on the novel, see Peter Brooks's *The Melodramatic Imagination* (1976; rpt. New Haven: Yale University Press, 1995), which finds Balzac's *Pére Goriot*—which Carrie is reading in Dreiser's final chapter—to be exemplary of a literary tradition that "applies pressure to the gesture, pressure through interrogation, through the evocation of more and more fantastic possibilities, to make it yield meaning, to make it give up to consciousness its full potential as 'parable'" (1).

21. Morgan, *An Hour with Delsarte*, 113.

22. Bertolt Brecht, *Brecht on Theatre: The Development of an Aesthetic* (New York: Hill and Wang, 2001), 42.

23. The editors of the Pennsylvania edition of *Sister Carrie*, for example, refer to *Under the Gaslight* as "that piece of lightweight melodrama" and argue that Carrie must "trans-form" it if it is to be emotionally compelling in any genuine way (533).

24. George Jean Nathan, *The Theatre, the Drama, the Girls* (New York: Alfred A. Knopf, 1921), 276–277.

25. Theodore Dreiser, *Dawn* (New York: Horace Liveright, 1931), 362–363. Dreiser at one point aspired to be "an author of comic opera books," a goal that he in a very real sense accomplished in *Sister Carrie*, if not quite in the manner he had first imagined (*Newspaper* 238). Before he turned to novel writing, Dreiser penned a musical (never produced and now lost) titled *Jeremiah I*, in which an American farmer strikes a magical stone with his shovel and is transported back in time to Aztec Mexico. He wrote a great deal of theater journalism in later years, evincing a growing distaste for the popular and musical stage; the most useful collections of it are *Theodore Dreiser's Ev'ry Month* (edited by Nancy Warner Barrineau) and

Art, Music, and Literature, 1897–1902 (edited by Yoshinobu Hakutani). He continued writing plays after his reputation as one of America's preeminent novelists was secured, though they tended toward Expressionism.

26. Amy Kaplan, for example, argues that the theater is palliative in Dreiser's text, serving "to translate the threats of city life into a form of art that can be instantly consumed by an audience," while James Livingston finds it offering a means of self-creation, of fashioning "new divisions and extensions of the self that had become possible and necessary under the regime of antebellum accumulation." See Kaplan, *The Social Construction of American Realism* (Chicago: University of Chicago Press, 1988), 158; and Livingston, *Pragmatism and the Political Economy of Cultural Revolution, 1850–1940* (Chapel Hill: University of North Carolina Press, 1994), 143.

27. Theodore Dreiser, *Twelve Men* (1919; rpt: New York: Boni and Liveright, 1927), 76; Theodore Dreiser, "Introduction," *The Songs of Paul Dresser* (New York: Boni and Liveright, 1927), vii.

28. Dreiser, *Dawn*, 112.

29. Dreiser on occasion flattered himself that his own literary talent might have been transferable to Broadway. One of his more well-known anecdotes revolves around his writing the lyrics for "On the Banks of the Wabash," which his brother set to music; it is today the state song of Indiana. In his essay "Birth and Growth of a Popular Song" (1891), Dreiser pats himself on the back thus: "the words of 'On the Banks of the Wabash' were written in less than an hour of an April Sunday afternoon," a feat that he finds all the more remarkable considering that "there is not more than one good popular song turned out a year, and a great success such as 'On the Banks of the Wabash' is not written once in ten years." Such success, he declares, is a matter of inherent ability: "It looks easy, and the truth is, it really is easy for the person who has the popular-song vein in him." See Dreiser, *Art, Music, and Literature* 130–131.

30. Of particular interest to scholars has been the extent to which Dreiser expresses this perpetual social observation in urban architecture, with one of his favorite symbols being the display window. On this subject see Bill Brown, "The Matter of Dreiser's Modernity," in *The Cambridge Companion to Theodore Dreiser* (Cambridge: Cambridge University Press, 2004) 83–99; Fisher, *Hard Facts*; Deborah M. Garfield, "Taking a Part: Actor and Audience in Theodore Dreiser's *Sister Carrie*," *American Literary Realism* 16:2 (Autumn 1983), 223–239; and Hana Wirth-Nesher, *City Codes: Reading the Modern Urban Novel* (Cambridge: Cambridge University Press, 1996).

31. Theodore Dreiser, *A Hoosier Holiday* (New York: John Lane, 1916), 226.

32. Lewis A. Erenberg's history of New York City nightlife contains an overview of the ways in which the restaurants and businesses of Broadway took on a showy, theatrical air and marketed themselves as extensions of the stage. In regard to the "lobster palaces" that celebrities frequented in this era, for example, Erenberg notes that their floor plans were designed to facilitate spectatorship: "It was but a short step from the fantasy on stage to the fantasies portrayed by the restaurants themselves." See Erenberg, *Steppin' Out: New York Nightlife and the Transformation of American Culture, 1890–1930* (Westport: Greenwood Press, 1981), 41. Even so famous a woman as Evelyn Nesbit, the former *Florodora* chorine and inspiration for the sensational murder of the architect Stanford White, thrilled at the memory of these theatrical restaurants in her memoir: "There you saw everybody who was anybody in the Broadway *milieu*. My reactions I shall never forget. The restaurant was

divided in two: the famous—and infamous—sitting on the right table; hoi polloi on the left. And *we* were given a table on the *right*! I couldn't help noticing that men at surrounding tables hardly took their eyes off me. Years have dimmed the recollection, but I am sure I could not have said, even then, which gave me the greater thrill: supping at Rector's—or having so many men of the world regarding me with evident admiration." See Nesbit, *Prodigal Days: The Untold Story* (London: John Long, 1934), 36. Emphasis original.

33. Donald Pizer, *The Novels of Theodore Dreiser: A Critical Study* (Minneapolis: University of Minnesota Press, 1976), 14, 16.

34. Henry James, *The Tragic Muse* (1890; rpt. New York: Penguin, 1995), 305; Willa Cather, *The Song of the Lark* (1915; rpt. New York: Oxford University Press, 2000), 255.

35. Cather, *The Song of the Lark*, 109.

36. Lionel Trilling, *The Liberal Imagination: Essays on Literature and Society* (New York: Viking, 1950), 13. Paul Giles provides an overview of the critical debate that Dreiser's style has inspired in the century since *Sister Carrie* was published, and concludes that his apparently doubled voice is deployed not to depict "the collapse of an attenuated idealism" but rather to illustrate "the tantalizing points of transition between one state and another." See Giles, "Dreiser's Style," in *The Cambridge Companion to Theodore Dreiser* (Cambridge: Cambridge University Press, 2004), 51.

37. Will A. Page, *Behind the Curtains of the Broadway Beauty Trust* (New York: Edward A. Miller, 1927), 2.

38. Jennifer L. Fleissner, *Women, Compulsion, Modernity: The Moment of American Naturalism* (Chicago: University of Chicago Press, 2004), 164.

39. Dreiser, *Dawn*, 198–199.

40. Dreiser, *Carrie*, 322; Christophe Den Tandt, *The Urban Sublime in American Literary Naturalism* (Urbana: University of Illinois Press, 1998), 3.

41. Dreiser, *Art, Music, and Literature*, 197.

42. Dreiser, *Art, Music, and Literature*, 197.

43. Richard Lehan, *Theodore Dreiser: His World and His Novels* (Carbondale: Southern Illinois University Press, 1969), xiii.

44. John Dos Passos, *Manhattan Transfer* (1925; rpt. New York: Library of America, 2003), 667, 494. Further references to this edition will appear parenthetically in the text.

45. Scholars who engage with this problem often refer to *Manhattan Transfer* as a "collectivist" novel, one whose narrative is essentially synecdotal: as Joseph Warren Beach has put it, "it is the structure itself which interests the collectivist, the pattern made from innumerable individual cases, the interplay, the working together—the 'organic filaments' . . . that bind together man to man, and class to class, in the orderly complex of 'society.'" See Beach, "*Manhattan Transfer*: Collectivism and Abstract Composition," in *Dos Passos, the Critics, and the Writer's Intention*, ed. Allen Belkind (Carbondale: Southern Illinois University Press, 1971), 61. For more on the tension between order, disorder, and literary form in *Manhattan Transfer*, see Robert M. Crunden, *Body and Soul: The Making of American Modernism* (New York: Basic Books, 2000); and Desmond Harding, *Writing the City: Urban Visions and Literary Modernism* (New York: Routledge, 2003).

46. Guy Bolton, *Sally of the Alley*, 1920 (Florenz Ziegfeld-Billie Burke Papers, Billy Rose Theater Collection, New York Public Library), I-19; III-2.

47. John Dos Passos, *Three Plays* (New York: Harcourt, Brace, 1934), xix.

48. The same cannot be said for Dos Passos's seldom-read novel *Streets of Night*, which was published two years before *Manhattan Transfer* and whose protagonist thinks of chorus girls as "those unfortunate women who have rendered themselves unworthy of the society of our mothers and sisters," such that they are only slightly less degraded than "common prostitutes." See Dos Passos, *Streets of Night* (1923; rpt. Cranbury: Associated University Presses, 1990), 30.

49. Michael Trask, *Cruising Modernism: Class and Sexuality in American Literature and Social Thought* (Ithaca: Cornell University Press, 2003), 180.

50. James Forbes, *The Chorus Lady* (1906; rpt. in *The Famous Mrs. Fair and Other Plays*, New York: George H. Doran, 1920), 78. Emphasis original.

51. Avery Hopwood, *The Gold Diggers* (1919; photocopy of unpublished manuscript), I:56. For analysis of *The Gold Diggers* and its sexual politics, see Glenn, *Female Spectacle*; and Latham, *Posing a Threat*. My thanks to Latham for sharing her copy of the play.

52. Janet Galligani Casey, *Dos Passos and the Ideology of the Feminine* (Cambridge: Cambridge University Press, 1998), 118.

53. Philip Fisher, *Still the New World: American Literature in a Culture of Creative Destruction* (Cambridge: Harvard University Press, 1999), 257.

54. Phillip Arrington, "The Sense of an Ending in *Manhattan Transfer*," *American Literature* 54:3 (October 1982), 441. For other readings of Ellen as essentially urban, mechanical, and robotic, see William Brevda, "How Do I Get to Broadway? Reading Dos Passos's *Manhattan Transfer* Sign," *Texas Studies in Literature and Language* 38:1 (Spring 1996), 79–114; Michael Clark, *Dos Passos's Early Fiction, 1912–1938* (Selingsgrove: Susquehanna University Press, 1987); Iain Colley, *Dos Passos and the Fiction of Despair* (London: Macmillan, 1978); and E. D. Lowry, "*Manhattan Transfer*: Dos Passos' Wasteland," in *Dos Passos: A Collection of Critical Essays* (Englewood Cliffs: Prentice-Hall, 1974), 53–60.

55. Joel Dinerstein, *Swinging the Machine: Modernity, Technology, and African American Culture between the World Wars* (Amherst: University of Massachusetts Press, 2003), 183.

56. Edmund Wilson, *The American Earthquake: A Documentary of the Twenties and Thirties* (Garden City: Doubleday, 1958), 51.

57. Gilbert Seldes, *The Seven Lively Arts* (New York: Harper and Brothers, 1924), 132.

58. Siegfried Kracauer, *The Mass Ornament: Weimar Essays* (Cambridge: Harvard University Press, 1995), 76, 79.

59. John Dos Passos, *John Dos Passos: The Major Nonfictional Prose* (Detroit: Wayne State University Press, 1988), 81; Glenn, *Female Spectacle*, 179.

60. Michael Denning, *The Cultural Front: The Laboring of American Culture in the Twentieth Century* (New York: Verso, 1996), 178.

61. John Dos Passos, *The 42nd Parallel.* (1930; rpt New York: Modern Library, 1937), 4.

62. Dos Passos, *The Major Nonfictional Prose*, 75, 77.

63. T. S. Eliot, *Selected Prose* (New York: Harcourt Brace Jovanovich, 1975), 174. The debate over the relative "passivity" of audiences in an era of mechanically reproduced popular culture is addressed by nearly every history of twentieth-century entertainment. For theorizations of the fused performer-spectator dynamic that Dos Passos admired and its implications for the avant-garde, see Lisa Appignanesi, *The Cabaret* (New Haven: Yale University Press, 2004); and Miriam Hansen, *Babel and Babylon: Spectatorship in American Silent Film* (Cambridge: Harvard University Press, 1991).

64. Dos Passos, *Three Plays*, xix. For more on Dos Passos and the cinema, see Lowry, "The Lively Art of *Manhattan Transfer*," *Publications of the Modern Language Association (PMLA)* 84:6 (October 1969), 1628–1638; Lisa Nannney, *John Dos Passos* (New York: Twayne, 1998); Michael North, *Camera Works: Photography and the Twentieth Century Word* (Oxford: Oxford University Press, 2005); Carol Shloss, *In Visible Light: Photography and the American Writer: 1840–1940* (Oxford: Oxford University Press, 1987); and Michael Spindler, "John Dos Passos and the Visual Arts," *Journal of American Studies* 15 (1981), 391–405.

65. John Dos Passos, "Foreword," in John Howard Lawson, *Roger Bloomer: A Play in Three Acts* (New York: Thomas Seltzer, 1923), vi–vii.

66. John Dos Passos, *The Garbage Man: A Parade with Shouting* (New York: Harper and Brothers, 1926), 159.

67. Several decades later, Dos Passos remained unwilling to look down on the popular arts or people with sincere attachments to them: "It was the sort of smug repudiation that put me off Sinclair Lewis' *Main Street*. What right did we have to rate ourselves higher than successful businessmen or the corner grocer or the whitewings who swept the streets for that matter? It wasn't that I accepted their standards: it was that I felt that to challenge a man's notions you had to meet him on his own ground." See Dos Passos, *The Best Times: An Informal Memoir* (New York: New American Library, 1966), 135. For more on Dos Passos's engagement with the stage, see George A. Knox and Herbert M. Stahl, *Dos Passos and "The Revolting Playwrights"* (Upsala: Lund, 1964).

68. John Dos Passos, *The Big Money* (1936; rpt. New York: Modern Library, 1937), 261.

69. Dos Passos, *The Big Money*, 425–426.

70. Beth Brown, *Applause* (New York: Horace Liveright, 1928), 190.

71. Ropes, *42nd Street*, 314.

72. Nathan, *The Theatre, the Drama, the Girls*, 61.

73. Peter Gay, *Modernism: The Lure of Heresy, from Baudelaire to Beckett and Beyond* (New York: W. W. Norton, 2008), 509.

CHAPTER 6

1. Jennifer Egan, *A Visit from the Goon Squad* (New York: Alfred A. Knopf, 2010), 18. Emphasis original.

2. Zachary Lazar, *Sway* (New York: Little, Brown, 2008), 246.

3. Roddy Doyle, *The Commitments* (1987; rpt. New York: Vintage, 1989), 55.

4. Matthew Specktor, *That Summertime Sound* (New York City: MTV Press, 2009), 245.

5. Specktor, *That Summertime Sound*, 263.

6. Paul Beatty, *Slumberland* (New York: Bloomsbury, 2008), 34–35.

7. Beatty, *Slumberland*, 16. Emphasis original.

8. Nick Hornby, *Juliet, Naked* (New York: Riverhead, 2009), 28.

9. Geoff Dyer, *But Beautiful: A Book about Jazz* (New York: North Point Press, 1996), viii. Further references to this edition will appear parenthetically in the text.

Works Cited

Abbate, Carolyn. *Unsung Voices: Opera and Musical Narrative in the Nineteenth Century.* Princeton: Princeton University Press, 1991.

Adorno, Theodor W. *Essays on Music.* Trans. Susan H. Gillespie. Ed. Richard Leppert. Berkeley: University of California Press, 2002.

Ahlquist, Karen. *Democracy at the Opera: Music, Theater, and Culture in New York City, 1815–60.* Urbana: University of Illinois Press, 1997.

———. "Mrs. Potiphar at the Opera: Satire, Idealism, and Cultural Authority in Post-Civil War New York." *Music and Culture in America, 1861–1918.* Ed. Michael Saffle. New York: Garland, 1998.

Albright, Daniel. *Music Speaks: On the Language of Opera, Dance, and Song.* Rochester: University of Rochester Press, 2009.

———. *Untwisting the Serpent: Modernism in Music, Literature, and Other Arts.* Chicago: University of Chicago Press, 2000.

Alda, Frances and the Orpheus Quartet. "Deep River." Victor, 1917.

Allen, Robert C. *Horrible Prettiness: Burlesque and American Culture.* Chapel Hill: University of North Carolina Press, 1991.

Altman, Rick. *The American Film Musical.* Bloomington: University of Indiana Press, 1987.

———. *Silent Film Sound.* New York: Columbia University Press, 2004.

Anderson, Paul Allen. *Deep River: Music and Memory in Harlem Renaissance Thought.* Durham: Duke University Press, 2001.

Anderson, T. J. III. *Notes to Make the Sound Come Right: Four Innovators of Jazz Poetry.* Fayetteville: University of Arkansas Press, 2004.

Appel, Alfred Jr. *Jazz Modernism: From Ellington and Armstrong to Matisse and Joyce.* New York: Alfred A. Knopf, 2002.

Appignanesi, Lisa. *The Cabaret.* New Haven: Yale University Press, 2004.

Ardis, Ann L. and Lewis, Leslie W., eds. *Women's Experience of Modernity, 1875–1945.* Baltimore: Johns Hopkins University Press, 2003.

Armstrong, Tim. *Modernism: A Cultural History.* Cambridge: Polity, 2005.

——. *Modernism, Technology, and the Body: A Cultural Study*. Cambridge: Cambridge University Press, 1998.

Aronson, Alex. *Music and the Novel: A Study in Twentieth-Century Fiction*. Totowa: Rowman and Littlefield, 1980.

Arrington, Phillip. "The Sense of an Ending in *Manhattan Transfer*." *American Literature* 54:3 (October 1982). 438–443.

Atkinson, Brooks. *Broadway*. New York: Macmillan, 1974.

Attali, Jacques. *Noise: The Political Economy of Music*. Trans. Brian Massumi. 1977. Rpt. Minneapolis: University of Minnesota Press, 1985.

Babbitt, Irving. *The New Laokoon: An Essay on the Confusion of the Arts*. Boston: Houghton Mifflin, 1910.

Baker, Houston A. Jr. *Afro-American Poetics: Revisions of Harlem and the Black Aesthetic*. Madison: University of Wisconsin Press, 1988.

——. *Blues, Ideology, and Afro-American Literature: A Vernacular Theory*. Chicago: University of Chicago Press, 1984.

——. *Modernism and the Harlem Renaissance*. Chicago: University of Chicago Press, 1987.

Banner, Lois W. *American Beauty*. New York: Alfred A. Knopf, 1983.

Banta, Martha. *Imaging American Women: Ideas and Ideals in Cultural History*. New York: Columbia University Press, 1987.

Barksdale, Richard K. *Langston Hughes: The Poet and His Critics*. Chicago: American Library Association, 1977.

Barlow, William. *"Looking Up at Down": The Emergence of Blues Culture*. Philadelphia: Temple University Press.

Barricelli, Jean-Pierre. *Melopoiesis: Approaches to the Study of Literature and Music*. New York: New York University Press, 1988.

Barth, John. *Lost in the Funhouse*. 1968. Rpt. New York: Anchor, 1988.

Barthes, Roland. *S/Z: An Essay*. Trans. Richard Miller. New York: Hill and Wang, 1970.

Battenfeld, Mary. "'Been Shapin Words T Fit M Soul': *Cane*, Language, and Social Change." *Callaloo* 25:4 (Autumn 2002). 1238–1249.

Bauerlein, Mark. *Whitman and the American Idiom*. Baton Rouge: Louisiana State University Press, 1991.

Baurle, Ruth H., ed. *The James Joyce Songbook*. New York: Garland, 1982.

——. *Picking Up Airs: Hearing the Music in Joyce's Text*. Urbana: University of Illinois Press, 1993.

Bawer, Bruce. "'I Could Still Hear the Music': Jay Gatsby and the Musical Metaphor." *Notes on Modern American Literature* 5:4 (1981). 6–10.

Beach, Christopher. *The Politics of Distinction: Whitman and the Discourses of Nineteenth-Century America*. Athens: University of Georgia Press, 1996.

Beach, Joseph Warren. "*Manhattan Transfer*: Collectivism and Abstract Composition." *Dos Passos, the Critics, and the Writer's Intention*. Ed. Allen Belkind. Carbondale: Southern Illinois University Press, 1971. 54–69.

Beard, George M. *American Nervousness: Its Causes and Consequences; A Supplement to Nervous Exhaustion (Neurasthenia)*. New York: G.P. Putnam's Sons, 1881.

Beatty, Paul. *Slumberland*. New York: Bloomsbury, 2008.

Beavers, Herman. "Dead Rocks and Sleeping Men: Aurality in the Aesthetic of Langston Hughes." *Langston Hughes Review* 11:1 (1992). 1–5.

Bedient, Calvin. *He Do the Police in Different Voices: The Waste Land and Its Protagonist.* Chicago: University of Chicago Press, 1986.

Bell, Clive. *Since Cézanne.* New York: Harcourt, Brace, 1922.

Bell, Kevin. *Ashes Taken for Fire: Aesthetic Modernism and the Critique of Identity.* Minneapolis: University of Minnesota Press, 2007.

Bellamy, Edward. *Looking Backward, 2000–1887.* 1888. Rpt. New York: Signet, 2000.

Bellini, Vincenzo. *Norma.* 1831. Achivio R.A.I., 1983.

Bendix, Regina. *In Search of Authenticity: The Formation of Folklore Studies.* Madison: University of Wisconsin Press, 1997.

Benjamin, Walter. *The Work of Art in the Age of Its Technological Reproducibility, and Other Writings on Media.* Ed. Michael W. Jennings, Brigid Doherty, and Thomas Y. Levin. Trans. Edmund Jephcott, Rodney Livingstone, Howard Eiland, and Others. Cambridge: Harvard University Press, 2008.

Bentley, Nancy. *Frantic Panoramas: American Literature and Mass Culture, 1870–1920.* Philadelphia: University of Pennsylvania Press, 2009.

Berley, Marc. *After the Heavenly Tune: English Poetry and the Aspiration to Song.* Pittsburgh: Duquesne University Press, 2000.

Berlin, Irving and Snyder, Ted. "That Mysterious Rag." New York: Ted Snyder Co. 1911.

Berman, Ronald. *The Great Gatsby and Modern Times.* Urbana: University of Illinois Press, 1994.

Bernstein, Charles, ed. *Close Listening: Poetry and the Performed Word.* Oxford: Oxford University Press, 1988.

Bernstein, Leonard. *The Unanswered Question: Six Talks at Harvard.* Cambridge: Harvard University Press, 1976.

Bertolini, Vincent J. "'Hinting' and 'Reminding': The Rhetoric of Performative Embodiment in *Leaves of Grass." English Literary History* 69 (2002). 1047–1082.

Blake, David Haven. *Walt Whitman and the Culture of American Celebrity.* New Haven: Yale University Press, 2006.

Blanning, Tim. *The Triumph of Music: The Rise of Composers, Musicians, and Their Art.* Cambridge: Harvard University Press, 2008.

Blissett, William. "Wagner in *The Waste Land." The Practical Vision: Essays in English Literature in Honour of Flora Ray.* Ed. James Campbell and James Doyle. Waterloo: Wilfred Laurier University Press, 1978. 71–85.

Block, Geoffrey. *Enchanted Evenings: The Broadway Musical from Show Boat to Sondheim.* Oxford: Oxford University Press, 1997.

Bluestein, Gene. "The Blues as a Literary Type." *Massachusetts Review* 8:4 (1967). 593–617.

———. *Poplore.* Amherst: University of Massachusetts Press, 1994.

Bochner, Jay and Edwards, Justin D, eds. *American Modernism across the Arts.* New York: Peter Lang, 1999.

Bolden, Tony. *Afro-Blue: Improvisations in African American Poetry and Culture.* Urbana: University of Illinois Press, 2004.

Bolgan, Anne C. *What the Thunder Really Said: A Retrospective Essay on the Making of* The Waste Land. Montreal: McGill-Queen's University Press, 1973.

Bolton, Guy. *Sally of the Alley.* 1920. Available as part of the Florenz Ziegfeld-Billie Burke Papers in the Billy Rose Theater Collection, New York Public Library.

Bonds, Mark Evan. *Music as Thought: Listening to the Symphony in the Age of Beethoven.* Princeton: Princeton University Press, 2006.

Bone, Robert. *Down Home: A History of Afro-American Short Fiction from Its Beginnings to the End of the Harlem Renaissance.* New York: G. P. Putnam's Sons, 1975.

Bonner, Patricia E. "Cryin' the Jazzy Blues and Livin' Blue Jazz: Analyzing the Blues and Jazz Poetry of Langston Hughes." *West Georgia College Review* 20 (1990). 15–29.

Booker, Peter. "Modernism Deferred: Langston Hughes, Harlem and Jazz Montage." *Locations of Literary Modernism: Region and Nation in British and American Modernist Poetry.* Ed. Alex Davis and Lee M. Jenkins. Cambridge: Cambridge University Press, 2000. 231–248.

Booth, Mark W. *The Experience of Songs.* New Haven: Yale University Press, 1981.

Bordman, Gerald. *American Musical Comedy: From Adonis to Dreamgirls.* Oxford: Oxford University Press, 1982.

Borshuk, Michael. *Swinging the Vernacular: Jazz and African American Modernist Literature.* New York: Routledge, 2006.

Bosman, Julie. "Bells and Whistles for a Few E-Books." *New York Times,* August 23, 2011. Accessed August 23, 2011. www.nytimes.com/2011/08/24/books/booktrack-introduces-e-books-with-soundtracks.html?ref=arts.

Botshon, Lisa and Goldsmith, Meredith, eds. *Middlebrow Moderns: Popular American Women Writers of the 1920s.* Boston: Northeastern University Press, 2003.

Bowen, Barbara E. "Untroubled Voice: Call and Response in *Cane*." *Black Literature and Literary Theory.* Ed. Henry Louis Gates Jr. New York: Methuen, 1984. 187–203.

Bowen, Zack. *Musical Allusions in the Works of James Joyce: Early Poetry through Ulysses.* Albany: State University of New York Press, 1974.

Bowlby, Rachel. *Just Looking: Consumer Culture in Dreiser, Gissing, and Zola.* New York: Methuen, 1985.

Bowman, Wayne D. *Philosophical Perspectives on Music.* Oxford: Oxford University Press, 1998.

Bradbury, Malcolm and McFarlane, James. *Modernism: A Guide to European Literature, 1890–1930.* 1976. Rpt. London: Penguin Books, 1991.

Brady, Erika. *A Spiral Way: How the Phonograph Changed Ethnography.* Jackson: University of Mississippi Press, 1999.

Brecht, Bertolt. *Brecht on Theatre: The Development of an Aesthetic.* Ed. and trans. John Willett. New York: Hill and Wang, 2001.

Breitwieser, Mitchell. "*The Great Gatsby*: Grief, Jazz and the Eye-Witness." *Arizona Quarterly* 47:3 (1991). 17–70.

——. "Jazz Fractures: F. Scott Fitzgerald and Epochal Representation." *American Literary History* 12:3 (2000). 359–381.

Brevda, William. "How Do I Get to Broadway? Reading Dos Passos's Manhattan Transfer Sign," *Texas Studies in Literature and Language* 38:1 (Spring 1996). 79–114.

Bromell, Nicholas Knowles. *Tomorrow Never Knows: Rock and Psychedelics in the 1960s.* Chicago: University of Chicago Press, 2002.

Brooker, Jewel Spears and Bentley, Joseph. *Reading* The Waste Land: *Modernism and the Limits of Interpretation.* Amherst: University of Massachusetts Press, 1990.

Brooks, Cleanth. *Modern Poetry and the Tradition.* Chapel Hill: University of North Carolina Press, 1939.

Brooks, Daphne. *Bodies in Dissent: Spectacular Performances of Race and Freedom, 1850–1910*. Durham: Duke University Press, 2006.

Brooks, Peter. *The Melodramatic Imagination: Balzac, Henry James, Melodrama, and the Mode of Excess*. 1976. Rpt. New Haven: Yale University Press, 1995.

Brooks, Tim. *Lost Sounds: Blacks and the Birth of the Recording Industry, 1890–1919*. Urbana: University of Illinois Press, 2004.

Brooks, Van Wyck. *America's Coming-of-Age*. 1915. Rpt. New York: Viking, 1930.

Brougher, Kerry et al. *Visual Music: Synaesthesia in Art and Music since 1900*. New York: Thames and Hudson, 2005.

Browder, Laura. *Rousing the Nation: Radical Culture in Depression America*. Amherst: University of Massachusetts Press, 1998.

Brown, Beth. *Applause*. New York: Horace Liveright, 1928.

Brown, Bill. "The Matter of Dreiser's Modernity." *The Cambridge Companion to Theodore Dreiser*. Ed. Leonard Cassuto and Clare Virginia Eby. Cambridge: Cambridge University Press, 2004. 83–99.

Brown, Calvin S. *Music and Literature: A Comparison of the Arts*. Athens: University of Georgia Press, 1948.

———. *Tones into Words: Musical Compositions as Subjects of Poetry*. Athens: University of Georgia Press, 1953.

Brown, Fahamisha Patricia. *Performing the Word: African-American Poetry as Vernacular Culture*. New Brunswick: Rutgers University Press, 1999.

Brown, Sterling A. "The Blues as Folk Poetry." *Folk-Say: A Regional Miscellany*. Ed. B. A. Botkin. Norman: University of Oklahoma Press, 1930. 324–339.

———. *A Son's Return: Selected Essays of Sterling A. Brown*. Ed. Mark. A Sanders. Boston: Northeastern University Press, 1996.

Broyles, Michael. *"Music of the Highest Class": Elitism and Populism in Antebellum Boston*. New Haven: Yale University Press, 1992.

Bruccoli, Matthew J., ed. *New Essays on* The Great Gatsby. Cambridge: Cambridge University Press, 1985.

Bruccoli, Matthew J. *Some Sort of Epic Grandeur: The Life of F. Scott Fitzgerald*. Columbia: University of South Carolina Press, 2002.

Buck, Gene and Ruby, Herman. "That Shakespearian Rag." 1912. Rpt. in T. S. Eliot, *The Waste Land* (New York: Norton, 2001). 51–54.

Bucknell, Brad. *Literary Modernism and Musical Aesthetics: Pater, Pound, Joyce, and Stein*. Cambridge: Cambridge University Press, 2001.

Bull, Michael. *Sounding Out the City: Personal Stereos and the Management of Everyday Life*. New York: Berg, 2000.

Bull, Michael and Les Black, eds. *The Auditory Culture Reader*. Oxford: Berg, 2003.

Bürger, Peter. *Theory of the Avant-Garde*. Trans. Michael Shaw. Minneapolis: University of Minnesota Press, 1984.

Burleigh, H. T. *Album of Negro Spirituals*. New York: F. Colombo, 1917.

Burlin, Natalie Curtis. *Negro Folk-Songs*. New York: G. Schirmer, 1918.

Butler, Christopher. *Early Modernism: Literature, Music, and Painting in Europe, 1900–1916*. Oxford: Clarendon Press, 1994.

Cahill, Marie. "The Dallas Blues." Victor, 1917.

Caldiera, Maria Isabel. "Jean Toomer's *Cane*: The Anxiety of the Modern Artist." *Callaloo* 25 (Autumn 1985). 544–550.

Callahan, John F. *In the African-American Grain: The Pursuit of Voice in Twentieth-Century Black Fiction*. Urbana: University of Illinois Press, 1988.

Cantwell, Robert. *When We Were Good: The Folk Revival*. Cambridge: Harvard University Press, 1996.

Carman, Bryan K. *A Race of Singers: Whitman's Working-Class Hero from Guthrie to Springsteen*. Chapel Hill: University of North Carolina Press, 2000.

Caryll, Ivan and McLellan, C. M. S. "My Beautiful Lady." New York: Chappell, 1910.

———. "My Beautiful Lady." Perf. Elizabeth Spencer. Edison: 1913.

Casey, Janet Galligani. *Dos Passos and the Ideology of the Feminine*. Cambridge: Cambridge University Press, 1998.

Cather, Willa. *The Song of the Lark*. 1915. Rpt. New York: Oxford University Press, 2000.

———. *Willa Cather in Person: Interviews, Speeches, and Letters*. Ed. L. Brent Bohlke. Lincoln: University of Nebraska Press, 1986.

Chanan, Michael. *Repeated Takes: A Short History of Recording and Its Effect on Music*. New York: Verso, 1995.

Chancellor, Paul. "The Music of 'The Waste Land.'" *Comparative Literature Studies* 6:1 (1969). 21–32.

Charters, Samuel B. *The Country Blues*. London: Michael Joseph, 1959.

Chion, Michel. *Audio-Vision: Sound on Screen*. 1990. Trans. Claudia Gorbman. Rpt. New York: Columbia University Press, 1994.

Chinitz, David E. "A Jazz-Banjorine, not a Lute: Eliot and Popular Music before *The Waste Land*." In *T.S. Eliot's Orchestra: Critical Essays on Poetry and Music*. Ed. John Xiros Cooper. New York: Garland, 2000. 3–24.

———. "A Vast Wasteland? Eliot and Popular Culture." *A Companion to T. S. Eliot*. Ed. David E. Chinitz. Oxford: Wiley-Blackwell, 2009. 66–78.

———. "In the Shadows: Popular Song and Eliot's Construction of Emotion." *Modernism/Modernity* 11:3 (2004). 449–467.

———. "Literacy and Authenticity: The Blues Poems of Langston Hughes." *Callaloo* 19.1 (1996). 177–192.

———. "The Problem of Dullness: T. S. Eliot and the 'Lively Arts' in the 1920s." *T. S. Eliot and Our Turning World*. Ed. Jewel Spears Brooker. London: Macmillan, 2001. 127–140.

———. *T. S. Eliot and the Cultural Divide*. Chicago: University of Chicago Press, 2003.

———. "T. S. Eliot's Blue Verses and Their Sources in the Folk Tradition." *Journal of Modern Literature* 23 (1999). 329–333.

Chopin, Kate. *The Awakening*. 1899. Rpt. New York: W.W. Norton, 1976.

Chua, Daniel K. L. *Absolute Music and the Construction of Meaning*. Cambridge: Cambridge University Press, 1999.

Clark, Michael. *Dos Passos's Early Fiction, 1912–1938*. Selingsgrove: Susquehanna University Press, 1987.

Clark, Suzanne. *Sentimental Modernism: Women Writers and the Revolution of the Word*. Bloomington: Indiana University Press, 1991.

Cockrell, Dale. *Demons of Disorder: Early Blackface Minstrels and Their World*. Cambridge: Cambridge University Press, 1997.

Coghill, Sheila and Tammaro, Thom, eds. *Visiting Walt: Poems Inspired by the Life and Work of Walt Whitman*. Iowa City: University of Iowa Press, 2003.

Cohan, George M. "We Do All the Dirty Work." New York: Cohan and Harris, 1911.

Cohn, Lawrence. *Nothing but the Blues: The Music and the Musicians*. New York: Abbeville Press, 1993.

Colley, Iain. *Dos Passos and the Fiction of Despair*. London: Macmillan, 1978.

Conrad, Joseph. *The Nigger of the "Narcissus."* 1897. Rpt. New York: Dover, 1999.

Cooke, Alice L. "Notes on Whitman's Musical Background." *New England Quarterly* 19.2 (June 1946). 224–235.

Cooke, Deryck. *The Language of Music*. Oxford: Oxford University Press, 1959.

Cooper, James Fenimore. *The Last of the Mohicans*. 1826. Rpt. New York: Modern Library, 2001.

Cooper, John Xiros. *Modernism and the Culture of Market Society*. Cambridge: Cambridge University Press, 2004.

——. *T. S. Eliot and the Politics of Voice: The Argument of The Waste Land*. Ann Arbor: UMI Research Press, 1987.

Cooper, John Xiros, ed. *T. S. Eliot's Orchestra: Critical Essays on Poetry and Music*. New York: Garland, 2000.

Correa, Delia da Sousa. *Phrase and Subject: Studies in Literature and Music*. London: LEGENDA, 2006.

Crafts, Susan D., Cavicchi, Daniel, and Keil, Charles, eds. *My Music*. Hanover: University Press of New England, 1993.

Crane, Hart. *Complete Poems and Selected Letters and Prose*. Ed. Brom Weber. New York: Liveright, 1966.

Crawford, Richard. *America's Musical Life: A History*. New York: W.W. Norton, 2001.

Crawford, Robert. *Devolving English Literature*. Oxford: Oxford University Press, 1992.

——. *The Savage and the City in the Work of T. S. Eliot*. Oxford: Clarendon Press, 1987.

Crunden, Robert M. *Body and Soul: The Making of American Modernism*. New York: Basic Books, 2000.

Cruz, Jon. *Culture on the Margins: The Black Spiritual and the Rise of American Cultural Interpretation*. Princeton: Princeton University Press, 1999.

Cuda, Anthony. *The Passions of Modernism: Eliot, Yeats, Woolf, and Mann*. Columbia: University of South Carolina Press, 2010.

Cullen, Countee. *Color*. 1925. Rpt. New York, Arno Press, 1969.

Cunningham, Michael. *Specimen Days*. New York: Picador, 2005.

Curnutt, Kirk. "Fitzgerald's Consumer World." *A Historical Guide to F. Scott Fitzgerald*. Ed. Kirk Curnutt. Oxford: Oxford University Press, 2004. 85–128.

Dahlhaus, Carl. *The Idea of Absolute Music*. 1978. Trans. Roger Lustig. Chicago: University of Chicago Press, 1989.

Daly, Nicholas. *Literature, Technology, and Modernity, 1860–2000* Cambridge, Cambridge University Press, 2004.

Dana, Margaret E. "Orchestrating *The Waste Land*: Wagner, Leitmotiv, and the Play of Passion." In *T. S. Eliot's Orchestra: Critical Essays on Poetry and Music*. Ed. John Xiros Cooper. New York: Garland, 2000. 267–295.

Danius, Sara. *The Senses of Modernism: Technology, Perception, and Aesthetics*. Ithaca: Cornell University Press, 2002.

Davidson, Cathy N. and Davidson, Arnold E. "Carrie's Sisters: The Popular Prototypes for Dreiser's Heroine." *Modern Fiction Studies* 23:3 (Autumn 1977). 395–408.

Davis, Francis. *The History of the Blues*. 1995. Rpt. New York: Da Capo Press, 2003.

Day, Timothy. *A Century of Recorded Music: Listening to Musical History*. New Haven: Yale University Press, 2000.

De Jongh, James. *Vicious Modernism: Black Harlem and the Literary Imagination*. Cambridge: Cambridge University Press, 1990.

DeKoven, Marianne. *Rich and Strange: Gender, History, Modernism*. Princeton: Princeton University Press, 1991.

Den Tandt, Christophe. *The Urban Sublime in American Literary Naturalism*. Urbana: University of Illinois Press, 1998.

Denning, Michael. *The Cultural Front: The Laboring of American Culture in the Twentieth Century*. New York: Verso, 1996.

Dettmar, Kevin J. H., ed. *Rereading the New: A Backward Glance at Modernism*. Ann Arbor: University of Michigan Press, 1992.

Dettmar, Kevin J. H. and Watt, Stephen, eds. *Marketing Modernisms: Self-Promotion, Canonization, Rereading*. Ann Arbor: University of Michigan Press, 1996.

DiBattista, Maria and McDiarmid, Lucy, eds. *High and Low Moderns: Literature and Culture, 1889–1939*. Oxford: Oxford University Press, 1996.

Dinerstein, Joel. *Swinging the Machine: Modernity, Technology, and African American Culture between the World Wars*. Amherst: University of Massachusetts Press, 2003.

Dixon, Robert M.W. and Godrich, John. *Recording the Blues*. London: Studio Vista, 1970.

Dixon, Wheeler Winston. *The Cinematic Vision of F. Scott Fitzgerald*. Ann Arbor: UMI Research Press, 1986.

Dizikes, John. *Opera in America: A Cultural History*. New Haven: Yale University Press, 1993.

Doctorow, E. L. *Ragtime*. 1975. Rpt. New York: Modern Library, 1997.

Dos Passos, John. *The 42nd Parallel*. 1930. Rpt. New York: Modern Library, 1937.

———. *The Best Times: An Informal Memoir*. New York: New American Library, 1966.

———. *The Big Money*. 1936. Rpt. New York: Modern Library, 1937.

———. "Foreword." John Howard Lawson, *Roger Bloomer: A Play in Three Acts*. New York: Thomas Seltzer, 1923.

———. *The Garbage Man: A Parade with Shouting*. New York, London: Harper and Brothers, 1926.

———. *John Dos Passos: The Major Nonfictional Prose*. Ed. Donald Pizer. Detroit: Wayne State University Press, 1988.

———. *Manhattan Transfer*. 1925. Rpt. in *Novels 1920–1925*. New York: Library of America, 2003.

———. *Streets of Night*. 1923. Rpt. Cranbury: Associated University Presses, 1990.

———. *Three Plays*. New York: Harcourt, Brace, 1934.

———. *Three Soldiers*. 1921. Rpt. in *Novels 1920–1925*. New York: Library of America, 2003.

Douglas, Ann. *Terrible Honesty: Mongrel Manhattan in the 1920s*. New York: Farrar, Straus and Giroux, 1995.

Doyle, Roddy. *The Commitments*. 1987. Rpt. New York: Vintage, 1989.

Dreiser, Theodore. *A Hoosier Holiday*. New York: John Lane, 1916.

———. *An American Tragedy*. 1925. Rpt. New York: Dell, 1959.

———. *Art, Music, and Literature, 1897–1902*. Ed. Yoshinobu Hakutani. Urbana: University of Illinois Press, 2001.

———. *Dawn*. New York: Horace Liveright, 1931.

———. "Introduction." *The Songs of Paul Dresser*. New York: Boni and Liveright, 1927. v–x.

———. *Newspaper Days*. Ed. T. D. Nostwich. Philadelphia: University of Pennsylvania Press, 1991.

———. *Sister Carrie*. 1900. Ed. Donald Pizer. New York: Norton, 2006.

———. *Sister Carrie*. 1900. Ed. Neda M. Westlake. Philadelphia: University of Pennsylvania Press, 1981.

———. *Theodore Dreiser's Ev'ry Month*. Ed. Nancy Warner Barrineau. Athens: University of Georgia Press, 1996.

———. *Twelve Men*. 1919. Rpt: New York: Boni and Liveright, 1927.

Du Bois, W. E. B. *Essays and Articles*. New York: Library of America, 1987.

———. *The Souls of Black Folk*. 1903. Rpt. New York: Penguin, 1996.

Dudden, Faye E. *Women in the American Theatre: Actresses and Audiences, 1790–1870*. New Haven: Yale University Press, 1994.

Dunlop, M. H. "Carrie's Library: Reading the Boundaries between Popular and Serious Fiction." In *Theodore Dreiser: Beyond Naturalism*. Ed. Mariam Gogol. New York: New York University Press, 1995. 201–215.

DuPlessis, Rachel Blau. *Genders, Races, and Religious Cultures in Modern American Poetry, 1908–1934*. Cambridge: Cambridge University Press, 2001.

Dyer, Geoff. *But Beautiful: A Book about Jazz*. New York: North Point Press, 1996.

Eagleton, Terry. *Against the Grain: Essays 1975–1985*. London: Verso, 1986.

Early, Gerald. "The Lives of Jazz." *American Literary History* 5:1 (1993). 129–146.

Eckstein, Lars. *Reading Song Lyrics*. New York: Rodopi, 2010.

Edwards, Brent Hayes. *The Practice of Diaspora: Literature, Translation, and the Rise of Black Internationalism*. Cambridge: Harvard University Press, 2003.

Egan, Jennifer. *A Visit from the Goon Squad*. New York: Alfred A. Knopf, 2010.

Eisenberg, Evan. *The Recording Angel: Music, Records and Culture from Aristotle to Zappa*. New Haven: Yale University Press, 2005.

Eisenstein, Sergei. *Film Form: Essays in Film Theory*. Trans. Jay Leyda. New York: Harcourt, Brace and World, 1949.

Eliot, T. S. *The Complete Poems and Plays, 1909–1950*. New York: Harcourt Brace, 1980.

———. *Inventions of the March Hare: Poems 1909–1917*. Ed. Christopher Ricks. New York: Harcourt Brace, 1996.

———. "London Letter." *The Dial* 73: 6 (December 1922). 659–663.

———. "Marianne Moore." *The Dial* 75:6 (December 1923). 594–597.

———. *The Sacred Wood: Essays on Poetry and Criticism*. 1920. Rpt. London: Methuen, 1934.

———. *Selected Prose*. Ed. Frank Kermode. New York: Harcourt Brace Jovanovich, 1975.

———. *The Use of Poetry and the Use of Criticism: Studies in the Relation of Criticism to Poetry in England*. 1933. Rpt. Cambridge: Harvard University Press, 1986.

——. *The Waste Land: A Facsimile and Transcript of the Original Drafts including the Annotations of Ezra Pound*. Ed. Valerie Eliot. New York: Harcourt Brace Jovanovich, 1971.

Elliott, Bridget and Wallace, Jo-Ann. *Women Artists and Writers: Modernist (im)positionings*. London: Routledge, 1994.

Ellis, Steve. "*The Waste Land* and the Reader's Response." In *The Waste Land*. Ed. Tony Davies and Nigel Wood. Buckingham: Open University Press, 1994. 83–104.

Ellison, Ralph. *Invisible Man*. 1952. Rpt. New York: Vintage, 1995.

——. *Shadow and Act*. 1964. Rpt. New York: Vintage, 1995.

Ellmann, Maud. *The Poetics of Impersonality: T. S. Eliot and Ezra Pound*. Cambridge: Harvard University Press, 1987.

Emerson, Ralph Waldo. *The Early Lectures of Ralph Waldo Emerson, 1833–1836*. Ed. Stephen E. Whicher and Robert E. Spiller. Cambridge: Harvard University Press, 1959.

——. *Essays and Lectures*. Ed. Joel Porte. New York: Library of America, 1983.

Epstein, Dena J. *Sinful Tunes and Spirituals: Black Folk Music to the Civil War*. 1977. Rpt. Urbana: University of Illinois Press, 1981.

Erenberg, Lewis A. *Steppin' Out: New York Nightlife and the Transformation of American Culture, 1890–1930*. Westport: Greenwood Press, 1981.

Erlmann, Veit, ed. *Hearing Cultures: Essays on Sound, Listening, and Modernity*. Oxford: Berg, 2004.

Ertan, Deniz. "When Men and Mountains Meet: Ruggles, Whitman, and Their Landscapes." *American Music* (Summer 2009). 227–253.

Evans, David. *Big Road Blues: Tradition and Creativity in the Folk Blues*. Berkeley: University of California Press, 1982.

Evans, Nicholas M. *Writing Jazz: Race, Nationalism, and Modern Culture in the 1920s*. New York: Garland, 2000.

Everett, William A. and Laird, Paul R., eds. *The Cambridge Companion to the Musical*. Cambridge: Cambridge University Press, 2002.

Ewen, David. *The Complete Book of the American Musical Theater*. New York: Holt, Rinehart and Winston, 1958.

Eyman, Scott. *The Speed of Sound: Hollywood and the Talkie Revolution*. New York: Simon and Schuster, 1997.

Fabre, Geneviève. "Dramatic and Musical Structures in 'Harvest Song' and 'Kabnis': Toomer's *Cane* and the Harlem Renaissance." *Jean Toomer and the Harlem Renaissance*. Ed. Geneviève Fabre and Michel Feith. New Brunswick: Rutgers University Press, 2001. 109–127.

Fabre, Geneviève and Feith, Michel, eds. *Jean Toomer and the Harlem Renaissance*. New Brunswick: Rutgers University Press, 2001.

——. *Temples for Tomorrow: Looking Back at the Harlem Renaissance*. Bloomington: Indiana University Press, 2001.

Faner, Robert D. *Walt Whitman and Opera*. 1951. Rpt. Carbondale: Southern Illinois University Press, 1972.

Farebrother, Rachel. "'Adventuring through the Pieces of a Still Unorganized Mosaic': Reading Jean Toomer's Collage Aesthetic in Cane." *Journal of American Studies* 40:3 (2006). 503–521.

Faulk, Barry J. "Modernism and the Popular: Eliot's Music Halls," *Modernism/Modernity* 8:4 (2001). 603–621.

——. *Music Hall and Modernity: The Late-Victorian Discovery of Popular Culture*. Athens: Ohio University Press, 2004.

——. "T. S. Eliot and the Symbolist City." *A Companion to T. S. Eliot*. Ed. David E. Chinitz. Oxford: Wiley-Blackwell, 2009. 27–39.

Favor, J. Martin. *Authentic Blackness: The Folk in the New Negro Renaissance*. Durham: Duke University Press, 1999.

Feinstein, Sascha. *Jazz Poetry: From the 1920s to the Present*. Westport: Greenwood Press, 1997.

Feinstein, Sascha and Komunyakaa, Yusef, eds. *The Jazz Poetry Anthology*. Bloomington: Indiana University Press, 1999.

——. *The Second Set: The Jazz Poetry Anthology*. Bloomington: Indiana University Press, 1996.

Feldman, Jessica R. *Gender on the Divide: The Dandy in Modernist Literature*. Ithaca: Cornell University Press, 1993.

Felski, Rita. *The Gender of Modernity*. Cambridge: Harvard University Press, 1995.

Ferber, Edna. *Show Boat*. Garden City: Doubleday, Page, 1926.

Fiedler, Leslie A. *Love and Death in the American Novel*. New York: Criterion Books, 1960.

Filene, Benjamin. *Romancing the Folk: Public Memory and American Roots Music*. Chapel Hill: University of North Carolina Press, 2000.

Fisher, Philip. *Hard Facts: Setting and Form in the American Novel*. Oxford: Oxford University Press, 1985.

——. *Still the New World: American Literature in a Culture of Creative Destruction*. Cambridge: Harvard University Press, 1999.

Fisher, Rudolph. "The Caucasian Storms Harlem." *American Mercury* 11:44 (August 1927). 393–398.

Fisk Jubilee Singers. *Fisk Jubilee Singers in Chronological Order, Vol. 3*. Document, 1997.

Fitzgerald, F. Scott. *The Apprentice Fiction of F. Scott Fitzgerald, 1909–1917*. Ed. John Kuhel. New Brunswick: Rutgers University Press, 1965.

——. *The Basil and Josephine Stories*. Ed. Jackson R. Bryer and John Kuehl. New York: Charles Scribner's Sons, 1973.

——. *The Beautiful and Damned*. 1922. Ed. James L.W. West III. Cambridge: Cambridge University Press, 2008.

——. *F. Scott Fitzgerald: A Life in Letters*. Ed. Matthew J. Bruccoli. New York: Scribner's, 1994.

——. *F. Scott Fitzgerald in His Own Time: A Miscellany*. Ed. Matthew J. Bruccoli and Jackson R. Bryer. New York: Popular Library, 1971.

——. *F. Scott Fitzgerald on Authorship*. Ed. Matthew J. Bruccoli and Judith S. Baughman. Columbia: University of South Carolina Press, 1996.

——. *F. Scott Fitzgerald's Ledger: A Facsimile*. Washington, DC: NCR/Microcard Editions, 1972.

——. *The Great Gatsby*. 1925. Ed. Matthew J. Bruccoli. Cambridge: Cambridge University Press, 1991.

——. *The Last Tycoon: An Unfinished Novel*. Ed. Edmund Wilson. 1941. Rpt. New York: Scribner's, 1970.

——. *The Letters of F. Scott Fitzgerald*. Ed. Andrew Turnbull. New York: Charles Scribner's Sons, 1963.

——. *The Lost Decade: Short Stories from Esquire, 1936–1941.* Ed. James L. W. West III. Cambridge: Cambridge University Press, 2008.

——. *My Lost City: Personal Essays, 1920–1940.* Ed. James L. W. West III. Cambridge: Cambridge University Press, 2005.

——. *This Side of Paradise.* 1920. Ed. James L.W. West III. Cambridge: Cambridge University Press, 1995.

Fitzgerald, Zelda. *Save Me the Waltz.* 1932. Rpt. Carbondale: Southern Illinois University Press, 1974.

Fleissner, Jennifer L. *Women, Compulsion, Modernity: The Moment of American Naturalism.* Chicago: University of Chicago Press, 2004.

Floyd, Samuel A. Jr., ed. *Black Music in the Harlem Renaissance: A Collection of Essays.* Westport: Greenwood Press, 1990.

Foley, Barbara. "'In the Land of Cotton': Economics and Violence in Jean Toomer's *Cane*." *African American Review* 32: 2 (Summer 1998). 181–198.

——. "Jean Toomer's Sparta." *American Literature* 67: 4 (1995). 747–775.

——. "Jean Toomer's Washington and the Politics of Class: from 'Blue Veins' to Seventh-street Rebels." *Modern Fiction Studies* 42.2 (1996). 289–321.

Folsom, Ed, ed. *Walt Whitman: The Centennial Essays.* Iowa City: University of Iowa Press, 1994.

Forbes, James. *The Chorus Lady.* 1906. Rpt. in *The Famous Mrs. Fair and Other Plays.* New York: George H. Doran, 1920.

Ford, Ford Madox. *Henry James: A Critical Study.* 1913. Rpt. New York: Octagon Books, 1964.

Ford, Karen Jackson. *Split-Gut Song: Jean Toomer and the Poetics of Modernity.* Tuscaloosa: University of Alabama Press, 2005.

——. "These Old Writing Paper Blues: The Blues Stanza and Literary Poetry." *College Literature* 24:3 (October 1997). 84–103.

Frank, Waldo. "Foreword." *Cane.* 1923. Rpt. New York: Norton, 1988. 138–140.

——. *The Re-Discovery of America: An Introduction to a Philosophy of American Life.* New York: Charles Scribner's Sons, 1929.

Fredrickson, George M. *The Black Image in the White Mind: The Debate on Afro-American Character and Destiny, 1817–1914.* New York: Harper and Row, 1971.

Frith, Simon. *Performing Rites: On the Value of Popular Music.* Cambridge: Harvard University Press, 1996.

Furia, Philip. *The Poets of Tin Pan Alley: A History of America's Great Lyricists.* Oxford: Oxford University Press, 1990.

Gardner, Helen. *The Art of T. S. Eliot.* London: Cresset Press, 1949.

Garfield, Deborah M. "Taking a Part: Actor and Audience in Theodore Dreiser's *Sister Carrie*." *American Literary Realism* 16:2 (Autumn 1983). 223–239.

Garofalo, Reebee. *Rockin' Out: Popular Music in the USA.* Boston: Allyn and Bacon, 1997.

Gates, Henry Louis Jr. *Figures in Black: Words, Signs, and the "Racial" Self.* Oxford: Oxford University Press, 1987.

——. *The Signifying Monkey: A Theory of African-American Literary Criticism.* Oxford: Oxford University Press, 1988.

Gates, Henry Louis Jr., and Jarrett, Gene Andrew. "Introduction." *The New Negro: Readings on Race, Representation, and African American Culture, 1892–1938*. Princeton: Princeton University Press, 2007. 1–20.

Gay, Peter. *Modernism: The Lure of Heresy, from Baudelaire to Beckett and Beyond*. New York: Norton, 2008.

Gelfant, Blanche H. "What More Can Carrie Want? Naturalistic Ways of Consuming Women." *The Cambridge Companion to American Realism and Naturalism: Howells to London*. Ed. Donald Pizer. Cambridge: Cambridge University Press, 1995. 178–210.

Gendron, Bernard. *Between Montmartre and the Mudd Club: Popular Music and the Avant-Garde*. Chicago: University of Chicago Press, 2002.

Gilbert, Sandra M. and Gubar, Susan. *No Man's Land: The Place of the Woman Writer in the Twentieth Century*. 3 vols. New Haven: Yale University Press, 1988–1994.

Giles, Paul. "Dreiser's Style." *The Cambridge Companion to Theodore Dreiser*. Ed. Leonard Cassuto and Clare Virginia Eby. Cambridge: Cambridge University Press, 2004. 47–62.

Gilroy, Paul. *The Black Atlantic: Modernity and Double Consciousness*. Cambridge: Harvard University Press, 1993.

Gioia, Ted. *Delta Blues: The Life and Times of the Mississippi Masters Who Revolutionized American Music*. New York: W.W. Norton, 2008.

Gitelman, Lisa. *Always Already New: Media, History, and the Data of Culture*. Cambridge: MIT Press, 2006.

——. *Scripts, Grooves, and Writing Machines: Representing Technology in the Edison Era*. Stanford: Stanford University Press, 1999.

Glenn, Susan A. *Female Spectacle: The Theatrical Roots of Modern Feminism*. Cambridge: Harvard University Press, 2000.

Goldsmith, Oliver. *Poems and Essays*. New York: William A. Barrow, 1824.

Gordon, Lyndall. *T. S. Eliot: An Imperfect Life*. New York: W.W. Norton, 1998.

Gottlieb, Robert and Kimball, Robert. "Introduction." *Reading Lyrics*. New York: Pantheon, 2000. xxiii–xxvi.

Grandel, Hartmut. "The Role of Music in the Self-Reflexive Poetry of the Harlem Renaissance." *Poetics in the Poem: Critical Essays on American Self-Reflexive Poetry*. Ed. Dorothy Z. Baker. New York: Peter Lang, 1997. 119–131.

Grandt, Jürgen E. *Kinds of Blue: The Jazz Aesthetic in African American Narrative*. Columbus: Ohio State University Press, 2004.

Grant, Mark N. *The Rise and Fall of the Broadway Musical*. Boston: Northeastern University Press, 2004.

Grant, Nathan. *Masculinist Impulses: Toomer, Hurtson, Black Writing, and Modernity*. Columbia: University of Missouri Press, 2004.

Greenspan, Ezra. *Walt Whitman and the American Reader*. Cambridge: Cambridge University Press, 1990.

Greenspan, Ezra, ed. *The Cambridge Companion to Walt Whitman*. Cambridge: Cambridge University Press, 1995.

Griffin, Farah Jasmine. *"Who Set You Flowin'?": The African-American Migration Narrative*. Oxford: Oxford University Press, 1995.

Gubar, Susan. *Racechanges: White Skin, Black Face in American Culture*. Oxford: Oxford University Press, 1997.

Gussow, Adam. *Seems Like Murder Here: Southern Violence and the Blues Tradition*. Chicago: University of Chicago Press, 2002.

Guterl, Matthew Pratt. *The Color of Race in America, 1900–1940*. Cambridge: Harvard University Press, 2001.

Hamilton, Marybeth. *In Search of the Blues*. New York: Basic Books, 2008.

Hamm, Charles. *Yesterdays: Popular Song in America*. New York: W. W. Norton, 1979.

Handy, W.C. *Father of the Blues*. 1941. Rpt. New York, Collier, 1970.

Handy, W.C. and Niles, Abbe. *Blues: An Anthology*. New York: Albert and Charles Boni, 1926.

Hansell, William H. "Black Music in the Poetry of Langston Hughes: Roots, Race, Release." *Obsidian* 4:3 (1978). 16–38.

Hansen, Miriam. *Babel and Babylon: Spectatorship in American Silent Film*. Cambridge: Harvard University Press, 1991.

Hanslick, Eduard. *The Beautiful in Music*. 1854. Trans. Gustav Cohen. Ed. Morris Weitz. Rpt. New York: Liberal Arts Press, 1957.

Harding, Desmond. *Writing the City: Urban Visions and Literary Modernism*. New York: Routledge, 2003.

Harmon, Charles. "*Cane*, Race, and 'Neither/Norism.'" *Southern Literary Journal* 32:2 (2000). 90–101.

——. "Cuteness and Capitalism in *Sister Carrie*." *American Literary Realism* 32:2 (Winter 2000). 125–139.

Harris, Benard. "'This music crept by me': Shakespeare and Wagner." In *The Waste Land in Different Voices*. Ed. A. D. Moody. London: Edward Arnold. 105–116.

Harris, Charles K. *After the Ball: Forty Years of Melody, an Autobiography*. New York: Frank-Maurice, 1926.

Harris, Marion. "St. Louis Blues." Columbia, 1920.

Hartman, Charles O. *Jazz Text: Voice and Improvisation in Poetry, Jazz, and Song*. Princeton: Princeton University Press, 1991.

Hasse, John Edward. *Beyond Category: The Life and Genius of Duke Ellington*. New York: Da Capo Press, 1993.

Havelock, Eric A. *The Muse Learns to Write: Reflections on Orality and Literacy from Antiquity to the Present*. New Haven: Yale University Press, 1986.

Hebdige, Dick. *Subculture: The Meaning of Style*. 1979. Rpt. London: Routledge, 1991.

Hegeman, Susan. *Patterns for America: Modernism and the Concept of Culture*. Princeton: Princeton University Press, 1999.

Heller, Adele and Rudnick, Lois, eds. *1915, The Cultural Moment: The New Politics, the New Woman, the New Psychology, the New Art and the New Theatre in America*. New Brunswick: Rutgers University Press, 1991.

Helmholtz, Hermann L. F. *On the Sensations of Tone as a Physiological Basis for the Theory of Music*. 1885. Trans. Alexander J. Ellis. Rpt. New York: Dover, 1954.

Hemenway, Robert E. *Zora Neale Hurston: A Literary Biography*. Champaign: University of Illinois Press, 1980.

Henderson, Stephen. *Understanding the New Black Poetry: Black Speech and Black Music as Poetic References*. New York: William Morrow, 1973.

Herbert, Victor and Blossom, Henry. "If I Were on the Stage." New York: M. Witmark and Sons, 1905.

———. "Kiss Me Again." New York: M. Witmark and Sons, 1915.

———. "Kiss Me Again." Perf. Marie Tiffany. Edison, 1919.

Hershey, Burnet. "Jazz Latitude." *New York Times*, June 25, 1922, p. SM5.

Hertz, David Michael. *The Tuning of the Word: The Musico-Literary Poetics of the Symbolist Movement*. Carbondale: Southern Illinois University Press, 1987.

Hill, Errol G. and Hatch, James V. *A History of African American Theatre*. Cambridge: Cambridge University Press, 2003.

Hobsbaum, Philip. "Eliot, Whitman and American Tradition." *Journal of American Studies* 3:2 (December 1969). 239–264.

Hochman, Barbara. "A Portrait of the Artist as a Young Actress: The Rewards of Representation in *Sister Carrie*." *New Essays on Sister Carrie*. Cambridge: Cambridge University Press, 1991. 43–64.

Hoffman, Frederick J. *The Twenties: American Writing in the Postwar Decade*. New York: Collier, 1962.

Hollander, John. *Images of Voice: Music and Sound in Romantic Poetry*. Cambridge: Heffer, 1970.

———. *Poetry and Music*. London: Routledge, 2007.

———. *The Untuning of the Sky: Ideas of Music in English Poetry, 1500–1700*. Princeton: Princeton University Press, 1961.

Hollis, C. Carroll. *Language and Style in Leaves of Grass*. Baton Rouge: Louisiana State University Press, 1983.

Holton, Sylvia Wallace. *Down Home and Uptown: The Representation of Black Speech in American Fiction*. Cranbury: Associated University Presses, 1984.

Hopwood, Avery. *The Gold Diggers*. Photocopy of unpublished manuscript.

Hornby, Nick. *Juliet, Naked*. New York: Riverhead, 2009.

Horowitz, Joseph. *Classical Music in America: A History of Its Rise and Fall*. New York: W.W. Norton, 2005.

"How Popular Song Factories Manufacture a Hit." *New York Times*, September 18, 1910, p. SM11.

Howard, June. *Form and History in American Literary Naturalism*. Chapel Hill: University of North Carolina Press, 1985.

Howarth, Herbert. *Notes on Some Figures behind T. S. Eliot*. Boston: Houghton Mifflin, 1964.

Howes, David, ed. *Empire of the Senses: The Sensual Culture Reader*. Oxford: Berg, 2005.

Hubbell, Raymond and Golden, John L. "Poor Butterfly." New York: T. B. Harms and Francis, Day and Hunter, 1916.

———. "Poor Butterfly." Perf. Elizabeth Spencer. Edison, 1917.

Huggins, Nathan Irvin. *Harlem Renaissance*. 1971. Rpt. Oxford: Oxford University Press, 2007.

Hughes, Langston. *The Collected Poems of Langston Hughes*. Ed. Arnold Rampersad and David Roessel. New York: Vintage, 1995.

———. *The Collected Works of Langston Hughes*, Volume 1: *The Poems, 1921–1940*. Ed. Arnold Rampersad. Columbia: University of Missouri Press, 2001.

——. *The Collected Works of Langston Hughes,* Volume 9: *Essays on Art, Race, Politics, and World Affairs.* Ed. Christopher C. De Santis. Columbia: University of Missouri Press, 2002.

——. *The Collected Works of Langston Hughes,* Volume 13: *Autobiography: The Big Sea.* Ed. Joseph McLaren. Columbia: University of Missouri Press, 2002.

Hughes, Langston and Hurston, Zora Neale. *Mule Bone: A Comedy of Negro Life.* 1931. Ed. George Houston Bass and Henry Louis Gates Jr. New York: Harper Perennial, 1991.

Hurston, Zora Neale. *Folklore, Memoirs, and Other Writings.* Ed. Cheryl A. Wall. New York: Library of America, 1995.

Hutchinson, George. "*Cane* and the New Negroes of Washington." *American Literature* 63:4 (1991). 683–692.

——. *The Harlem Renaissance in Black and White.* Cambridge: Harvard University Press, 1995.

——. "Jean Toomer and American Racial Discourse." *Texas Studies in Literature and Language* 35 (Summer 1993). 226–250.

Hutchinson, George, ed. *The Cambridge Companion to the Harlem Renaissance.* Cambridge: Cambridge University Press, 2007.

Huyssen, Andreas. *After the Great Divide: Modernism, Mass Culture, Postmodernism.* Bloomington: Indiana University Press, 1986.

Hyman, Alan. *The Gaiety Years.* London: Cassell, 1975.

Ikonné, Chidi. *From Du Bois to Van Vechten: The Early New Negro Literature, 1903–1926.* Westport: Greenwood Press, 1981.

"Inherent Vice." Accessed September 11, 2011. www.amazon.com/Inherent-Vice-Novel-Thomas-Pynchon/dp/0143117564/ref=sr_1_1?s=books&ie=UTF8&qid=1315760137&sr=1-1.

Irwin, John T. *American Hieroglyphics: The Symbol of the Egyptian Hieroglyphics in the American Renaissance.* New Haven: Yale University Press, 1980.

Ives, Charles. *Essays before a Sonata and Other Writings.* Ed. Howard Boatwright. New York: W.W. Norton, 1961.

Jackson, Papa Charlie. *Complete Recorded Works, Vol. 1.* Document Records, 1991.

Jaidka, Manju. *T. S. Eliot's Use of Popular Sources.* Lewiston: Edwin Mellen Press, 1997.

James, Henry. *The Tragic Muse.* 1890. Rpt. New York: Penguin, 1995.

James, Jamie. *The Music of the Spheres: Music, Science, and the Natural Order of the Universe.* New York: Grove Press, 1993.

James, Pearl. "History and Masculinity in F. Scott Fitzgerald's *This Side of Paradise.*" *Modern Fiction Studies* 51:1 (2005). 1–33.

Jay, Gregory S. *T. S. Eliot and the Poetics of Literary History.* Baton Rouge: Louisiana State University Press, 1983.

Jefferson, Blind Lemon. *Blind Lemon Jefferson.* Milestone Records, 1992.

Jemie, Onwuchekwa. *Langston Hughes: An Introduction to the Poetry.* New York: Columbia University Press, 1976.

Jerving, Ryan. "Early Jazz Literature (And Why You Didn't Know)." *American Literary History* 16:4 (2004). 648–674.

——. "Jazz Language and Ethnic Novelty." *Modernism/modernity* 10:2 (2003). 239–268.

Johnson, James Weldon. *Black Manhattan.* 1930. Rpt. New York: Arno Press, 1968.

——. *Writings*. Ed. William L. Andrews. New York: Library of America, 2004.

Johnson, James Weldon and Johnson, J. Rosamond. *The Book of American Negro Spirituals*. 1925. Rpt. New York: Viking, 1964.

Johnson, James William. "Lyric." *The New Princeton Encyclopedia of Poetry and Poetics*. Ed. Alex Preminger and T. V. F. Brogan. Princeton: Princeton University Press, 1993.

Johnson, Patricia A. and Farrell, Walter C. Jr. "How Langston Hughes Used the Blues." *MELUS* 6:1 (Spring 1979). 55–63.

Jones, Gavin. *Strange Talk: The Politics of Dialect Literature in Gilded Age America*. Berkeley: University of California Press, 1999.

Jones, Gayl. *Liberating Voices: Oral Tradition in African American Literature*. Cambridge: Harvard University Press, 1991.

Jones, LeRoi. *Blues People: Negro Music in White America*. New York: Morrow Quill, 1963.

Jones, Meta DuEwa. "Listening to What the Ear Demands: Langston Hughes and His Critics." *Callaloo* 25: 4 (Autumn 2002). 1145–1175.

——. *The Muse Is Music: Jazz Poetry from the Harlem Renaissance to Spoken Word*. Urbana: University of Illinois Press, 2011.

Jourdain, Robert. *Music, the Brain, and Ecstasy: How Music Captures Our Imagination*. New York: Quill, 1997.

Kadlec, David. *Mosaic Modernism: Anarchism, Pragmatism, Culture*. Baltimore: Johns Hopkins University Press, 2000.

Kahn, Douglas. *Noise Water Meat: A History of Sound in the Arts*. Cambridge: MIT Press, 1999.

Kahn, Douglas and Gregory Whitehead, eds. *Wireless Imagination: Sound, Radio, and the Avant-Garde*. Cambridge: MIT Press, 1992.

Kalaidjian, Walter. *American Culture between the Wars: Revisionary Modernism and Postmodern Critique*. New York: Columbia University Press, 1993.

Kalaidjian, Walter, ed. *The Cambridge Companion to American Modernism*. Cambridge: Cambridge University Press, 2005.

Kammen, Michael. *American Culture, American Tastes: Social Change and the 20th Century*. New York: Alfred A. Knopf, 2000.

——. *The Lively Arts: Gilbert Seldes and the Transformation of Cultural Criticism in the United States*. Oxford: Oxford University Press, 1996.

Kaplan, Amy. *The Social Construction of American Realism*. Chicago: University of Chicago Press, 1988.

Katz, Mark. *Capturing Sound: How Technology Has Changed Music*. Berkeley: University of California Press, 2004.

Keats, John. *The Major Works*. Oxford: Oxford World's Classics, 2008.

Kehl, D.G. "Thalia Does the Charleston: Humor in the Fiction of F. Scott Fitzgerald." *F. Scott Fitzgerald in the Twenty-First Century*. Ed. Jackson R. Breyer, Ruth Prigozy, and Milton R. Stern. Tuscaloosa: University of Alabama Press, 2003. 202–222.

Kenner, Hugh. *A Homemade World: The American Modernist Writers*. Baltimore: Johns Hopkins University Press, 1989.

——. *The Mechanic Muse*. Oxford: Oxford University Press, 1987.

——. *The Pound Era*. Berkeley: University of California Press, 1971.

Kenney, William Howland. *Recorded Music in American Life: The Phonograph and Popular Memory, 1890–1945*. Oxford: Oxford University Press, 1999.

Kerkering, Jack. "'Of Me and Mine': The Music of Racial Identity in Whitman and Lanier, Dvorak and Du Bois." *American Literature* 73:1 (March 2001). 147–184.

Kerman, Cynthia Earl and Eldridge, Richard. *The Lives of Jean Toomer: A Hunger for Wholeness.* Baton Rouge: Louisiana State University Press, 1987.

Kern, Jerome and Green, Schuyler. "Babes in the Wood." New York: T. B. Harms and Francis, Day and Hunter, 1915.

———. "Babes in the Woods." Perf. Harry MacDonough and Lucy Isabelle Marsh. Victor, 1917.

Killingsworth, M. Jimmie. "Whitman's Physical Eloquence." *Walt Whitman: The Centennial Essays.* Ed. Ed Folsom. Iowa City: University of Iowa Press, 1994. 68–78

Kirk, Elise K. *American Opera.* Urbana: University of Illinois Press, 2001.

Kittler, Friedrich A. *Discourse Networks, 1800/1900.* 1985. Trans. Michael Metteer and Chris Cullens. Rpt. Stanford: Stanford University Press, 1990.

———. *Gramophone, Film, Typewriter.* 1986. Trans. Geoffrey Winthrop-Young and Michael Wutz. Stanford: Stanford University Press, 1999.

Kivy, Peter. *Antithetical Arts: On the Ancient Quarrel between Literature and Music.* Oxford: Clarendon Press, 2009.

———. *The Fine Art of Repetition: Essays in the Philosophy of Music.* Cambridge: Cambridge University Press, 1993.

———. *New Essays on Musical Understanding.* Oxford: Clarendon Press, 2001.

———. *Osmin's Rage: Philosophical Reflections on Opera, Drama, and Text.* Princeton: Princeton University Press, 1988.

———. *Philosophies of Arts: An Essay in Differences.* Cambridge: Cambridge University Press, 1997.

———. *Sound and Semblance: Reflections on Musical Representation.* Princeton: Princeton University Press, 1984.

———. *Sound Sentiment: An Essay on the Musical Emotions.* Philadelphia: Temple University Press, 1989.

Knapp, Raymond. *The American Musical and the Formation of National Identity.* Princeton: Princeton University Press, 2005.

———. *The American Musical and the Performance of Personal Identity.* Princeton: Princeton University Press, 2006.

Knowles, Sebastian D. G. "Death by Gramophone." *Journal of Modern Literature* 27:1 (2003). 1–14.

———. "'Then You Wink the Other Eye': T. S. Eliot and the Music Hall." *American Notes and Queries* 11:4 (Fall 1998). 20–32.

Knox, George A. and Stahl, Herbert M. *Dos Passos and "The Revolting Playwrights."* Upsala: Lund, 1964.

Kodat, Catherine Gunther. "To 'Flash White Light from Ebony': The Problem of Modernism in Jean Toomer's *Cane*." *Twentieth Century Literature.* 46:1 (2000). 1–19.

Koritz, Amy. *Gendering Bodies/Performing Art: Dance and Literature in Early Twentieth-Century British Culture.* Ann Arbor: University of Michigan Press, 1995.

Kracauer, Siegfried. *The Mass Ornament: Weimar Essays.* Trans. and ed. Thomas Y. Levin. Cambridge: Harvard University Press, 1995.

Kramer, Lawrence. *After the Lovedeath: Sexual Violence and the Making of Culture.* Berkeley: University of California Press, 1997.

———. *Music and Poetry: The Nineteenth Century and After*. Berkeley: University of California Press, 1984.

Kramer, Lawrence, ed. *Walt Whitman and Modern Music: War, Desire, and the Trials of Nationhood*. New York: Garland, 2000.

Kramer, Victor A. and Russ, Robert A., eds. *Harlem Renaissance Re-Examined: A Revised and Expanded Edition*. Troy: Whitson, 1997.

Krasner, David. *A Beautiful Pageant: African American Theatre, Drama, and Performance in the Harlem Renaissance, 1910–1927*. New York: Palgrave Macmillan, 2002.

———. *Resistance, Parody, and Double Consciousness in African American Theatre, 1895–1910*. New York: St. Martin's Press, 1997.

Krause, Sydney J. "Whitman, Music, and Proud Music of the Storm." *Publications of the Modern Language Association (PMLA)* 72:4 (September 1957). 705–721.

Krehbiel, Henry Edward. *Afro-American Folksongs: A Study in Racial and National Music*. 1913. Rpt. New York: Frederick Ungar, 1962.

Lambert, Constant. *Music Ho! A Study of Music in Decline*. 1934. Rpt. London: Hogarth, 1985.

Lange, Art and Mackey, Nathaniel, eds. *Moment's Notice: Jazz in Poetry and Prose*. Minneapolis: Coffee House Press, 1993.

Lanier, Sidney. *The Centennial Edition of the Works of Sidney Lanier*, Volume II: *The Science of English Verse and Essays on Music*. Ed. Paull Franklin Baum. Baltimore: Johns Hopkins University Press, 1945.

Lanza, Joseph. *Elevator Music: A Surreal History of Muzak, Easy-Listening, and Other Mood-song*. New York: St. Martin's Press, 1994.

Lastra, James. *Sound Technology and the America Cinema: Perception, Representation, Modernity*. New York: Columbia University Press, 2000.

Latham, Angela J. *Posing a Threat: Flappers, Chorus Girls, and Other Brazen Performers of the American 1920s*. Hanover: Wesleyan University Press, 2000.

Lawrence, D. H. *Phoenix: The Posthumous Papers of D. H. Lawrence*. Ed. Edward D. McDonald. New York: Viking, 1936.

Lazar, Zachary. *Sway*. New York: Little, Brown, 2008.

Leavis, F.R. *New Bearings in English Poetry: A Study of the Contemporary Situation*. 1932. Rpt. London: Chatto and Windus, 1938.

Leggio, James, ed. *Music and Modern Art*. New York: Routledge, 2002.

Lehan, Richard. *Theodore Dreiser: His World and His Novels*. Carbondale: Southern Illinois University Press, 1969.

Lemke, Sieglinde. *Primitivist Modernism: Black Culture and the Origins of Transatlantic Modernism*. Oxford: Oxford Universy Press, 1998.

Lenhart, Charmenz S. *Musical Influence on American Poetry*. Athens: University of Georgia Press, 1956.

Leppert, Richard. *The Sight of Sound: Music, Representation, and the History of the Body*. Berkeley: University of California Press, 1993.

Levenson, Michael. *A Genealogy of Modernism: A Study of English Literary Doctrine, 1908–1922*. Cambridge: Cambridge University Press, 1984.

Levine, Lawrence W. *Black Culture and Black Consciousness: Afro-American Folk Thought from Slavery to Freedom*. Oxford: Oxford University Press, 1977.

———. *Highbrow/Lowbrow: The Emergence of Cultural Hierarchy in America*. Cambridge: Harvard University Press, 1990.

Levith, Murray J., ed. *Musical Masterpieces in Prose*. Neptune: Paganiniana, 1981.

Levitin, Daniel J. *This Is Your Brain on Music: The Science of a Human Obsession*. New York: Dutton, 2006.

Lewis, David Levering. *When Harlem Was in Vogue*. 1979. Rpt. New York: Vintage, 1982.

Lewis, Pericles. *The Cambridge Introduction to Modernism*. Cambridge: Cambridge University Press, 2007.

Lewis, Sinclair. *Main Street*. 1920. Rpt. New York: Library of America, 1992.

Leypoldt, Günter. "Democracy's 'Lawless Music': The Whitmanian Moment in the U.S. Construction of Representative Literariness." *New Literary History* 38 (2007). 333–352.

Lhamon, W.T. Jr. *Raising Cain: Blackface Performance from Jim Crow to Hip Hop*. Cambridge: Harvard University Press, 1998.

Linett, Maren Tova, ed. *The Cambridge Companion to Modernist Women Writers*. Cambridge: Cambridge University Press, 2010.

Livingston, James. *Pragmatism and the Political Economy of Cultural Revolution, 1850–1940*. Chapel Hill: University of North Carolina Press, 1994.

Lock, Graham and Murray, David. *Thriving on a Riff: Jazz and Blues Influences*. Oxford: Oxford University Press, 2009.

Locke, Alain, ed. *The New Negro*. 1925. Rpt. New York: Simon and Schuster, 1992.

Lomax, Alan. *The Land Where the Blues Began*. New York: New Press, 1993.

——. *Mister Jelly Roll: The Fortunes of Jelly Roll Morton, New Orleans Creole and "Inventor of Jazz."* 1950. Rpt. Berkeley: University of California Press, 1973.

——. *Selected Writings, 1934–1997*. Ed. Ronald D. Cohen. New York: Routledge, 2003.

Longenbach, James. *Modernist Poetics of History: Pound, Eliot, and the Sense of the Past*. Princeton: Princeton University Press, 1987.

Longhurst, Brian. *Popular Music and Society*. Cambridge: Polity, 1995.

Lott, Eric. *Love and Theft: Blackface Minstrelsy and the American Working Class*. Oxford: Oxford University Press, 1993.

Lovell, John Jr. *Black Song: The Forge and the Flame: The Story of How the Afro-American Spiritual Was Hammered Out*. New York: Paragon House, 1972.

Lowry, E. D. "The Lively Art of *Manhattan Transfer*." *PMLA* 84:6 (October 1969). 1628–1638.

——. "*Manhattan Transfer*: Dos Passos' Wasteland." *Dos Passos: A Collection of Critical Essays*. Ed. Andrew Hook. Englewood Cliffs: Prentice-Hall, 1974. 53–60.

Mackenzie, Compton. *My Record of Music*. London: Hutchinson, 1955.

Mackey, Nathaniel. "Sound and Sentiment, Sound and Symbol." *Callaloo* 30 (Winter 1987). 29–54.

Malek, James S. *The Arts Compared: An Aspect of Eighteenth-Century British Aesthetics*. Detroit: Wayne State University Press, 1974.

Manganaro, Marc. *Myth, Rhetoric, and the Voice of Authority: A Critique of Frazer, Eliot, Frye, and Campbell*. New Haven: Yale University Press, 1992.

Mansell, Darrel. "*The Jazz History of the World* in *The Great Gatsby*." *English Language Notes* 25:2 (1987). 57–62.

Mao, Douglas and Walkowitz, Rebecca L., eds. *Bad Modernisms*. Durham: Duke University Press, 2006.

Marcus, Greil. *Mystery Train: Images of America in Rock 'n' Roll Music*. 1975. Rpt. New York: Plume, 1990.

Maretzek, Max. *Crotchets and Quavers, or, Revelations of an Opera Manager in America.* 1855. Rpt. New York: Da Capo Press, 1966.

Marinetti, F. T. "Destruction of Syntax—Radio Imagination—Words-in-Freedom." *Futurism: An Anthology.* Ed. Lawrence Rainey, Christine Poggi, and Laura Wittman. New Haven: Yale University Press, 2009. 143–151.

Matthews, Artie. *Weary Blues.* St. Louis: Stark Music, 1915.

Matthiessen, F. O. *The Achievement of T. S. Eliot.* New York: Houghton Mifflin, 1935.

——. *American Renaissance: Art and Expression in the Age of Emerson and Whitman.* 1941. Rpt. Oxford: Oxford University Press, 1968.

Mayer, David and Day-Mayer, Helen. "A 'Secondary Action' or Musical Highlight? Melodic Interludes in Early Film Melodrama Reconsidered." *The Sounds of Early Cinema.* Ed. Richard Abel and Rick Altman. Bloomington: Indiana University Press, 2001. 220–231.

Mayer, John T. *T. S. Eliot's Silent Voices.* Oxford: Oxford University Press, 1989.

McCall, Dan. "'The Self-Same Song that Found a Path': Keats and *The Great Gatsby*." *American Literature* 42:4 (January 1971), 521–530.

McCann, Paul. *Race, Music, and National Identity: Images of Jazz in American Fiction, 1920–1960.* Madison: Farleigh Dickinson University Press, 2008.

McGurl, Mark. *The Novel Art: Elevations of American Fiction after Henry James.* Princeton: Princeton University Press, 2001.

McKay, Claude. *Banjo: A Story without a Plot.* New York: Harper and Brothers, 1929.

McKeever, B. F. "*Cane* as Blues." *Negro American Literature Forum* 4 (July 1970). 61–64.

McLuhan, Marshall. *The Gutenberg Galaxy: The Making of Typographic Man.* Toronto: University of Toronto Press, 1962.

——. "Pound, Eliot, and the Rhetoric of *The Waste Land*." *New Literary History* 10:3 (Spring 1979). 557–580.

——. *Understanding Media: The Extensions of Man.* New York: McGraw-Hill, 1964.

McNamara, Kevin R. *Urban Verbs: Arts and Discourses of American Cities.* Stanford: Stanford University Press, 1996.

Melville, Herman. *Pierre; or, The Ambiguities.* 1852. Rpt. New York: Library of America, 1984.

Menand, Louis. *Discovering Modernism: T. S. Eliot and His Context.* Oxford: Oxford University Press, 1987.

Meyer-Baer, Kathi. *The Music of the Spheres and the Dance of Death: Studies in Musical Iconology.* Princeton: Princeton University Press, 1970.

Michaels, Walter Benn. *The Gold Standard and the Logic of Naturalism: American Literature at the Turn of the Century.* Berkeley: University of California Press, 1987.

——. *Our America: Nativism, Modernism, and Pluralism.* Durham: Duke University Press, 1995.

Michlin, Monica. "Langston Hughes's Blues." *Temples for Tomorrow: Looking Back at the Harlem Renaissance.* Ed. Geneviève Fabre and Michel Feith. Bloomington: Indiana University Press, 2001. 236–253.

Middleton, Richard, *Studying Popular Music.* Philadelphia: Open University Press, 1990.

——. *Voicing the Popular: On the Subjects of Popular Music.* New York: Routledge, 2006.

Millard, Andre. *America on Record: A History of Recorded Sound*. Cambridge: Cambridge University Press, 2005.

Miller, Dayton Clarence. *The Science of Musical Sounds*. New York: Macmillan, 1916.

Miller, James E. Jr. *The American Quest for a Supreme Fiction: Whitman's Legacy in the Personal Epic*. Chicago: University of Chicago Press, 1979.

———. *T. S. Eliot's Personal Waste Land: Exorcism of the Demons*. University Park: Pennsylvania State University Press, 1977.

Miller, Karl Hagstrom. *Segregating Sound: Inventing Folk and Pop Music in the Age of Jim Crow*. Durham: Duke University Press, 2010.

Milner, Greg. *Perfecting Sound Forever: An Aural History of Recorded Music*. New York: Faber and Faber, 2009.

Minnick, Lisa Cohen. *Dialect and Dichotomy: Literary Representations of African American Speech*. Tuscaloosa: University of Alabama Press, 2004.

Minter, David. *A Cultural History of the American Novel: Henry James to William Faulkner*. Cambridge: Cambridge University Press, 1994.

Mizejewski, Linda. *Ziegfeld Girl: Image and Icon in Culture and Cinema*. Durham: Duke University Press, 1999.

Moers, Ellen. *Two Dreisers*. New York: Viking, 1969.

Moody, A. D. *Thomas Stearns Eliot: Poet*. Cambridge: Cambridge University Press, 1979.

Moon, Michael. *Disseminating Whitman: Revision and Corporeality in* Leaves of Grass. Cambridge: Harvard University Press, 1991.

Mordden, Ethan. *Make Believe: The Broadway Musical in the 1920s*. Oxford: Oxford University Press, 1997.

Morgan, Anna. *An Hour with Delsarte: A Study of Expression*. 1889. Rpt. Boston: Lee and Shepard, 1895.

Morris, Adalaide, ed. *Sound States: Innovative Poetics and Acoustical Technologies*. Chapel Hill: University of North Carolina Press, 1997.

Morris, Timothy. *Becoming Canonical in American Poetry*. Urbana: University of Illinois Press, 1995.

Morrisson, Mark S. *The Public Face of Modernism: Little Magazines, Audiences, and Reception, 1905–1920*. Madison: University of Wisconsin Press, 2001.

Morton, Jelly Roll. *New Orleans Rhythm Kings and Jelly Roll Morton*. Milestone Records, 1992.

Moten, Fred. *In the Break: The Aesthetics of the Black Radical Tradition*. Minneapolis: University of Minnesota Press, 2003.

Murphet, Julian. *Multimedia Modernism: Literature and the Anglo-American Avant-Garde*. Cambridge: Cambridge University Press, 2009.

Murray, Albert. *Stomping the Blues*. New York: McGraw-Hill, 1976.

Musgrove, S. *T. S. Eliot and Walt Whitman*. Wellington: New Zealand University Press, 1952.

Nanney, Lisa. *John Dos Passos*. New York: Twayne, 1998.

Nathan, George Jean. *Another Book on the Theatre*. New York: B. W. Heuebsch, 1915.

———. *The Entertainment of a Nation, or, Three-Sheets in the Wind*. New York: Alfred A. Knopf, 1942.

———. *The Theatre, the Drama, the Girls*. New York: Alfred A. Knopf, 1921.

Nathanson, Tenney. *Whitman's Presence: Body, Voice, and Writing in Leaves of Grass.* New York: New York University Press, 1992.

Negus, Keith. *Popular Music in Theory: An Introduction.* Hanover: Wesleyan University Press, 1996.

Nelson, Cary. *Repression and Recovery: Modern American Poetry and the Politics of Cultural Memory, 1910–1945.* Madison: University of Wisconsin Press, 1989.

Nesbit, Evelyn. *Prodigal Days: The Untold Story.* London: John Long, 1934.

Nicholls, David G. *Conjuring the Folk: Forms of Modernity in African America.* Ann Arbor: University of Michigan Press, 2000.

Nicholls, Peter. *Modernisms: A Literary Guide.* Berkeley: University of California Press, 1995.

Nielsen, Aldon Lynn. *Black Chant: Languages of African-American Postmodernism.* Cambridge: Cambridge University Press, 1997.

———. *Reading Race: White American Poets and the Racial Discourse in the Twentieth Century.* Athens: University of Georgia Press, 1988.

———. *Writing between the Lines: Race and Intertextuality.* Athens: University of Georgia Press, 1994.

Nielsen, Aldon Lynn, ed. *Reading Race in American Poetry: "An Area of Act."* Urbana: University of Illinois Press, 2000.

Niles, Abbe. "Introduction: Sad Horns." *Blues: An Anthology.* By Handy, W.C. and Niles, Abbe. New York: Albert and Charles Boni, 1926. 1–24.

Norris, Frank. *McTeague: A Story of San Francisco.* 1899. Rpt. New York: W.W. Norton, 1997.

North, Michael. *Camera Works: Photography and the Twentieth Century Word.* Oxford: Oxford University Press, 2005.

———. *The Dialect of Modernism: Race, Language, and Twentieth Century Literature.* Oxford: Oxford University Press, 1994.

———. *Reading 1922: A Return to the Scene of the Modern.* Oxford: Oxford University Press, 1999.

———. "Visual Culture." *The Cambridge Companion to American Modernism.* Ed. Walter Kalaidjian. Cambridge: Cambridge University Press, 2005. 177–194.

Nye, Russel. *The Unembarrassed Muse: The Popular Arts in America.* New York: Dial Press, 1970.

O'Daniel, Therman B., ed. *Jean Toomer: A Critical Evaluation.* Washington, DC: Howard University Press, 1988.

Ogren, Kathy J. *The Jazz Revolution: Twenties America and the Meaning of Jazz.* Oxford: Oxford University Press, 1989.

Oliver, Paul. *Aspects of the Blues Tradition.* 1968. Rpt. New York: Oak Publications, 1970.

———. *The Meaning of the Blues.* 1960. Rpt. New York: Collier Books, 1963.

———. *Songsters and Saints: Vocal Traditions on Race Records.* Cambridge: Cambridge University Press, 1984.

———. *The Story of the Blues.* Philadelphia: Chilton, 1969.

Omry, Keren. *Cross-Rhythms: Jazz Aesthetics in African-American Literature.* New York: Continuum, 2008.

Ong, Walter J. *Orality and Literacy: The Technologizing of the Word.* 1982. Rpt. New York: Methuen, 1988.

Orvell, Miles. *The Real Thing: Authenticity and Imitation in American Culture, 1880–1940*. Chapel Hill: University of North Carolina Press, 1989.

Ottenberg, June C. *Opera Odyssey: Toward a History of Opera in Nineteenth-Century America*. Westport: Greenwood Press, 1994.

Page, Brett. *Writing for Vaudeville*. Springfield: Home Correspondence School, 1915.

Page, Will A. *Behind the Curtains of the Broadway Beauty Trust*. New York: Edward A. Miller, 1927.

Palmer, Robert. *Deep Blues*. New York: Viking, 1981.

Parker, Derek and Parker, Julia. *The Natural History of the Chorus Girl*. Indianapolis: Bobbs-Merrill, 1975.

Pascal, Richard. "Walt Whitman and Woody Guthrie: American Prophet-Singers and Their People." *Journal of American Studies* 24:1 (April 1990). 41–59.

Pater, Walter. *The Renaissance: Studies in Art and Poetry*. 1888. Rpt. Oxford: Oxford University Press, 2010.

Paulson, William R. *The Noise of Culture: Literary Texts in a World of Information*. Ithaca: Cornell University Press, 1988.

Pavlic, Edward M. *Crossroads Modernism: Descent and Emergence in African-American Literary Culture*. Minneapolis: University of Minnesota Press, 2002.

Pearce, Roy Harvey. *The Continuity of American Poetry*. Princeton: Princeton University Press, 1961.

Pease, Allison. *Modernism, Mass Culture, and the Aesthetics of Obscenity*. Cambridge: Cambridge University Press, 2000.

Peckham, Joel B. "Jean Toomer's *Cane*: Self as Montage and the Drive toward Integration." *American Literature* 72:2 (2000). 275–290.

Perloff, Marjorie and Dworkin, Craig. *The Sound of Poetry/The Poetry of Sound*. Chicago: University of Chicago Press, 2009.

Perloff, Nancy Lynn. *Art and the Everyday: Popular Entertainment and the Circle of Erik Satie*. Oxford: Clarendon Press, 1991.

Peterson, Richard A. "Understanding Audience Segmentation: From Elite and Mass to Omnivore and Univore." *Poetics* 21:4 (August 1992). 243–258.

Philip, Robert. *Performing Music in the Age of Recording*. New Haven: Yale University Press, 2004.

Phillips, Gene D. *Fiction, Film, and F. Scott Fitzgerald*. Chicago: Loyola University Press, 1986.

Picker, John M. *Victorian Soundscapes*. Oxford: Oxford University Press, 2003.

Pizer, Donald. *The Novels of Theodore Dreiser: A Critical Study*. Minneapolis: University of Minnesota Press, 1976.

Ponce, Martin Joseph. "Langston Hughes's Queer Blues." *Modern Language Quarterly* 66:4 (December 2005). 505–537.

Porter, Eric. *What Is This Thing Called Jazz?: African American Musicians as Artists, Critics, and Activists*. Berkeley: University of California Press, 2002.

Posnock, Ross. *Color and Culture: Black Writers and the Making of the Modern Intellectual*. Cambridge: Harvard University Press, 1998.

Pound, Ezra. *The Cantos of Ezra Pound*. New York: New Directions, 1996.

——. *Literary Essays*. Ed. T. S. Eliot. 1918. Rpt: New York: New Directions, 1968.

——. "Vortex." *Blast* 1. London: John Land, 1914. 153–154.

Powers, Richard. *The Time of Our Singing*. New York: Picador, 2003.

Prendergast, Mark. *The Ambient Century: From Mahler to Moby—The Evolution of Sound in the Electronic Age*. New York: Bloomsbury, 2003.

Price, Kenneth M. *Whitman and Tradition: The Poet in His Century*. New Haven: Yale University Press, 1990.

Prieto, Eric. *Listening In: Music, Mind, and the Modernist Narrative*. Lincoln: University of Nebraska Press, 2002.

Prigozy, Ruth. "'Poor Butterfly': F. Scott Fitzgerald and Popular Music." *Prospects* 2 (1976). 41–68.

Quinn, Arthur Hobson. *Edgar Allan Poe: A Critical Biography*. 1941. Rpt. Baltimore: Johns Hopkins University Press, 1998.

Radano, Ronald. *Lying up a Nation: Race and Black Music*. Chicago: University of Chicago Press, 2003.

Rado, Lisa, ed. *Modernism, Gender, and Culture: A Cultural Studies Approach*. New York: Garland, 1997.

———. *Rereading Modernism: New Directions in Feminist Criticism*. New York: Garland, 1994.

Railton, Stephen. "'As If I Were with You': The Performance of Whitman's Poetry." *The Cambridge Companion to Walt Whitman*. Ed. Ezra Greenspan. Cambridge: Cambridge University Press, 1995. 7–26.

Rainey, Lawrence. *Institutions of Modernism: Literary Elites and Public Culture*. New Haven: Yale University Press, 1998.

———. *Revisiting* The Waste Land. New Haven: Yale University Press, 2005.

Ramazani, Jahan. *Poetry of Mourning: The Modern Elegy from Hardy to Heaney*. Chicago: University of Chicago Press, 1994.

———. "'Sing to Me Now': Contemporary American Poetry and Song." *Contemporary Literature* 52:4 (2011). 716–755.

Ramey, Lauri. *Slave Songs and the Birth of African American Poetry*. New York: Palgrave Macmillan, 2008.

Rampersad, Arnold. *The Life of Langston Hughes*, Volume I: *1902–1941: I, Too, Sing America*. Oxford: Oxford University Press, 1986.

Raso, Manuel Villar. "Musical Structure of Whitman's Poems." *Utopia in the Present Tense: Walt Whitman and the Language of the New World*. Ed. Marina Camboni. Rome: Università degli Studi di Macerata, 1994. 189–202.

Rasula, Jed. "Jazz and American Modernism." *The Cambridge Companion to American Modernism*. Ed. Walter Kalaidjian. Cambridge: Cambridge University Press, 2005. 157–176.

Raussert, Wilfried. *Negotiating Temporal Differences: Blues, Jazz and Narrativity in African American Culture*. Heidelberg: Universitätsverlag C. Winter Heidelberg, 2000.

Redding, Patrick. "Whitman Unbound: Democracy and Poetic Form, 1912–1931." *New Literary History* 41:3 (Summer 2011). 669–690.

Reynolds, David S. *Beneath the American Renaissance: The Subversive Imagination in the Age of Emerson and Melville*. Cambridge: Harvard University Press, 1988.

———. *Walt Whitman's America: A Cultural Biography*. 1995. Rpt. New York: Vintage, 1996.

Rhodes, Chip. *Structures of the Jazz Age: Mass Culture, Progressive Education, and Racial Discourse in American Modernism*. New York: Verso, 1998.

Richards, I. A. *Principles of Literary Criticism*. 1934. Rpt. New York: Routledge, 2001.

Ricks, Christopher B. *Dylan's Visions of Sin*. London: Viking, 2003.

Robertson, Michael. *Worshipping Walt: The Whitman Disciples*. Princeton: Princeton University Press, 2008.

Robledo, Julian and Terriss, Dorothy. "Three O'clock in the Morning." London: West's Limited, 1921.

———. "Three O'clock in the Morning." Perf. John McCormack. Victrola, 1922.

Ropes, Bradford. *42nd Street*. New York: Grosset and Dunlap, 1932.

Rorem, Ned. "Words without Song." *The Artistic Legacy of Walt Whitman: A Tribute to Gay Wilson Allen*. Ed. Edwin Haviland Miller. New York: New York University Press, 1970.

Ross, Alex. *Listen to This*. New York: Farrar, Straus and Giroux, 2010.

Rubin, Joseph Jay. *The Historic Whitman*. University Park: Pennsylvania State University Press, 1973.

Ruotolo, Cristina. "'Whence the Song:' Voice and Audience in Dreiser's *Sister Carrie*." *Sister Carrie*. New York: Norton, 2006. 584–603.

Rusch, Frederik L. "Form, Function, and Creative Tension in Cane: Jean Toomer and the Need for the Avant-Garde." *MELUS* 17:4 (Winter, 1991–1992). 15–28.

Rushdie, Salman. *The Ground beneath Her Feet*. London: Jonathan Cape, 1999.

Russell, Tony. *Blacks, Whites, and Blues*. 1970. Rpt. in *Yonder Come the Blues*. Cambridge: Cambridge University Press, 2001.

Ryan, Jennifer D. *Post-Jazz Poetics: A Social History*. New York: Palgrave Macmillan, 2010.

Sacks, Oliver. *Musicophilia: Tales of Music and the Brain*. New York: Alfred A. Knopf, 2007.

Saffle, Michael, ed. *Music and Culture in America, 1861–1918*. New York: Garland, 1998.

Sand, George. *Consuelo*. 1842–3. Trans. Fank H. Potter. 2 vols. Rpt. Boston: Estes and Lauriat, 1897.

Sanjek, Russell. *American Popular Music and Its Business: The First Four Hundred Years*. 3 vols. Oxford: Oxford University Press, 1988.

Scandura, Jani and Thurston, Michael, eds. *Modernism, Inc.: Body, Memory, Capital*. New York: New York University Press, 2001.

Scarborough, Dorothy. *On the Trail of Negro Folk-Songs*. Cambridge: Harvard University Press, 1925.

"Scenes in 'Black America.'" *New York Times*, May 26, 1895, p. 16.

Schafer, R. Murray. *The Tuning of the World*. New York: Alfred A. Knopf, 1977.

Scher, Steven Paul, ed. *Music and Text: Critical Inquiries*. Cambridge: Cambridge University Press, 1992.

Schleifer, Ronald. *Modernism and Popular Music*. Cambridge: Cambridge University Press, 2011.

Scholes, Robert. *Paradoxy of Modernism*. New Haven: Yale University Press, 2006.

Schopenhauer, Arthur. *The World as Will and Representation*. 1818. Trans. E. F. J. Payne. 2 vols. Rpt. Mineola: Dover, 1969.

Schuchard, Ronald. *Eliot's Dark Angel: Intersections of Life and Art*. Oxford: Oxford University Press, 1999.

Schwartz, Jean and Jerome, William. "Ring Ting-a-Ling." New York: Jerome and Schwartz, 1912.

————. "Ring Ting-a-Ling." Perf. Ada Jones. Columbia: 1912.

Schweighauser, Philipp. *The Noises of American Literature, 1890–1985: Toward a History of Literary Acoustics*. Gainesville: University Press of Florida, 2006.

Schwenger, Peter. "The Obbligato Effect." *New Literary History* 42:1 (Winter 2011). 115–128.

Scofield, Martin. *T. S. Eliot: The Poems*. Cambridge: Cambridge University Press, 1988.

Scott, Bonnie Kime, ed. *The Gender of Modernism: A Critical Anthology*. Bloomington: Indiana University Press, 1990.

————. *Gender in Modernism: New Geographies, Complex Intersections*. Urbana: University of Illinois Press, 2007.

Scott, Derek B. *Sounds of the Metropolis: The Nineteenth-Century Popular Music Revolution in London, New York, Paris, and Vienna*. Oxford: Oxford University Press, 2008.

Scruggs, Charles. "'All Dressed Up but No Place to Go': The Black Writer and His Audience during the Harlem Renaissance." *American Literature* 48: 4 (1977). 543–563.

Scruggs, Charles and VanDemarr, Lee. *Jean Toomer and the Terrors of American History*. Philadelphia: University of Pennsylvania Press, 1998.

Seabrook, John. *Nobrow: The Culture of Marketing, the Marketing of Culture*. New York: Vintage, 2001.

See, Sam. "'Spectacles in Color': The Primitive Drag of Langston Hughes." *PMLA* 124:3 (Winter 2009). 798–816.

Seldes, Gilbert. *The Seven Lively Arts*. New York: Harper and Brothers, 1924.

Shephard, Esther. *Walt Whitman's Pose*. New York: Harcourt, Brace, 1938.

Sherry, Vincent. *Ezra Pound, Wyndham Lewis, and Radical Modernism*. Oxford: Oxford University Press, 1993.

Shirley, Wayne D. "The Coming of 'Deep River.'" *American Music* 15:4 (Winter 1996). 493–534.

Shloss, Carol. *In Visible Light: Photography and the American Writer: 1840–1940*. Oxford: Oxford University Press, 1987.

Shteir, Rachel. *Striptease: The Untold History of the Girlie Show*. Oxford: Oxford University Press, 2004.

Sidran, Ben. *Black Talk*. New York: Holt, Rinehart and Winston, 1971.

Sigg, Eric. *The American T. S. Eliot: A Study of the Early Writings*. Cambridge: Cambridge University Press, 1989.

————. "Eliot as a Product of America." *The Cambridge Companion to T. S. Eliot*. Ed. A. David Moody. Cambridge: Cambridge University Press, 1994. 14–30.

Singer, Ben. *Melodrama and Modernity: Early Sensational Cinema and Its Contexts*. New York: Columbia University Press, 2001.

Singh, Amritjit, Shiver, William S., and Brodwin, Stanley, eds. *The Harlem Renaissance: Revaluations*. New York: Garland, 1989.

Skaggs, Carmen Trammell. *Overtones of Opera in American Literature from Whitman to Wharton*. Baton Rouge: Louisiana State University Press, 2010.

Sklar, Robert. *F. Scott Fitzgerald: The Last Laocoön*. Oxford: Oxford University Press, 1967.

Small, Christopher. *Music of the Common Tongue: Survival and Celebration in Afro-American Music*. Hanover: Wesleyan University Press, 1998.

——. *Musicking: The Meanings of Performing and Listening*. Hanover: Wesleyan University Press, 1998.

Smethurst, Brian. "Lyric Stars: Countee Cullen and Langston Hughes." *The Cambridge Companion to the Harlem Renaissance*, ed. George Hutchison. Cambridge: Cambridge University Press, 2007. 112–125.

Smith, Carol H. "Sweeney and the Jazz Age." *Critical Essays on T. S. Eliot: The Sweeney Motif.* Ed. Kinley E. Roby. Boston: G. K. Hall, 1985. 87–99.

Smith, Grover. *T. S. Eliot's Poetry and Plays: A Study in Sources and Meaning*. 1950. Rpt. Chicago: University of Chicago Press, 1968.

——. *The Waste Land*. London: George Allen and Unwin, 1983.

Smith, Mark M., ed. *Hearing History: A Reader*. Athens: University of Georgia Press, 2004.

Snodgrass, W. D. "The Rhythm That Rocks Walt's Cradle." *Sewanee Review* 116:3 (2008). 398–410.

Sollors, Werner. *Ethnic Modernism*. 2002. Rpt. Cambridge: Harvard University Press, 2008.

——. "Jean Toomer's *Cane*: Modernism and Race in Interwar America." *Jean Toomer and the Harlem Renaissance*. Ed. Geneviève Fabre and Michel Feith. New Brunswick: Rutgers University Press, 2001. 1–37.

Soto, Michael. "Jean Toomer and Horace Liveright; or, A New Negro Gets 'into the Swing of It.'" *Jean Toomer and the Harlem Renaissance*. Ed. Geneviève Fabre and Michel Feith. New Brunswick: Rutgers University Press, 2001. 162–187.

——. *The Modernist Nation: Generation, Renaissance, and Twentieth-Century American Literature*. Tuscaloosa: University of Alabama Press, 2004.

Sousa, John Philip. "The Menace of Mechanical Music." *Appleton's Magazine* 8 (August 1906). 278–284.

Southern, Eileen. *The Music of Black Americans: A History*. 1971. Rpt. New York: W.W. Norton, 1983.

Spears, Monroe K. *Dionysus and the City: Modernism in Twentieth-Century Poetry*. Oxford: Oxford University Press, 1970.

Specktor, Matthew. *That Summertime Sound*. New York City: MTV Press, 2009.

Spencer, Jon Michael. *The New Negroes and Their Music: The Success of the Harlem Renaissance*. Knoxville: University of Tennessee Press, 1997.

Spengemann, William C. *Three American Poets: Walt Whitman, Emily Dickinson, and Herman Melville*. Notre Dame: University of Notre Dame Press, 2010.

Spindler, Michael. "John Dos Passos and the Visual Arts." *Journal of American Studies* 15 (1981). 391–405.

Springer, Robert, ed. *Nobody Knows Where the Blues Come From: Lyrics and History*. Jackson: University of Mississippi Press, 2006.

Stead, C. K. *The New Poetic: Yeats to Eliot*. 1964. Rpt. Philadelphia: University of Pennsylvania Press, 1987.

——. *Pound, Eliot and the Modernist Movement*. London: Macmillan, 1986.

Stearns, Harold. *America and the Young Intellectual*. New York: George H. Doran, 1921.

Stein, Gertrude. *Selected Writings*. Ed. Carl Van Vechten. New York: Vintage, 1962.

Steinman, Lisa M. *Made in America: Science, Technology, and American Modernist Poets*. New Haven: Yale University Press, 1987.

Stepto, Robert. *From Behind the Veil: A Study of Afro-American Narrative.* Urbana: University of Illinois Press, 1979.

Stern, Milton R. *The Golden Moment: The Novels of F. Scott Fitzgerald.* Urbana: University of Illinois Press, 1970.

Sterne, Jonathan. *The Audible Past: Cultural Origins of Sound Reproductions.* Durham: Duke University Press, 2003.

Stewart, Garrett. *Reading Voices: Literature and the Phonotext.* Berkeley: University of California Press, 1990.

Stewart, Susan. *Poetry and the Fate of the Senses.* Chicago: University of Chicago Press, 2002.

Stoddard, Martin. *Wagner to "The Waste Land": A Study of the Relationship of Wagner to English Literature.* London: Macmillan, 1982.

Stovall, Floyd. *The Foreground of Leaves of Grass.* Charlottesville: University of Virginia Press, 1974.

Strausbaugh, John. *Black Like You: Blackface, Whiteface, Insult and Imitation in American Popular Culture.* New York: Penguin, 2006.

Strychacz, Thomas. *Modernism, Mass Culture, and Professionalism.* Cambridge: Cambridge University Press, 1993.

Suárez, Juan A. *Pop Modernism: Noise and the Reinvention of the Everyday.* Urbana: University of Illinois Press, 2007.

Suisman, David. *Selling Sounds: The Commercial Revolution in American Music.* Cambridge: Harvard University Press, 2009.

Sundquist, Eric J. *The Hammers of Creation: Folk Culture in Modern African-American Fiction.* Athens: University of Georgia Press, 1992.

———. *To Wake the Nations: Race in the Making of American Literature.* Cambridge: Harvard University Press, 1993.

Surette, Leon. *The Birth of Modernism: Ezra Pound, T. S. Eliot, W. B. Yeats, and the Occult.* Montreal: McGill-Queen's University Press, 1993.

Swirski, Peter. *From Lowbrow to Nobrow.* Montreal: McGill-Queen's University Press, 2005.

Symes, Colin. "From *Tomorrow's Eve* to *High Fidelity*: Novel Responses to the Gramophone in Twentieth Century Literature." *Popular Music* 24:2 (2005). 193–206.

Syrotinski, Michael and Ian Maclachlan, eds. *Sensual Reading: New Approaches to Reading in Its Relation to the Senses.* Lewisburg: Bucknell University Press, 2001.

Tawa, Nicholas E. *The Way to Tin Pan Alley: American Popular Song, 1866–1910.* New York: Schirmer Books, 1990.

Taylor, Deems. "Music." *Civilization in the United States: An Inquiry by Thirty Americans.* Ed. Harold E. Stearns. New York: Harcourt, Brace, 1922.

Terris, Daniel. "Waldo Frank, Jean Toomer, and the Critique of Racial Voyeurism." Hathaway, Heather, et al., eds. *Race and the Modern Artist.* Oxford: Oxford University Press, 2003. 92–114.

Thompson, Emily. *The Soundscape of Modernity: Architectural Acoustics and the Culture of Listening in America, 1900–1933.* Cambridge: MIT Press, 2002.

Thoreau, Henry David. *Journal IX (August 16, 1856–August 7, 1857).* Ed. Bradford Torrey. Rpt. Cambridge: Riverside Press, 1906.

Thurman, Wallace. *The Collected Writings of Wallace Thurman: A Harlem Renaissance Reader*. Ed. Amritjit Singh and Daniel M. Scott III. New Brunswick: Rutgers University Press, 2003.

———. *Infants of the Spring*. 1932. Rpt. Boston: Northeastern University Press, 1992.

Tichi, Cecelia. *Shifting Gears: Technology, Literature, Culture in Modernist America*. Chapel Hill: University of North Carolina Press, 1987.

Titon, Jeff Todd. *Early Downhome Blues: A Musical and Cultural Analysis*. 1977. Rpt. Chapel Hill: University of North Carolina Press, 1994.

Toll, Robert C. *Blacking Up: The Minstrel Show in Nineteenth-Century America*. New York: Oxford University Press, 1974.

Toomer, Jean. *Cane*. 1923. Rpt. New York: Norton, 1988.

———. *A Jean Toomer Reader: Selected Unpublished Writings*. Ed. Frederick L. Rusch. Oxford: Oxford University Press, 1993.

———. "Karintha." *Broom* 4 (January 1923). 83–85.

———. *The Letters of Jean Toomer, 1919–1924*. Ed. Mark Whalan. Knoxville: University of Tennessee Press, 2006.

———. *Selected Essays and Literary Criticism*. Ed. Robert B. Jones. Knoxville: University of Tennessee Press, 1996.

———. *The Wayward and the Seeking: A Collection of Writings by Jean Toomer*. Ed. Darwin T. Turner. Washington, DC: Howard University Press, 1980.

Tosches, Nick. *Where Dead Voices Gather*. Boston: Little, Brown, 2001.

Towbridge, John Townsend. "Reminiscences of Walt Whitman." *Atlantic Monthly* (February 1902). 163–175.

Tracy, Steven C. *Langston Hughes and the Blues*. Urbana: University of Illinois Press, 1988.

Trask, Michael. *Cruising Modernism: Class and Sexuality in American Literature and Social Thought*. Ithaca: Cornell University Press, 2003.

Traubel, Horace. *With Walt Whitman in Camden*. Vol. II. New York: Michell Kennerley, 1915.

———. *With Walt Whitman in Camden*. Vol. III. New York: Michell Kennerley, 1914.

Trilling, Lionel. *The Liberal Imagination: Essays on Literature and Society*. New York: Viking, 1950.

Trombold, John. "Popular Songs as Revolutionary Culture in John Dos Passos' *U.S.A.* and Other Early Works." *Journal of Modern Literature* 19:2 (Autumn 1995). 289–316.

Turner, Catherine. *Marketing Modernism: Between the Two World Wars*. Amherst: University of Massachusetts Press, 2003.

Untermeyer, Louis. "Disillusion vs. Dogma." 1923. Rpt. *T. S. Eliot: The Contemporary Reviews*. Ed. Jewel Spears Brooker. Cambridge: Cambridge University Press, 2004. 93–95.

Van Vechten, Carl. *"Keep A-Inchin' Along": Selected Writings of Carl Van Vechten about Black Art and Letters*. Ed. Bruce Kellner. Westport: Greenwood, 1979.

Varnedoe, Kirk and Gopnik, Adam, eds. *Modern Art and Popular Culture: Readings in High and Low*. New York: Harry N. Abrams, 1990.

Vendler, Helen. "The Unweary Blues." *New Republic* (March 6, 1995). 37–42.

Vergo, Peter. *The Music of Painting: Music, Modernism, and the Visual Arts from the Romantics to John Cage*. London: Phaidon Press, 2012.

Verlaine, Paul. *Jadis et Naguére*. 1885; rpt. Paris: Le Club du meilleur livre, 1959.

Vogel, Shane. *The Scene of Harlem Cabaret: Race, Sexuality, Performance*. Chicago: University of Chicago Press, 2009.

Walcutt, Charles Child. *American Literary Naturalism, a Divided Stream*. Minneapolis: University of Minnesota Press, 1956.

Wald, Elijah. *Escaping the Delta: Robert Johnson and the Invention of the Blues*. New York: HarperCollins, 2004.

Waldron, Edward E. "The Blues Poetry of Langston Hughes." *Negro American Literature Forum* 5:4 (Winter 1971). 140–149.

Waldron, Philip. "The Music of Poetry: Wagner in *The Waste Land*." *Journal of Modern Literature* 18:4 (Fall 1993). 421–434.

Walker, Alice. *In Search of Our Mothers' Gardens*. New York: Harcourt Brace Jovanovich, 1983.

Wall, Cheryl A. *Worrying the Line: Black Women Writers, Lineage, and Literary Tradition*. Chapel Hill: University of North Carolina Press, 2005.

"Walt Whitman as Musical Prophet." *Musical America* (July 3, 1915). 18.

Waskow, Howard J. *Whitman: Explorations in Form*. Chicago: University of Chicago Press, 1966.

Waters, William. *Poetry's Touch: On Lyric Address*. Ithaca: Cornell University Press, 2003.

Watson, Steven. *Strange Bedfellows: The First American Avant-Garde*. New York: Abbeville Press, 1991.

Webb, Jeff. "Literature and Lynching: Identity in Jean Toomer's *Cane*." *English Literary History* 67:1 (2000). 205–228.

Weber, William. *The Great Transformation of Musical Taste: Concert Programming from Haydn to Brahms*. Cambridge: Cambridge University Press, 2008.

Weheliye, Alexander G. *Phonographies: Grooves in Sonic Afro-Modernity*. Durham: Duke University Press, 2005.

Weiss, Jeffrey. *The Popular Culture of Modern Art: Picasso, Duchamp, and Avant-Gardism*. New Haven: Yale University Press, 1994.

Werner, Craig Hansen. *Playing the Changes: From Afro-Modernism to the Jazz Impulse*. Urbana: University of Illinois Press, 1994.

Whalan, Mark. *Race, Manhood, and Modernism in America: The Short Story Cycles of Sherwood Anderson and Jean Toomer*. Knoxville: University of Tennessee Press, 2007.

Whitcomb, Ian. *After the Ball: Pop Music from Rag to Rock*. Baltimore: Penguin, 1972.

White, LeRoy. "Nigger Blues." Dallas: Bush and Gerts, 1913.

———. "Nigger Blues." Perf. Al Bernard. Edison, 1919.

Whiteman, Paul and McBride, Mary Margaret. *Jazz*. New York: J. H. Shears, 1926.

Whitman, Walt. "All about a Mocking-Bird." 1860. Rpt. in *Walt Whitman: The Contemporary Reviews*. Ed. Kenneth M. Price. Cambridge: Cambridge University Press, 1996. 74–76.

———. *Complete Poetry and Collected Prose*. Ed. Justin Kaplan. New York: Library of America, 1982.

———. *Faint Clews and Indirections: Manuscripts of Walt Whitman and His Family*. Ed. Clarence Gohdes and Rollo G. Silver. Durham: Duke University Press, 1949.

———. *The Journalism: Volume I, 1834–1846*. Ed. Herbert Bergman. New York: Peter Lang, 1998.

──. *New York Dissected: A Sheaf of Recently Discovered Newspaper Articles by the Author of* Leaves of Grass. New York: Rufus Rockwell Wilson, 1936.

──. *Notebooks and Unpublished Prose Manuscripts, Volume 1.* Ed. Edward F. Grier. New York: New York University Press, 1984.

──. *Notes and Fragments: Left by Walt Whitman.* Ed. Richard Maurice Burke. London: Talbot, 1899.

──. *Prose Works 1892.* 2 vols. Ed. Floyd Stovall. New York: New York University Press, 1963.

──. *The Uncollected Poetry and Prose of Walt Whitman, Much of Which Has Been but Recently Discovered with Various Early Manuscripts Now First Published.* 2 vols. Ed. Emory Holloway. New York: Peter Smith, 1932.

Willard, Charles B. *Whitman's American Fame: The Growth of His Reputation after 1892.* Menasha: George Banta, 1950.

Williams, C. K. *On Whitman.* Princeton: Princeton University Press, 2010.

Williams, Sherley A. "The Blues Roots of Contemporary Afro-American Poetry." *Chant of Saints: A Gathering of Afro-American Literature, Art, and Scholarship.* Ed. Michael S. Harper and Robert B. Stepto. Urbana: University of Illinois Press, 1979. 123–135.

Williams, William Carlos. *Spring and All.* 1923. Rpt. New York: New Directions, 1986.

Willmott, Glenn. *Modernist Goods: Primitivism, the Market, and the Gift.* Toronto: University of Toronto Press, 2008.

Wilson, Carl. *Let's Talk about Love: A Journey to the End of Taste.* New York: Continuum, 2007.

Wilson, Edmund. *The American Earthquake: A Documentary of the Twenties and Thirties.* Garden City: Doubleday, 1958.

──. *Axel's Castle: A Study in the Imaginative Literature of 1870–1930.* 1931. Rpt. New York: Macmillan, 1991.

──. "F. Scott Fitzgerald." 1922. Rpt. in *F. Scott Fitzgerald in His Own Time*, ed. Matthew J. Bruccoli and Jackson R. Bryer. New York: Popular Library, 1971. 404–409.

──. *The Shores of Light: A Literary Chronicle of the Twenties and Thirties.* New York: Farrar, Straus and Young, 1952.

Winn, James Anderson. *Unsuspected Eloquence: A History of the Relations between Poetry and Music.* New Haven: Yale University Press, 1981.

Wintz, Cary D. *Black Culture and the Harlem Renaissance.* Houston: Rice University Press, 1988.

Wirth-Nesher, Hana. *City Codes: Reading the Modern Urban Novel.* Cambridge: Cambridge University Press, 1996.

Wojcik, Pamela Robertson, and Knight, Arthur, eds. *Soundtrack Available: Essays on Film and Popular Music.* Durham: Duke University Press, 2001.

Wolf, Werner. *The Musicalization of Fiction: A Study in the Theory and History of Intermediality.* Amsterdam: Rodopi, 1999.

Woll, Allen. *Black Musical Theatre: From Coontown to Dreamgirls.* Baton Rouge: Louisiana State University Press, 1989.

Wood, Clement. *Nigger: A Novel.* New York: E. P. Dutton, 1922.

Woolf, Virginia. *A Room of One's Own.* 1929. Rpt. Oxford: Oxford University Press, 2008.

Work, John W. *Folk Song of the American Negro*. 1915. Rpt. New York, Negro Universities Press, 1969.

Wright, Richard. "Blueprint for Negro Writing." *New Challenge* 2:2 (Fall 1937). 53–65.

Yaffe, David. *Fascinating Rhythm: Reading Jazz in American Writing*. Princeton: Princeton University Press, 2006.

Index